THE CONSERVATIVE GOVERNMENTS AND SOCIAL POLICY

Edited by
Hugh Bochel and Martin Powell

P

First published in Great Britain in 2024 by

Policy Press, an imprint of
Bristol University Press
University of Bristol
1–9 Old Park Hill
Bristol
BS2 8BB
UK
t: +44 (0)117 374 6645
e: bup-info@bristol.ac.uk

Details of international sales and distribution partners are available at policy.bristoluniversitypress.co.uk

British Library Cataloguing in Publication Data
A catalogue record for this book is available from the British Library

ISBN 978-1-4473-6582-2 hardcover
ISBN 978-1-4473-6583-9 paperback
ISBN 978-1-4473-6584-6 ePub
ISBN 978-1-4473-6585-3 ePdf

Cover design: Lyn Davies Design
Front cover image: Alamy Stock Photo/PA Images

Contents

List of tables and figures   v

Notes on contributors   vii

1   Introduction: The Conservative governments from Cameron to Sunak (2015–23)   1
Hugh Bochel and Martin Powell

2   The Conservatives and public spending since 2015   20
Nick Ellison

3   Turning up the thermostat: the Conservatives, social policy and public opinion   45
Andrew Defty

4   Brexit and the Conservative Party's social policies   65
Steven Corbett

5   The Johnson Conservative government, its conservatism and the pandemic response   81
Ian Greener

6   The governance of social policy under the Conservatives   100
Catherine Bochel and Hugh Bochel

7   Conservative health policy, 2015–23   116
Martin Powell

8   The less things change: conservatism, COVID-19 and incoherence in education policy   133
Stephen J. Ball

9   Conservative housing policy in England   151
Peter Somerville

10   Social security policies under the Conservatives 2015–22: austerity, COVID-19 and the living cost crisis   174
Stephen McKay and Karen Rowlingson

11   Labour market strategies and welfare policies: the Conservative record   192
Anne Daguerre and David Etherington

12   The Conservatives and adult social care   208
Jon Glasby

13   The Conservatives, family policy and the data revolution   225
Val Gillies and Rosalind Edwards

14   Troubling social policy during turbulent times: children and UK Conservative governments since 2015   243
Harriet Churchill

15   Conservative criminal justice: a strange rediscovery of   260
      'law and order' politics
      Peter Squires
16   Equalities and the Conservatives: the widening of   280
      social divisions?
      Kirstein Rummery
17   The Conservative governments, devolution and social policy   298
      Ann Marie Gray
18   Conclusions   317
      Hugh Bochel and Martin Powell

Index   330

List of tables and figures

Tables

1.1	Dimensions of political approaches	14
2.1	COVID-19-related spending by function (billions, estimated)	32
5.1	Conservatism and cronyist populism	95
9.1	Trends in tenure, households in England (thousands)	152
9.2	Housing completions, England	152
10.1	Secretaries of State for Work and Pensions, 2010–22	177
10.2	Rates of selected social security benefits (including state pensions), 2014–22	179
10.3	Rates of Universal Credit, 2014–22	180
17.1	Dimensions of political approaches and the devolved administrations	311
18.1	Dimensions of political approaches	319

Figures

2.1	Gross domestic product and total managed expenditure (real terms, billions at 2019 prices), 2005–06 to 2014–15	22
2.2	Total managed expenditure (real terms, billions at 2019 prices), 2005–06 to 2014–15	23
2.3	Deficit (percentage of GDP), 2005–06 to 2020–21	24
2.4	UK debt (percentage of GDP), 2005–06 to 2020–21	25
2.5	Total managed expenditure and gross domestic product (real terms, billions), 2015–16 to 2019–20	27
2.6	Total managed expenditure outturns by function (percentage of GDP), 2015–16 to 2019–20	28
2.7	Total managed expenditure outturns by function (real terms, billions), 2015–16 to 2019–20	29
2.8	Spending on COVID-19 by lead department (billions)	33
2.9	UK business investment (chained volume, seasonally adjusted), 2007Q4–2022Q1	38
2.10	Gross fixed capital formation for selected countries (percentage of GDP), 2005–20	39
3.1	Attitudes to tax and spend (per cent), 1983–2021	49
3.2	Perceptions of benefit levels (per cent), 1983–2021	52
3.3	Do you think the way that the government is cutting spending is being done fairly or unfairly? (per cent) July 2010–March 2016	55

5.1   COVID-19 deaths in the UK, 2020–22   88
5.2   COVID-19 deaths in selected European nations, 2020–22   90
5.3   COVID-19 cases per million population in the UK, 2020–22   91
10.1 Social security spending (percentage of GDP),   178
      2010–11 to 2022–23

Notes on contributors

Stephen J. Ball is Emeritus Professor of Sociology of Education at the University College London, Institute of Education. He was elected Fellow of the British Academy in 2006, and is also Fellow of the Society of Educational Studies, and a Laureate of Kappa Delta Phi; he has honorary doctorates from the Universities of Turku (Finland) and Leicester. He is co-founder of the *Journal of Education Policy*. His main areas of interest are in sociologically informed education policy analysis and the relationships between education, education policy and social class. He has written 20 books and a series of detective stories (*The Enemies of Truth*, KDP, 2023), and he has published over 140 journal articles. Recent books include *Edu.Net* (Routledge, 2017) and *Foucault as Educator* (Springer, 2017).

Catherine Bochel is Visiting Fellow at the School of Social and Political Sciences, University of Lincoln. She has published widely on the policy process, participation and petitions systems, including *Making and Implementing Public Policy* (Palgrave, 2018; with Hugh Bochel).

Hugh Bochel is Emeritus Professor of Public Policy at the University of Lincoln. He has published widely in the fields of social and public policy, including editing (with Martin Powell) *The Coalition Government and Social Policy* (Policy Press, 2016).

Harriet Churchill is Lecturer in Social Work (Children and Families, Social Policy) in the Department of Sociological Studies at the University of Sheffield. Harriet's research interests are in the areas of social policy, family studies, child welfare, parental support and family support. She is co-investigator on the EurofamNet project, and her recent publications have compared and evaluated family and parenting support reforms in the UK and among European countries.

Steven Corbett is Senior Lecturer in Social Policy at Liverpool Hope University. His research interests include participatory democracy, Brexit and nationalist populism, critiques of the neoliberal state, and alternative approaches to social policy. He has recently published on the impact of Brexit and nationalist populism on the European Social Model (in *Social Policy and Society*) and is currently developing a comparative political economy analysis of state responses to the COVID-19 pandemic.

Anne Daguerre is Reader in Social Justice in the School of Business and Law at the University of Brighton. An alumna of the Woodrow Wilson Center in Washington DC, she has held visiting appointments at George Mason University, the University of Pittsburgh and George Washington University. Anne's areas of expertise are welfare reform, labour market policies, and social policy and administration. Recent publications include 'Federalism in a time of coronavirus: the Trump administration, intergovernmental relations, and the fraying social compact' (in *State and Local Government Review*, 2020; with T. Conlan). Anne is Principal Investigator for a major Economic and Social Research Council grant: 'Activating employers: the politics of regulation in the UK, the US and Australia' (2023–25).

Andrew Defty is Associate Professor of Politics in the School of Social and Political Sciences at the University of Lincoln. He has published widely on parliamentary scrutiny and the politics of welfare, including *Welfare Policy under New Labour: views from inside Westminster* (Policy Press, 2007; with Hugh Bochel) and *Watching the Watchers: Parliament and the Intelligence Services* (Palgrave Macmillan, 2014; with Hugh Bochel and Jane Kirkpatrick).

Rosalind Edwards is Professor of Sociology at the University of Southampton, where she is also a Fellow of the National Centre for Research Methods. She is also a Fellow of the Academy of Social Sciences. She has published widely on families and family policies, and in the fields of qualitative and mixed methods and methodology.

Nick Ellison is Professor of Social Policy at the University of York. His wide-ranging research interests include UK and comparative social policy, the politics of social policy and citizenship theory. Recent publications include the *Handbook on Social Policy and Society* (Edward Elgar, 2020; edited with Tina Haux), 'Neoliberalism' in *The Student's Companion to Social Policy* (Wiley Blackwell, 2022; P. Alcock et al, eds) and 'Covid (in)equalities: labor market protection, health and residential care in Germany, Sweden and the UK' (in *Policy and Society*, 2022; with Paula Blomqvist and Timo Fleckenstein).

David Etherington is Professor of Local and Regional Economic Development in the School of Justice, Security and Sustainability at Staffordshire University. David's research interests are in labour market and welfare policies, including comparative perspectives on labour studies. Recent research includes collaborative work on poverty in Stoke on Trent with Citizens Advice North Staffordshire Stoke on Trent: *Families on the Brink in Stoke-on-Trent: How Austerity and the Cost-of-living Is Driving Poverty and Destitution* (Staffordshire University, 2023; with M. Jones, L. Telford, S. Harris and S. Hubbard). Other publications include 'Political economy of the inclusive labour market revisited: welfare through work in Denmark' (in J. Ingold and P. McGurk, eds, *Employer Engagement: Making Active Labour*

Market Policies Work, Policy Press, 2023; with Martin Jones) and 'Trade union strategies to tackle labour market insecurity: geography and the role of Sheffield TUC' (*Industrial Relations*, 2023; with B. Jeffery, B. Thomas, M. Jones and B Ledger-Jessop).

Val Gillies is Professor of Social Policy and Criminology at the University of Westminster. She has researched and published in the area of family, social class and marginalised children and young people, producing a wide range journal articles and books and chapters.

Jon Glasby is Professor of Health and Social Care at the University of Birmingham and Director of IMPACT, the UK centre for implementing evidence in adult social care. Jon trained as a social worker and specialises in research and policy advice around adult social care, health and social care partnerships, personalisation and evidence-based practice. In 2022, he was a special adviser to the House of Lords Adult Social Care Committee.

Ann Marie Gray is Professor of Social Policy at Ulster University. Her research interests include social care policy, gender and social policy and devolution and social policy. Recent publications include: 'Devolution and Social Policy' (in P. Alcock, T. Haux, V. McCall and M. May, eds, *The Student's Companion to Social Policy*, Blackwell Wiley, 2022), 'Is public opinion in support of decriminalisation?' (in S. Sheldon and K. Wells, eds, *Decriminalising Abortion in the UK*, Policy Press, 2020; with K. Wellings) 'From principles to practice: social security in the Scottish Laboratory of Democracy' (*Journal of Social Security Law*, 2019; with M. Simpson and G. McKeever).

Ian Greener is Professor of Applied Social Science and Head of School of Social Science at the University of Aberdeen. Ian has published monographs on a range of topics, including *Comparing Health Systems* (Policy Press, 2023) and an update of the Beveridge report: *The Welfare State in the 21st Century: The New Five Giants Confronting Societal Progress* (Edward Elgar, 2022). He has authored and co-authored a range of peer-reviewed journal articles over the last 20 years. He lives in Monifieth in Angus, where he can be found walking on a beach with his dog, Archie.

Stephen McKay is Distinguished Professor in Social Research at the University of Lincoln, where he has worked since 2013. Prior to that, he worked at the University of Birmingham, where he directed the Economic and Social Research Council Doctoral Training Centre. His research interests cover poverty and inequality, and much of his research involves quantitative methods applied to large-scale data. Recent work includes articles on 'rainy-day savers' (*Applied Economics*, 2023) and on shaping local social care markets (*Journal of Social Policy*, 2022).

Martin Powell is Professor of Health and Social Policy at the Health Services Management Centre, School of Social Policy, University of Birmingham. He has research interests in health and social policy in the UK. He is the editor of three books on the New Labour Governments in the UK (Policy Press), and co-editor (with Hugh Bochel) of *The Coalition Government and Social Policy* (Policy Press, 2016).

Karen Rowlingson is Professor of Social Policy and Dean of the Faculty of Social Sciences at the University of York. Prior to that, she spent 15 years at the University of Birmingham in a number of leadership roles, including as Founding Director of CHASM (Centre on Household Assets and Savings Management). Other leadership roles include: Chair of the Social Policy Association; Specialist Advisor to the House of Lords Select Committee on Financial Exclusion; and Vice Chair of the Economic and Social Research Council's Research Committee. Karen's research focuses on issues of poverty, wealth and economic inequality, with a particular interest in social security and tax systems.

Kirstein Rummery is Professor in the Department of Sociology, Social Policy and Criminology at the University of Stirling. She has undertaken research in areas such as comparative care policy and gender equality, disability support and women's politicisation, and is currently working on a project funded by the National Institute for Health and Care Research/Economic and Social Research Council on 'Dementia Friendly Neighbourhoods' and a project funded by the Big Lottery Fund (DRILL Programme) on 'Costing Good Self-Directed Support'. Recent publications include 'Dangerous care: developing theory to safeguard older adults in caring relationships in the UK' (*Journal of Adult Protection*, 2023; with F. Sherwood-Johnson, J. Lawrence, K. Mackay, K. Ramsay and R. McGregor) and 'Getting lost with dementia: encounters with the time-space of not knowing' (*Health and Place*, 2022; with R. Ward, E. Odzakovic, K. Manji, A. Kullberg, A. Clark and S. Campbell).

Peter Somerville is Emeritus Professor of Social Policy at the University of Lincoln. His research interests include housing policy, homelessness, community development and climate change policy. Recent publications include 'A critique of climate change mitigation policy' (*Policy & Politics*, 2020), 'The continuing failure of UK climate change mitigation policy' (*Critical Social Policy*, 2020), 'Revisiting the connections between capital and nature I: the importance of labour' (*Capitalism Nature Socialism*, 2020),

'Revisiting the connections between capital and nature II: the case of climate change' (*Capitalism Nature Socialism*, 2021) and Zero Hour (2022) *Net Zero Ambition Report.*

Peter Squires is Professor Emeritus of Criminology and Public Policy at the University of Brighton, where he worked for over thirty years. His work has covered a wide range of issues, including community safety, policing, youth crime, gangs, violence and anti-social behaviour management and firearm-related crime. He was President of the British Society for Criminology (2015–19). He is the author of several books, including *Rethinking Knife Crime* (Palgrave, 2021; with Elaine Williams) and an edited collection on *Southern & Postcolonial Perspectives on Policing, Security and Social Order* (Policy Press, 2023).

Introduction: The Conservative governments from Cameron to Sunak (2015–23)

Hugh Bochel and Martin Powell

Introduction

This book considers the evolution of the Conservative Party's social policies following the 2015 general election. The period from 2015 was remarkable in a number of respects, including the Brexit process, the COVID-19 pandemic and the turnover of prime ministers, each of which had implications for the development and implementation of social policies. The 2015 election led to a Conservative government with a narrow majority in the House of Commons, and this was followed by another general election in 2017, when the Conservatives lost their majority, and subsequently by the 2019 general election, which resulted in a substantial Conservative majority of 80 seats. However, those Conservative governments were subject to significant new influences over which they had only limited control, with many of the consequences of the Brexit referendum and the COVID-19 pandemic being notable examples, while other key developments, such as 'austerity' and attempts at 'levelling up', were much more clearly driven by decisions within the Conservative Party and governments themselves. One of the ramifications of these developments was that the Conservative Party had five leaders (and the UK, five prime ministers) within seven years, with equally rapid turnover in many Cabinet positions, and each individual arguably had different preferences that would be expected to influence the shape of social policy, as is discussed later.

This chapter seeks to provide the context, and to some extent a framework, for the chapters that follow, through:

- briefly considering the main features of policy and underlying themes in the social policies of the Conservative governments from 2015;
- examining the extent to which the Cameron, May, Johnson, Truss and Sunak administrations of 2015 onwards had similar approaches to social policy compared with each other, and with their immediate predecessor, the Coalition government;

- outlining the major influences on Conservative policy during the period, including in relation to both key philosophical positions and the impact of events; and
- considering the implications of developments under the Conservatives for social policy in the UK in the post-Brexit and COVID-19 era.

Conservative social policy, 2010–15

The general election of May 2010 brought to an end 13 years of New Labour governments. With no overall majority for any party in the House of Commons, it led to a Coalition government of the Conservative and Liberal Democrat parties. While the Conservatives had presented themselves as a more 'compassionate' party at the 2010 general election (see, for example, Bochel, 2011), the reality of social policy as it developed under the Coalition government was generally rather different (Bochel and Powell, 2016; Lupton et al, 2016). David Cameron presented the 'Big Society' as his vision to replace Labour's 'Third Way'. Stressing active citizenship, civil society, devolution and 'localism', this would replace the 'big state'. However, it failed to become the defining approach of the Coalition, with many critics regarding it as camouflage for the dominant theme of the Coalition and then Conservative governments, austerity (see, for example, Crossley, 2020; Vizard and Hills, 2021a; Powell, 2022), an approach which also fitted well with the ideological leanings of many of the key individuals in government at the time.

Following the global financial crisis, by the end of 2009–10 the budget deficit was £104 billion (6.9 per cent of gross domestic product – GDP), while the net public sector debt was £956 billion (62 per cent of GDP). The Coalition government sought to end the budget deficit and reduce public sector debt by 2015, largely through spending cuts alongside much more limited use of tax increases, which the government argued was a necessary response to the increase in government borrowing. However, while public expenditure fell dramatically, there were differential cuts between spending departments (with some areas, such as health and education, being relatively protected, while others were hit disproportionately), nations and groups, but with unprecedented reductions in funding for local authorities and large cuts in working-age benefits. Indeed, Vizard and Hills point out that the Coalition government's approach might be more accurately characterised as 'selective austerity' (2021a, p 2). Nevertheless, taken together with the idea of localism and the Big Society, the narratives clearly pointed towards a smaller state.

Aside from austerity, arguably the most significant social policy reforms by the Coalition government were in social security, where reducing benefits and raising the income tax threshold were seen as key elements in 'making work pay', as well as contributing to the deficit reduction, albeit with the flagship Universal Credit reforms seeing significant challenges in respect of their implementation. In addition, a broadly deregulatory approach could be seen across many areas of social policy, including education, health care and pensions, while in others, such as housing and social care, there was little new in terms of policy, with, for example, the government initially accepting but then effectively abandoning Dilnot's (2011) proposal for a 'cap' on social care costs for individuals.

While the early days of the government had seen elements of rhetoric that might have been associated with 'compassionate' or 'One Nation' conservatism (Bochel and Powell, 2018), there were stronger echoes of the New Right-influenced Thatcher governments of the 1980s, with austerity, and the neoliberal emphasis on a small state and belief in the efficiency and effectiveness of the market, and encouraging self-reliance among individuals, dominating many areas of social policy.

However, it is also important to note that during this period devolution led to a greater divergence of approaches within the constituent elements of the UK (see Chapter 17), and that while the Coalition government might be seen as pursuing neoliberal policies, in contrast, although affected by public expenditure cuts determined in Westminster and Whitehall, the governments of Scotland and Wales broadly continued to maintain and even extend social democratic social policies.

Conservative social policy, 2015–22

At the general election of 2015, most opinion polls and commentators were suggesting a hung parliament, but, albeit with only 37 per cent of the vote, the Conservatives, led by David Cameron, achieved a majority of 12 seats and were able to form a government. As in 2010, the Conservative manifesto (Conservative Party, 2015) emphasised the need to reduce the national deficit and debt, signalling significant continuity with the Coalition's approach. It set out two phases for the deficit reduction plan, with the first two years of the government intended to see government spending cut by 1 per cent per year in real terms and then, in 2018–19, a move into surplus, with government spending growing in line with inflation. The reductions were planned to involve further cuts of £13 billion in departmental savings, £12 billion of welfare savings and at least £5 billion from action to tackle tax evasion and aggressive tax avoidance.

Where social policy was concerned, key policies in the manifesto included:

- creating two million jobs over the next five years;
- 'major reforms of tax and welfare', including raising the income tax threshold, reducing the household benefit cap and continuing to roll out Universal Credit, while expanding free childcare;

- continuing the process of academisation of schools and the spread of free schools;
- spending at least an additional £20 billion above inflation on the National Health Service (NHS) by 2020 and delivering seven-days-a-week hospital care by 2020;
- building the 'Big Society';
- building more affordable homes, introducing new Help to Buy Individual Savings Accounts and extending Right to Buy to tenants of housing associations;
- taking the family home out of Inheritance Tax for all but the richest; continuing to increase the State Pension through the triple lock, so that it would rise by 2.5%, inflation or earnings, whichever is the highest; giving people the freedom to invest and spend their pension how they like; and making sure no one is forced to sell their home to pay for care.

Although the Liberal Democrats were no longer part of the government, there was initially considerable continuity in the Cabinet for key areas for social policy, including the Chancellor of the Exchequer (George Osborne), the Home Secretary (Theresa May), the Secretary of State for Work and Pensions (Iain Duncan Smith), the Secretary of State for Health (Jeremy Hunt) and the Secretary of State for Education (Nicky Morgan).

Similarly, the government's plans for public expenditure initially remained the same, with Osborne announcing in the July 2015 Budget that the deficit would be cut at the same pace as in the previous Parliament, and also that 'in normal economic times we should continue to raise more than we spend. ... It is as simple as that, we should always fix the roof while the sun is shining' (Hansard, 2015). He argued that would mean that it was necessary to find another £12 billion of welfare savings.

While the government was able to pursue some of its economic and social aims, constitutional issues were to play a significant part in policy debate over the next few years. These included devolution to the nations of the UK (see Chapter 17). However, the 2015 manifesto promised to hold an in/out referendum on the UK's membership of the European Union (EU). The referendum, on 23 June 2016, resulted in a narrow (51.9 per cent to 48.1 per cent) victory for the 'Leave' campaign, which set in train a series of events which were to dominate British politics for the next four years. Cameron immediately resigned as Prime Minister and was replaced by 'Remainer' Theresa May on 13 July. In her first speech as Prime Minister, May (2016), like Cameron before her, drew on rhetoric and ideas that appeared to set out a more compassionate approach, focusing on reducing inequalities:

> That means fighting against the burning injustice that, if you're born poor, you will die on average 9 years earlier than others.

If you're black, you're treated more harshly by the criminal justice system than if you're white.

If you're a white, working-class boy, you're less likely than anybody else in Britain to go to university.

If you're at a state school, you're less likely to reach the top professions than if you're educated privately.

If you're a woman, you will earn less than a man. If you suffer from mental health problems, there's not enough help to hand. [...]

We will do everything we can to help anybody, whatever your background, to go as far as your talents will take you.

On 29 March 2017, she triggered Article 50, which started the official process for the UK leaving the EU. Shortly after, seeking to increase her parliamentary majority in order to strengthen her hand in negotiations with the EU, she called a general election, for 8 June 2017. Reflecting May's speech (above), the Conservatives' 2017 manifesto included the goals of improving opportunities for more disadvantaged citizens, enhancing intergenerational justice and remedying long-standing inequities (Conservative Party, 2017). Key policies included:

- real terms increases in NHS spending, reaching £8 billion extra per year by 2022–23;
- scrapping the triple lock on the State Pension after 2020 and replacing it with a 'double lock', rising with earnings or inflation;
- increasing the National Living Wage to 60% of median earnings by 2020;
- raising the cost of the social care threshold from £23,000 to £100,000, although including the value of the home in the calculation of assets for home care as well as residential care;
- increasing spending on schools by £4 billion by 2022;
- cutting net migration to below 100,000.

However, the Conservatives immediately ran into difficulties, with the promises to reform social care being widely criticised and attempts to clarify and alter the policy contributing to a poor campaign that contrasted markedly with the 'strong and stable' message with which it had sought to commence.

Despite going into the election campaign with a significant lead in opinion polls, the Conservatives lost their majority in the House of Commons, although they remained the largest party and were able to command a small majority with the support of the Democratic Unionist Party. The Queen's Speech, setting out the government's legislative agenda, saw a variety of changes from the manifesto, with the proposed funding reforms for social care being dropped, while the national minimum wage was to be increased and there were commitments to tackle high energy prices and unacceptable corporate practices. Only days after the general election, a fire destroyed Grenfell Tower, a 23-storey block of largely social housing in North Kensington, West London, and 72 people died. The fire, in one of the richest areas of the UK, and evidence to the subsequent inquiry, were widely seen as raising questions over inequality, but also arguably contributed further to debates over the regulatory role of central and local government (Apps, 2021) and the use of contracting out to manage some forms of social provision.

In October 2018, in her speech to the Conservative Party conference, May declared that the austerity programme was over, with the Chancellor, Phillip Hammond, promising a £30 billion increase in public spending by 2024, including on schools and Universal Credit. However, the lack of a clear majority and the difficulties of achieving any agreement on Brexit, and the amount of government activity focused on that issue, meant that there was relatively little attention paid to the mechanisms of making and delivering such policies, and for much of the public sector, including schools and the NHS, financial pressures remained significant.

Having failed to get her Brexit 'deal' through Parliament, May resigned in July 2019, to be replaced by Boris Johnson (who had supported Leave at the referendum), promising to 'get Brexit done'. In his first speech as Prime Minister, Johnson undertook to 'fix the crisis in social care once and for all with a clear plan we have prepared' (Johnson, 2019), and introduced the idea of levelling up, albeit with no detail provided. During the first few months of his government, there were again claims that austerity was ending – for example, by the Chancellor, Sajid Javid (Jordan, 2019) – with plans for a £100 billion National Infrastructure Fund and for spending on hospital construction (Berry, 2019).

However, when Johnson called a general election for December 2019, the Conservatives scaled back their plans for public spending. The manifesto, *Get Brexit Done: Unleash Britain's Potential*, reflected the Party's attempt to appeal to Labour-voting areas. It talked about 'levelling up every part of the UK – not just investing in our great towns and cities, as well as rural and coastal areas, but giving them far more control of how that investment is made' (Conservative Party, 2019, p 26), along with:

- increasing spending on the NHS and building more new hospitals;
- improving social care, including through seeking cross-party consensus;
- increasing funding for schools and giving greater powers for heads and teachers over discipline;
- promising not to increase Income Tax, National Insurance or VAT (Value Added Tax);
- introducing a points-based immigration system;
- delivering thousands of affordable homes; and alongside these

- more positive references than usual to subjects such as wages, working conditions and pensions, albeit frequently framed as opportunities associated with Brexit (Allen and Bara, 2021).

In some respects, the manifesto could be seen, in terms of Andrew Gamble's (1988) famous formulation, as marking something of an apparent shift back to 'strong state conservatism' and its grasp of law and order, and away from the low-tax neoliberalism of the Coalition.

Johnson had previously described himself as a One Nation Conservative, in an interview with the *Daily Telegraph* when campaigning to be Mayor of London. Although the term had hardly featured during the campaign, let alone in the Conservative manifesto, on the morning following the general election Johnson branded not only himself but also his party as One Nation Conservatives when he said, 'we now speak as a One Nation Conservative Party … from Woking to Workington … to Wolverhampton' (BBC News, 2019). The NHS was a substantial part of this early focus, including a pledge to increase the NHS budget by £34 billion during the Parliament (Mornington, 2020), with another significant element appearing to be the promise to 'level up' the country, although, while many commentators assumed that it was about levelling up prosperity across the regions, there was little clarity in Johnson's speeches. However, Johnson appeared equally willing to declare himself to be a 'Thatcherite' – for example, in early 2022, when in an article defending an increase in National Insurance despite the manifesto promise not to do so, he and the Chancellor, Rishi Sunak, described themselves as 'tax-cutting Conservatives' and Thatcherites (Bowden, 2022).

From a social policy perspective, levelling up was arguably the key idea of the Johnson governments. However, there were significant questions over the meaning of the term and the lack of clarity about the emphasis – for example, the extent to which it distinguished, or not, between economic inequality and social inequality, and between regions and individuals.

However, in part as a result of the COVID-19 pandemic, which, particularly in tandem with the ongoing demands of Brexit, resulted in a 'becalming' of much of the policy agenda, but arguably also because of the lack of clarity and thought associated with Johnson's earlier pronouncements, the levelling up agenda largely stalled, and while the Prime Minister and other ministers continued to refer to it (for example, Johnson, 2020), there was little by way of significant immediate policy development (see Chapter 6). In addition, in May 2020, in the first Budget of the Johnson premiership, there was no real evidence of increased spending on social services, and instead the consequences of the major public spending cuts since 2010 continued to dominate (see Chapter 2).

While other factors and 'events' have always had an impact on governments and their aims, the COVID-19 pandemic provided an unanticipated shock to a government that was always likely to be facing other significant challenges, including the ramifications of Brexit and the ongoing implications of austerity. The emergence of the pandemic in early 2020 (see Chapter 5; see also, for example, Pomati et al, 2021) had major ramifications for public expenditure and for many parts of the welfare state. For example, there was a massive procurement effort for personal protective equipment, support for business and workers through a 'furlough' scheme, the setting up of the Test and Trace system and, later, the largest vaccination programme in the history of the NHS. The government was forced to use the social security system as it promised to, in the words of Chancellor Rishi Sunak, 'do whatever it takes' (for example, Hansard, 2020) to help people get through the crisis, with changes to the level of some benefits, including Working Tax Credit and Universal Credit, expansions of eligibility for some groups and suspension of elements of conditionality, although most of the measures introduced were temporary. In the narrow sense of total public expenditure, the pandemic clearly signalled the end of austerity. According to the House of Commons Library (Harari et al, 2021), estimates of the cost of government measures announced ranged from about £315 billion to £410 billion, the equivalent of about £4,700 to £6,100 per person in the UK. The Office for Budget Responsibility (2021) expected that in 2021–22 the government would 'spend £1,045 billion, equivalent to around £37,000 per household or 45.1 per cent of national income'. Government borrowing in December 2020 pushed the national debt to £2.1 trillion, or 104.5 per cent of GDP, the highest debt ratio since 1962 (ONS, 2021; see Chapter 2).

However, as had been widely pointed out during the early phase of austerity, it was clear that again we were not 'all in it together'. It quickly became apparent that COVID-19 had differing affects across social groups, with both the direct and indirect effects of COVID-19 reflecting and exacerbating existing inequalities and differences while also creating new ones (for example, British Academy, 2021). In addition, there were claims that those close to the government appeared to benefit disproportionately from government procurement (Public Accounts Committee, 2021). Moreover, the Johnson government was also damaged by accusations that those in government behaved differently during the pandemic from the guidance given to the wider population, with revelations in late 2021 and early 2022 that there were a number of parties in Downing Street during periods of lockdown being particularly damaging, along with the publication of a report by senior civil servant Sue Gray (Cabinet Office, 2022) and an investigation by the Metropolitan Police.

Despite the pressures on the government arising from Brexit and the pandemic, the rhetoric of levelling up continued to be a core policy theme, albeit with concrete policies developing fairly slowly. The idea of levelling up formed a central part of the Queen's Speech in May 2021 and continued to feature in Johnson's speeches. For example:

> No one believes ... that there is any basic difference in the potential of babies born across this country. Everyone knows that talent and energy and enthusiasm and flair are evenly spread across the UK, evenly spread. It is opportunity that is not and it is the mission of this government to unite and level up across the whole UK. (Johnson, 2021)

The 2020 Spending Review saw the announcement of a Levelling Up Fund, with £4 billion to be spent in England and £0.8 billion in Northern Ireland, Scotland and Wales, with the stated intention of investing in 'local infrastructure that has a visible impact on people and their communities and will support economic activity' (HM Treasury, 2020, p 4). That was accompanied by the Community Renewal Fund for 2021–22, worth £220 million, and the Towns Fund, worth £3.6 billion (see, for example, House of Commons Library, 2021).

A key document was widely expected to be the White Paper, *Levelling Up the United Kingdom* (HM Government, 2022). However, although it contained a variety of ideas and initiatives, including targets and metrics for measuring change in relation to the economy, education and health, critics argued that many of them simply reiterated previous government statements and that some of the targets appeared very ambitious. They also focused on the lack of detail about funding and the apparent lack of funding in relation to that which would be required to achieve the desired degree of change. The Institute for Fiscal Studies (2021) noted that 'deliberate policy choices since 2010 have made achieving some of the "missions" in the White Paper more difficult to achieve. ... To deliver on its new ambitions, the government may first have to unpick some of the choices made over the past 12 years.' Critics pointed as well to the gap between rhetoric and practice, with broken promises and some perverse examples of funding by the Future High Streets Fund, the Community Renewal Fund and the Towns Fund, as some of the wealthiest parts of England were allocated ten times more funding per capita for levelling up than the poorest (for example, McIntyre et al, 2022).

Of course, devolution continued to prove important during the Johnson premiership, with the governments of Scotland and Wales frequently deciding to pursue different policy directions from Westminster, including in relation to the COVID-19 pandemic, where they frequently exercised greater caution in seeking to protect their populations and in 'opening up' at times when case numbers were dropping. They also tended to seek to continue to pursue broadly social democratic policies, albeit with their capacities for spending being considerably limited by a dependence on government at the UK level and an unwillingness to raise taxes where they had such powers. In Northern

Ireland, there were again differences, including over the impact of Brexit and the effective creation of a 'border' in the sea between Northern Ireland and the rest of the UK, with the main unionist parties being strongly opposed to that, and this had implications for the government of the province more broadly, as was highlighted in February 2022 when Northern Ireland's First Minister, Paul Givan, resigned, triggering the collapse of the power-sharing executive, although the Northern Ireland Assembly was able to continue to operate.

The Chancellor's 'Spring Statement' (or 'mini-budget') of March 2022 took place in the context of the UK facing a cost of living crisis, with the highest inflation in forty years and a major squeeze on incomes in prospect. Sunak responded to surging inflation with what the Resolution Foundation described as a 'significant, but poorly targeted, package of support' (Bell et al, 2022, p 2) for 2022–23, including raising the National Insurance threshold from £9,880 to £12,570 in July, a 5p cut to Fuel Duty rates and a £500 million increase to the Household Support Fund. He also promised a 'jam tomorrow' pre-election cut of 1p in income tax. However, the Resolution Foundation claimed that only £1 in every £3 for the measures announced would go to the bottom half of the income distribution and that a further 1.3 million people would fall into absolute poverty in 2023, including 500,000 children – the first time Britain would have seen such a rise in poverty outside of recessions (Bell et al, 2022).

Johnson's position as Prime Minister was undermined by the COVID-19 pandemic, with a slow and inadequate initial response to the severity of the pandemic, but more significantly by what became known as 'Partygate', with evidence, mentioned earlier, that government staff and politicians, including Johnson and Sunak, attended parties and other gatherings at a time when they were generally banned for public health reasons. Other issues, including an increase in inflation and the Prime Minister's attempts to excuse or support the Members of Parliament (MPs) Owen Paterson and Chris Pincher following misbehaviours added to discontent. In particular, Johnson steadily lost the support of Conservative MPs, and even after winning a 'no confidence' vote on 6 June 2022, with 59 per cent of the vote, he faced considerable opposition from within his own party. In July 2022, he was forced to resign following a revolt by a number of Cabinet members and another contest for the leadership of the Conservative Party and the post of Prime Minister began.

Following ballots by MPs and the Party membership, Liz Truss was appointed Prime Minister on 6 September 2022. However, a disastrous mini-budget of unfunded tax cuts led to the sacking of the new Chancellor, Kwasi Kwarteng, quickly followed by the resignation of Truss, making her the prime minister with the shortest time in office in UK history. Indeed, even before her resignation she was forced to allow the new Chancellor,

Jeremy Hunt, to reverse many of the tax changes that she and Kwarteng had proposed.

With no other candidate in the new Conservative leadership election achieving the support of the 100 MPs necessary to progress to a run-off ballot of the Party's membership (although Johnson claimed to have met this but decided not to stand), the runner-up to Truss in the previous ballot, and former Chancellor, Rishi Sunak, was appointed as Prime Minister on 25 October. Reflecting a desire to move on from the chaos of the previous months, Sunak's (2022) first speech as Prime Minister promised 'integrity, professionalism and accountability at every level'. In appointing his Cabinet, Sunak appeared to seek to draw on different factions of the Conservative Party and to present a picture of unity and stability in contrast to the short Truss government. He retained Hunt as Chancellor, while the reappointment of Michael Gove as Levelling Up Secretary suggested that there was still some potential for developments in that area. However, his choices were not unproblematic: Gavin Williamson, Minister without Portfolio, was forced to resign after less than three weeks following bullying accusations; Deputy Prime Minister and Justice Secretary Dominic Raab was also facing an investigation into bullying and subsequently resigned in April 2022; and Suella Braverman, reappointed as Home Secretary only a week after having been forced to resign for breaching the Ministerial Code, continued to make often controversial statements, particularly in relation to asylum seekers and immigration. Sunak was also slow to appoint an ethics adviser following Lord Geidt's resignation in the face of Boris Johnson's behaviour as Prime Minister.

Many of the difficult financial decisions facing the government were delayed until the Autumn Statement of 17 November 2022 (BBC News, 2022; Hansard, 2022). The Chancellor, Jeremy Hunt, presented what he called a 'balanced plan for stability' of £55 billion consolidation with just under half coming from tax and just over half from spending (col 846). He stated that '[i]n the face of unprecedented global headwinds', the government's priorities were stability, growth and public services, and to protect the vulnerable, because 'this is a compassionate Conservative Government' (Hansard, 2022). The key points were that plans for public spending would be maintained until 2025, with increases for the NHS, social care and education, but would then grow more slowly than previously expected. The introduction of the lifetime cap on social care costs in England, due in October 2023, was delayed by two years, and social housing rent increases were capped at a below-inflation rate of 7 per cent from April 2023. Major benefits were increased by about 10 per cent, in line with inflation, with an increase in the UK National Living Wage for people over 23. The household energy price cap was extended for one year beyond April, but made less generous with typical bills capped at £3,000 a year instead of £2,500, and there were additional payments for households on means-tested benefits, pensioner households and individuals on disability benefits. A windfall tax on profits of oil and gas firms was increased from 25 per cent to 35 per cent and extended until March 2028. Income Tax Personal Allowance, higher-rate thresholds, the main National Insurance and Inheritance Tax thresholds were all frozen until April 2028. The threshold of the top 45 per cent additional rate of Income Tax was reduced from £150,000 to £125,140. Tax-free allowances for dividend income and Capital Gains Tax were cut for 2023 and 2024. Local councils in England were enabled to increase Council Tax up to 5 per cent a year without a local vote, instead of the previous figure of 3 per cent.

With high inflation and economic uncertainty persisting at the time of the Budget statement in March 2023, albeit with the Office for Budget Responsibility taking a slightly less pessimistic view of the state of the economy, the Chancellor sought to focus on encouraging people, particularly those over 50, who had left their jobs to return to the workforce, to boost business investment. However, some of the major changes, such as removing the cap on the lifetime allowance for pensions savings, would only affect the highest paid, while plans to increase the amount of free childcare for working parents were also criticised for not being underpinned by sufficient funding. The government did, however, extend the Energy Price Guarantee to July 2023, helping to some extent to lower household energy bills, although it was again criticised for not targeting the £3 billion cost towards those on lower incomes.

Ideology and policy preferences

Although explored further in the subsequent chapters, and in more detail in the Conclusion to this book, at this stage it is worth providing some overall consideration of the ideological and policy preferences of the governments of this period. One obvious starting point, although not unproblematic, particularly given the turnover of prime ministers, is election manifestos. In a general exploration of manifestos, Allen and Bara (2021), drawing on the Manifesto Project,[1] examined issue salience, claiming that the 2019 Conservative manifesto saw an increase in positive references to labour groups (a category that covers support for workers' rights, wages, conditions and pensions – commitments traditionally associated with the Labour Party), with the score almost doubling between 2017 and 2019. They note also that the term 'levelling up' featured four times in the 2019 manifesto. More generally, they point out that 3 of the Manifesto Project's 56 categories featured in the set of ten most prominent categories in each of the manifestos (2015, 1017 and 2019): 'Welfare State Expansion', 'Technology and Infrastructure' and 'Equality: Positive'. Over the three Conservative manifestos, the most salient category in 2015 was 'Welfare State Expansion' (8.7 per cent), whereas it was 'Technology and Infrastructure' in 2017 (14.5 per cent) and again in 2019 (8.1 per cent), with 'Welfare State Expansion' second in 2017 (10.8 per cent) and fourth in 2019 (7.3 per cent).

Turning to the Manifesto Project's 'left-right' scale, Allen and Bara claim that the 2019 Conservative manifesto represented the biggest shift to the Right since the 1970s, reversing the move to the Left under David Cameron in 2015 and Theresa May in 2017. Then, examining the 'left-right' dimension along with a second dimension of 'cosmopolitan-traditionalist', which reflects sociocultural issues, they argue, perhaps unsurprisingly, that the Conservatives have tended to be the party of the free market and traditionalist values, and suggest that the Conservatives were slightly less neoliberal in 2019 than in 2017 but more neoliberal than in 2015, and more traditionalist in 2019 and 2015 than in 2017.

However, the implications of some of these claims for social policy are far from clear. First, as we have already hinted, manifestos represent rhetoric or intentions rather than policy action. Second, some of the conclusions appear to be confusing. It is hard to see how positive references to labour groups and welfare state expansion square with much social policy analysis over the last decade or so (for example, Bochel and Powell, 2016; McEnhill and Taylor-Gooby, 2018; Vizard and Hills, 2021b), although they might clearly be rhetorical mechanisms for the purpose of electoral advantage.

In order to provide an examination of changes to the provision of social policy under the Conservatives since 2015, this book seeks to set them against a framework of alternative political approaches, including the New Right and the Third Way, initially developed for Powell's (1999) discussion of New Labour. These approaches are shown in Table 1.1 according to the main dimensions for the Coalition government identified in Bochel and Powell (2016).

These dimensions, although fairly broad and inevitably with considerable overlaps, can help us consider the differing approaches and key features of the Conservative governments under successive prime ministers from 2015. The Old Left can be seen as being concerned with the redistribution of wealth; One Nation with maintaining a welfare state for paternalistic reasons and to support the development of the economy; the Third Way with an 'investor's' welfare state; and the New Right as desiring a reduction in the welfare state and increased reliance on the market. The final category seeks to summarise the social policy of the Conservative–Liberal Coalition government from 2010 to 2015 (Commission on Social Justice, 1994; Powell, 1999; Bochel and Powell, 2016).

As outlined earlier, three successive Conservative leaders and prime ministers – Cameron, May and Johnson – sought to identify themselves with forms of Conservative thinking that were concerned with inequality and to portray an interest in addressing certain economic and social inequalities (for

Table 1.1: Dimensions of political approaches

Dimension	Old Left	Third Way	One Nation	New Right	Coalition
Approach	Leveller	Investor	Investor	Deregulator	Deregulator
Citizenship	Rights	Rights and responsibilities	Rights and responsibilities	Responsibilities	Responsibilities
Outcome	Equality	Inclusion	Inclusion/some inequality	Inequality	Inequality
Mixed economy of welfare	State	State/private; civil society	State/private	Private	Private
Mode	Command and control	Cooperation/ partnership	Command and control/ cooperation	Competition	Competition
Expenditure	High	Pragmatic	Pragmatic	Low	Low
Benefits	High	Low/medium	Low/medium	Low	Low
Services	High	Medium	Medium	Low	Low/medium
Accountability	Central state/ upwards	Central state/upwards and market/downwards	Central state/upwards and market/downwards	Market/ downwards	Market/downwards and civil society
Politics	Left	Left/post-ideological	Right/ pragmatic	Right	Right

Source: Bochel and Powell (2016, Table 1.1), adapted from Powell (1999, Table 1.1)

example, Kilty, 2020). It might be argued that perhaps the main reason for each espousing such rhetoric was recognition of significant national divisions within the UK (and indeed divisions within England), which bring with them potential dangers for the Conservative Party and its electoral appeal; thus, the breadth and flexibility of the One Nation label has been used to make the Party appear more attractive. The brief Truss government appeared to move, or perhaps lurch, towards a different position, with an even clearer emphasis on a low-tax economy and greater tolerance for inequality. In contrast, Jeremy Hunt's Autumn Statement as Chancellor for the Sunak government mentioned a 'compassionate Conservative government', 'levelling up', 'protecting the vulnerable', and 'record' increases for services (which follow from the high rate of inflation), funded by asking for more tax 'from those who have more means' (Hansard, 2022). Similarly, the 2023 Budget speech claimed that the Conservatives had 'cut inequality' and 'lifted 2 million people out of absolute poverty, after housing costs', although it also highlighted further sanctions for some jobseekers (Hunt, 2023). However, critics pointed out that the UK was in a mess resulting from '12 weeks of Conservative chaos and 12 years of Conservative economic failure: growth dismal, investment down, wages squeezed and public services crumbling' (Reeves, Hansard, 2022, col 856), along with the highest inflation for many years and reduced living standards.

Conclusion

This chapter has outlined the evolution of the Conservative Party's social policies from the 2015 general election. The dominant feature of policy under the Coalition government, austerity, saw some reduction, and was followed by a large increase in public expenditure during the pandemic, only to see something of a return to 'austerity mark 2' from 2022 onwards, albeit that the 2022 Autumn Statement pushed many of the major constraints on public expenditure beyond the likely date for the next general election. Far from a 'European welfare state with American taxes', the immediate future appeared likely to involve an American-style welfare state with European taxes.

As noted earlier, during this period 'events' arguably played even more of a role in influencing government decisions and directions than usual. For example, Brexit dominated much of the machinery of government and had a becalming effect on policy, including on the development of new initiatives, given the difficulties of getting almost any significant policies through Parliament. Similarly, 'policy making as usual' was made impossible by the COVID-19 pandemic. Finally, the Russian invasion of Ukraine in 2022 was followed by high fuel costs and the highest levels of inflation for thirty years. Moreover, the period saw a rapid turnover of key government personnel during this period, with five prime ministers, seven secretaries of state for justice, five secretaries of state for health and social care and eight secretaries of state for education between 2015 and 2023.

There were some similarities in the approaches of the first three Conservative prime ministers over the period from 2015, with each making significant claims about reducing inequality, whether it was Cameron's 'Big Society', May's 'burning injustices' or Johnson's 'levelling up'. In each case, however, it was equally possible to question the extent to which policy change, let alone outcomes, matched the rhetoric. In general, as the following chapters illustrate, any achievements in reducing the inequalities identified by the three prime ministers were modest, at best. However, as noted, while prime ministers appeared to embrace ideas that might be seen as associated with traditional One Nation Conservatism, at the same time they displayed emphases, such as tax cuts, lower levels of public expenditure and greater individual responsibility, that were more clearly linked with New Right thinking. The brief period of the Truss premiership promised a clearer ideological position of inequality before it was brutally ended in a fashion that Conservatives used to lecture Labour governments about: 'You can't buck the markets'. That was followed by the Sunak administration putting forward an unappealing package of tax rises and expenditure cuts (even if largely delayed until after the likely date of the next general election), set against a context of cost of living and energy crises, rising unemployment and multiple strikes by workers seeking increased pay.

This Introduction has sketched out some of the main contours of Conservative social policy during the years 2015 to 2022. It has raised some broad issues (see Table 1.1) that are explored in more detail in subsequent individual chapters and in the concluding chapter.

Note

[1]   See more on the Manifesto Project at https://manifesto-project.wzb.eu.

References

Allen, N. and Bara, J. (2021) 'Clear blue water? The 2019 party manifestos', *The Political Quarterly*, 92(3): 531–40.

Apps, P. (2021) 'Government "deeply sorry" for failures in oversight of regulatory system before Grenfell', *Inside Housing*, 7 December. Available at: www.insidehousing.co.uk/news/government-deeply-sorry-for-failu res-in-oversight-of-regulatory-system-before-grenfell-73615 (accessed 19 July 2023).

BBC News (2019) 'Election results 2019: Boris Johnson's victory speech in full', 13 December. Available at: www.bbc.co.uk/news/election-2019-50777071 (accessed 4 December 2020).

BBC News (2022) 'Autumn Statement: key points at a glance', 17 November. Available at: www.bbc.co.uk/news/business-63555313 (accessed 5 December 2022).

Bell, T., Brewer, M., Corlett, A., Hale, S., Handscomb, K., Judge, L., Leslie, J., Marshall, J., Murphy, L., Shah, K., Smith, J., Slaughter, H. and Thwaites, G. (2022) *Inflation nation: putting Spring Statement 2022 in context*, London: Resolution Foundation.

Berry, C. (2019) 'Austerity: resurrection? The main parties' positions on fiscal policy and welfare spending at the 2019 general election', *People Place and Policy*, 13(2): 55–62.

Bochel, H. (ed) (2011) *The Conservative Party and social policy*, Bristol: Policy Press.

Bochel, H. and Powell, M. (eds) (2016) *The Coalition government and social policy*, Bristol: Policy Press.

Bochel, H. and Powell, M. (2018) 'Whatever happened to compassionate Conservatism under the Coalition government?', *British Politics*, 13(2): 146–70.

Bowden, G. (2022) 'National Insurance: Boris Johnson and Rishi Sunak confirm rise from April', *BBC News*, 30 January. Available at: www.bbc.co.uk/news/uk-60185741 (accessed 31 January 2022).

British Academy (2021) *The COVID decade: understanding the long-term societal impacts of COVID-19*, London: British Academy.

Cabinet Office (2022) *Investigation into alleged gatherings on government premises during Covid restrictions: update*, London: Cabinet Office.

Commission on Social Justice (1994) *Social justice: strategies for national renewal*, London: Vintage.

Conservative Party (2015) *Strong leadership, a clear economic plan, a brighter, more secure future. The Conservative Party manifesto 2015*, London: Conservative Party.

Conservative Party (2017) *Forward together: our plan for a stronger Britain and a prosperous future. The Conservative and Unionist Party Manifesto 2017*, London: Conservative Party.

Conservative Party (2019) *Get Brexit done, unleash Britain's potential: The Conservative and Unionist Party manifesto 2019*, London: Conservative Party.

Crossley, S. (2020) '"Everywhere and nowhere": interventions and services under austerity', in J. Rees, M. Pomati and E. Heins (eds) *Social Policy Review 32*, Bristol: Policy Press/Social Policy Association, pp 271–90.

Dilnot, A. (2011) *Fairer care funding*, London: Commission on Funding of Care and Support.

Gamble, A. (1988) *The free economy and the strong state: the politics of Thatcherism*, Basingstoke: Palgrave Macmillan.

Hansard, House of Commons (2015) 14 October, vol 600, col 427.

Hansard, House of Commons (2020) 11 March, vol 673, col 281.

Hansard, House of Commons (2022) *Autumn Statement*, 17 November, vol 722, cols 844–93.

Harari, D., Hutton, G., Keep, M., Powell, A., Sandford, M. and Ward, M. (2021) *The levelling up agenda*, Debate pack, London: House of Commons Library.

HM Government (2022) *Levelling up the United Kingdom*, London: HMSO.

HM Treasury (2020) *Spending Review 2020*, London: HMSO.

Hunt, J. (2023) 'Spring Budget 2023 speech', *Gov.uk*, 15 March. Available at: www.gov.uk/government/speeches/spring-budget-2023-speech (accessed 18 April 2023).

Institute for Fiscal Studies (2021) 'An initial IFS response to the government's Levelling up White Paper', 2 February. Available at: https://ifs.org.uk/articles/initial-ifs-response-governments-levelling-white-paper (accessed 19 July 2023).

Johnson, B. (2019) 'Boris Johnson's first speech as Prime Minister: 24 July 2019', *Gov.uk*, 24 July. Available at: www.gov.uk/government/speeches/boris-johnsons-first-speech-as-prime-minister-24-july-2019 (accessed 9 February 2022).

Johnson, B. (2020) 'PM economy speech: 30 June 2020', *Gov.uk*, 30 June. Available at: www.gov.uk/government/speeches/pm-economy-speech-30-june-2020 (accessed 9 February 2022).

Johnson, B. (2021) 'The Prime Minister's levelling up speech: 15 July 2021', *Gov.uk*, 15 July. Available at: www.gov.uk/government/speeches/the-prime-ministers-levelling-up-speech-15-july-2021 (accessed 9 February 2022).

Jordan, D. (2019) 'Chancellor Sajid Javid declares the end of austerity', *BBC News*, 4 September. Available at: www.bbc.co.uk/news/business-49577250 (accessed 25 January 2022).

Kilty, R. (2020) 'What does it mean to be leader of a "One Nation Conservative government"? The case of Boris Johnson', *Revue Français de Civilisation Britannique*, XXV(3). Available at: https://journals.openedition.org/rfcb/5862 (accessed 25 January 2022).

Lupton, R., Burchardt, T., Hills, J., Stewart, K. and Vizard, P. (eds) (2016) *Social policy in a cold climate*, Bristol: Policy Press.

May, T. (2016) 'Statement from the new Prime Minister Theresa May', *Gov.uk*, 13 July. Available at: www.gov.uk/government/speeches/statement-from-the-new-prime-minister-theresa-may (accessed 15 February 2022).

McEnhill, L. and Taylor-Gooby, P. (2018) 'Beyond continuity? Understanding change in the UK welfare state since 2010', *Social Policy & Administration*, 52(1): 252–70.

McIntyre, N., Duncan, P. and Halliday, J. (2022) 'Levelling-up: some wealthy areas of England to see 10 times more funding than poorest', *The Guardian*, 2 February. Available at: www.theguardian.com/inequality/2022/feb/02/levelling-up-funding-inequality-exposed-by-guardian-research (accessed 9 February 2022).

Mornington, A.-D. (2020) 'Was Boris Johnson's One-Nation post-electoral pledge sincere?', *Revue Français de Civilisation Britannique*, XXV(3). Available at: https://journals.openedition.org/rfcb/5693 (accessed 25 January 2022).

Office for Budget Responsibility (2021) 'A brief guide to the public finances'. Available at: https://obr.uk/docs/dlm_uploads/BriefGuide-AB21-1.pdf (accessed 19 July 2023).

Office for National Statistics (2021) *UK government debt and deficit: December 2020*, London: Office for National Statistics. Available at: https://www.ons.gov.uk/economy/governmentpublicsectorandtaxes/publicspending/bulletins/ukgovernmentdebtanddeficitforeurostatmaast/december2020 (accessed 1 August 2023).

Pomati, M., Jolly, A. and Rees, J. (eds) *Social Policy Review 33*, Bristol: Policy Press/Social Policy Association.

Powell, M. (1999) 'Introduction', in M. Powell (ed) *New Labour: new welfare state*, Bristol: Policy Press.

Powell, M. (2022) 'Austerity politics and beyond, 2010–2021', in P. Alcock, T. Haux, V. McCall and M. May (eds) *The student's companion to social policy*, Chichester: Wiley Blackwell.

Public Accounts Committee (2021) *COVID-19: government procurement and supply of personal protective equipment*, London: House of Commons.

Sunak, R. (2022) 'Rishi Sunak's first speech as Prime Minister: 25 October 2022', *Gov.uk*, 25 October. Available at: www.gov.uk/government/speeches/prime-minister-rishi-sunaks-statement-25-october-2022 (accessed 18 April 2023).

Vizard, P. and Hills, J. (2021a) 'Introduction and overview', in P. Vizard and J. Hills (eds) *The Conservative governments' record on social policy from May 2015 to pre-COVID 2020: policies, spending and outcomes*, London: Centre for Analysis of Social Exclusion, LSE, pp 1–12.

Vizard, P. and Hills, J. (eds) (2021b) *The Conservative governments' record on social policy from May 2015 to pre-COVID 2020: policies, spending and outcomes*, London: Centre for Analysis of Social Exclusion, LSE.

2

The Conservatives and public spending since 2015

Nick Ellison

Introduction

Caught between the neoliberal desire for low-tax, free market, small state solutions, and a 'One Nationism' that demands higher spending and greater state intervention, Conservative governments from 2015 failed to establish a coherent and consistent approach to public expenditure. Five spending phases distinguish the 2015–23 period, oscillating between two variants of New Right/neoliberalism and three more or less reluctant iterations of One Nationism (see Chapter 1 and Tables 1.1 and 18.1). First was the continuation of 'Osborne economics', best understood as a phase of 'neoliberal austerity' despite efforts to cloak it in a 'we're all in it together' rhetoric. Second, a pragmatic Brexit-induced One Nationism appeared towards the end of Theresa May's premiership when 'austerity' was pronounced over and spending constraints were relaxed somewhat, this position extending into the Johnson era with its post-Brexit promise to 'level up'. Third, a reluctant, ad hoc One Nationism was evident in the state-sponsored COVID-19 support packages and subsequent efforts to limit the effects of post-pandemic inflation and the cost of living crisis that accompanied the Russian invasion of Ukraine – reluctant because packages were either less inclusive (COVID-19) or on occasion less generous (cost of living support) than they could have been; ad hoc because throughout this period the government found itself at the mercy of events, continually having to revise proposed spending measures to keep abreast of the challenges it faced. Fourth, a radical neoliberal variant briefly appeared in the shape of the Truss government's tax-cut-driven approach to economic and fiscal policy, this interlude being replaced, fifth, by a paradoxical approach in the shape of the 2022 Autumn Statement and March 2023 Budget, which contain both One Nation and neoliberal elements – epitomising the Conservatives' One Nation/neoliberal dilemma.

Beginning in 2015, the next section briefly examines Conservative assumptions about public spending during the run-up to the Brexit referendum. Attention is paid to spending under Cameron's second government (2015–16) and May's two governments (2016–19), a period that witnessed the eventual easing of austerity in the aftermath of the Brexit vote. The chapter then explores government reactions to the economic and fiscal rollercoaster that includes the COVID-19 pandemic, its inflationary aftermath, the subsequent energy and cost of living crises provoked by Russia's war in Ukraine, and the self-inflicted harm of the disastrous Truss episode.

Public spending, 2015–20

The 2010–15 Coalition government's public spending strategy, billed as a necessary response to the 2008 financial/banking crisis, established a double-edged approach to (specifically social) spending that afforded some protection to certain services and population groups while significantly reducing protection for others. Pensioners, for instance, benefited from continuity with Labour's pension reforms and particularly the introduction of the triple lock, which guaranteed pension increases according to whichever was the greater among prices (based on the Consumer Prices Index), earnings and 2.5 per cent (Ellison, 2016; Vizard and Obolenskaya, 2021). Of the spending departments, the Department of Health was among only three (alongside International Development and Energy and Climate Change) to benefit from real terms budget increases, although these were 'exceptionally low' (Vizard et al, 2016, p 157), lagging behind the very modest increases in gross domestic product (GDP) and, more importantly, the ever-growing need for health and social care principally caused by the UK's rapidly ageing population. Conversely, from 2013, a series of tax and benefit changes, including the imposition of a 'benefits cap' on many social security recipients and a 'welfare cap' on spending devoted to social protection, resulted in 'substantial losses at the bottom of the income distribution' with 'single parent families, larger families and those with young children' being particularly affected (Vizard and Obolenskaya, 2021, p 28; see also Beatty and Fothergill, 2017). The majority of spending departments saw their budgets significantly reduced, with the Department for Communities and Local Government, for example, experiencing a 40 per cent real terms cut, while local authorities were simultaneously prevented from offsetting this loss of central government support by a government-imposed cap on Council Tax rises (Hastings et al, 2012). Looking at total managed expenditure (TME), real terms public spending fell from £929 billion in 2010–11 to a low of £910 billion in 2013–14 before recovering to £919 billion in 2014–15. TME stood at 45.8 per cent of GDP in 2010–11 and 41 per cent in 2015–16. Figure 2.1 provides an overview of UK GDP and TME between 2005–06 and 2014–15, while Figure 2.2 focuses specifically on real terms TME during that period.

Not surprisingly, as the key personnel did not immediately change, the transition from a Conservative-dominated Coalition government to a

Figure 2.1: Gross domestic product and total managed expenditure (real terms, billions at 2019 prices), 2005–06 to 2014–15

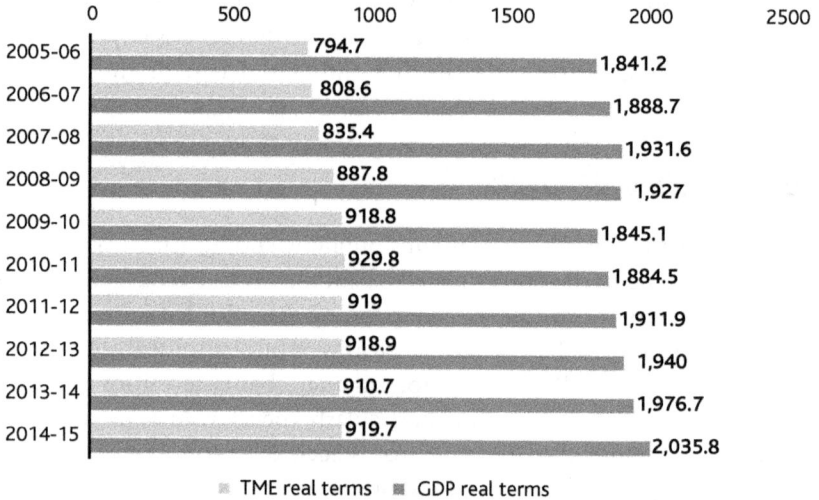

	0	500	1000	1500	2000	2500

2005-06	794.7 / 1,841.2
2006-07	808.6 / 1,888.7
2007-08	835.4 / 1,931.6
2008-09	887.8 / 1,927
2009-10	918.8 / 1,845.1
2010-11	929.8 / 1,884.5
2011-12	919 / 1,911.9
2012-13	918.9 / 1,940
2013-14	910.7 / 1,976.7
2014-15	919.7 / 2,035.8

■ TME real terms ■ GDP real terms

Source: Adapted from HM Treasury (2021a, Table 4.1)

Conservative administration following the 2015 general election resulted in public spending continuity. Chancellor George Osborne stated in his July 2015 Budget speech that further reducing the deficit and cutting the UK's level of debt remained the key priorities that informed a proposed £37 billion 'consolidation' during the Parliament, £12 billion of which was to come from further welfare reductions. Success here, Osborne (2015) argued, would accelerate the move from a 'low-wage, high-tax, high-welfare society to a higher-wage, lower-tax, lower-welfare economy'. Reiterating the points frequently made during his time as Coalition Chancellor, Osborne (2015) stressed that social protection was for those who could not work and that '[t]hose who can work will be expected to look for work and take it when it is offered', pointing out that '[i]t is not acceptable that in an economy moving towards full employment, some young people leave school and go straight on to a life on benefits'.

This neoliberal tone echoed the aims that Osborne had set out in his Mais Lecture of February 2010. And, in general terms, the underpinning principles of constrained departmental spending, tight control of local authority expenditure and downward pressure on welfare costs did not change substantially until the latter phase of May's premiership. In terms of 'results', as Figure 2.3 indicates, boosted by the combination of controlled public spending and rising GDP, net borrowing fell from a height of 10 per cent of GDP in 2009–10 to 2.6 per cent in 2019–20, immediately before the onset of the COVID-19 pandemic. UK debt also declined over the period, although not to levels below 80 per cent as Osborne had hoped (see Figure 2.4).

Figure 2.2: Total managed expenditure (real terms, billions at 2019 prices), 2005–06 to 2014–15

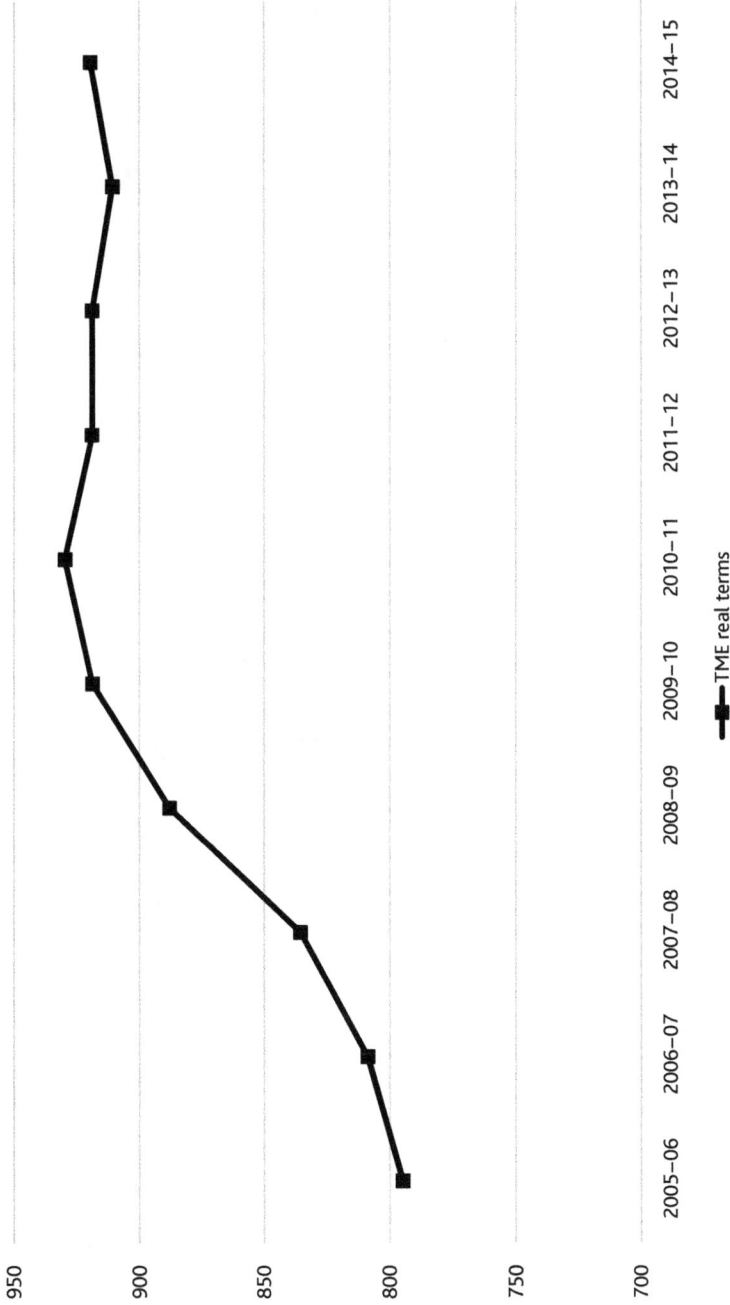

Source: Adapted from HM Treasury (2021a, Table 4.1)

Figure 2.3: Deficit (percentage of GDP), 2005–06 to 2020–21

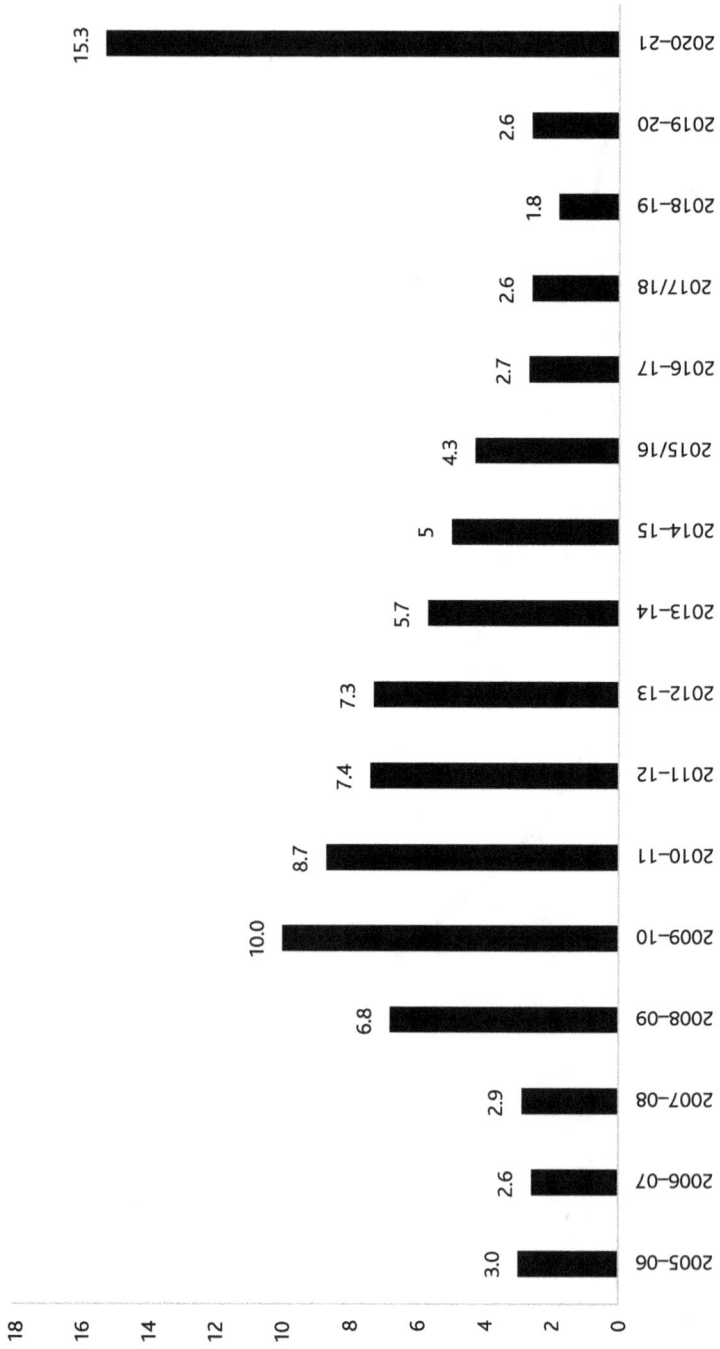

Year	Deficit
2005–06	3.0
2006–07	2.6
2007–08	2.9
2008–09	6.8
2009–10	10.0
2010–11	8.7
2011–12	7.4
2012–13	7.3
2013–14	5.7
2014–15	5
2015/16	4.3
2016–17	2.7
2017/18	2.6
2018–19	1.8
2019–20	2.6
2020–21	15.3

Source: Adapted from ONS (2022)

Figure 2.4: UK debt (percentage of GDP), 2005–06 to 2020–21

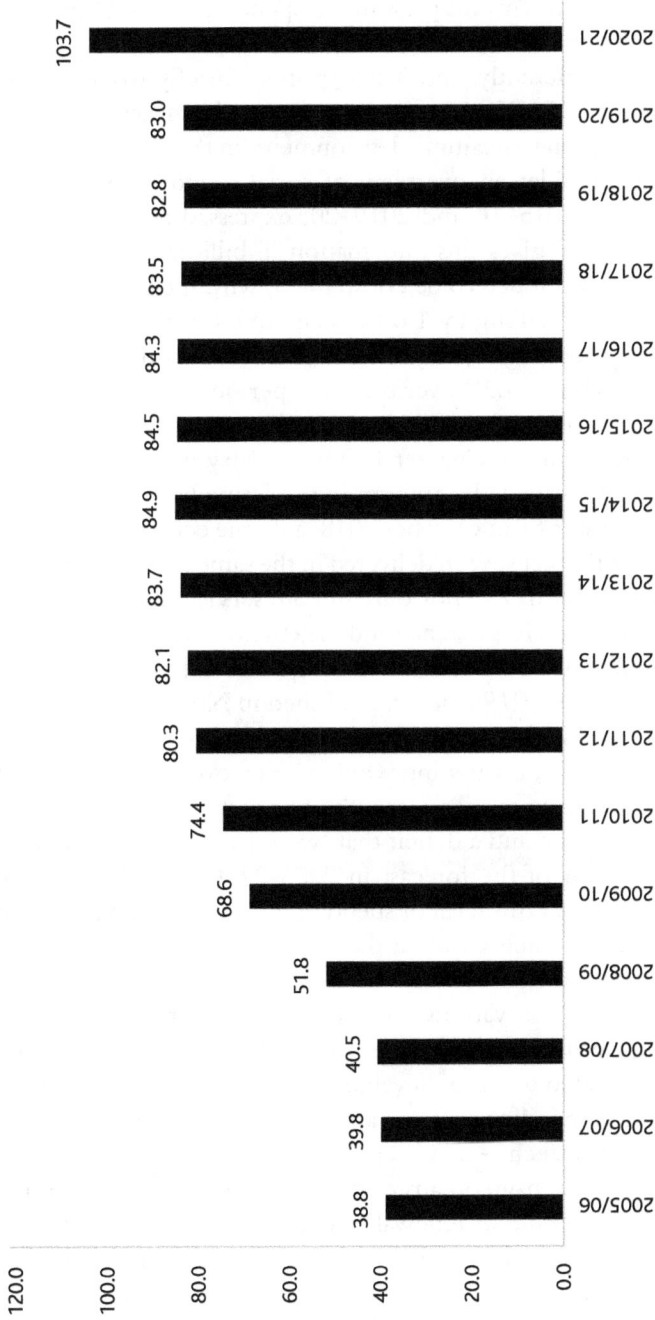

Year	Value
2020/21	103.7
2019/20	83.0
2018/19	82.8
2017/18	83.5
2016/17	84.3
2015/16	84.5
2014/15	84.9
2013/14	83.7
2012/13	82.1
2011/12	80.3
2010/11	74.4
2009/10	68.6
2008/09	51.8
2007/08	40.5
2006/07	39.8
2005/06	38.8

Source: Adapted from ONS (2022)

Although spending increased by 2.4 per cent in the five years to 2019–20, GDP rose by just under 8 per cent between 2015–16 and 2019–20, continuing the downward pressure on spending set by Osborne during the Coalition government (see Figures 2.1 and 2.5). Nevertheless, different areas were treated differently, and it is important briefly to explore the general nature of pre-COVID-19 spending, especially in key social policy areas, before moving on to examine developments in the post-COVID-19 period. Figure 2.6 provides an overview of social spending by function in core areas between 2015–16 and 2019–20, expressed as a percentage of GDP, while Figure 2.7 gives this information in billions of pounds (real terms). Expenditure continued to be constrained, with spending on education and social protection falling by 1.6 per cent and 4 per cent respectively, while total health spending slightly bucked the trend, rising by 9.2 per cent, or 1.3 per cent above GDP, over the same period.

This period of tightly controlled spending was relaxed in the wake of the Brexit referendum (see Chapter 4). Theresa May, who, in a chaotic leadership election, had succeeded Cameron in the immediate aftermath, announced the 'end of austerity' in October 2018, a theme echoed in Chancellor Philip Hammond's Budget speech delivered in the same month (Hammond, 2018). Spending was set to rise not only in core services like health and housing, but also in areas such as defence and the environment. The Office for Budget Responsibility (OBR) noted 'the rapid growth in public services spending' in its *Restated March 2019 Forecast*, published in November of that year (2019, p 4), and expressed concern about renewed pressure on the deficit. In the OBR's estimation, borrowing would rise by over 16 per cent in the 2019–20 forecast, leading to increases in 'public sector net borrowing by roughly £20 billion a year' and a deficit that 'would still be in excess of £30 billion in the final year of the forecast in 2023-24' (OBR, 2019, pp 2, 3) – the anxiety being that this level of spending risked breaching the government's fiscal mandate, which required the 'cyclically adjusted budget to lie below 2 per cent of GDP in 2020-21' (OBR, 2019, p 15).

Despite these reservations, on taking power in the summer of 2019, the Johnson government pressed on with spending promises, now framed in the Brexit-related terms of 'levelling up'. Further commitments included a £13.8 billion spending increase announced by Sajid Javid in his September 2019 Budget speech – a speech in which he claimed that 'we can now afford to turn the page on austerity ... and move forward from a decade of recovery to a decade of renewal' – with a promise of another £13 billion targeted specifically at the National Health Service, education and law and order (Javid, 2019). With the prospect of a 'hard' Brexit looking increasingly likely, it was not surprising that the politico-economic tone shifted significantly. Javid's spending announcement, which effectively marked the emergence in policy terms of the levelling up agenda, was accompanied by

Figure 2.5: Total managed expenditure and gross domestic product (real terms, billions), 2015–16 to 2019–20

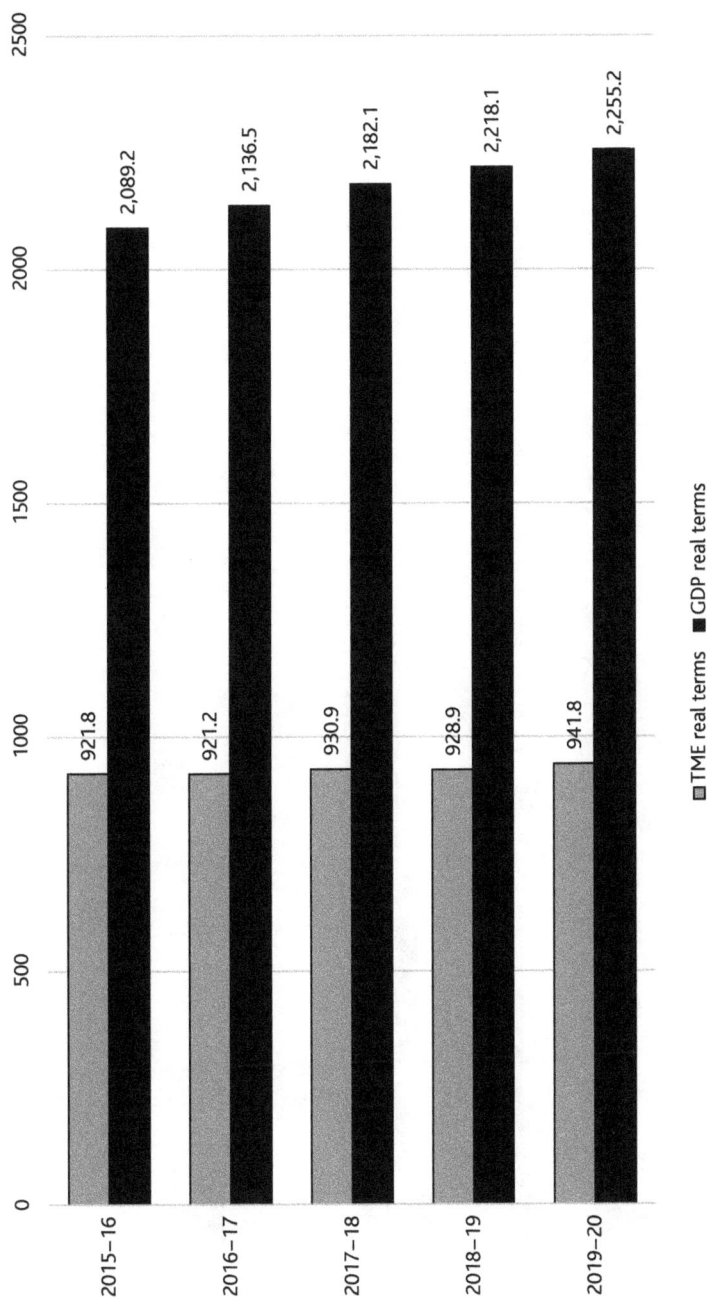

Note: Figures are adjusted to 2020–21 price levels using ONS GDP deflators released in June 2021.
Source: Adapted from HM Treasury (2021a, Table 4.1)

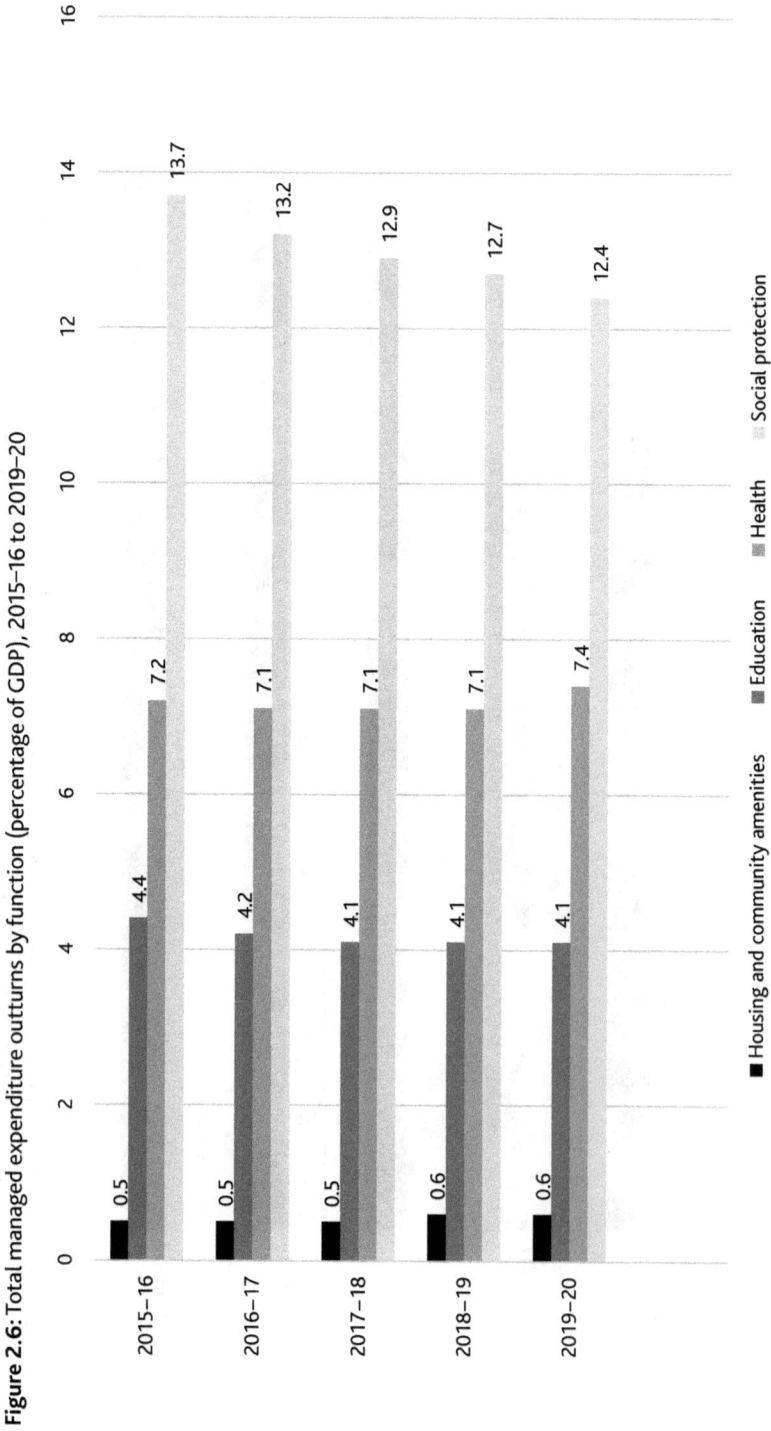

Figure 2.6: Total managed expenditure outturns by function (percentage of GDP), 2015–16 to 2019–20

Source: Adapted from HM Treasury (2021a, Table 4.4)

Housing and community amenities ■ Education ■ Health ■ Social protection

Figure 2.7: Total managed expenditure outturns by function (real terms, billions), 2015–16 to 2019–20

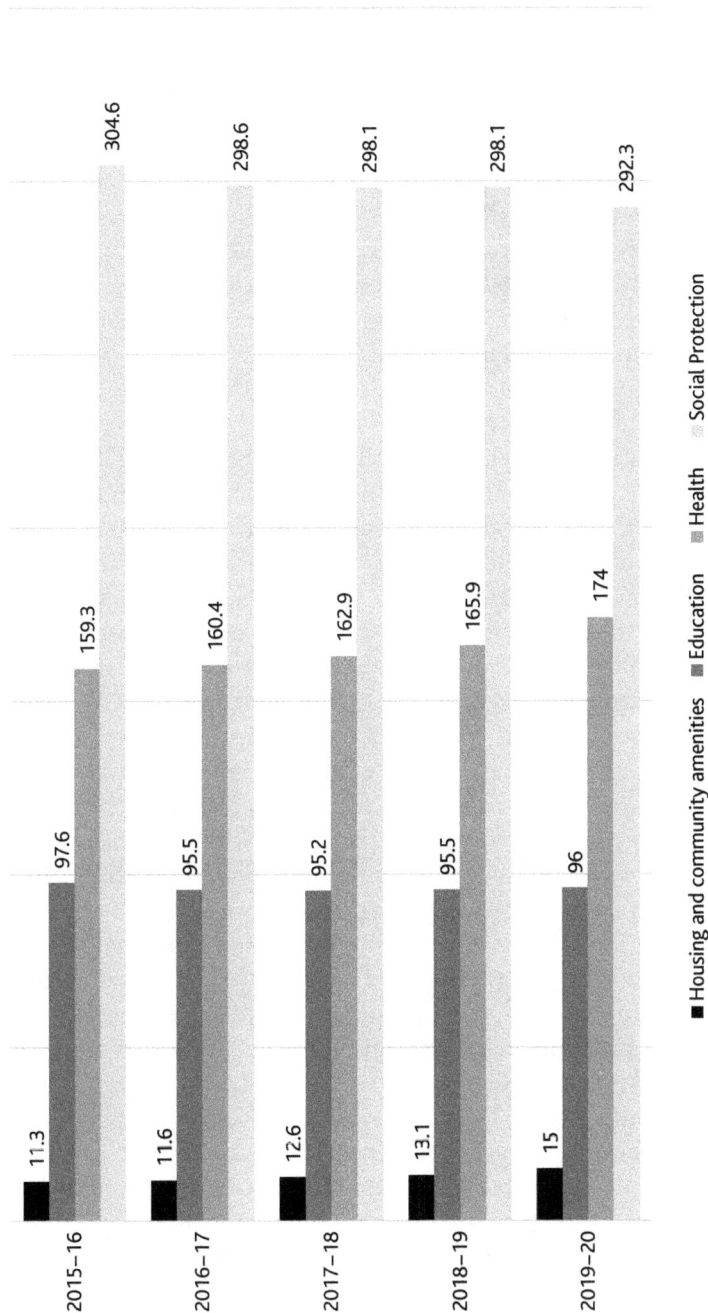

■ Housing and community amenities ■ Education ■ Health ▨ Social Protection

Year	Housing and community amenities	Education	Health	Social Protection
2015–16	11.3	97.6	159.3	304.6
2016–17	11.6	95.5	160.4	298.6
2017–18	12.6	95.2	162.9	298.1
2018–19	13.1	95.5	165.9	298.1
2019–20	15	96	174	292.3

Note: Figures are adjusted to 2020–21 price levels using ONS GDP deflators released in June 2021.
Source: Adapted from Public Expenditure Statistical Analysis release (HM Treasury, 2021a)

the confirmation of increased amounts of funding for 'Brexit and no-deal preparedness' and 'Brexit delivery', initially announced by Hammond – and this in the context of the timely rediscovery of a 'Global Britain', requiring the ushering in of a 'new economic era' and a 'genuinely independent free trade policy with the rest of the world' (Javid, 2019).

The fate of Javid's plans will of course never be known. Not only did he leave office in January 2020, following a heated disagreement with Boris Johnson and Dominic Cummings about the dismissal of his advisors, but also, with the onset of the COVID-19 pandemic in February/March of that year, it quickly became clear that existing public spending provision could not hope to deal with the burden placed on the public finances by the crisis. Indeed, the reality of COVID-19 made earlier concerns about the size of the deficit appear decidedly quaint. The £152 billion deficit recorded at the height of the financial crisis pales against the £323 billion reached at the height of the pandemic in 2020–21.

This brief account of public spending during the 2015–2020 period, pre COVID-19, is important because it tracks the economic and fiscal direction of travel that Conservative governments effectively *had* to take if they were to succeed politically after the Brexit referendum. Austerity remained a guiding principle for the first two years of Hammond's Chancellorship, and, without doubt, its effects continued to be experienced by key services and vulnerable sections of the population throughout this period and beyond (Beatty and Fothergill, 2017; McEnhill and Taylor-Gooby, 2018). However, austerity as an explicit ideological and economic objective was rendered unsustainable in the face of the referendum result. Neutralising the Brexit Party in the run-up to the 2019 general election in order to maximise the votes of 'identity conservative' (Sobolewska and Ford, 2020) 'Leave' supporters necessitated attention not only to 'getting Brexit done' but also, as an intrinsic part of that process, promising more investment for Leave-voting English constituencies – something facilitated immensely by the popular (and populist) figure of Boris Johnson (Evans et al, 2021). The difficulty, though, was how to pursue a potentially expensive levelling up agenda in newly won 'red wall' constituencies while retaining the loyalty of traditional Conservative voters in true blue areas, particularly in the south and south-east of England, some of whom were sympathetic One Nationers, though unconvinced by Brexit, and others of whom were pro-Brexit, small state free marketeers. While these lines of division were successfully managed for short-term electoral purposes (possibly aided by a weak opposition and the forced removal of many long-serving One Nation Members of Parliament – MPs) and subsequently masked by COVID-19, their continuance has hindered the pursuit of a coherent spending *strategy*. Unsurprisingly, tensions relating to this central concern, exacerbated but also muddied by Johnson's personal ambivalence about spending and the role of the state, re-emerged in the wake of the pandemic. Before engaging directly with this matter, however, it is important to explore the spending impact of COVID-19 itself and, beyond that, the challenges posed by recent events, most obviously the Russian invasion of Ukraine.

COVID-19, Ukraine and public spending

Without question, COVID-19 placed an immediate and, excepting the last World War, unprecedented burden on the UK's public finances. Initially slow to appreciate the severity of the pandemic, and with a legacy of underspending in key services, particularly social care (National Audit Office, 2018; King's Fund, 2021), the government nevertheless responded to the economic and financial dimensions of the crisis in ad hoc fashion, though with some agility, from roughly mid-April 2020 onwards (see also Chapter 5). On the employment front, faced with the prospect of a 14 per cent drop in output and a dramatic rise in unemployment as businesses went into lockdown, Javid's successor, Rishi Sunak, established two schemes designed to protect both workers and businesses from the worst effects of the pandemic. The Coronavirus Job Retention Scheme, first announced on 20 March 2020, allowed employers to claim 80 per cent of their usual monthly wage costs up to a maximum of £2,500 per employee per month, while the Self-Employment Income Support Scheme provided cash grants of 80 per cent of profits for the self-employed up to the same amount. Additional measures included temporary changes to Universal Credit and Working Tax Credit, the former seeing certain eligibility criteria removed and recipients of both benefits receiving a payment increase of £20 per week (Ellison et al, 2022).

As has been noted elsewhere, the two central support packages alongside the benefit measures – while they undoubtedly prevented economic collapse, rocketing unemployment and a dramatic rise in poverty – were implemented without too much One Nation concern for equality (Bambra et al, 2021; Calvert and Arbuthnot, 2021; Summers et al, 2021), the poorest and most vulnerable sections of the population not being fully included in the schemes (see Platt and Warwick, 2020; British Academy, 2021). Nevertheless, in straightforward spending terms, the financial commitment was, by any measure, exceptional in peacetime. Using figures taken from the National Audit Office's 'COVID-19 cost tracker', the total *lifetime* cost of COVID-19 was estimated at £370 billion in May 2021 (National Audit Office, 2021), although figures from other sources vary depending on the chosen timeframe (see, for example, OBR, 2022a, p 84). Table 2.1 displays the National Audit Office's estimates of overall COVID-19-related spending by function while Figure 2.8 shows the major departments involved with COVID-19-associated spending and the original estimated lifetime cost,

Table 2.1: COVID-19-related spending by function (billions, estimated)

Type of support	£ (billion)
Support for businesses	154
Health and Social Care	84
Other services, including emergency services	67
Support for individuals	60
Other support	5
Total	370

Source: National Audit Office (2021)

the estimated lifetime cost as of 2021 and the spend as of 2021 associated with each.

How was this level of spending financed, and what was its impact on the UK's deficit and debt ratios in relation to GDP? According to Brien and Keep, the government raised £792 billion from taxes and other revenues, but 'receipts were 9.3% lower in 2020/21 than forecast before the pandemic and 4.4% lower compared with 2019/20' (2022, p 17). Although these receipts 'were larger relative to the size of the economy in 2020/21 compared with 2019/20', probably because government protection of incomes through the support schemes meant that taxes continued to be paid, the pressure on public spending inevitably led to enhanced government borrowing, which rose to £323 billion (just over 15 per cent of GDP in 2020–21; see Figure 2.3), compared to the £57 billion borrowed in 2019–20 (Brien and Keep, 2022, pp 18–19). Crucially, of course, this level of borrowing funded what was effectively *temporary* relief. Public expenditure fell by 60 per cent through 2021 as pandemic pressures eased, the economy revived and the support schemes were wound down (including the controversial decision to withdraw the £20 weekly uplift to Universal Credit).

As spending declined from its COVID-19 peak, other pressures began to emerge. Manifesto commitments made before the 2019 general election awaited fulfilment, not least the promise to invest £1 billion per year in social care over the course of the Parliament (Conservative Party, 2019, p 14) – a pledge given additional significance following the demonstrable failings of the care system in the early stages of the pandemic (Daly, 2020). These considerations prompted short-term 'tax and spend' measures in the March and October 2021 Budgets. The OBR confirmed as much in its October *Economic and Fiscal Outlook*, stating that 'the Government has announced a significant discretionary increase in both the tax burden and the size of the post-pandemic state' (2021, p 7). Tax rises included the 1.25 per cent increase in National Insurance contributions announced in October for April 2022,

Figure 2.8: Spending on COVID-19 by lead department (billions)

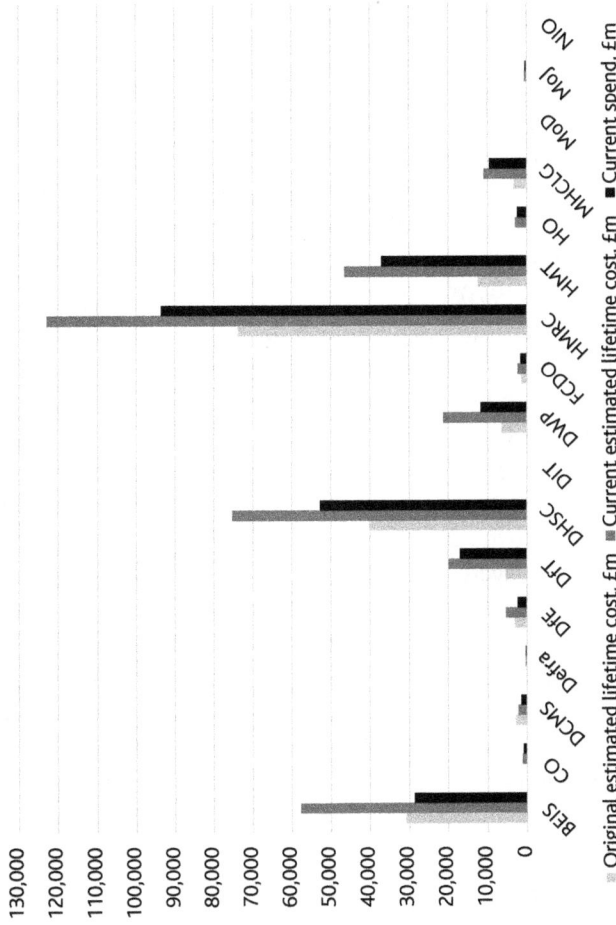

Notes: BEIS is the Department for Business, Energy and Industrial Strategy; CO is the Cabinet Office; DCMS is the Department for Culture Media and Sport; Defra is the Department for Environment, Food and Rural Affairs; DfE is the Department for Education; DfT is the Department for Transport; DHSC is the Department for Health and Social Care; DIT is the Department for International Trade; DWP is the Department for Work and Pensions; FCDO is the Foreign, Commonwealth and Development Office; HMRC is HM Customs and Revenue; HMT is HM Treasury; HO is the Home Office; MHCLG is the Ministry of Housing, Communities and Local Government; MoD is the Ministry of Defence; MoJ is the Ministry of Justice; NIO is the Northern Ireland Office.
Source: National Audit Office (2021)

which was to be permanently succeeded by a new Health and Social Care Levy from April 2023, and other increases previously declared in March, including a significant rise in Corporation Tax (from 19 per cent to 25 per cent) and a five-year freeze on personal tax thresholds. Despite Sunak's assurance that he would cut Income Tax in 2024, the OBR estimated that the measures in place at that time would take 'the tax burden from 33.5% of GDP before the pandemic to 36.2% of GDP by 2026–27, its highest since the early 1950s' (2021, p 8). Meanwhile, departmental expenditure was increased, with 'roughly £30 billion on average added to departmental budgets in each year of the Spending Review'. About half that figure would go 'directly from the new levy to health and social care with the other half undoing the £18 billion of unspecified cuts to pre-pandemic spending totals made in the last two fiscal events' (OBR, 2021, p 8). Overall, this tax and spend approach was judged by the OBR in its March 2022 *Economic and Fiscal Outlook* (OBR, 2022a) to allow the Chancellor to achieve his fiscal target of total public spending at 41 per cent of GDP by 2025–26, the largest share of GDP since the 1970s.

Prefiguring stronger critiques, and indeed the tone of the July–September 2022 Tory leadership campaign, this strategy was not received well by certain sections of the Parliamentary Conservative Party. Ex-Housing Secretary Robert Jenrick's warning against 'the current level of public spending and the size of the state' (quoted in Mason, 2021) was not an isolated instance and reflected the Conservatives' deep-seated ambivalence about the proposed levels of public expenditure. It is of course difficult to be sure how Sunak's strategy would have played out, because, by January 2022, the global economic and political environment was changing radically. In the ensuing months, the UK economy was confronted by a plethora of challenges that demanded immediate spending responses, returning the government to the ad hoc policy space that had characterised the COVID-19 pandemic period. Price increases due to rapidly rising levels of economic activity and consequent supply bottlenecks resulted in a 5 per cent inflation rate in January 2022. This deteriorating situation worsened dramatically following the Russian invasion of Ukraine on 24 February. Food and energy prices rose further, and by April Consumer Prices Index inflation stood at 9 per cent, rising to double figures by August and with further increases forecast (Bank of England, 2022). The headline feature of the developing crisis was the increase in the energy price cap, which rose by 54 per cent to £1,971 in April 2022, with another hike to £3,549 promised for October and a further increase to £4,279 set for January 2023. Following urgent demands from opposition parties, charities and pressure groups for a swift and generous reaction to the rising cost of living (see Brown, 2022), the government's spending response came in four instalments: a 'Sunak response' delivered in two parts; a generous, though uncosted, 'Truss/Kwarteng response', rapidly concocted in the wake of Truss' leadership election victory; and a 'Hunt response' in the November Autumn Statement, which removed much of its immediate predecessor's apparent generosity (Hunt, 2022).

Such was the speed of change between late spring and autumn 2022 that little is to be gained from rehearsing the Sunak response in any detail. Suffice it to say that Sunak part one saw some hastily – and reluctantly – conceived ameliorative measures announced in the Spring Spending Review. The National Insurance floor was raised, removing those on very low incomes from this 'tax' altogether and taking some of the sting out of the upcoming Health and Social Care Levy for others. Elsewhere a series of temporary reliefs saw, inter alia, 2022–23 Council Tax rebates of £150 provided for 80 per cent of households and a repayable £200 rebate on energy bills. However, at around £5 billion, the giveaway was modest, as the Institute for Fiscal Studies (IFS) pointed out (IFS, 2022b), and the measures were swiftly exposed as inadequate, leading to Sunak part two in late May 2022. This saw the introduction of what the IFS (2022a) heralded as a 'genuinely big package of support for households' with 'the poorest households ... now [being] approximately compensated for the rising cost of living this year'. Tax cuts favoured by Right-wing Conservative MPs such as Iain Duncan Smith and Steve Baker were not included in the package – anticipating the key point of division in the Sunak–Truss leadership debates. Indeed, the headline takeaway was a tax *rise* in the form of the controversial Energy (Oil and Gas) Profits Levy, a 'windfall tax' levied on the excess profits made by oil and gas companies. Combining the March and May packages, the IFS estimated a net injection of £14 billion (£37 billion gross).

Truss, Sunak and the longer view

Reviewing the Tory leadership election in early September 2022, it was unlikely that Sunak's approach to dealing with rising inflation and the fuel crisis was ever going to convince MPs and Party members on the neoliberal Right. A steady chorus of objections to the windfall tax from Conservative tax cutters (Woodcock, 2021; Maidment, 2022) was a harbinger of things to come – and this even though the measures taken in March and May reflected, at best, a 'reluctant' One Nationism that Sunak intended to last for just one year. Comments by him as Chancellor support this view. In a statement made at the Confederation of British Industry's annual dinner in May 2022, he claimed that 'even as we protect people from the worst of the crisis, we must continue to be responsible with the public finances and get borrowing sustainably under control and debt falling' (quoted in Brown, 2022). In a foretaste of his leadership campaign, Sunak went on to outline a longer-term, neoliberal-friendly plan to cut the deficit, control spending and rely on 'higher productivity [as] the only way to raise living standards' (quoted in Brown, 2022).

This relative caution about immediate tax cuts in fact appealed to a majority of Conservative MPs, although not to key Right-wingers associated with the influential European Research Group, nor to a majority of Party members for whom Truss' 'tax cuts now' approach proved more compelling. In the event, of course, the Truss government's 'sugar-rush boost to demand' (Bell et al, 2022a, p 24) contained in Kwasi Kwarteng's infamous September 'mini-budget', and the uncosted £43 billion of borrowing it relied on, fell foul of both the markets (see Easton, 2022) and the Bank of England, leaving the government in a dangerous strategy-free zone from which it then had to attempt to escape. The tone of Jeremy Hunt's – the fourth Chancellor of 2022 – Autumn Statement in 2022 and his March 2023 Budget signalled a part reversion to the One Nation tax and spend approach adopted by Sunak, though with significant medium-term pressure on spending indicating a reluctance, or possibly an inability, to engage with long-term solutions.

The Statement heralded a £55 billion consolidation, roughly half coming from delayed spending cuts and around half from restored tax rises. Hunt reintroduced Sunak's Corporation Tax increase following its abolition by Kwarteng, extended the freeze on Income Tax thresholds, increased the Energy Profits Levy from 25 per cent to 35 per cent and lowered the Income Tax additional rate tax threshold from £150,000 to £125,140. Apart from the Health and Social Care Levy, removed by Kwarteng and not restored, these adjustments reversed the tax cuts instigated by the Truss regime, steadying the markets in doing so. Nevertheless, although progressive, with '70% of the new taxes for individuals ... paid by the richest fifth of households' (Bell et al, 2022b, p 3), Hunt recognised there were political limits, both outside and inside the Conservative Party, to tax rises and spending cuts. Consequently, he decided to meet the immediate costs of a reduced, though still expensive, energy support package, higher interest rates on government debt and the fact that some spending increases could not be delayed for fear of risking social dislocation (see Bell et al, 2022a) through increased borrowing. On this basis, the Chancellor was able to increase benefits in line with inflation and continue with the levelling up programme, though somewhat reduced (OBR, 2022b, pp 41–2). The overall package, which also included a 10.1 per cent rise in the State Pension in line with the triple lock principle, was estimated to leave the UK with a 97 per cent debt-to-GDP ratio, a historically high tax burden and the prospect of significant future reductions in public spending (Bell et al, 2022b).

Much of this was confirmed in the March 2023 Budget, which, like the Statement, exhibited elements of One Nationism – with a neoliberal twist. Lower-than-expected expenditure on energy support and the UK's better-than-expected economic performance offered a modicum of relief compared to November's pessimism. Even so, the predicted 6 per cent increase in the cost of living between 2022–23 and 2024–25, steadily rising tax-to-GDP ratio to 2027–28 (OBR, 2023, pp 8–10) and rapidly increasing interest rates, combined with the electorally delicate legacy of Osbornian austerity, meant the Chancellor chose not to reduce the level of borrowing set out in the Autumn Statement. This was less a recognition of the importance of public spending in straitened times than an acceptance that he had little room for manoeuvre. Tax cuts, however desirable to the small state mindset, would risk market scepticism, falling receipts, further interest rate hikes and, therefore, additional pressure on public services, all of which would disturb One Nationers. Conversely, further rises would not only provoke the neoliberal Right but also, depending on their precise nature, contribute to already declining living standards. In the event, with borrowing levels maintained, the Budget provided a tentative stimulation to growth through a temporary investment allowance to offset the impact of the Corporation Tax rise and a welcome, though problematic and largely delayed, increase in support for childcare to encourage greater labour market participation. These measures, together with increased defence spending, amount to an additional £6.4 billion per annum over five years. Whether these modest adjustments to the Autumn Statement are sufficient to resolve the UK's labour market issues, encourage investment and achieve the fiscal mandate of a debt-to-GDP ratio of 94.6 per cent together with the supplementary target of net borrowing not exceeding 3 per cent of GDP by 2027–28 remains unclear (see OBR, 2023, p 125).

What is clear, however, is that, except for health and the part exception of education, the spending cuts are set to increase (see Bell et al, 2023). Those announced in the autumn remain in place and, according to the OBR, a 'declining path of public spending … across the forecast' will see TME fall as a share of GDP in the last three years of the period (2023, p 94). Of course, it is possible that predictions of a backloaded dose of neoliberal austerity could be unduly pessimistic, with energy costs and inflation turning out lower, and growth higher, than expected, but two closely related 'structural' factors are likely to perpetuate the Conservative spending dilemma. First, sustained business investment and productivity have proved elusive despite the promises of successive chancellors. Second, with Brexit remaining far from 'done' in terms of its economic fallout, there is a danger that this record will be compounded as the UK struggles to adjust to the post-Brexit economic era.

According to the Bank of England, business investment has been weak in recent years, with confidence suffering from Brexit fallout and the further uncertainty caused by the pandemic (Bank of England, 2021; Dhingra et al, 2022). Figure 2.9 illustrates the problem, showing that business investment has lagged gross fixed capital formation (GFCF) since 2020 quarter 2. In fact it has been sluggish since the financial crisis, and following COVID-19, it

Figure 2.9: UK business investment (chained volume, seasonally adjusted), 2007Q4–2022Q1

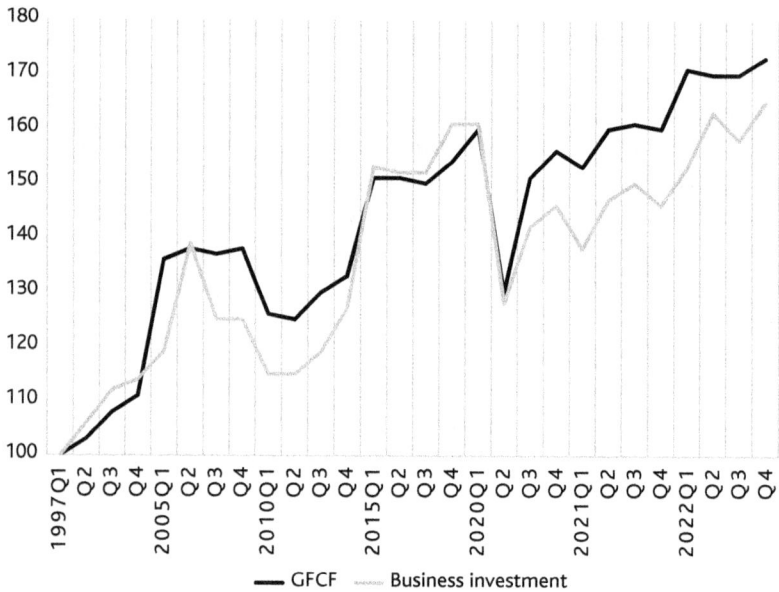

Note: 1997Q1 = 100.
Source: Adapted from ONS (2023)

only reached its 2019 level in the last quarter of 2022. Although UK GFCF has grown somewhat since the end of the pandemic, it has been lower than comparable economies, as Figure 2.10 demonstrates – the point being not only that the UK's capital base is weaker than that in other advanced economies, but also that business is seemingly cautious about supporting it. And improvement is not guaranteed. For example, Conservative hostility to migrant labour, combined with post-COVID-19 changes in attitudes to work, could adversely affect labour market flexibility, while the temporary nature of the investment allowance announced in the Budget may act as a disincentive to long-term investment planning. As Du and Shepotylo note, 'in a scenario where productivity is strained … and capital flow remains free, it is possible that private investment may decay, exacerbated by the fact that there is still so much uncertainty about the future of the UK-EU [European Union] trading relationship' (2022, p 50).

Brexit indeed seems to be a – arguably *the* – problem where trade is concerned (Parker and Giles, 2022). Successive editions of the OBR's *Economic and Fiscal Outlook* have forecast a Brexit-induced 15 per cent reduction in imports and exports, leading to a '4 per cent reduction in the potential productivity of the UK economy' (OBR, 2023, pp 46–7). With alternative trade agreements nowhere near sufficient to offset the decline

Figure 2.10: Gross fixed capital formation for selected countries (percentage of GDP), 2005–20

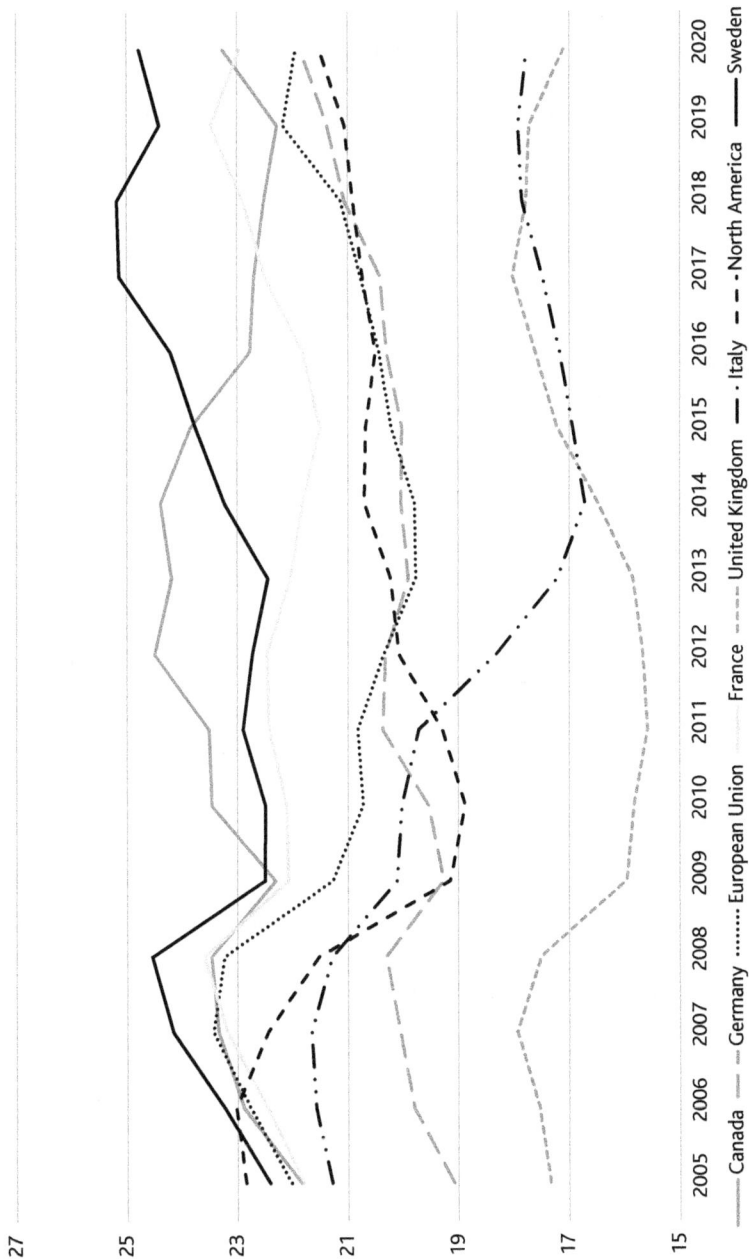

Source: Adapted from World Bank (2022)

in trade with the EU, one recent inquiry into the consequences of Brexit predicts that a progressive loss of trade openness will be the long-term result of leaving Europe, the upshot being 'a poorer and less productive [UK] by the end of the decade' with exports 'expected to be 38% lower than they would have been inside the EU by 2030' (Dhingra et al, 2022, pp 14, 51). In the shorter term, trade disruption is already adversely affecting parts of the country, Bailey and Rajic noting that the Midlands and northern England are particularly vulnerable because they are 'most dependent on the EU for both their exports and imports (not least in manufacturing)' (2022, p 16).

Conclusion

On the evidence set out in this chapter, there is reason to suppose that Conservative governments – and indeed the Conservative Party – will struggle to resolve the divide between those whose desire for low-tax, low-spend market outcomes remains the pre-eminent goal of macroeconomic policy and those who recognise, however reluctantly, that significant levels of public spending are necessary to support not only public services but also investment. Although, the external shocks experienced since early 2020, together with the self-imposed economic shock of Brexit, would have tested any government, the ad hoc deployment of One Nation policies like the COVID-19 income replacement measures and the energy support packages, which compare reasonably well with those of EU countries (Jurkovic, 2023), do not themselves signal a resolution to this fundamental dilemma. Neither does the ambiguous character of the March 2023 Budget. As discussed, at the time of writing, budgetary arrangements, though containing One Nation elements, are accompanied by others designed to appeal to the Conservative Party's neoliberal wing. The likely upshot is that Conservative attitudes to the state and public spending will remain inherently faction ridden and, to avoid persistent intra-party strife, vulnerable to short-term, pragmatic 'solutions'. Meanwhile, in difficult economic times, the UK continues to lack the levels of state support necessary to underpin the long-term public and private sector investment needed for sustainable growth – this supply-side commitment, accompanied by a reformed and progressive tax base (see Johnson, 2023), being an essential prerequisite for the well-funded public services on which social inclusion and cohesion ultimately depend.

References

Bailey, D. and Rajic, I. (2022) *Manufacturing after Brexit*, London: UK in a Changing Europe.

Bambra, C., Lynch, J. and Smith, K.E. (2021) *The unequal pandemic: COVID-19 and health inequalities*, Bristol: Policy Press.

Bank of England (2021) 'Influences on investment by UK businesses: evidence from the Decision Maker Panel', *Quarterly Bulletin*, Q2. Available at: www.bankofengland.co.uk/quarterly-bulletin/2021/2021-q2 (accessed 20 June, 2022).

Bank of England (2022) 'Monetary policy report, August 2022', 4 August. Available at: www.bankofengland.co.uk/monetary-policy-report/2022/august-2022 (accessed 5 September 2022).

Beatty, C. and Fothergill, S. (2017) 'Welfare reform in the United Kingdom 2010–16: expectations, outcomes and local impacts', *Social Policy and Administration*, 52(5): 950–68.

Bell, T., Broome, M., Cominetti, N., Corlett, A., Fry, E., Handscomb, K., Judge, L., Leslie, J., Murphy, L., Shah, K., Slaughter, H., Smith, J., Thwaites, G. and Try, L. (2022a) *Blowing the budget: assessing the implications of the September 2022 fiscal statement*, Resolution Foundation Briefing, London: Resolution Foundation.

Bell, T., Brewer, M., Broome, M., Cominetti, N., Corlett, A., Fry, E., Hale, S., Handscomb, K., Leslie, J., Marshall, J., McCurdy, C., Shah, K., Smith, J., Thwaites, G. and Try, L. (2022b) *Help today, squeeze tomorrow: putting the 2022 Autumn Statement in context*, Resolution Foundation Briefing, London: Resolution Foundation.

Bell, T., Brewer, M., Broome, M., Cominetti, N., Corlett, A., Fry, E., Hale, S., Handscomb, K., McCurdy, C., Murphy, L., Odamtten, F., Pacitti, C., Pittaway, S., Shah, K., Smith, J., Thwaites, G. and Try, L. (2023) *We're going on a growth Hunt: putting the 2023 Spring Budget in context*, London: Resolution Foundation.

Brien, P. and Keep, M. (2022) *Public spending during the Covid-19 pandemic*, London: House of Commons Library. Available at: https://researchbriefings.files.parliament.uk/documents/CBP-9309/CBP-9309.pdf (accessed 15 June 2022).

British Academy (2021) *Shaping the COVID decade: understanding the long-term societal impacts of COVID-19*, London: British Academy.

Brown, T. (2022) 'In focus: cost of living, economic resilience and government policy', *House of Lords Library*. Available at: https://lordslibrary.parliament.uk/cost-of-living-economic-resilience-and-government-policy/ (accessed 17 June 2022).

Calvert, J. and Arbuthnot, G. (2021) *Failures of state: the inside story of Britain's battle with coronavirus*, London: Mudlark.

Conservative Party (2019) *Get Brexit done, unleash Britain's potential: the Conservative and Unionist Party manifesto 2019*, London: Conservative Party.

Daly, M. (2020) 'COVID-19 and care homes in England: what happened and why', *Social Policy and Administration*, 54(7): 985–98.

Dhingra, S., Fray, E., Hale, S. and Ningyuan, J. (2022) *The big Brexit: an assessment of the scale of change to come in Britain*, London: Resolution Foundation.

Du, J. and Shepotylo, O. (2022) *TCA, non-tariff measures and UK trade*, ERC Research Paper 8, Birmingham: Aston Business School, Aston University.

Easton, J. (2022) '"Uninvestable" UK market lost £300 billion in Truss's first month', *Bloomberg*, 6 October. Available at: www.bloomberg.com/news/articles/2022-10-06/-uninvestable-uk-market-lost-300-billion-in-truss-first-month?in_source=embedded-checkout-banner (accessed 19 July, 2023).

Ellison, N. (2016) 'The Coalition government, public spending and social policy', in H. Bochel and M. Powell (eds) *The Coalition government and social policy*, Bristol: Policy Press, pp 27–52.

Ellison, N., Blomqvist, P. and Fleckenstein, T. (2022) 'Covid (in)equalities: labor market protection, health and residential care in Germany, Sweden and the UK', *Policy and Society*, 41(2): 247–59.

Evans, G., de Geuss, R. and Green, J. (2021) 'Boris Johnson to the rescue? How the Conservatives won the radical-right vote in the 2019 general election', *Political Studies*. Available at: https://doi.org/10.1177/003232 17211051191 (accessed 19 July, 2023).

Hammond, P. (2018) 'Budget 2018: Philip Hammond's speech', *Gov.uk*, 29 October. Available at: www.gov.uk/government/speeches/budget-2018-philip-hammonds-speech (accessed 23 May 2019).

Hastings, A., Bailey, N., Gannon, M., Besemer, K. and Bramley, G. (2012) 'Coping with the cuts: the management of the worst financial settlement in living memory', *Local Government Studies*, 41(4): 601–21.

HM Treasury (2021) *Public expenditure statistical analysis*, London: HM Treasury.

HM Treasury (2022) *Autumn Statement 2022*, CP 751, London: HMSO. Available at: https://assets.publishing.service.gov.uk/government/uploads/system/uploads/attachment_data/file/1118417/CCS1022065440-001_SECURE_HMT_Autumn_Statement_November_2022_Web_accessible__1_.pdf (accessed 19 July 2023).

Hunt, J. (2022) *Autumn Statement: Chancellor Jeremy Hunt's speech to House of Commons*, London: HM Treasury. Available at: https://assets.publishing.service.gov.uk/government/uploads/system/uploads/attachment_data/file/1118417/CCS1022065440-001_SECURE_HMT_Autumn_Statement_November_2022_Web_accessible__1_.pdf (accessed 25 November 2022).

IFS (Institute for Fiscal Studies) (2022a) 'IFS response to government cost of living support package'. Available at: https://ifs.org.uk/publications/16066 (accessed 16 June 2022).

IFS (Institute for Fiscal Studies) (2022b) 'Spring Statement 2022 – Paul Johnson's opening remarks from the event'. Available at: https://ifs.org.uk/collections/spring-statement-2022 (accessed 16 June 2022).

Javid, S. (2019) 'Spending round 2019: Chancellor Sajid Javid's speech to House of Commons', 4 September. Available at: www.gov.uk/government/speeches/spending-round-2019-sajid-javids-speech (accessed 11 May, 2022).

Johnson, P. (2023) *Follow the money: how much does Britain cost?* London: Abacus Books.

Jurkovic, P. (2023) 'Energy price support schemes', *UK in a Changing Europe*. Available at: https://ukandeu.ac.uk/explainers/energy-price-support-sche mes/ (accessed 30 March 2023).

King's Fund (2021) *Adult social care funding and eligibility: our position*, London: King's Fund.

Maidment, J. (2022) 'Rishi Sunak accused of "throwing red meat to socialists" with windfall tax', *Daily Telegraph*, 26 May.

Mason, R. (2021) 'Rishi Sunak faces backlash over "big state, high tax" budget', *The Guardian*, 28 October. Available at: www.theguardian.com/uk-news/2021/oct/28/rishi-sunak-faces-tory-backlash-over-big-state-high-tax-budget (accessed 23 June 2022).

McEnhill, L. and Taylor-Gooby, P. (2018) 'Beyond continuity? Understanding change in the UK welfare state since 2010', *Social Policy and Administration*, 52(1): 252–70.

National Audit Office (2018) *Adult social care at a glance*, London: National Audit Office. Available at: www.nao.org.uk/reports/adult-social-care-at-a-glance/ (accessed 15 April 2019).

National Audit Office (2021) 'COVID-19 cost tracker'. Available at: www.nao.org.uk/covid-19/cost-tracker/ (accessed 23 May 2021).

OBR (Office for Budget Responsibility) (2019) *Restated March 2019 forecast*, London: Office for Budget Responsibility. Available at: https://obr.uk/docs/dlm_uploads/Restated_March_2019.pdf (accessed 19 July 2023).

OBR (Office for Budget Responsibility) (2021) *Economic and Fiscal Outlook: October 2021*, London: HMSO. Available at: https://obr.uk/efo/economic-and-fiscal-outlook-october-2021/ (accessed 22 April 2022).

OBR (Office for Budget Responsibility) (2022a) *Economic and Fiscal Outlook: March 2022*, London: HMSO. Available at: https://obr.uk/efo/economic-and-fiscal-outlook-march-2022/ (accessed 19 July 2023).

OBR (Office for Budget Responsibility) (2022b) *Economic and Fiscal Outlook: November 2022*, London: HMSO. Available at: https://obr.uk/efo/economic-and-fiscal-outlook-november-2022/ (accessed 19 July 2023).

OBR (Office for Budget Responsibility) (2023) *Economic and Fiscal Outlook: March 2023*, London: HMSO. Available at: https://obr.uk/efo/economic-and-fiscal-outlook-march-2023/ (accessed 19 July 2023).

ONS (Office for National Statistics) (2022) 'UK government debt and deficit, March 2022'. Available at: www.ons.gov.uk/economy/governmentpubli csectorandtaxes/publicspending/bulletins/ukgovernmentdebtanddeficitf oreurostatmaast/march2022#:~:text=1.-,Main%20points,equivalent%20 to%202.6%25%20of%20GDP (accessed 19 July 2023).

ONS (Office for National Statistics) (2023) 'Business investment in the UK: October-December 2022, provisional results'. Available at: www.ons.gov.uk/economy/grossdomesticproductgdp/bulletins/businessinvestment/octobertodecember2022provisionalresults (accessed 21 June 2023).

Osborne, G. (2015) 'Chancellor George Osborne's Summer Budget 2015 speech', *Gov.uk*, 8 July. Available at: www.gov.uk/government/speeches/chancellor-george-osbornes-summer-budget-2015-speech (accessed 14 April 2022).

Parker, G. and Giles, C. (2022) 'The deafening silence over Brexit's economic fallout', *Financial Times*, 20 June.

Platt, L. and Warwick, R. (2020) 'COVID-19 and ethnic inequalities in England and Wales', *Fiscal Studies*, 41(2): 259–89.

Sobolewska, M. and Ford, R. (2020) *Brexit land*, Cambridge: Cambridge University Press.

Summers, K., Scullion, L., Geiger Baumberg, B., Robertshaw, D., Edmiston, D., Gibbons, A., Karagiannaki, E., de Vries, R. and Ingold, J. (2021) *Claimants' experiences of the social security system during the first wave of COVID-19*, Canterbury: University of Kent.

Vizard, P. and Obolenskaya, P. (2021) 'Context and inheritance', in P. Vizard and J. Hills (eds) *The Conservative governments' record on social policy reform from May 2015 to pre-COVID 2020: policies, spending and outcomes*, London: Centre for Analysis of Social Exclusion, LSE, pp 13–30.

Vizard, P., Obolenskaya, P. and Jones, E. (2016) 'Health', in R. Lupton, T. Burchardt, K. Stewart and P. Vizard (eds) *Social policy in a cold climate: policies and their consequences since the crisis*, Bristol: Policy Press, pp 147–86.

Woodcock, A. (2021) 'Boris Johnson faces open warfare with his own party over National Insurance hike', *Independent*, 5 September.

World Bank (2022) 'Gross fixed capital formation (% of GDP)'. Available at: https://data.worldbank.org/indicator/NE.GDI.FTOT.ZS (accessed 28 June 2022).

3

Turning up the thermostat: the Conservatives, social policy and public opinion

Andrew Defty

Introduction

This chapter examines shifts in public attitudes towards public spending and welfare provision in the period from 2015, following five years of austerity under the Coalition government. In the period leading up to and following the 2010 general election, there was some evidence of declining support for public spending and a hardening of attitudes towards benefits recipients, which aligned, in some respects closely, with the austerity agenda of the incoming Coalition government (Taylor-Gooby and Martin, 2008; Curtice, 2010b; Defty, 2011). Recent studies have highlighted a further hardening of attitudes towards those in receipt of state benefits under the Coalition government (Pearce and Taylor, 2013; Taylor-Gooby and Taylor, 2015; Defty, 2016).

While there is a growing body of evidence of anti-welfare attitudes in the UK, studies of public attitudes have long highlighted the contested, and sometimes contradictory, nature of public opinion in this area (Hudson et al, 2016b; van Oorshot, 2000). Drawing on historical data on public attitudes, Hudson et al (2016a) have questioned whether recent claims for declining public support are based in part on 'nostalgia narratives' of a 'golden age' of public support for welfare, which is not supported by historical polling data. Others have argued that fluctuations in support for tax and spend can be explained by reference to a thermostatic effect in which support for spending is linked to public perceptions about whether government is increasing spending or implementing cuts. According to this argument, cuts to public spending prompt a rise in support for tax-funded increases in provision, while increased investment in services will eventually prompt the public to urge spending restraint (Stuart and Wlezien, 2005; Curtice, 2010a, 2010b; Curtice et al, 2021). Some have questioned whether public attitudes may be impacted by factors other than public spending, such as the level of unemployment (van Oorschot, 2006), while recent studies have suggested that after a prolonged period of declining public support the thermostat of public sympathy may become stuck in the 'off' position (Taylor-Gooby and Taylor, 2015; Defty, 2016).

This chapter traces shifting public attitudes towards austerity, focusing on changing attitudes towards tax and spend, changes in public priorities for state support and a gradual softening of attitudes towards those in receipt of benefits. It also examines public attitudes towards inequality in the context of the impact of austerity and more particularly the government's 'levelling up' agenda, and the impact of the COVID-19 pandemic on public attitudes towards state provision. The chapter uses data from the annual British Social Attitudes survey to examine long-term trends in public attitudes towards public expenditure and welfare provision. British Social Attitudes has tracked changes in public support for state provision in a range of areas since 1983 and is widely regarded as having high methodological standards. The chapter also draws on polling data from a range of polling companies, most notably Ipsos and YouGov. These data provide more detailed and frequent snapshots of public responses to government policy. As such data may be more likely to be subject to variation or polling error, wherever possible conclusions have not been based on the results of individual polls.

Tax and spend and priorities

There is some evidence that the public accepted a need for significant spending cuts in the wake of the financial crisis of 2007 to 2008. In a poll published on the eve of the Coalition government's first Budget in 2010, 58 per cent of respondents agreed with the statement that 'there is a real need to cut spending on public services in order to pay off the very high national debt we now have' (Ipsos, 2010b). In a series of monthly polls undertaken by YouGov from early 2011 until the end of 2015, more than 50 per cent of respondents agreed that spending cuts were necessary, while around 30 per cent thought that cuts were unnecessary (YouGov, 2015). There were concerns about the speed and depth of government cuts, but the gap between those who felt the government was cutting too deeply and too fast and those who thought the government's approach was about right narrowed over the course of the 2010 Parliament. In February 2011, YouGov reported that 51 per cent thought the government was cutting too deeply, while only 25 per cent thought that the level of cuts was about right. Similarly, 58 per cent thought the government was cutting spending too quickly, compared to 27 per cent who thought the speed of cuts was about right. By the time of the 2015 general election, those who felt that cuts were too deep had fallen to 39 per cent, while the proportion of those who felt that cuts were about right had risen to 36 per cent. Similarly, the proportion who felt that the government was cutting too quickly had fallen to 40 per cent, while those who thought the speed of cuts was about right had increased to 36 per cent (YouGov, 2015; Defty, 2016).

The public, however, remained divided on the government's policy of austerity. In a poll undertaken by YouGov in October 2018, shortly after Theresa May had announced an end to austerity, while 31 per cent agreed that austerity was 'the right policy at the time but it is now right to end it', 27 per cent agreed with the statement that it was 'never the right policy and should never have happened at all'. A larger proportion (36 per cent) thought that austerity had not helped the economy, compared to 30 per cent who thought that it had, and a much larger proportion (43 per cent) thought that austerity policies had been applied unfairly, while only 20 per cent thought they had been fair. Moreover, there was considerable scepticism about whether the government's austerity policies had really come to an end in 2018 and what that might mean. Only 10 per cent of those polled thought that austerity had ended, while 50 per cent thought government austerity policies had not ended (YouGov, 2018b). The public were more divided on what the end of austerity might actually mean. In a separate poll, 35 per cent thought that the end of austerity meant there was no longer any need for spending cuts, but 32 per cent thought it did not mean this. Similarly, while 38 per cent thought the end of austerity meant the government would be spending more on public services, 26 per cent did not think this would be the case (YouGov, 2018a).

Fluctuation in public support for spending restraint was also reflected in the data from British Social Attitudes. Although support for cutting taxes has remained at a low level, consistently supported by fewer than one in ten respondents since the survey began, support for increasing taxes and spending, and support for keeping taxes and spending at current levels, have fluctuated over time (see Figure 3.1). In the period leading up to and beyond the 2010 general election, there was a fall in support for increased public spending on health, education and social benefits and a commensurate rise in the proportion who felt that taxes and spending should remain the same. In 2007, for the first time since the mid–1980s, more people expressed support for keeping taxes and spending at the same level than supported increasing taxes in order to spend more on public services. Support for keeping taxes and spending at the same level remained higher than support for increasing taxes and spending throughout the period of the Coalition government. However, support for tax-funded increases in public spending began to rise in the later years of the Coalition and 2016 was the first year since the financial crisis that more people wanted an increase in taxes and spend than wanted taxes and spending to stay at the same level. In every survey since 2016, more than half of respondents have supported an increase in taxes and spending, while support for keeping taxes and spending at the same level dipped to 31 per cent in 2017 and did not go above 40 per cent in the period reported on here. Although during 2017–20 there was a narrowing of the gap between those who supported an increase in tax and spend and those who wanted it to keep at the same level, the 2021 survey saw a slight upturn in support for tax and spend and a further downturn in support for keeping them the same (British Social Attitudes, 1983–2021; Curtice, 2022).

The fluctuations in support for tax and spend, as shown in Figure 3.1, can be explained by a thermostatic effect in which support for increased taxes and spending remained at a relatively high level during the period of Conservative rule in the 1980s and 1990s, when government policy was characterised by fiscal restraint, while a decline in support for higher taxes and spending followed the election of a Labour government committed to investing in public services. In contrast, after several years of austerity under the Coalition government, during which the majority of the public supported spending restraint, since 2016 public support has shifted back in favour of increasing taxes and spending (Curtice, 2022). There was a fall in support for tax and spend between 2017 and 2020, which may have been the result of a combination of factors, including the government's announcement that austerity was over, the well-publicised aspiration to provide support to more deprived areas through the levelling up agenda and, more recently, the government's response to the COVID-19 pandemic.

What is not clear, however, is how long the majority of the public are prepared to accept spending restraint before deciding that there is a need for tax-funded increases in provision, or how generous or how long a period of increased spending needs to be before it triggers a rise in support for spending restraint. Looking at the most recent data, despite a significant increase in state support during the COVID-19 pandemic, there was actually a slight increase in support for extra provision in 2021, suggesting that a short, albeit significant, increase in state support may not be sufficient to satisfy demands for increased provision and may even whet the public's appetite for further support. The thermostatic effect may pose a particular challenge to the Conservatives in the period leading up the next general election, particularly if they continue to pursue policies based on spending restraint.

Public priorities and attitudes towards benefits recipients

Data on public priorities for welfare spending indicate a long-standing distinction between those groups considered to be more deserving of state support and those considered to be less deserving. Annual data from British Social Attitudes since the 1980s has consistently indicated strong support for mass public services such as health and education, while support for spending on social security benefits has by comparison been consistently low, and some studies suggested that there has been a particular hardening of attitudes towards those in receipt of state benefits following the election of

Figure 3.1: Attitudes to tax and spend (per cent), 1983–2021

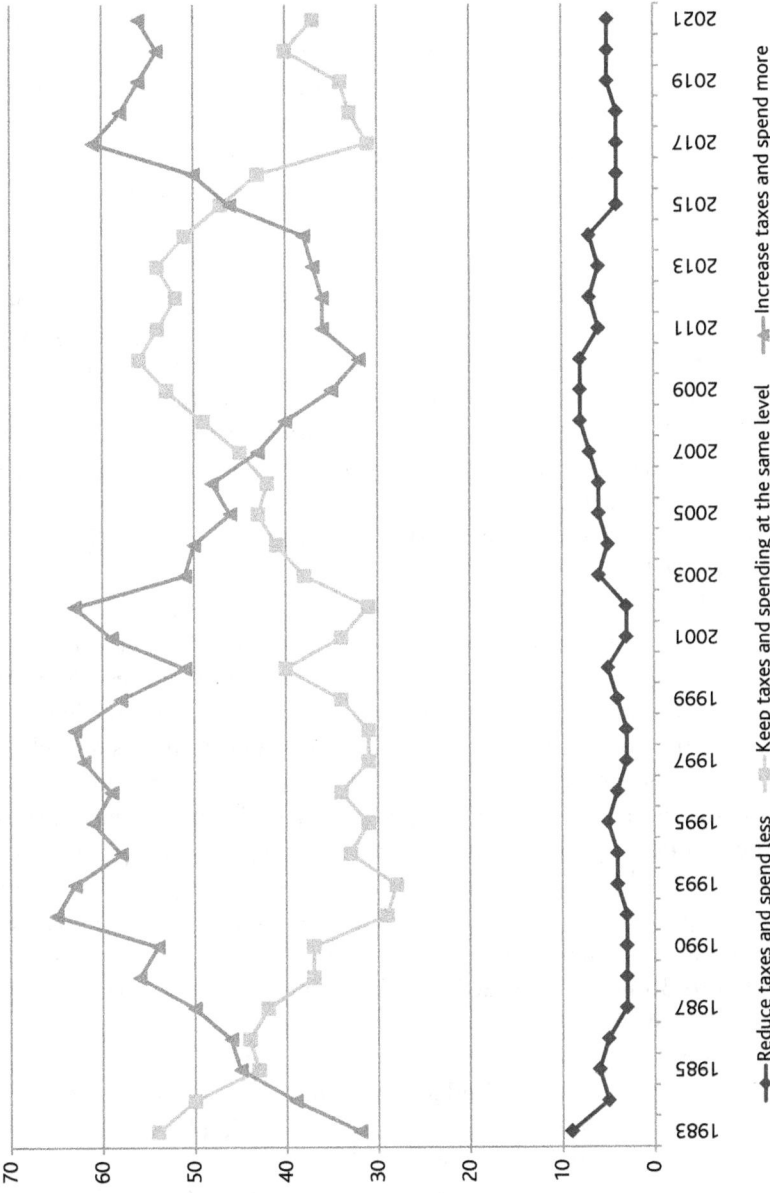

Note: These questions were not asked in the surveys done in 1988 and 1992.
Source: Author's adaptation from British Social Attitudes survey data

Reduce taxes and spend less — Keep taxes and spending at the same level — Increase taxes and spend more

the Coalition government in 2010 (Pearce and Taylor, 2013; Taylor-Gooby and Taylor, 2015).

In this context, the government appeared to be on fairly safe ground in cutting spending on welfare while protecting services such as health and education. There has, however, been some shift in priorities for additional spending since 2010. While health and education continued to be the public's top priorities, support for extra spending on both has fallen back in recent years. The proportion who said that education should be the highest priority for extra spending fell from 32 per cent in 2010 to 14 per cent in 2021. While the proportion prioritising extra spending on health increased in the same period, from 41 per cent to 54 per cent, this was down from a peak of 58 per cent in 2018. There is also some evidence that public sympathy for those in receipt of benefits has increased in recent years. While additional spending on social security benefits was seen as the highest priority by only a small minority, consistently supported by less than 2 per cent of respondents between 2010 and 2018, support for this had more than doubled to 5 per cent by 2021. While still low, this was a level of support which had not been reported since before the election of the Labour government in 1997. There has also been a marked increase in those prioritising extra spending on housing, from 5 per cent in 2010 to 10 per cent in 2021 (British Social Attitudes, 2010–21).

A similar pattern was seen when the public were asked to identify their priorities for extra spending on social benefits. Again, the public appeared to make a distinction between those who are more and less deserving of support, with unemployed people and single parents typically viewed as less deserving than other groups in receipt of state support, such as retired people, disabled people and carers, and those working on a low income. However, during the time in which the Conservatives have been in government, there has been a decline in support for extra spending on some of those groups typically viewed as more deserving and an increase in support for benefits for the unemployed and single parents. The proportion identifying retirement pensions as their highest priority for extra spending fell from 51 per cent in 2010 to 36 per cent in 2020. In the same period, the proportion who felt that unemployment benefits should be the highest priority for extra spending increased from 4 per cent to 13 per cent.

When British Social Attitudes posed the question of priorities slightly differently, in terms of whether respondents would like to see more or less spending on particular social benefits, the proportion who supported more spending on retired people fell from 72 per cent in 2008 to 44 per cent in 2021. In the same period, the proportion who supported more spending on unemployed people increased from 14 per cent to 29 per cent, while those supporting an increase in spending on single parents also rose, albeit more modestly from 37 per cent to 42 per cent. Although unemployed people remain the only group for which a larger proportion would like to see less spending than those who support more spending, the proportion advocating for less spending on unemployed people fell from 55 per cent to 32 per cent between 2008 and 2021, while those advocating less spending on single parents fell from 17 per cent to 15 per cent (British Social Attitudes, 2008–21).

Evidence of some softening of attitudes towards those in receipt of benefits can also be seen in questions about the public's perception of the level of benefits. One question regularly asked since the British Social Attitudes survey began in 1983 is whether benefits are 'too high and discourage work' or 'too low and cause hardship' (Figure 3.2). The proportion who thought that benefits were too high and discouraged work began to rise steeply from 1997 and peaked at 64 per cent in 2011. In contrast, those who felt that benefits were too low and cause hardship fell significantly across the same period. However, the proportion who thought that benefits are too low and cause hardship has been trending upwards since 2011, when less than one in five thought this to be the case. Indeed, 2019 was the first year since 2000 that more people thought that benefits were too low and cause hardship (37 per cent) than those who thought that benefits are too high and discourage work (34 per cent). Moreover, the proportion who thought that benefits were too low increased markedly in 2020 to 52 per cent, the first year since 1995 that more than half of respondents felt that benefits were too low (British Social Attitudes, 1997–2020).

A similar question, asking whether people agreed or disagreed with the statement that 'if welfare benefits were not so generous, people would learn to stand on their own two feet', also indicated that attitudes towards benefits have changed in recent years. There was a majority of respondents agreeing with that statement from 1998 until 2019, when 37 per cent disagreed and 34 per cent agreed, with the gap widening slightly in 2020, with 40 per cent disagreeing and 34 per cent agreeing (Curtice, 2022).

The COVID-19 pandemic may provide one possible explanation for a shift in public opinion towards more generous support. Polling data indicate a broad measure of public support for policies introduced to help those in financial difficulty as a result of the pandemic. For example, in November 2020, YouGov reported that 59 per cent of those polled supported extending the suspension of the requirement that recipients of Universal Credit look for work (YouGov, 2020d). In a separate poll in the same month, 80 per cent supported providing free school meal vouchers during school holidays for as long as the coronavirus outbreak continued (YouGov, 2020a).

A series of questions revealed overwhelming support for the 'furlough' scheme, with 82 per cent agreeing that it was essential to protect people's livelihoods, 90 per cent agreeing it helped people who were facing difficult times through no fault of their own, and 77 per cent agreeing it helped to

Figure 3.2: Perceptions of benefit levels (per cent), 1983–2021

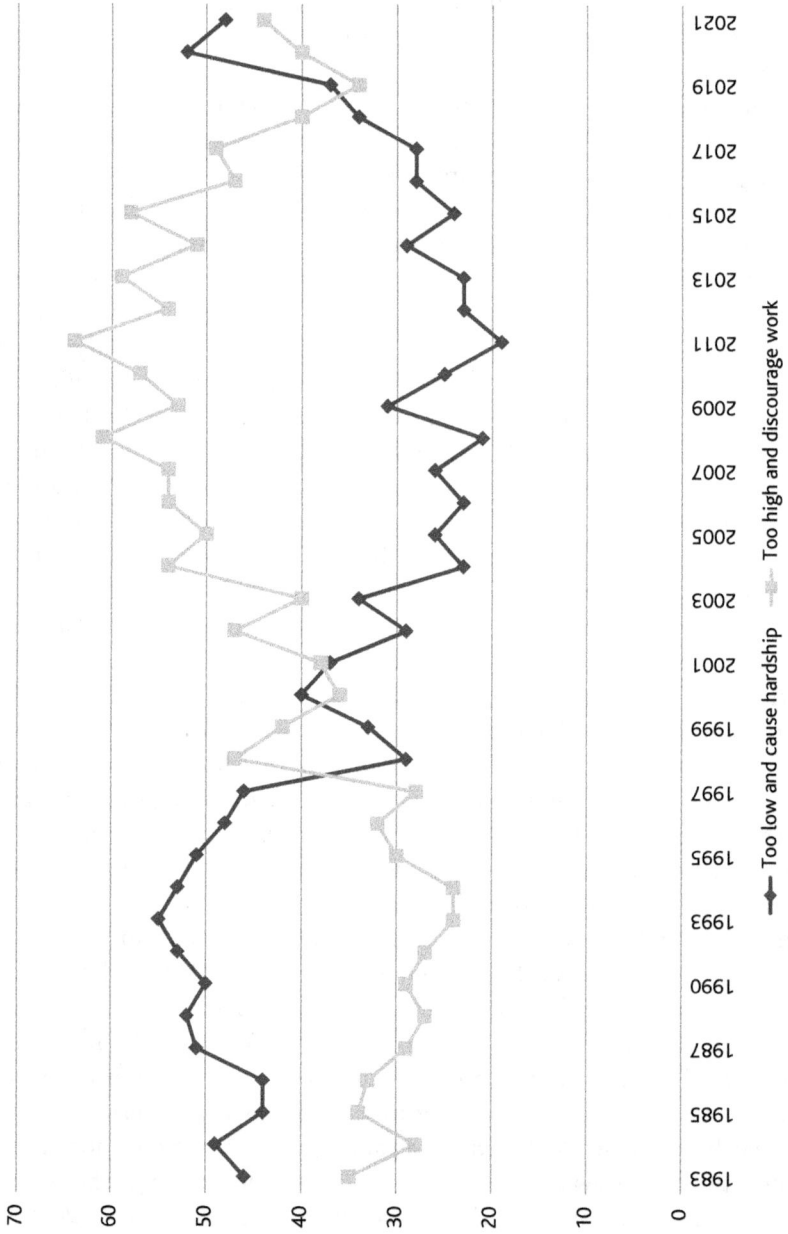

Note: These questions were not asked in the surveys done in 1988 and 1992.
Source: Author's adaptation from British Social Attitudes survey data

Legend: Too low and cause hardship — Too high and discourage work

prevent child poverty and hunger. In contrast, only 21 per cent thought it discouraged people from looking for work and 25 per cent agreed it encouraged reliance on the state, while 53 per cent and 49 per cent, respectively, disagreed (YouGov, 2020b).

Later, when polled about the success of various policies introduced in response to the pandemic, 49 per cent thought the Universal Credit uplift had been a success compared to only 7 per cent who thought it had been a failure and 27 per cent who thought it had been neither a success nor a failure. Similarly, 59 per cent thought the furlough scheme had been a success, compared to 7 per cent who thought it was a failure and 26 per cent who thought it had been neither (YouGov, 2021c).

There is also some evidence of support for the continuation of measures introduced to help those in need beyond the end of the pandemic. In November 2020, 56 per cent thought that the provision of free school meals during school holidays should be made permanent, compared to 33 per cent who were opposed (YouGov, 2020a). In September 2021, in response to the impending end of the £20 uplift in Universal Credit, 38 per cent of those polled supported it being made permanent, while a further 18 per cent thought it should come to an end, but not yet. In contrast, only 20 per cent thought the furlough scheme should be extended beyond its scheduled end date in September 2021 (YouGov, 2021e).

A number of studies have examined the impact of the pandemic on attitudes towards those in receipt of state support (Curtice et al, 2021, 2022; de Vries et al, 2021; Duffy et al, 2021). These did find some evidence of a softening of attitudes towards benefits recipients during the pandemic, but also raised questions about the extent to which the pandemic has led to a long-term shift in attitudes.

Two broad conclusions can be drawn from these studies. First, although there is evidence of a softening of attitudes during the pandemic, this was part of a shift which began some years earlier. For example, Curtice et al argue that rather than representing a turning point in public opinion, it is perhaps surprising that the shifts in public opinion during the pandemic were so marginal. This, they suggest, was because the pandemic occurred 'at a time when some important attitudes had already recently shifted' – for instance, the reaction against austerity policies pursued since 2010, such as that illustrated in Figures 3.1 and 3.2, 'ensured that the climate of public opinion was more likely to be supportive of the help the government provided during the pandemic' (Curtice et al, 2022, p 31).

Second, while there is evidence of some shifts in public opinion during the pandemic leading to a more generous attitude to those in receipt of state support, this was short-lived and attitudes quickly rebounded as the impact of the pandemic diminished. For example, using polling data from YouGov, de Vries et al show that while attitudes towards benefits claimants softened during the first and second waves of the pandemic, in both cases 'attitudes rebounded following lockdowns, with only small changes being sustained' (2021, p 26). Rather than engendering a meaningful increase in solidarity with welfare claimants, they argue that more generous attitudes might be explained as 'Covid exceptionalism' (de Vries et al, 2021, p 26).

Poverty, inequality and levelling up

Under the leadership of Theresa May and then Boris Johnson, the Conservatives sought to shift the agenda away from austerity and place greater emphasis on combating inequality through levelling up. This focus on inequality and fairness was, perhaps, an appropriate response to the challenges posed by the government's austerity policies. While the public broadly accepted the need for spending cuts and were divided on the speed and depth of cuts, polling data consistently indicated that the majority of the public felt that the burden of spending cuts was being applied unfairly. Monthly polling for YouGov on the question of whether the government had cut spending in a way that was fair to all sections of society indicated that although for a very short period after the 2010 general election a higher share of people thought the government was cutting spending in a fair way, the proportion who thought that cuts were unfair began to rise from mid-2010 (Figure 3.3). In each month from October 2010 until the end of 2015, more than half of those polled thought that cuts had been unfair, while, for the most part, less than one in three believed they had been instituted fairly (YouGov, 2015). YouGov polled less frequently on this question after 2015, but in two polls in 2016, over half (57 per cent and 53 per cent) agreed that cuts had been made unfairly, while only around a fifth (19 per cent and 21 per cent) thought cuts had been applied fairly, a smaller proportion than for any of the monthly polls conducted by YouGov between 2010 and the end of 2015 (YouGov, 2016a, 2016b).

Public concern about inequality is also reflected in long-term data from British Social Attitudes. From 1990 to 2018, more than three quarters of respondents consistently responded that the gap between those with high and low incomes in the UK is too large. While the Conservatives under Theresa May promised to support 'ordinary working families', over a long period of time a large proportion of respondents to British Social Attitudes surveys have agreed with the statement that 'ordinary working people do not get their fair share of the nation's wealth'. On average between 1986 and 2021, 61 per cent of respondents agreed with this statement. The level of agreement has, however, varied somewhat depending on which party was in government. The average level of agreement between 1986 and 1996 was 65 per cent. Between 1998 and 2009, when Labour was in power, the average level of agreement was 59 per cent. Although the average level of

Figure 3.3: Do you think the way that the government is cutting spending is being done fairly or unfairly? (per cent) July 2010–March 2016

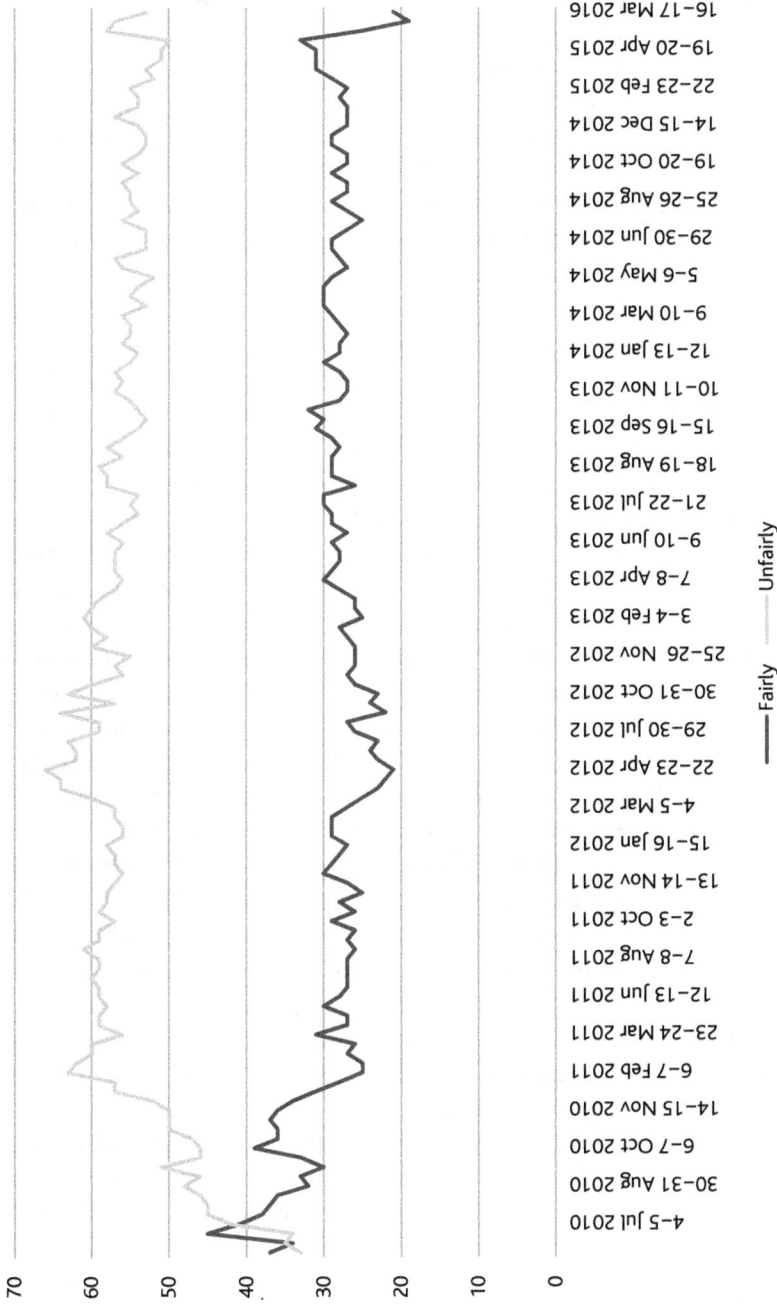

——— Fairly ——— Unfairly

Source: Constructed by the author from YouGov (2015, 2016a, 2016b)

agreement since 2010 was only slightly higher, at 61 per cent, between 2019 and 2021 there was a particularly steep rise in those agreeing, from 57 per cent to 67 per cent, the highest level since 1995 (British Social Attitudes, 1986–2021; Curtice, 2022).

Responses to another statement about inequality, that there is 'one law for the rich and one for the poor', indicated similar levels of agreement, with an average of 61 per cent since 2010, and a similarly steep rise in agreement between 2019 and 2021, from 56 per cent to 66 per cent. However, as Curtice (2022) observes, responses to this question may have less to do with financial inequality than the well-publicised breaches of COVID-19 restrictions in Downing Street under Boris Johnson.

Growing public concern about inequality is also reflected in opinion polling, particularly in the period since 2010. The Ipsos Issues Index tracks public perceptions of the most important issues facing Britain. In the period after 2015, this has unsurprisingly been dominated by Britain's relationship with Europe; this reached a peak in April 2019, when 72 per cent saw it as the most important issue facing the country. The second most prevalent issue was the COVID-19 pandemic, peaking in April 2020, when 85 per cent saw it as the most important issue for the country. Nevertheless, while the proportion identifying Brexit and COVID-19 as the most important issues facing the country have risen steeply and fallen back, albeit not to pre-2015 levels, public concern about the level of poverty and inequality stayed on an upward trajectory after 2010. In May 2010, only 6 per cent of those polled identified poverty and inequality as one of the most important issues facing the country (Ipsos, 2010a), but by the time of the 2015 general election this had risen to 17 per cent (Ipsos, 2015). Concern about poverty and inequality continued to rise, peaking at 22 per cent in January 2020, when it was ranked fourth on the Issues Index, after Brexit, the National Health Service and climate change (Ipsos, 2020). This was the highest level since 1997, when Ipsos first coded 'poverty/inequality' on the Issues Index. Although concern about poverty and inequality has since fallen back, identified by 14 per cent as one of the most important issues in August 2022, these concerns have perhaps been subsumed into broader worry about inflation and price rises, which has topped the index since April 2022, when it reached the highest level since 1990 (Ipsos, 2022b).

There is also a wealth of data which indicates that the public has grown more pessimistic about the economic situation. British Social Attitudes has consistently shown that more than half of those surveyed think there is 'quite a lot' of poverty in Britain, and that in recent years the public has become more pessimistic about levels of poverty (Clery and Dangerfield, 2019). The proportion agreeing that there is 'quite a lot' of poverty in Britain increased from 60 per cent in 2009 to 68 per cent in 2019, while the share of those who felt 'there is very little real poverty' fell from 40 per cent to 28 per cent in the same period. Moreover, the proportion who felt that poverty had increased over the previous ten years increased from 50 per cent in 2009 to 66 per cent in 2019, and 61 per cent of those surveyed in 2019 thought that poverty would increase in the next ten years (British Social Attitudes, 2009–2019).

More recent polling data suggest that the level of public pessimism about the economy grew significantly worse during 2022. The Ipsos Economic Optimism Index is calculated by measuring those who feel the general economic conditions in the country will improve or get worse over the next 12 months. Economic optimism actually rose during the pandemic; in June 2021, it reached its highest point since 2015, with 53 per cent thinking economic conditions would improve in the next 12 months, while 31 per cent thought they would get worse – a net optimism figure of +22 (Ipsos, 2021a). However, public optimism about the economy dropped steeply over the next twelve months. In January 2022, more than half of those polled thought that the country's economic condition would get worse in the 12 months after that (Ipsos, 2022a), and by March 2022, economic optimism had fallen to its lowest level since the financial crisis, with 76 per cent of those polled thinking the economy would get worse in the coming 12 months. According to Ipsos, this matched the worst-ever levels in 44 years of tracking economic optimism, recorded in 1980 and 2008. With only 14 per cent thinking that the economy would improve, this gave a net optimism score of −62, the worst score since July 2008 (Ipsos, 2022c). Economic optimism reached a new low in June 2022, shortly before the resignation of Boris Johnson: 77 per cent said they thought the economy would get worse, while only 13 per cent thought it would improve (Ipsos, 2022d). Unsurprisingly, the short tenure of Liz Truss as Prime Minister did little to relieve public concerns about the economy, and there was little evidence of an improvement following the election of Rishi Sunak. In the first Ipsos poll following Sunak's appointment, 72 per cent said they thought the economy would get worse, while just 16 per cent expected it to improve (Ipsos, 2022e). Six months into Sunak's tenure, there had been some improvement in economic optimism, but 58 per cent still expected the economic situation to get worse, while 22 per cent thought it would improve (Ipsos, 2023).

Sustained and growing public concern about levels of poverty and the state of the economy suggest that statements by government ministers have done little to convince the public that the government is committed to combating inequality. In particular, the Johnson government's well-publicised levelling up agenda appears to have had little impact on the public. Rather like the 'Big Society' agenda perpetuated by the Coalition government, a large proportion of the public appear to have little awareness of the levelling up agenda, and those who do claim to understand it are sceptical about its likely success (Defty, 2014). In December 2020, one year after levelling up was introduced in the Conservative manifesto for the 2019 election (Conservative Party, 2019), only a third of those polled by YouGov claimed to have heard of levelling up and to know what it meant, while 12 per cent had heard of it but had no idea what it meant and 31 per cent said they had never heard of it (YouGov, 2020c). Moreover, public awareness does not appear to have improved over time. An Ipsos poll from July 2021 found that 43 per cent knew nothing about or had not heard of levelling up (Ipsos, 2021c). In two further polls by YouGov in November and December 2021, 31 per cent and 24 per cent, respectively, claimed never to have heard the phrase 'levelling up' (YouGov, 2021a, 2021d).

Even when provided with some details about what levelling up aimed to achieve, there was considerable scepticism about the likelihood of success. One of the central features of this agenda was the claim that it would reduce inequalities between different parts of the UK. When YouGov asked the public to choose between various options for what levelling up might mean, the largest proportion (30 per cent), agreed that it was 'mostly about making sure that people in the North and Midlands have the same opportunities as people in the South East'. However, the second-largest group (28 per cent) thought 'it doesn't really mean anything at all' (YouGov, 2021b). In October 2021, Ipsos asked whether government policies would reduce inequalities between different regions of the UK; 39 per cent thought that this was 'fairly' or 'very' likely, but 52 per cent thought it was 'not very likely' or 'not likely at all' (Ipsos, 2021b). Similarly, when YouGov asked in December 2021 whether people thought levelling up would mean more money being spent in the area in which they lived, only 7 per cent thought it would, while 44 per cent thought it would make no difference and 18 per cent thought it would mean less money being spent in their local area (YouGov, 2021d).

While it is not clear whether the commitment to levelling up will continue to be a centrepiece of Conservative policy up to the next election (which will take place in 2025 at the latest), there is little evidence that changes in leadership have convinced the public that Conservative policies will improve the economic situation or reduce inequality. Polling indicated strong public opposition to a number of policies in the mini-budget introduced by the Truss government in September 2022. YouGov reported that 57 per cent thought that overall the measures included in the mini-budget were unfair, with only 19 per cent thinking the proposals were fair, the worst score for any financial statement since the Conservatives entered government in 2010. There was particularly strong opposition to removing the cap on bankers' bonuses, which was seen as the wrong priority by 71 per cent of those polled, and abolishing the 45 per cent top rate of income tax, which was opposed by 72 per cent (Smith, 2022). The public were somewhat more divided on the proposals brought forward in the Autumn Statement introduced by the Sunak government in November 2022. YouGov reported that 31 per cent thought the government's economic plans were fair, while 30 per cent thought they were unfair and 38 per cent said they did not know if the proposals were fair or not. However, only 15 per cent of those polled, and 25 per cent of Conservative voters polled, thought the Autumn Statement would leave the country better off (Morris, 2022).

Conclusion

After a sustained period of austerity during which there was significant public support for spending restraint and a hardening of attitudes towards benefits recipients, the period since 2015 has seen a gradual turning up of the thermostat with a decline in public support for austerity and a softening of attitudes towards those in most need. Support for increased taxes and public spending has risen markedly since 2015, and although the gap has recently narrowed between those in favour of tax and spend and those who would like to keep this at current levels, since 2017 more than 50 per cent of the public have supported tax-funded increases in provision. There has also been a shift in public priorities for government spending. Although the public continue to make a distinction between those who are viewed as more and less deserving of state support and the majority of the public continue to prioritise mass services, such as health, education and pensions, there is some evidence of a decline in support for additional help for groups typically seen as more deserving and a rise in support for those often seen as less deserving, such as those in receipt of state benefits.

This shift in attitudes is perhaps underpinned by the widespread public perception that the burden of austerity has been unfairly borne by the poorest in society. While there is some evidence that the public accepted the need for austerity policies and were divided on the level and speed of cuts, polling data consistently indicate that a significant majority of the public believe austerity has been applied unfairly. This is supported by longer-term data from British Social Attitudes, which has long indicated that the public believe levels of poverty and inequality in British society are too high.

This shift in public attitudes has coincided to some extent with a shift in government rhetoric and to some extent policy, particularly under Theresa May and Boris Johnson. Both May and Johnson emphasised the need to combat inequalities, and Johnson in particular placed this at the centre of his policy agenda through the idea of levelling up. There is, however, little evidence that the public believe Conservative policies have had any impact on inequality, and there is even some evidence to indicate that the public believe inequality has got worse, particularly since 2019. There is also scepticism about claims that austerity has come to an end and strong evidence that a large proportion of the public have little awareness or understanding of what 'levelling up' means.

However, perhaps the most significant problem facing the Conservatives as they head towards another general election is that the government's approach to public spending and welfare appears to be moving in the opposite direction to public opinion. Under both Truss and Sunak, the Conservatives announced significant cuts to tax and public spending at a time when, after more than ten years of austerity, the public would like to see an increase in tax-funded public provision. The Conservatives have also continued to adopt a restrictive approach to the provision of benefits at a time when the public has become more generous in its attitudes towards benefits recipients. This apparent reintroduction of austerity has generated opposition within the Parliamentary Conservative Party, prompting a number of U-turns in the first months of the Truss government. There is also evidence of significant opposition to this approach among Conservative voters. If the Conservatives are to win the next election, they may need to change direction once again, or hope for a significant shift in public opinion.

References

British Social Attitudes (1983–2021), *UK Data Archive*. Available at: www.data-archive.ac.uk/ (accessed 10 October 2022).

Clery, E. and Dangerfield, P. (2019) 'Poverty and inequality', in J. Curtice, E. Clery, J. Pery, M. Phillips and N. Rahim (eds) *British Social Attitudes 36*, London: National Centre for Social Research.

Curtice, J. (2010a) 'Debate: election 2010: a new mood on tax and spend?', *Policy & Politics*, 38(2): 325–9.

Curtice, J. (2010b) 'Thermostat or weathervane? Public reactions to spending and redistribution under New Labour', in A. Park, J. Curtice, K. Thomson, M. Philips, E. Clery and S. Butt (eds), *British Social Attitudes 26*, London: Sage, pp 19–38.

Curtice, J. (2022) 'Taxation, welfare and inequality: the shape of post-COVID public attitudes', in S. Butt, E. Clery and J. Curtice (eds) *British Social Attitudes 39*, London: National Centre for Social Research.

Curtice, J., Abrams, D. and Jessop, C. (2021) 'New values, new divides? The impact of the COVID-19 pandemic on public attitudes', in E. Clery, J. Curtice, S. Frankenburg, H. Morgan and S. Reid (eds) *British Social Attitudes 38*, London: National Centre for Social Research.

Curtice, J., Abrams, D. and Jessop, C. (2022) *A turning point in history? Social and political attitudes in Britain in the wake of the pandemic*, London: National Centre for Social Research.

Defty, A. (2011) 'The Conservatives, social policy and public opinion', in H. Bochel (ed) *The Conservative Party and social policy*, Bristol: Policy Press, pp 61–76.

Defty, A. (2014) 'Can you tell what it is yet? Public attitudes towards "the Big Society"', *Social Policy and Society*, 13(1): 13–24.

Defty, A. (2016) 'The Coalition, social policy and public opinion', in H. Bochel and M. Powell (eds) *The Coalition government and social policy*, Bristol: Policy Press, pp 79–98.

de Vries, R., Baumberg Geiger, B., Scullion, L., Summers, K., Edmiston, D., Ingold, J., Robertshaw, D. and Young, D. (2021) *Solidarity in a crisis? Trends in attitudes to benefits during COVID-19*, Welfare – At a Social Distance project report. Available at: www.distantwelfare.co.uk/attitudes (accessed 10 October 2022).

Duffy, B., Hewlett, K., Hesketh, R., Benson, R. and Wager, A. (2021) *Unequal Britain: attitudes to inequalities after Covid-19*, London: The Policy Institute/UK in a Changing Europe. Available at: www.kcl.ac.uk/policy-institute/assets/unequal-britain.pdf (accessed 10 October 2022).

Hudson, J., Lunt, N., Hamilton, C., Mackinder, S., Meers, J. and Swift, C. (2016a) 'Nostalgia narratives? Pejorative attitudes to welfare in historical perspective: survey evidence from Beveridge to the British Social Attitudes survey', *Journal of Poverty and Social Justice*, 24(3): 227–43.

Hudson, J., Patrick, R. and Wincup, E. (2016b) 'Introduction to themed special issue: exploring "welfare" attitudes and experiences', *Journal of Poverty and Social Exclusion*, 24(3): 215–26.

Ipsos (2010a) 'May 2010 Issues Index', 18 May. Available at: www.ipsos.com/en-uk/may-2010-issues-index (accessed 10 October 2022).

Ipsos (2010b) 'June 2010 Political Monitor', 21 June. Available at: www.ipsos.com/en-uk/june-2010-political-monitor (accessed 10 October 2022).

Ipsos (2015) 'Economist/Ipsos May 2015 Issues Index', 28 May. Available at: www.ipsos.com/en-uk/economistipsos-mori-may-2015-issues-index (accessed 10 October 2022).

Ipsos (2020) 'Ipsos Issues Index – January 2020', 19 February. Available at: www.ipsos.com/en-uk/ipsos-mori-issues-index-january-2020 (accessed 10 October 2022).

Ipsos (2021a) 'Political Monitor June 2021'. Available at: www.ipsos.com/en-uk/starmers-ratings-fall-further-now-same-levels-corbyn-14-months (accessed 10 October 2022).

Ipsos (2021b) 'The levelling up diaries part 2', 3 December. Available at: www.ipsos.com/en-uk/levelling-diaries-part-2 (accessed 10 October 2022).

Ipsos (2021c) 'The public's expectations for levelling up', 5 October. Available at: www.ipsos.com/en-uk/publics-expectations-for-levelling-up (accessed 10 October 2022).

Ipsos (2022a) 'Political Monitor January 2022'. Available at: www.ipsos.com/en-uk/7-10-britons-dissatisfied-boris-johnson-prime-minister (accessed 10 October 2022).

Ipsos (2022b) 'Ipsos Issues Index: August 2022', 24 August. Available at: www.ipsos.com/en-uk/ipsos-issues-index-august-2022 (accessed 10 October 2022).

Ipsos (2022c) 'Ipsos poll shows economic optimism falls to lowest since 2008 financial crash', 18 March. Available at: www.ipsos.com/en-uk/ipsos-poll-shows-economic-optimism-falls-lowest-2008-financial-crash (accessed 10 October 2022).

Ipsos (2022d) 'Political Monitor 22–29 June 2022'. Available at: www.ipsos.com/en-uk/conservative-party-image-weakens-lowest-score-2011-being-seen-fit-govern (accessed 10 October 2022).

Ipsos (2022e) 'Political Monitor 9-16 November 2022'. Available at: https://www.ipsos.com/sites/default/files/ct/news/documents/2022-11/November%202022%20Political%20Monitor%20Topline_181122_PUBLIC.pdf (accessed 21 November 2022).

Ipsos (2023) 'Rishi Sunak's personal poll ratings improve but Labour retain strong lead in voting intention', 4 April. Available at: www.ipsos.com/en-uk/rishi-sunaks-personal-poll-ratings-improve-labour-retain-strong-lead-voting-intention (accessed 10 May 2023).

Morris, J. (2022) 'Half of Britons believe the Autumn Statement will leave families worse off', *YouGov*, 23 November. Available at: https://yougov.co.uk/topics/politics/articles-reports/2022/11/23/half-britons-believe-autumn-statement-will-leave-f (accessed 2 December 2022).

Pearce, N. and Taylor, E. (2013) 'Changing attitudes towards the role of the state', in A. Park, C. Bryson, E. Clery, J. Curtice and M. Phillips (eds) *British Social Attitudes 30*, London: National Centre for Social Research, pp 33–61.

Smith, M. (2022) 'Mini-budget gets worst reception of any financial statement since Tories took charge in 2010', *YouGov*, 27 September. Available at: https://yougov.co.uk/topics/politics/articles-reports/2022/09/27/mini-budget-gets-worst-reception-any-financial-sta (accessed 10 October 2022).

Stuart, N. and Wlezien, C. (2005) 'Opinion-policy dynamics: public preferences and public expenditure in the United Kingdom', *British Journal of Political Science*, 35(4): 665–89.

Taylor-Gooby, P. and Martin, R. (2008) 'Trends in sympathy for the poor', in A. Park, J. Curtice, K. Thomson, M. Phillips, M. Johnson and E. Clery (eds) *British Social Attitudes 24*, London: Sage, pp 229–57.

Taylor-Gooby, P. and Taylor, E. (2015) 'Benefits and welfare: long-term trends or short-term reactions?', in J. Curtice and R. Ormston (eds), *British Social Attitudes 32*, London: National Centre for Social Research, pp 74–101.

van Oorschot, W. (2000) 'Who should get what and why? On deservingness criteria and the conditionality of solidarity among the public', *Policy and Politics*, 28(1): 33–48.

van Oorschot, W. (2006) 'Making the difference in social Europe: deservingness perceptions among citizens of European welfare states', *Journal of European Social Policy*, 16(1): 23–42.

YouGov (2015) 'Political Tracker: government cuts 2010 – 2015'. Available at: https://d25d2506sfb94s.cloudfront.net/cumulus_uploads/document/umkary60am/YG-Archives-Pol-Trackers-Government%20Cuts-040515.pdf (accessed 10 October 2022).

YouGov (2016a) 'YouGov survey results: 13–14 March 2016'. Available at: https://docs.cdn.yougov.com/rpbw4bk27a/InternalResults_160214_PreBudget_W.pdf (accessed 10 October 2022).

YouGov (2016b) 'YouGov / Times survey results: 16–17 March 2016'. Available at: https://d25d2506sfb94s.cloudfront.net/cumulus_uploads/document/iwe2t5mo0i/TimesResults_160317_Budget&VI_W.pdf (accessed 10 October 2022).

YouGov (2018a) 'YouGov / Peston survey results: 29–30 October 2018'. Available at: https://docs.cdn.yougov.com/3ak4cqb6q6/Peston_181030_Results_w.pdf (accessed 10 October 2022).

YouGov (2018b) 'YouGov / The Times survey results: 29–30 October 2018'. Available at: https://d25d2506sfb94s.cloudfront.net/cumulus_uploads/document/y8iwpyuaaf/TimesResults_181030_VI_Trackers_BudgetQs_bpcw.pdf (accessed 10 October 2022).

YouGov (2020a) 'YouGov / Channel 4 survey results: 9–10 November 2020'. Available at: https://docs.cdn.yougov.com/k5ae44met3/Channel4_UCResults_201110.pdf (accessed 10 October 2022).

YouGov (2020b) 'YouGov / KCL survey results: 11–12 November'. Available at: https://docs.cdn.yougov.com/kzi666gg1s/KCL_Inequality1stRelease_201113.pdf (accessed 10 October 2022).

YouGov (2020c) 'YouGov / Matt Chorley survey results: 15–16 December 2020'. Available at: https://docs.cdn.yougov.com/y9yyeo1wvx/Internal_Chorley_201216.pdf (accessed 10 October 2022).

YouGov (2020d) 'YouGov / Rethink survey results: 4–5 November 2020'. Available at: https://docs.cdn.yougov.com/ml9p82h68w/Rethink_UniversalCredit_201105.pdf (accessed 10 October 2022).

YouGov (2021a) 'YouGov / SEETEC survey results: 12–15 November 2021'. Available at: https://docs.cdn.yougov.com/tfxw0lih90/SEETEC_LevellingUp_211115_W.pdf (accessed 10 October 2022).

YouGov (2021b) 'YouGov survey results: 1–11 June 2021'. Available at: https://docs.cdn.yougov.com/6jso6mipuf/Copy%20of%20DWF_YouGov_Survey_Results_20210611_W.pdf (accessed 10 October 2022).

YouGov (2021c) 'YouGov survey results: 22–23 September 2021'. Available at: https://docs.cdn.yougov.com/4hdbxyt780/Internal_Furlough_210923_V2_W.pdf (accessed 10 October 2022).

YouGov (2021d) 'YouGov survey results: 30 November – 13 December 2021'. Available at: https://docs.cdn.yougov.com/li2af8iulc/Internal_LevellingUp_merge_211214_W.pdf (accessed 10 October 2022).

YouGov (2021e) 'YouGov / The Times survey results: 2–3 September 2021'. Available at: https://docs.cdn.yougov.com/n0w90jr18i/TheTimes_VI_UC_Results_210903_W.pdf (accessed 10 October 2022).

4

Brexit and the Conservative Party's social policies

Steven Corbett

Introduction

The UK's decision, in a referendum on 23 June 2016, to end its 43-year membership of 'the European project' was based on a difference of just over one million voters, which enabled the 'Leave' campaign to win the referendum by 51.9 per cent of the vote to 48.1 per cent. Prior to the referendum, the Conservative Party had been facing an onslaught from the radical Right. The United Kingdom Independence Party (UKIP) received the largest vote share in the 2014 European Parliament elections in the UK and got almost four million votes in the 2015 UK general election on an anti-European Union (EU) and anti-immigration ticket. While UKIP made gains in the Labour heartlands by appealing to the nationalism of 'old' Labour voters who rejected 'modernised' Blairite social democracy, it also acted as a weight in pulling the largely neoliberal Conservative Party to the nationalist Right (Ford and Goodwin, 2014).

The post-vote Brexit process is analysed here as an attempt to manage the internal contradictions of the Conservative Party under a succession of different prime ministers (Teresa May, Boris Johnson, Elizabeth Truss and Rishi Sunak). These developments indicate the continuance of neoliberalism in the social policy field as a form of social control, prioritisation of markets and corporate interests, and emphasis on welfare chauvinism – a focus, in both rhetoric and policy, on restricting welfare entitlements to 'our own' people, based on ethnonational demarcations, which promises (but rarely delivers) ontological security (Donoghue and Kuisma, 2022). Often in conflict with the neoliberals, an ascendant radical Right libertarian authoritarian wing of the Conservative Party is drawing on support from Eurosceptic Members of Parliament (MPs), radical Right financial actors and think tanks, such as Global Britain, the Adam Smith Institute and the TaxPayers' Alliance. It ignores societal and environmental crises, and prioritises a turbo-capitalism of tax-free zones (such as free ports) and financial accumulation located in private equity, hedge funds and other 'alt-finance' organisations (Benquet and Bourgeron, 2022). It is often contemptuous of the limited democratic scrutiny and accountability of the UK Parliament. During the period covered here (from 2016 onwards), this faction of the Conservative Party captured some of the major offices of state.

This chapter examines the roots of the referendum, the vote itself and the implications for social policy in the UK's post-Brexit transition process. Developments in post-Brexit social policy in relation to social and employment standards, migration policy, health care and the tensions between the devolved governments of the UK are assessed. While the welfare chauvinist shift has attempted to hold together the Conservative Party's coalition of factions and retain power following the end of the Coalition government, the continuing problems in the post-EU UK of poverty, insecurity and global economic competitiveness suggest increasingly fragmented and diverging social policy tensions.

Neoliberalism, libertarian authoritarianism and English nationalism

The myths of the British Empire and a specific English nationalism, connected to the impact of the Second World War on national discourse, have shaped Euroscepticism in the UK. This has found contemporary expression in nationalist populism in order to simplify complex cultural, political and economic phenomena as a matter of 'the people' versus 'elites' (Corbett, 2016) and a form of welfare chauvinism (Donoghue and Kuisma, 2022). While English nationalism characterises the English people as exceptionalist and socially conservative, this is problematic for the Conservative Party because its neoliberal direction has espoused a more open free market globalism that has often conflicted with the social conservative base. English nationalism is also a theme within Labour's working-class constituencies in former industrial areas (Winlow et al, 2017). The deployment of English nationalism conflicts with the established European neoliberalism associated with membership of the EU and a libertarian authoritarian tendency that seeks to render the UK (or at least England) as a site of accumulation for deregulated financial capital (Benquet and Bourgeron, 2022).

The Thatcherite turn in British politics shifted the terms of the European debate in the 1980s and 1990s, particularly with reference to the Maastricht Treaty 1992 and political and economic integration. Over the past four decades, this nationalist and chauvinist populism has been stoked by the Conservative Party, its European Research Group (ERG) caucus (comprised of many MPs who would later serve in the May, Johnson, Truss and Sunak administrations), UKIP, the Right-wing news media (the *Daily Mail*, *The Sun* and *The Telegraph* in particular) and radical Right think tanks and lobby groups with links to the US Atlas Foundation (the Institute of Economic Affairs, the Adam Smith Institute, the Centre for Policy Studies, the Global

Warming Policy Foundation, the Legatum Institute and the Taxpayers' Alliance, among others). All of these groups, while not antithetical to neoliberalism in principle, see an alternative 'global' future in which the UK, rather than operating within neoliberal EU structures, would be able to freely pursue financial deregulation and further flexibilisation and privatisation of social policy concerns, with access to Commonwealth, US and Asian consumers and labour markets.

The development of both the Eurozone and the European Social Model has entrenched this opposition (Walker, 2005). The European Social Model, purported to offer a specifically European regard for 'social' concerns as much as 'economic' ones, has been more of a weak rhetorical device to 'humanise' neoliberalism in the EU than a specifically European social policy approach (Corbett and Walker, 2019), although European citizens have benefited from some policies, such as the Working Time Directive. But in the post-financial crisis landscape, moves such as the adoption of the Stability and Growth Pact have further promoted economic integration and fiscal rules, over social concerns. There is a Left-wing critique of the neoliberal direction of the EU, stemming from earlier criticisms of the European Economic Community as a capitalist bosses' club, and many of the critical groups, such as the Socialist Workers Party, proposed 'Lexit' (Left exit) during the referendum, despite this not being an option on the referendum ballot. Relevant to this critique is the Maastricht Treaty's 3 per cent deficit spending limit and privatisations under the aegis of market competition, and this critique has solidified post 2008 with the banking and Eurozone crises. In this period of austerity neoliberalism, the treatment of southern European Member States, in particular Greece, has seen structural adjustment policies implemented to further neoliberalise these economies against the democratically expressed wishes of their populations, leading Benquet and Bourgeron to assert that the EU can be seen 'as a structurally neoliberal institution, constitutionally protected from any form of popular influence' (2022, p 94). Therefore, deepening dissatisfaction with neoliberal politics can be located both in the direction of the UK state and the EU. In this context, the EU referendum was a tinderbox for societal anger across the political spectrum, although the most powerful organisations for exiting the EU, and those currently using the levers of the British state to shape Brexit, have come from the libertarian authoritarian radical Right, marshalling a populist welfare chauvinist discourse of English nationalism.

The referendum

With the combination of pressure from the intake of hard-line Eurosceptic Conservative MPs in the 2010 election and an attempt to stymie the 'revolt on the Right' by UKIP, then Prime Minister David Cameron made a pledge in 2013 to hold a 'simple' in/out referendum on British membership of the EU. The risk taken by Cameron was mitigated by the assumption that the 2015 election result was likely to require another coalition government and that the pledge could be negotiated away with the pro-EU Liberal Democrats. When a surprise majority was achieved, this move ultimately put long-term societal stability and Cameron's political career (as a pro-'Remain' Tory) on the line for short-term electoral advantage.

The pledge stipulated that Cameron would provide his favoured offer of a renegotiated relationship between the UK and the EU against 'Brexit', which was entirely unspecified at this point. Four key principles were negotiated: a four-year 'emergency brake' on in-work benefits for migrants; a reduction in Child Benefit paid to EU migrants when their children remain overseas; the removal of the phrase 'ever closer union' from any future EU treaties involving the UK; and 'emergency safeguards' to protect the City of London and reduce 'red tape' for British businesses. While the first two principles were positioned to appeal to English nationalism and welfare chauvinism, the latter two were aimed squarely at Eurosceptics within the Conservative Party, with the aim to reduce social standards, and the alt-finance world of hedge funds and private equity traders who saw more opportunities for the accumulation of profit outside the EU (Benquet and Bourgeron, 2022).

In the three-month referendum campaign, the weight of the political and economic establishment presented the Remain case, with neoliberal elites positing the economic costs for families should the UK leave the EU. Meanwhile, a prominent Eurosceptic and Left-wing MP, Jeremy Corbyn, led the Labour Party's own lukewarm Remain campaign, proposing to 'remain and reform', which focused on workers' rights, despite this also not being an option on the referendum ballot. Other political, financial and media elites supported the Leave campaign, which also had two groupings. The official cross-party Vote Leave campaign comprised of leading Conservative MPs, such as Johnson (in an instrumental move to boost his own leadership chances), Michael Gove and the Labour grandee Frank Field. Leave.EU, a rival campaign, was led by UKIP leader Nigel Farage and bankrolled by Arron Banks and other members of the alt-finance world. Indeed, the financial sector provided 57 per cent of funding for the Leave campaigns, notably £1.9 million from private equity funds and £5.4 million from hedge funds (Benquet and Bourgeron, 2022).

With the majority of the British news media backing the Leave campaign, it engaged in emotive and 'positive' messages of English nationalism. This included the slogan 'Vote Leave, take control', emphasising the repatriation of sovereignty to the UK Parliament as representatives of 'the people'. Johnson appealed to 'hope' for the voiceless and restoration of democracy across Europe from a 'liberal cosmopolitan' perspective, while in response to the cataclysmic economic warnings of the Remain campaign, Gove claimed that 'the people' were 'tired of experts'. A defining image was the (false) claim about funding for the National Health Service (NHS) on the side of a red bus: 'We send the EU £350 million a week, let's fund our NHS instead'. When the referendum results were announced, the bellicose Farage declared that 23 June 2016 should be renamed the UK's 'Independence Day'.

'Getting Brexit done'

After the referendum, the shell-shocked Cameron resigned, and following a leadership campaign, Theresa May emerged as the new leader of the Conservative Party and Prime Minister charged with enacting Brexit. This period saw debate emerge on the terms 'soft Brexit' and 'hard Brexit', the former referring to regulatory alignment with the EU's single market and customs union and maintenance of free movement, while not being an EU member, akin to Iceland, Liechtenstein, Norway or Switzerland, and the latter indicating a dramatic break from EU-level regulations, in which the UK could, most likely, attempt to undercut the EU-27 on social, environmental and employment standards and financial deregulation. During this period, the anodyne phrase 'Brexit means Brexit' was used to reassure the Eurosceptics that May would follow through on a hard Brexit break from the EU, especially on social standards. Initially, May was heralded by the Right-wing news media and likened to Thatcher as someone able to fight both enemies in Europe over the UK's withdrawal and pro-EU enemies within, characterised as lawyers, judges, celebrities, politicians and other liberal elites seeking to undermine the referendum result.

May's Lancaster House speech in January 2017 signalled the government's intention that the UK would leave the single market and that 'no deal' would be better than a 'bad deal', indicating that the 'hardest' of Brexits, necessitating leaving the EU on World Trade Organization (WTO) terms, was on the table. May followed this by triggering Article 50, beginning the process of exiting the EU, in late March 2017. However, with her authority under threat, she called a snap election. After a poor election campaign, the Conservatives lost their majority in Parliament and were forced to rely on the Northern Irish Democratic Unionist Party to support the government's programme as a minority administration. This was significant in relation to one of the key sticking points of negotiations, concerning the border between Northern Ireland and the Republic of Ireland and the dangerous consequences of a return to a hard border in this region.

There were hints by spring 2018 that the UK was willing to make significant concessions around the free movement of people, the role of the European Court of Justice and budget contributions. In the end, the negotiations produced a soft Brexit plan, with 'managed divergence' from EU rules and a 'common rulebook'. In the following months, successive ministers resigned from May's government in protest over the Brexit agreement, including Brexit Minster David Davis and Foreign Secretary Boris Johnson. By the end of 2018, May had survived a confidence vote from within her own party and faced successive defeats and rebellions over the direction that the Brexit Bill was taking. By spring 2019, the government had endured three defeats on attempts to pass the Brexit Bill. On the eve of the European elections, scheduled for 27 May 2019, May announced her intention to step down once a new leader was elected over the summer. Meanwhile, the Conservatives, like Labour, endured a pitiful performance in the European elections, in which Farage's newly formed Brexit Party won the most votes.

In July 2019, Boris Johnson became Prime Minister and pursued a hard Brexit approach, whereby key aspects, such as the Irish backstop and the pledge not to dilute social, environmental and employment standards, were stripped from the Withdrawal Agreement. By the late summer, Johnson prorogued Parliament for five weeks in order to prevent increasing opposition from within his own party to the hard Brexit direction his government was taking, including the option of leaving the EU without a deal in place on 31 October 2019. Twenty-one Conservative MPs opposed to Brexit were expelled from the Party. Meanwhile, the suspension of Parliament was deemed by the UK's Supreme Court to be illegal, and a Bill, sponsored by Labour MP Hilary Benn, was passed that ensured the UK would not be able to leave the EU without a deal.

In a snap election on 12 December 2019, having repeated ad infinitum the slogan 'get Brexit done', Johnson won a huge 80-seat majority, a scale of victory not seen since the 1980s under Thatcher. However, more fragmentation was seen as Scotland and Northern Ireland returned strongly anti-Brexit candidates and England and Wales saw many seats change hands from Labour to the Tories. As a consequence of this decisive victory and the prior removal of anti-Brexit rebels from the Party, Johnson was able to ensure a relatively smooth passage of the EU Withdrawal Bill, leading to the UK's formal departure from the EU on 31 January 2020.

In this period of political chaos and with the eventual completion of the first stage of the post-referendum departure of the UK, the strongly Eurosceptic libertarian authoritarian faction was determined to ensure that the possibility of a soft Brexit did not come to pass. In the end, the essential difference between the Withdrawal Agreement that May failed to get through Parliament, precipitating her downfall, and the ratification of the eventual Bill in January 2020 was the removal of the commitment to EU social standards and the rewriting of the Irish backstop (Hantrais, 2020b). The prospect of regulatory divergence raises concerns for the further transformation of social policies under neoliberal and libertarian authoritarian influences if, as is likely, the UK seeks to undercut the social standards and provisions of the EU-27 Member States.

The shape of Brexit to come

Given the competing factions within both the Conservative Party and the financial sector, the government's direction during the post-Brexit period has largely embraced a combination of welfare chauvinism and libertarian authoritarianism in relation to the social policy field. The government has continued to look for vaguely defined 'Brexit opportunities' as part of the 'Global Britain' branding, in line with the clamour for further financial deregulation in striking trade and finance deals with other trading blocs and major economies. This includes the pledge to ratify the Comprehensive and Progressive Agreement for Trans-Pacific Partnership in July 2023, which requires pro-corporate policies and lower environmental standards for the UK. The implications for social policy include a much-reduced welfare state in terms of fiscal capacity and further privatisation of welfare needs. Given these dire circumstances, as Bochel and Powell argue in Chapter 1, the likely outcome would be 'an American-style welfare state with European taxes' (p 15). This owes much to the government's response to a succession of crises that the welfare state faces, from Brexit to the COVID-19 pandemic and the political economic consequences of Russia's invasion of Ukraine, along with long-term failures to strengthen both the UK's productivity and social policy provision in the context of austerity neoliberalism, and it favours the interests of big business.

Brexit, the economy and social policy

Rather than restoring democratic sovereignty to the British people, 'public and social policies are shaped more by the needs and interests of big business than any other policy actor' (Farnsworth, 2020, p 106). A cursory example is the sweetheart deal involving a direct grant made by then Prime Minister May to keep Nissan operating its car production plant in North East England amid Brexit uncertainty. The broader economic impact of Brexit has been estimated as a 5.5 per cent lower gross domestic product compared with similar economies in the summer of 2022, with investment 11 per cent lower, although this is compounded by the impact of COVID-19 and long-term weak productivity in the UK economy (Springford, 2022). This provides less room for manoeuvre in relation to social policy provision and is contributing to the current pressures on living standards. The possibilities for building a new economy and a new social contract outside of the fiscally restrained post-financial-crisis EU are very limited, but this does provide an opportunity for further libertarian authoritarian and chauvinist approaches within the social policy field. As Farnsworth argues:

> [i]n reality, any goods traded into the EU will still have to comply with regulations regarding quality and standards. Thus, the area that the UK government will have most scope to adjust regulations is in the sphere of labour and social policy regulations, especially governing working hours, holidays, equal pay, maternity and paternity leave, trade union rights, workplace consultations over redundancies and employers' national insurance contributions. (2017, p 713)

This, in part, relates to the unresolved tensions between the political economic direction of the UK state and its model of capitalism, in which a libertarian authoritarianism is increasingly dominant, and the social policy field, which remains under the influence of neoliberal approaches to policy making and public service delivery and is being reshaped by nationalist welfare chauvinism in practice.

Brexit and social rights

One of the major differences between May's failed Brexit deal and Johnson's successful Withdrawal Agreement is the removal of the commitment to regulatory alignment with respect to EU social and employment standards (Hantrais, 2020b). The likely consequences are that this will allow for increased flexibility and weakening of existing labour market regulation and social rights within the UK as a means to 'undercut' EU social rights, gain a competitive advantage and attract business investment under the auspices of 'Global Britain'. While the EU has insisted on a 'level playing field' with regards to social and environmental standards in a future trade deal, as Prime Minister, Johnson explicitly ruled out any form of regulatory alignment (Hantrais, 2020a). There are likely to be further tensions over this issue as Prime Minister Sunak moves on to trade negotiations.

The risk to existing levels of social and employment standards can be exemplified by the actions of a prominent Brexiter, Jacob Rees-Mogg, during his tenure as Business Secretary (and later from the back benches), in pushing for a 'sunset clause' in the Retained EU Law (Revocation and Reform) Bill, whereby 2,400 laws agreed with the EU were to be purged from the statute book on 31 December 2023 – although the scope of these changes was much reduced, though still significant, under Sunak. This narrow timeframe would have given the government (and devolved administrations) free rein to determine social and employment policy on a range of issues, including pension rights, equal pay legislation, minimum wages, food standards and other workplace and environmental protections, without adequate democratic scrutiny (O'Carroll, 2022). For Rees-Mogg, this was a necessary component of 'taking back control' from the EU, enacting Brexit and restoring 'parliamentary sovereignty', while trades union representatives and lawyers criticised the measure as giving ministers free rein to rewrite laws without adequate Parliamentary scrutiny. Moreover, Rees-Mogg and others have sought to end the jurisdiction of the European Court of Human Rights, and there are increasingly authoritarian clampdowns on social and environmental movements in the UK (Benquet and Bourgeron, 2022).

Brexit, immigration and work

In the immediate post-Brexit and post-COVID-19 pandemic period, net UK migration reached the highest levels recorded, despite promises by successive Conservative governments from Cameron onwards to reduce net migration to 'below 100,000 per year'. While there has been a significant increase in non-EU migration, especially in relation to international students and their families, migration from within the EU is now net negative (Sumption, 2022). Indeed, the most immediate social policy impact of Brexit pertains to the rights, in relation to social security and health care access, of citizens travelling across the UK–EU border for work, study or retirement (Stewart et al, 2020). Meanwhile, backlogs in asylum applications in the UK left around 143,000 people awaiting a decision in the autumn of 2022 (Casciani, 2022). This is in the context of the Johnson government attempting to enact a welfare chauvinist policy of 'rendition' of illegal immigrants and asylum seekers to Rwanda in 2022, under the notion of 'taking back control' of national borders.

The UK government has enacted a restricted, points-based immigration policy following the end of free movement, which includes requirements for English language proficiency and a job offer for skilled work with a minimum salary of £25,600, while student visas have been expanded (Stewart et al, 2020; Sumption, 2022). Despite mainstream perceptions of 'welfare tourism' in relation to jobs, benefits, housing and health care that have fuelled the populist marshalling of welfare chauvinism, Stewart et al (2020) argue that European Economic Area (EEA) migrants have been net contributors to the UK's economy, paying more in taxes than they receive in the form of service use. Further, restricting free movement while implementing a points-based system of immigration relies 'on skilled migrants continuing to see the UK as an attractive destination: a weaker economy, a depreciated currency and perceptions of a less tolerant society may work against this' (Stewart et al, 2020, p 512). As a consequence, the reduction in migration from the EU and broader EEA means that both the fiscal means to fund public services within a neoliberal economic framework and the availability of skilled workers in key jobs such as health and social care is coming under increasing pressure, with more than 10 per cent of NHS job vacancies – 133,446 positions – unfilled in England alone at the end of September 2022 (Gammie, 2022).

In this context, Labour opposition leader Keir Starmer, in a speech to the Confederation of British Industry in November 2022, called for UK business to invest more in training British citizens, rather than increasing immigration in order to address the shortage of workers in the UK (Allegretti, 2022). However, the UK's long-term approach, both inside and outside the EU, has favoured a lightly regulated, less coordinated market based on adversarial labour relations, lower levels of trade union representation and highly flexible and insecure employment policies, and this looks likely to deepen the uncoordinated liberal market economy, with an attendant weak, residual and conditional welfare state in the post-Brexit period (Farnsworth, 2020). Moving from an economy based on the exploitation of cheap, mobile and flexible labour to a smaller, more highly skilled workforce has related political economic and structural transformations that have not featured in Starmer's statements on how Labour would govern the country through the Brexit process.

Brexit and the NHS

While oversight of the form and extent of health care provision has always remained at the discretion of national governments within the EU (Hantrais, 2020b), the Brexit referendum saw the weaponisation of the NHS in relation to EU membership. A populist nativism was marshalled, with the infamous red bus claim that £350 million per week was sent to the EU, which might better be spent on the NHS, reflecting the status of the health service as a 'secular religion' in the UK (Wincott, 2020; Kettell and Kerr, 2021). While the figure was debunked as overinflating the cost of EU membership to the UK, key to the emotive connection and influence that the claim had on voters was the nativist focus on 'our NHS', which implies a welfare chauvinist claim in the face of presumed 'health tourism'. The focus on the NHS also indicates that welfare chauvinism in the field of social policy was mobilised in order to deepen the sense of in-groups and out-groups in othering non-British people in relation to the UK's relationship with the EU (Kettell and Kerr, 2021). This is despite long-term underfunding of the NHS, undoubtedly exacerbated by the COVID-19 pandemic, to the extent that the 'winter crisis', where NHS provision is stretched to breaking point, is seen as a regularity, life expectancies in northern England have started to decline, waiting lists have increased, with over 7.1 million people waiting for treatment in September 2022, and the first-ever strike over pay was called by nurses and emergency paramedics in December 2022. In addition, 10 per cent of patients on waiting lists have opted to go private through self-pay and credit, with over 60 per cent of private patients reporting that this is to avoid waiting for NHS treatment, some doing so despite the prospect of becoming severely indebted (Engage Britain, 2022). Meanwhile, think tanks associated with the libertarian authoritarian drivers of hard Brexit advocate running down the NHS in order to open it up to private health care providers in a future trade deal with the US (Benquet and Bourgeron, 2022).

Brexit and the devolved governments

Brexit also has significant social policy implications for the devolved governments of Northern Ireland, Scotland and Wales, indicating further divergence between the four nations of the UK and much tension over the border between Northern Ireland and the Republic of Ireland (Birrell and Gray, 2017). While EU directives in the social policy field are largely a matter of devolved governance in the UK, EU edicts on the Working Time Directive, the rights of agency workers and maternity policies, among other areas of social policy, were incorporated into the Equality Act 2010. Significantly, the European Social Fund has channelled funding into some of the poorest areas of the UK, non-British EU workers account for a third of the public sector workforce in Wales, Scotland has accessed a significant amount of Horizon 2020 funding for university research, and Northern Ireland has benefitted from billions in EU funding to support cohesion and integration of the country with the border counties of the Republic of Ireland (Birrell and Gray, 2017). In the vote, Wales, like England, returned a majority vote for Leave (52.5 per cent and 53.4 per cent, respectively), despite the Welsh Government's support for Remain. In Scotland, on the other hand, 62 per cent voted in favour of Remain, and the Scottish Government have made moves to secure a second independence referendum given the UK government's refusal to consider remaining within the single market and customs union and maintaining the free movement of workers, seen as red lines by those in Holyrood.

In Northern Ireland, 55.8 per cent voted for Remain, and the highly contentious politics of the border with the Republic of Ireland has featured prominently in post-Brexit negotiations. With concerns from the US and EU over the endurance of the Good Friday Agreement, which is key to peace in Northern Ireland. May's initial plan for a 'backstop' which would allow Northern Ireland to remain, to some extent, in the customs union and single market, avoiding the need for a hard border, was rejected; following this, Johnson's Withdrawal Agreement included a protocol which effectively established a border between the EU and UK across the Irish Sea. Sunak's subsequent Windsor Framework agreement was presented as a resolution to this contentious issue, with 'green' and 'red' lanes allowing for more nuance in the movement of goods and diverging EU and UK regulations, although the issue of regulatory divergence or convergence in relation to trade will remain prominent in the coming years (McCormick, 2023).

This contentious and uncertain state of affairs means that, on the one hand, EU funding for areas of poverty in all four countries has ended, with the much-reduced UK government Levelling Up Fund proposed to replace this, while on the other hand, further divergence in social policy direction is likely, with Scotland favouring a more 'social democratic' northern European welfare settlement, Wales prioritising funding for public services and Northern Ireland facing a debate around its future in the UK with the contentious operation of the Windsor Framework. The current balance of power suggests that further ruptures to the Union, especially in Northern Ireland and Scotland, are likely as the Brexit process continues.

The ideological transformation of the Conservative Party

After the 2008 financial crisis, there has been a shift in neoliberal societies, with the rise of Right-wing nationalist and nativist populism as both a cultural backlash to the dominance of social liberalism and an ethnonationalist retort to the economic consequences of neoliberal globalisation and austerity policies. The tensions within the Conservative Party revealed by Brexit suggest two dominant tendencies: neoliberalism and libertarian authoritarianism.

In regard to the first tendency, the long-established alliance between neoliberalism and social conservatism has dominated UK politics and society as far back as Thatcher's shift of the Conservative Party to the Right, and was expressed initially as authoritarian populism (Hall, 1988) and later as a form of social control and technocratic management of fiscal and social policies by both major parties (Miller and Rose, 2008). In the last decade, as austerity has laid waste to the social contract and welfare state in the UK, with an increasingly harsh workfare regime and marketised and privatised public services, the successive shocks of the financial crisis, the Brexit vote and the COVID-19 pandemic have transformed the contours of neoliberal hegemony. This has been described as a post-neoliberal phase of the political management of Anglo-American societies (Davies and Gane, 2021). In this period, the older shibboleths of the neoliberal technocratic political class have been increasingly exposed as incapable of providing a hegemonic framing ideology for politics and policy. With the breakdown of political consensus in the 2010s, populisms of the Left and Right attempted to establish a new framing ideology. However, despite some electoral gains for the social democratic Left in Europe, the revolt on the political Right in the austerity decade in the UK has been much more influential (Ford and Goodwin, 2014). In Gramscian terms, this represents an interregnum in which neoliberalism, with no social democratic or socialist counterhegemonic threat (Winlow and Hall, 2023), is evolving into a different form of social policy, less open to globalisation and more firmly rooted in welfare chauvinist, authoritarian and nationalist frameworks (Joppke, 2021).

The second tendency emerging in Conservative politics in this period is an increasingly prevalent strand of libertarian authoritarianism in recent politics and social policy from the Right of the Conservative Party and its outriders in the alt-finance world and alt-Right social movements. This represents a global challenge to the neoliberal global economic order and can be seen in the rise of Right-wing authoritarian populists in the UK, the US, Brazil, Denmark, Hungary, India, Italy, Poland and Sweden, in particular. This perspective has been an influential driver behind the push for Brexit as 'hard Brexit', 'no deal' and on 'WTO terms', which is shaping the post-Brexit social policy field and has also underpinned, to some extent, the UK government's COVID-19 policies. This second tendency embraces hard-Right populist politics and can be evidenced in the some of the actions of the UK government during and after the Brexit negotiations. For example, the pressure placed on May to ensure that Brexit takes the appropriate form and the repeated rejection of the terms of her soft Brexit Withdrawal Agreement, as well as the illegal proroguing of Parliament and the expulsion of 'Brexit rebels' from the Conservative Party, represent a hard-line approach that is not afraid of curtailing the limited democratic scrutiny offered by the British political system of the government's plans for Brexit. Other examples, from both the Johnson and Sunak administrations, include the post-Brexit attempt to run down the time limit of EU laws and the increasingly hostile migration policies, evidenced in the UK government's notorious Rwanda rendition policy and the 'stop the boats' approach to 'deter' asylum seekers, refugees and illegal migrants from entering the UK (see also Chapter 15).

Conclusion

Certainly, in the post-Brexit economic landscape, the future for the Conservative Party in power is challenging. This chapter has assessed the drivers on the Right behind Brexit and the emerging implications for Conservative social policies, in particular the impact on social rights, immigration and work, the NHS and the devolved governments. There are difficulties in holding together the increasingly unstable coalition of different factions that make up the Party, especially the neoliberal and the libertarian authoritarian wings.

Along with the powerful influence that the libertarian authoritarian ERG has held over the Party's internal battle over Britain's EU membership for several decades, emerging groups, modelled on the ERG, have differing agendas. The Covid Recovery Group advocates greater transparency in relation to COVID-19 policies but also provides a forum for the more Right-wing libertarian authoritarian strand of the Conservative Party to oppose state intervention, such as the quasi-Keynesian Coronavirus Job Retention Scheme. However, the disaster of the 45-day-long Truss administration and its infamous mini-budget reveals that the Party remains to some extent in hock to the needs of big business and first-wave finance (the mainstream neoliberal institutional investors, such as central and commercial banks, pension funds, and insurance companies), and any libertarian authoritarian 'economic revolution' would require a strategy that allows other fractions of capital to prosper also in achieving the goal of a minimal state dedicated primarily to deregulating financial capital and the preservation of private property.

In addition, the Northern Research Group seeks to advance the priorities of northern English Conservative MPs with respect to the 'levelling up' agenda, placing the leadership in a difficult position in negotiating the difference between electoral and governing rhetoric and concrete social policies aimed at improving the lives of people in English regions (Peele, 2021). This is especially challenging in light of the end of EU structural funds targeted at some of the poorest regions, given the poor economic performance of the UK. While the opposition Labour Party has accepted that there is no turning back on the referendum result, they are yet to illuminate a path beyond the constraints of neoliberalism and libertarian authoritarianism that develops social policies oriented towards meeting human needs. It is clear that Brexit will continue to shape the contours of British social policy for decades to come.

References

Allegretti, A. (2022) 'Keir Starmer walks fine line in shifting Labour's stance on immigration', *The Guardian*, 23 November. Available at: www.theguard ian.com/politics/2022/nov/23/keir-starmer-walks-fine-line-shifting-lab our-stance-immigration (accessed 19 July 2023).

Benquet, M. and Bourgeron, T. (2022) *Alt-finance: how the City of London bought democracy*, London: Pluto Press.

Birrell, D. and Gray, A.M. (2017) 'Devolution: the social, political and policy implications of Brexit for Scotland, Wales and Northern Ireland', *Journal of Social Policy*, 46(4): 765–82.

Casciani, D. (2022) 'UK net migration hits all-time record at 504,000', *BBC News*, 24 November. Available at: www.bbc.co.uk/news/uk-63743 259 (accessed 19 July 2023).

Corbett, S. (2016) 'The social consequences of Brexit for the UK and Europe: Euroscepticism, populism, nationalism, and societal division', *International Journal of Social Quality*, 6(1): 11–31.

Corbett, S. and Walker, A. (2019) 'Between neoliberalism and nationalist populism: what role for the "European Social Model" and social quality in post-Brexit Europe?', *Social Policy & Society*, 18(1): 93–106.

Davies, W. and Gane, N. (2021) 'Post-neoliberalism? An introduction', *Theory, Culture & Society*, 38(6): 3–28.

Donoghue, M. and Kuisma, M. (2022) 'Taking back control of the welfare state: Brexit, rational-imaginaries and welfare chauvinism', *West European Politics*, 45(1): 177–99.

Engage Britain (2022) 'Millions turning to private healthcare are forced into financial worry', *Engage Britain*, 18 August. Available at: https://engage britain.org/news-millions-turning-to-private-healthcare/ (accessed 19 July 2023).

Farnsworth, K. (2017) 'Taking back control or empowering big business? New risks to the welfare state in the post-Brexit competition for investment', *Journal of Social Policy*, 46(4): 699–718.

Farnsworth, K. (2020) 'Taking back control? Big business and the welfare state', in M. Donoghue and M. Kuisma (eds) *Whither social rights in (post-) Brexit Europe?* Berlin: Social Europe and the Friederich Ebert Stiftung, pp 100–8.

Ford, R. and Goodwin, M. (2014) *Revolt on the right: explaining support for the radical right in Britain*, London: Routledge.

Gammie, J. (2022) 'NHS vacancies in England rise to new record high', *The Independent*, 1 December. Available at: www.independent.co.uk/news/uk/nhs-job-vacancies-record-high-b2236960.html (accessed 19 July 2023).

Grey, C. (2021) *Brexit unfolded: how no one got what they wanted (and why they were never going to)*, London: Biteback.

Hall, S. (1988) *The hard road to renewal: Thatcherism and the crisis of the left*, London: Verso.

Hantrais, L. (2019) *What Brexit means for EU and UK social policy*, Bristol: Policy Press.

Hantrais, L. (2020a) 'Afterword: what Brexit and COVID-19 mean for EU and UK social policy'. Available at: https://policy.bristoluniversitypress.co.uk/asset/8562/hantrais-online-afterword.pdf (accessed 19 July 2023).

Hantrais, L. (2020b) 'Reconceptualising and delivering social policy: competing challenges in (post-)Brexit and pandemic Europe', in M. Donoghue and M. Kuisma (eds) *Whither social rights in (post-)Brexit Europe?* Berlin: Social Europe and the Friederich Ebert Stiftung, pp 26–33.

Joppke, C. (2021) *Neoliberal nationalism: immigration and the rise of the populist right*, Cambridge: Cambridge University Press.

Kettell, S. and Kerr, P. (2021) 'The Brexit religion and the holy grail of the NHS', *Social Policy & Society*, 20(2): 282–95.

McCormick, A. (2023) 'The Windsor Framework: a quick evaluation', *UK in a Changing Europe*, 28 February. Available at: https://ukandeu.ac.uk/the-windsor-framework-a-quick-evaluation/ (accessed 19 July 2023).

Miller, P. and Rose, N. (2008) *Governing the present: administering economic, social and personal life*, Bristol: Policy Press.

O'Carroll, C. (2022) 'Rees-Mogg move to axe 2,400 Laws is "anti-democratic"', say legal experts', *The Guardian*, 22 October. Available at: www.theguard ian.com/law/2022/oct/24/post-brexit-proposals-mean-2400-laws-could-disappear-lawyers-warn (accessed 19 July 2023).

Peele, G. (2021) 'Post Brexit and post-Covid: reflections on the contemporary Conservative Party', *The Political Quarterly*, 92(3): 404–11.

Springford, J. (2022) 'The cost of Brexit to June 2022', *Centre for European Reform*, 21 December. Available at: www.cer.eu/insights/cost-brexit-june-2022 (accessed 19 July 2023).

Stewart, K., Cooper, I. and Shutes, I. (2020) 'What will "taking back control" mean for social policy in the UK? Brexit, public services and social rights', *Journal of European Social Policy*, 30(4): 509–17.

Sumption, M. (2022) 'Why has non-EU migration to the UK risen?', *Migration Observatory*, 21 November. Available at: https://migrationobse rvatory.ox.ac.uk/resources/commentaries/why-has-non-eu-migration-to-the-uk-risen/ (accessed 19 July 2023).

Walker, A. (2005) 'Which way for the European social model: minimum standards or social quality?', in J. Goul Andersen, A.-M. Guillemard, P.H. Jensen and B. Pfau-Effinger (eds) *The changing face of welfare*, Bristol: Policy Press, pp 33–54.

Wincott, D. (2020) 'Imagined solidarities: Brexit, welfare, states, nations, and the EU', in M. Donoghue and M. Kuisma (eds) *Whither social rights in (post-) Brexit Europe?* Berlin: Social Europe and the Friederich Ebert Stiftung, pp 7–15.

Winlow, S. and Hall, S. (2023) *The death of the Left: why we must begin from the beginning again*, Bristol: Policy Press.

Winlow, S., Hall, S. and Treadwell, J. (2017) *Rise of the Right: English nationalism and the transformation of working class politics*, Bristol: Policy Press.

5

The Johnson Conservative government, its conservatism and the pandemic response

Ian Greener

Introduction

When considering the Conservative government's response to the COVID-19 pandemic, a chapter of this length cannot possibly examine every event and narrate the full story of the pandemic. That will be the job of longer work, as well as future public inquiries into what might be usefully learned from the events following 2019. This chapter has to be both narrower and broader than those responses. It is narrower as it has only limited space to consider a massively complex issue. This means focusing on a series of events which are key to the argument that the chapter will make. It is broader in that it attempts to make an argument about the pandemic and the kind of conservatism that the Johnson government, which was in place through the first two and a half years of the pandemic, can be located as representing.

The chapter argues that the Johnson government, in its leadership of the UK COVID-19 response, represents a particular form of conservatism, which will be called 'cronyist populism', and it locates this form of conservatism in relation to the typology of Conservatives presented in the opening chapter of the book but also in relation to the 'authoritarian populism' suggested by Hall (1979), which was based on the Thatcher government and remained a key reference point in the Conservative Party leadership elections of 2022.

The chapter discusses the idea of cronyist populism later on, but first it provides a periodisation of the pandemic response. This periodisation, while contestable, should at least be recognisable to those who either lived through it or have read about it from other accounts. It places a stronger emphasis on the first year of the pandemic because this period demonstrates the extent to which the government struggled in terms of its response and the contradictions presented in the particular form of conservatism present in the Johnson government. The chapter then explores the key elements of the pandemic response present in the periodisation before moving finally to locate those key elements in relation to the models of conservatism presented in Chapter 1 and developing them further into the concept of cronyist populism.

Periodising the pandemic response

The periodisation presented here has seven phases – going from 'complacency' to 'panic', then 'getting a grip', followed by 'getting back to normal', the 'winter disaster', 'freedom' and finally the 'living with the virus' phase. There is certainly overlap between these periods, so they do not neatly separate from one time period to the next. However, each captures something important and distinctive about the response and so is important in understanding the events of 2020–22. The primary focus of this periodisation is around the early phases – especially complacency and panic – since more happened in those periods as the virus emerged and the government struggled to come up with a response to it.

Complacency

In early 2020, the UK had a newly elected government with a substantial majority following an election where much debate had been based around Brexit. Therefore, 2020 was to be the year in which the government 'delivered' Brexit, with senior government members voicing scepticism about the role of 'experts' in policy making (Mance, 2016). In terms of pandemic preparedness, the UK was regarded as a 'leader in risk assessment', including for significant events such as pandemics (Comptroller and Auditor General, 2021b), and scored highly on an index of epidemic 'preparedness' in 2019 (Oppenheim et al, 2019). It is in this context that the initial spread of COVID-19 occurred. Previous governments (ostensibly of the same political persuasion as the Conservative government elected in 2019) had run a series of pandemic exercises, based on both simulations and models, in the five years before the COVID-19 pandemic, but refused to release the reports, especially for the coronavirus exercise that took place in 2016, claiming it would 'damage national security' to do so (Dyer, 2021).

It is also the case that the initial messaging about COVID-19 by the World Health Organization (WHO) could have been clearer. In January 2020, a shift took place from the WHO presenting the virus as being unlikely to be easily transmittable between humans to its gaining of a far better understanding of both the high probability of such transmission and the challenge of the virus being nonsymptomatic for some time on being transmitted.

The first phase of the UK response to COVID-19 can be characterised as one of 'complacency'. Some of this could be justified – international alarm bells had rung before in relation to the potential spread of novel viruses, in the cases of SARS (severe acute respiratory syndrome) and MERS (Middle East respiratory syndrome) in the previous decade, but these had not spread to the UK. The UK had this factor in common with several other European nations, and so an initial lack of engagement was not unique to it (Carroll et al, 2020).

The UK did have some features which marked its initial approach out as different, however. The government was newly elected and so still establishing itself, and it was preoccupied with other matters (not least Brexit, but also floods in the north of the country). It was led by a populist prime minister who was not known for engaging with detail. Finally, the UK was to prove a laggard in putting in place significant public health measures. Not only was it using an 'insider' model of scientific advice (Cairney, 2021a) that was based heavily around quantitative modelling subject to significant changes in results as new data emerged, but also behavioural scientists were suggesting that early action from the government might result in 'fatigue' and noncompliance by the public (Williams et al, 2021). The government also took a highly centralised approach to policy making (and, later, to pandemic response) that often sidelined expertise that was not a part of its committees (Cairney, 2021a).

The UK pandemic response must also be seen in the context of what was termed the 'austerity' of the previous ten years. After the financial crisis of 2007 to 2008, a Coalition government made up of the Conservatives and the Liberal Democrats was formed in 2010, which made significant reductions in public financing across a range of areas to try and deal with the significant fallout of the crisis. Public Health England saw budget cuts of around 40 per cent between 2012 and 2019, and public sector laboratories saw the continuation of a longer-term reduction in numbers from 30 in 2000 to 8 just before the pandemic. Though National Health Service budgets had grown between 2010 and the pandemic (in contrast to local authority budgets, which funded many of the care homes that were to prove so pivotal in the first year of the crisis), this was at half the historical average rate (Williams et al, 2021).

So, the first stage of the pandemic – complacency – was not unique to the UK, but the government was slow to engage and less well-prepared than governments in other countries. The next stage of the pandemic came when that complacency confronted rising cases and deaths.

Panic

As international concerns about COVID-19 grew in February 2020, the UK government was still being advised by its expert groups that there was nothing it needed to do as an urgent priority (Freedman, 2020, p 40). In early March, however, things began to escalate. The WHO's new messages about both transmissibility and incubation periods led to Prime Minister Johnson, in his particular style, suggesting the need for more careful hygiene and asking us to sing 'Happy Birthday' twice to ourselves while washing our hands, but still insisting that the UK was well-prepared for an outbreak of the virus. Initial communication about the pandemic, in line with the characterisation presented here, was labelled as 'complacent' and, being based on an ad hoc approach (such as the handwashing advocated by Johnson), likely to lead to 'low reliability practices' (Sanders, 2020, p 374). As the international situation grew more grave, however, Johnson's position quickly began to change, with him apparently admitting in a media interview on 5 March that the handwashing measures alone were unlikely to be enough.[1]

The UK had a test for the new viral strain of COVID-19 that was emerging as early as mid-January, and so could test those with possible symptoms very early on. However, the resources devoted to catching the entry of the virus into the country or to tracing cases were not significant, and by the second week of March cases were appearing that could not be explained via the tracing processes that had been implemented. It is likely that around this time Chief Medical Officer Chris Whitty concluded that such tracing could not match the scale of the challenge ahead, and attention moved away from testing and tracing (Freedman, 2020, p 44).

If there was a government strategy at this point, it seems to have been one premised on isolating the highest-risk groups (the elderly and those with long-term conditions) and achieving a kind of 'herd immunity' for the rest of the population. Although such an approach was never announced, language which clearly implies this approach as being at the front of thinking began to emerge in the media (Sanders, 2020).

The UK was now beginning to lag behind the more serious measures being introduced elsewhere in the world and also appeared distracted by the Budget scheduled for 11 March. After the Budget, a campaign began within government to persuade the Prime Minister to move to more significant measures. The problem here was that '[k]nown for his optimistic, blustery style and his inattention to detail, Johnson may have been naturally inclined to accept options that demanded the minimum rather than maximum, and so content to be advised to follow a gradual path of escalation' (Freedman, 2020, p 64). On 16 March, Johnson addressed the country with the message to stop nonessential contact with others and unnecessary travel. A week later, a 'lockdown' began, with the announcement that people must 'stay at home'.

At this point, the potential impact of the virus was labelled as 'unprecedented', and the government moved its position, asking people to show 'determination and resolve' and calling for 'national unity', but also presenting the belief that the path of the virus could turned 'within the next 12 weeks' (Jarvis, 2022, p 35). On 19 March, the Prime Minister made a national televised statement on the coronavirus, one to two weeks later than had been the case in most other European countries. Johnson himself tested positive for the virus on 26 March and was later admitted to hospital.

The National Audit Office has been highly critical of the government's response to COVID-19 during March 2020. They suggested that the government was 'not fully prepared for wide-ranging impacts that this pandemic has had on society, the economy and essential public services' (Comptroller and Auditor General, 2021b, p 8). They concluded that there was no explicit agreement about what level of risk the government was willing to accept for an event like COVID-19. Assessment of government plans in place in February and March 2020 found that most (82 per cent) were 'inadequate to meet the demands of any actual incident' (Comptroller and Auditor General, 2021b, p 9). Cairney found that in this phase ministers were guided by the advice of 'insider scientists' (often included in the government's 'SAGE' – Scientific Advisory Group for Emergencies – advisory committee), which they followed, the evidence that was produced being part of a political process that had to follow 'the rules of the game', or what the government would accept. This led to an approach in early March based on 'exhortation' to the public rather than the 'imposition' of rules (Cairney, 2021b, p 11).

During the panic stage, poor policy decisions were made, perhaps the most damaging being the discharge of older people from hospitals into nursing homes without a testing infrastructure in place to ensure the virus would not be transmitted to other vulnerable people in the homes. This decision was not unique to the UK, but appears to have been the result of a breakdown of communication and infrastructure that surely had a direct connection to the spread of the infection and deaths.

The next panic element was concerned with how health systems would have to be adapted to cope with the coming pandemic. One area where this was clear was the need to increase the number of ventilators to deal with the expected wave of people struggling to breathe. Prominent figures, such as James Dyson, made public announcements suggesting their companies could help. There was a focus on increasing the capacity of health services through the establishment of 'Nightingale hospitals' – effectively temporary wards located in a variety of different locations – but with apparently little planning for how these would be staffed or resourced.

The most discussed aspect of panic involved supplies of personal protective equipment (PPE) in health and social care, which quickly ran low. This issue became apparent with a global shortage appearing and the discovery that the UK's supplies were running out and there was limited capacity to quickly produce more within the country. An aeroplane was chartered to fly from China, full of PPE, with the flight covered on national television news (BBC News, 2020). Most of the materials, sadly, were later found to be below the standard needed for use in health and social care. This foreshadowed later purchases of PPE from certain businesses whose owners had connections with the government, as some of that equipment was also found to be unusable in care settings.

The panic stage saw some travel restrictions put in place (especially during the lockdown period), but little in the way of sensible debate about the potential to close borders as a mean of containing the virus – a strategy which was presented as key to controlling the virus even before the extent of the pandemic was clear (Sridhar, 2020). It is clear, looking back from the longer term, that countries which did put in place firm border controls were able to exert considerably stronger control over the virus in the first two years of the pandemic (Greener, 2021).

Clearly the UK Conservative government was not alone in finding the pandemic difficult. However, the time already lost in the 'complacency' phase, combined with the instinctual approach of the Johnson administration, which appeared to be based on a mix of distrust of expertise, a latent libertarianism and an emphasis on the presentation of policy rather than implementation – perhaps rooted in the approach taken in respect of Brexit – meant that the realisation that things were not going well resulted in a genuine sense of disorientation, with weeks being lost at a crucial time in terms of building capacity to cope with the pandemic ahead.

Getting a grip

As the government sought to get beyond the panic phase, it become apparent that coordinated action was needed. This period was one in which the need to 'get a grip' of the situation became the focus of activity. The key strategy here was based around growing the COVID-19 testing regime and, perhaps as importantly, reporting to the public that both testing and PPE were now widely available – therefore showing that the government was successfully addressing the pandemic.

The first element of getting a grip was around testing, and this emerged from the beginning of April 2020 as it became clear that countries such as Germany had in place an infrastructure that was far superior to that found in the UK (The Guardian, 2020). This led to the regular government COVID-19 televised briefings, which put a strong emphasis on reporting the growth in testing capacity, though also perhaps to a period of hitting the target but missing the point. Testing in a pandemic is about knowing how many people have the virus, but also about isolating those people, supporting them while they are ill and tracing the contacts. The UK did put in place a system to try and achieve these goals, but it seemed to fail under the strain of growing case numbers and its cost escalated to billions, with little accountability as to how that money was spent.

The government's lockdown measures, restrictions on travel and the issuing of rapid tests direct to households, and the increased practice of working from home for those who were fortunate enough to be able to, did lead to a situation where cases began to fall, and the government looked forward to removing restrictions and to things getting back to normal – the next phase.

Getting back to normal

As case numbers and daily deaths from the virus began to fall from their peak in March, the Johnson government moved to lift COVID-19 restrictions and reopen the economy. People were encouraged to 'eat out to help out', and what travel movement restrictions were in place were removed.

This was a period of optimism with signs that vaccines might be available soon (in record time), something the government began to take credit for on the grounds that, as their claim went, the fast-tracking of the vaccine was due to new freedoms coming from Brexit. The public responded by taking overseas holidays, but that created the space for new strains of the virus to enter to the UK.

The 'getting back to normal' phase also made it more difficult, especially for a government elected on the basis of achieving greater 'freedom' for the UK, to reintroduce restrictions when COVID-19 cases began to rise again. Moreover, the toll of ill health and deaths on the population was not addressed by the government, and by August there was evidence of a 'profound impact on the population', with survivors facing pressing mental and physical health needs, and of 'unprecedented' demands on intensive care unit spaces and equipment (Flynn et al, 2020, p 688).

This phase also saw rumours and then photographs and finally open admissions that the government had not been following its own guidance during the lockdown phase earlier in the year. The Prime Minister's Chief Advisor, Dominic Cummings, was forced to give a press conference to account for his own behaviour, and he resigned soon after. Public trust in the government response fell significantly following Cummings' statement, and after June a higher proportion distrusted the government than trusted it (Lalot et al, 2020; Davies et al, 2021). This loss of trust was to prove crucial as the government sought to introduce its vaccination programme later in the year, with low vaccine acceptance in 25 per cent of the population (Trent ct al, 2022).

Winter disaster

Winter 2020 represented something of a disaster for the pandemic response. If we look at the UK's official COVID-19 deaths plotted over time (Figure 5.1),

Figure 5.1: COVID-19 deaths in the UK, 2020–22

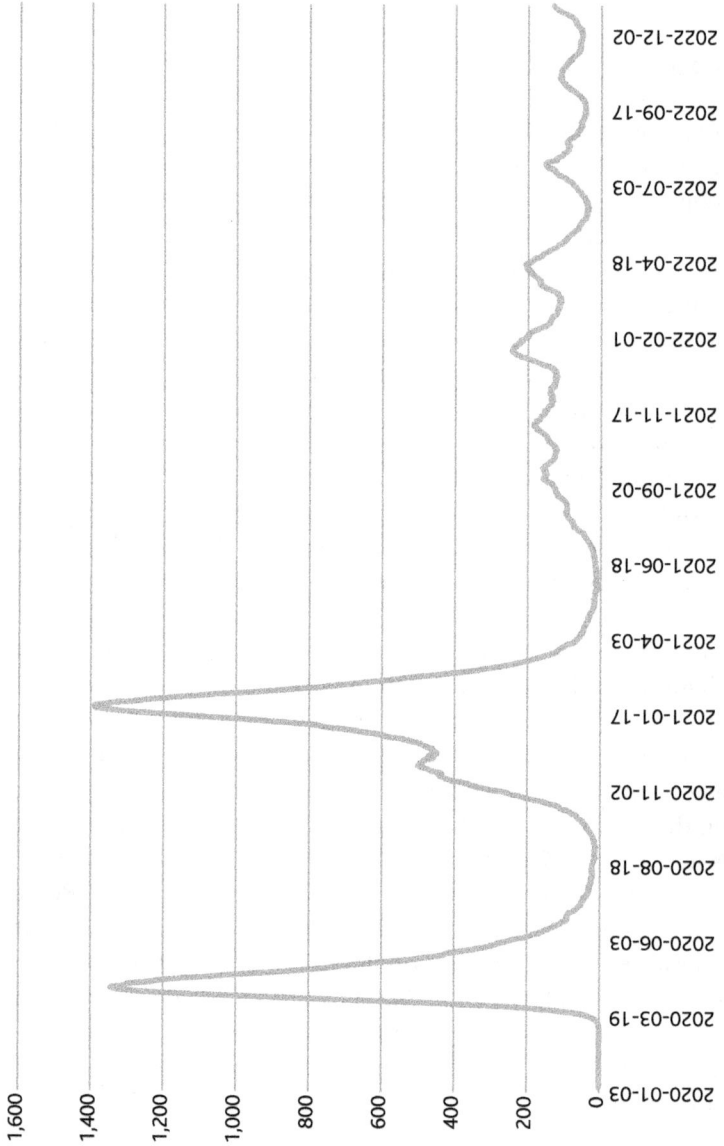

Source: Mathieu et al (2020)

the two big spikes appear as the pandemic first arrived and then again in winter 2020.

Comparison of COVID-19 deaths in the UK with those in France, Germany, Italy and Spain – several of the UK's nearest neighbours – shows a similar pattern, but with the UK doing worse at the peak levels than all of those other nations (Figure 5.2).

Winter saw the emergence of a variant of the virus which appeared to have originated in the UK, perhaps as a result of the very high case numbers post summer. It was also a time when the government reduced restrictions on household mixing so that people could try and enjoy a Christmas closer to the usual holiday, but with tragic effect. Winter 2020–21 saw daily COVID-19 deaths in the UK rise to the same levels as in the early months of the pandemic, and to higher levels than several comparable countries.

More positively, winter 2020 was also the period when it became clearer that a vaccine against the virus was emerging, and along with that the hope that case numbers and deaths would not be as high again.

Freedom

The rise in cases and deaths in the winter of 2020–21 began to abate by the beginning of March. The government response to this, along with the emergence of the vaccine programme, was to declare that 19 July 2021 would be 'Freedom Day', when all remaining restrictions would be removed. We can think of this as the second period of 'getting back to normal' (after the previous summer), but this time, backed by the vaccination programme, death rates, although they began to rise in late August/early September, did not reach the levels seen in the winter of 2020.

Living with the virus

The last phase (up to mid-2022 and beyond) is living with the virus. In this period, COVID-19 cases have become detached from COVID-19 deaths. Examining the rolling case rate, there was a clear peak in winter 2020–21, with a fall in the early months of 2021 (see Figure 5.3), which was replicated in the rate of deaths. By the middle of that year, around Freedom Day, cases rose significantly, but deaths did not. Perhaps the central reason for this was the vaccination programme, which by early 2021 was reaching the highest number of people yet.

After the middle of 2021, there was a rise in cases through the winter, again to the highest level seen so far but without the extreme death rates of 2020. As the winter of 2021 passed, the case rate again fell, but remained 'stuck' at around the same underlying level through 2022.

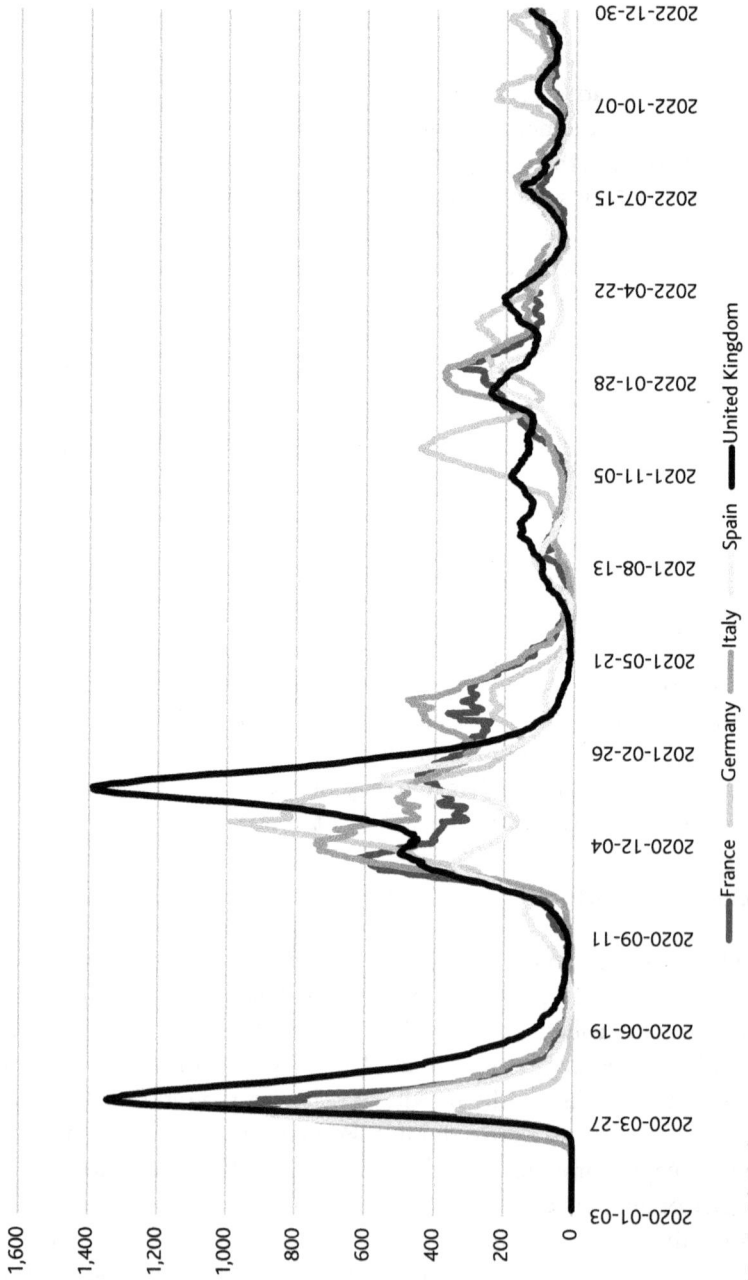

Figure 5.2: COVID-19 deaths in selected European nations, 2020–22

France ——— Germany ——— Italy ——— Spain ——— United Kingdom

Source: Mathieu et al (2020)

Figure 5.3: COVID-19 cases per million population in the UK, 2020–22

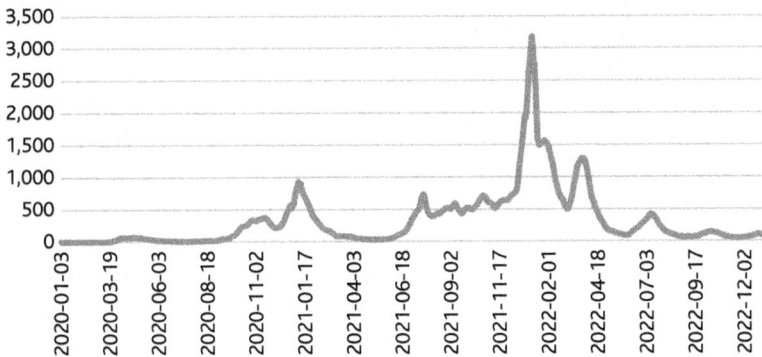

Source: Mathieu et al (2020)

Having summarised the phases of the UK response to COVID-19, we can now consider the key elements of the response and characterise the elements of conservatism present within each of them.

Key elements of the Conservative pandemic response

Reluctant, late action is the first key element of the Conservative pandemic response, This was evident in the first stages of the pandemic, when the response from government was a mix of denial and then panic. The government seemed unwilling to follow the basic principles of pandemic preparedness, even as these were rehearsed in the media (Sridhar, 2020). The Conservative government elected in 2019 on a populist Brexit-based mandate found itself having to consider unpopular things – limiting gatherings, closing borders, closing schools and even shutting down the economy. The government's reluctance to confront these realities and its delay (compared to close neighbours) in putting them in place is, in many respects, very much what we might expect from a populist Conservative government sceptical of large-scale government intervention, even when such intervention was necessary to adequately confront the pandemic. Reluctant, late action appeared to be a recurring theme through the first two years of the pandemic, combined with populist measures such as removing pandemic restrictions for Christmas 2020 (Comptroller and Auditor General, 2021a).

A second key element of the Conservative government response, derived from its reluctant, late responses, is the mixed messaging that was often present. The Prime Minister initially underplayed the seriousness of the situation and appeared desperate for the pandemic to end and for restrictions to be removed. At press conferences, scientific officers presented data and attempted to give public health messages, but these often appeared at odds with the message coming from the Prime Minister. This was not helped by the repeated media leaks of ministerial breaches of the pandemic restriction rules or the bizarre spectacle of the Prime Minister's own Chief Advisor giving a press conference to try and account for his apparent breach of the rules. This mixed messaging gave the impression of a government expecting others to follow rules when its own members and staff were not prepared to.

The third element, misreporting of data, came in the 'getting a grip' phase. The reporting of numbers of tests carried out and PPE issued was undermined by reports that those numbers were being 'gamed' by ministers – to boost the reported numbers, tests were being double-counted and the component parts of PPE were being counted separately. This apparent over-reporting further undermined the government's credibility, and this was added to by the misreporting on high-profile interventions such as the temporary Nightingale hospitals, which were presented to the media as the cornerstone of the pandemic response but were later dismantled, largely unused.

The misreporting of data linked to an additional element – an apparent short-termism, seen in the focus on elements of pandemic response that could be easily reported and presented to the media rather than considering long-term planning and investment. For instance, there has been little investment in longer-term thinking about ventilation and filtering of air in public and private workplaces and other buildings, or in what a smaller, more responsive Test and Trace system might look like, or in understanding the potential impacts of 'long COVID' and how people facing this diagnosis might be supported.

Finally, and perhaps least attractive of all, there have been widespread allegations of cronyism in the government's response. Work from the Good Law Project has highlighted the 'fast line' contracting arrangements for PPE, which often appeared to benefit contacts of government members while more qualified suppliers seem to have been often overlooked (Evans et al, 2022; Good Law Project, 2022). It is certainly the case that large amounts of the supplies purchased by the government proved unsuitable for use in the pandemic and ended up being stored in warehouses at further cost or were destroyed.

What kind of conservatism do these key themes in the government's pandemic response point to?

Conservatism and the Johnson government's pandemic response

A much-repeated trope of British politics is the idea of 'muddling through' (Hennessy, 1997). In normal times, incremental change, often from a Conservative government concerned with protecting the inheritance of the past and adapting slowly to the present, can seem like a sensible, pragmatic approach. In a pandemic, where rapid change is necessary, muddling through does not work as well. The tension between the Johnson government's emphasis on 'freedom' – originating in one of the central arguments for Brexit – and the need for restricting people's lives, in the first year of the pandemic especially, appears to have resulted in: laggardly responses to the challenge of COVID-19 as it unfolded; messaging being confused as the government sought to present an overly optimistic position; and a lack of long-term planning, indicative of a belief that current systems could be adapted to face the challenge of the pandemic when a bigger change was needed.

Another key element of the Johnson government's response was its populist tone. Johnson played down the virus in January, February and even March of 2020, continuing much as normal. After that, populist measures were common among Conservative politicians, such as conspicuously clapping for essential workers (they often filmed themselves doing this and posted the videos to social media), presenting responses in press conferences lined with Union flags to show their patriotism, claiming that the British vaccine response was 'world-leading' and would have been constrained had we remained within the European Union – the latter claim was especially contestable. The populism of removing restrictions for Christmas 2020 proved catastrophic in terms of the additional COVID-19 cases and deaths around that time, admittedly in a context where people may have broken the restrictions anyway, not least because of the confused messaging around them and lack of compliance by members of the government.

Finally, the government's response was rooted in closed networks around government ministers, with massive PPE and testing contracts going to people who were supportive of the government or connected to its members, whereas others, even with significant expertise to offer, found themselves with no opportunity to contribute. In some ways, it is understandable that in a crisis ministers chose to make use of existing connections to try and ensure a strong response. However, this does not explain either the colossal waste that appeared to result in terms of purchased PPE that remained unused as it was not fit for purpose or the very poor track record of the UK in preventing the spread of the virus, suggesting significant problems with its high-cost Track and Trace system.

Combining these elements, we can characterise the Conservative response as cronyist populism. This is a combination of the populism of a government faced with the challenge of coordinating a pandemic response – and which had been elected on a populist mandate to 'get Brexit done', based on distrust of experts and flag-waving patriotism – and the attempts to make that response in a way that often depended on, and directly benefitted, the social networks of those in power.[2]

Cronyist populism is a very British version of the 'authoritarian populism' originating in the 1980s, and which has experienced a resurgence in interest with the move Right in American politics under Trump (Morelock, 2018), as well as with European and UK leaders keen to emphasise their strength in the name of nationalistic approaches to government (Crewe et al, 2020). Whereas authoritarian populism often seeks, however, to emphasise the importance of law and order in the name of defending freedoms in a country, Cronyist populism is more about those in power giving populist messages about the national interest, while apparently not following the restrictions they have put in place for everyone else themselves, and acting in ways which sometimes appear as if they are utilising a national crisis to both award highly lucrative to their elite peers.

This mix of factors – of a populist government falling short of its promises but attempting to divert from that through conspicuous patriotism supported by a range of newspapers – entails government by an elite tier of people from a very narrow social background, supported by a media which is seeking to preserve its privileges and appears to promote the nationalism and populism that sustains the elite in power by presenting them as patriots in the face of challenges from 'woke' opposition and from the courts (with judges already being labelled as 'enemies of the people'[3] by one newspaper for requiring the consent of Parliament before Brexit could go ahead). There are authoritarian elements to this, but this element is undermined by elites breaking the rules they expected the public to follow.

Another key element of cronyist populism is that grand claims about success are made in an almost Trumpian way – that is, claims are made to activate a news cycle, but they bear little scrutiny in terms of accuracy. However, by moving onto another claim or another issue before the current claim has been checked, less room is left for scrutiny, even where the claims appear to be, in the Frankfurtian (1988) sense, 'bullshit', or they have some initial grounding in truth which is subsequently no longer the case. For instance, the claim that Brexit made the quick approval of the COVID-19 vaccination possible was highly questionable, and continued claims about the success of the vaccination programme have been undermined by the UK falling behind most comparable nations after an initially strong start. Equally, to avoid accepting that any failures in policy or delivery were due to the government, representatives of the government either directed blame at others or simply said it was time to 'move on' to other topics. These strategies meant it was difficult to actually make the hard business of a coordinated pandemic response happen, as this would have required concerted effort and an ability to engage in ongoing learning as the virus developed and mutated.

In Table 5.1, we compare the characterisation of Conservative governments from 2015 in this chapter, as cronyist populism, with that

Table 5.1: Conservatism and cronyist populism

Dimension	Conservative governments, 2015–	Cronyist populism
Approach	Deregulator	Reluctant, late regulation
Citizenship	Responsibilities	Populist/nationalist
Outcome	Inequality	Exacerbated inequality
Mixed economy of welfare	Private	Crony/private
Mode	Competition	Crony – supply limitation and cost increases
Expenditure	Low/pragmatic	High within contract networks
Benefits	Low/pragmatic	High in lockdowns but low/pragmatic afterwards
Services	Low/medium	Low – limited capacity
Accountability	Market	Via media and the public
Politics	Right	Cronyist/Right

provided in Chapter 1, It is clear that some significant tensions appear in the pandemic response.

The pandemic response saw a government initially reluctant to put in place regulations finding that an effective pandemic response required such action, but then failing to uphold those rules within its own employees and ministers. In addition, the previous years of deregulation and reduced investment had left the state with rather less capacity to achieve a successful response than it might have had (Williams et al, 2021). Johnson's instincts as Prime Minister might also have been to undermine the scale of the challenge and emphasise individual measures such as handwashing rather than imposing restriction. When this led to the need for a firmer response, this, in turn, led to a centralisation of policy response from a government which struggled to provide the leadership or coordinated capacity necessary while local authorities were not trusted or resourced to respond more adaptively to the changing conditions in their own areas.

Existing inequalities were further exacerbated further during the pandemic, which those on precarious contracts having to work through the pandemic despite the increased risks involved, and with those from non-White background being particularly affected (Bambra et al, 2021). Although the government put in place a system through which it subsidised the pay of many of those unable to work during the height of the pandemic (see Chapters 10 and 11), that support was withdrawn without evidence of long-term planning or thought of those who continue to be affected by the virus, or who have significant health conditions that put them at additional risk.

There is also clearly a tension between the mode of welfare governance based on competition and market accountability outlined here and the pandemic response, which saw 'fast-track' supplier links being given to associates of the government, with little accountability for those that conspicuously did not deliver value for those contracts. This appears to resemble more the distribution of largesse than the cut and thrust of market-based governance. Those outside of favoured networks, in the meantime, often found themselves struggling to recruit staff because of labour shortages (as a result of both the pandemic, but also Brexit), and facing increased costs for basic resources.

In terms of expenditure, the pandemic response represented a clear end to austerity, and saw a massive increase in debt. This appears to have acted as a double-edged sword, however, allowing the largesse distributed by the Johnson government but creating the space for a Right of centre critique of that expenditure to emerge, resulting in the disastrous Truss government in 2022, and the emphasis of the Sunak government (at time of writing) on public expenditure cuts.

Conclusion

The Conservative pandemic response occurred mostly under the Johnson government, which is characterised in this chapter as one of cronyist populism. Johnson's conservatism struggled to confront the reality of the challenges of the pandemic, making decisions to impose restrictions slower than other nations and then putting in place a centralised process for awarding pandemic contracts that favoured associates of his political party. Moreover, it set out restrictions that the public were expected to follow despite the government routinely appearing to breach them. This was combined with flag-waving patriotism, claiming the success of the vaccine was due to the government (and Brexit) and attempting to cover over the cracks that resulted. This populism claimed to be governing on behalf of the people, with the government 'getting the big calls right', but eventually it resulted in the removal of Johnson in 2022, and many of his own ministers and Conservative Members of Parliament, perhaps fearing for their own electoral futures, calling for his resignation.

The UK COVID-19 response is hard to read as a success, either on its own terms or in comparison to nations which have done significantly better in relation to case or death rates. The UK had all the advantages of being an island able to close borders effectively, but it squandered them through inaction and dithering in the first part of the pandemic, and it also wasted billions in terms of Test and Trace and contracting for PPE. Its legacy resulted in far greater deaths than were necessary in the first year of the pandemic, and the continuing high case numbers are raising significant concerns about long COVID going forward. Additional legacies include the brief and catastrophic Truss government, which was a response to the expenditure and debt incurred during the pandemic, and the probable return of austerity under Prime Minister Sunak.

Notes

[1] Find a transcript of what Boris Johnson said at: https://fullfact.org/health/boris-john son-coronavirus-this-morning/

[2] See My Little Crony at: www.sophie-e-hill.com/slides/my-little-crony/ – this is an interactive website about the relationships between Conservative government ministers and large-value contracts, including those awarded during the pandemic.

[3] *Daily Mail*, 4 November 2016.

References

Bambra, C., Lynch, J. and Smith, K.E. (2021) *The unequal pandemic: COVID-19 and health inequalities*, Bristol: Policy Press.

BBC News (2020) 'Coronavirus: plane carrying millions of pieces of PPE lands in Yorkshire', 7 May. Available at: www.bbc.co.uk/news/av/uk-engl and-south-yorkshire-52584253 (accessed 19 July 2023).

Cairney, P. (2021a) 'The UK government's COVID-19 policy: assessing evidence-informed policy analysis in real time', *British Politics*, 16(1): 90–116.

Cairney, P. (2021b) 'The UK government's COVID-19 policy: what does "guided by the science" mean in practice?', *Frontiers in Political Science*, 3: 624068. doi: 10.3389/fpos.2021.624068

Carroll, W.D., Strenger, V., Eber, E., Porcaro, F., Cutrera, R., Fitzgerald, D.A. and Balfour-Lynn, I.M. (2020) 'European and United Kingdom COVID-19 pandemic experience: the same but different', *Paediatric Respiratory Reviews*, 35: 50–6.

Comptroller and Auditor General (2021a) *Initial learning from the government's response to the COVID-19 pandemic: report session 2021–22*, London: National Audit Office.

Comptroller and Auditor General (2021b) *The government's preparedness for the COVID-19 pandemic: lessons for government on risk management*, London: National Audit Office.

Crewe, I., Sanders, D. and King, A.S. (eds) (2020) *Authoritarian populism and liberal democracy*, Cham: Palgrave Macmillan.

Davies, B., Lalot, F., Peitz, L., Heering, M.S., Ozkececi, H., Babaian, J., Davies Hayon, K., Broadwood, J. and Abrams, D. (2021) 'Changes in political trust in Britain during the COVID-19 pandemic in 2020: integrated public opinion evidence and implications', *Humanities and Social Sciences Communications*, 8(1): 166. doi: 10.1057/s41599-021-00850-6

Dyer, C. (2021) 'Pandemic preparedness: UK government kept coronavirus modelling secret', *British Medical Journal*, 373: n1501. doi: 10.1136/bmj. n1501

Evans, R., Pegg, D. and Lawrence, F. (2022) 'UK health department played "fast and loose" when awarding Covid contracts to Randox', *The Guardian*, 22 July. Available at: www.theguardian.com/politics/2022/jul/27/uk-health-department-played-fast-and-loose-when-awarding-covid-contracts-to-randox (accessed 19 July 2023).

Flynn, D., Moloney, E., Bhattarai, N., Scott, J., Breckons, M., Avery, L. and Moy, N. (2020) 'COVID-19 pandemic in the United Kingdom', *Health Policy and Technology*, 9(4): 673–91.

Frankfurt, H. (1988) *The importance of what we care about: philosophical essays*, Cambridge: Cambridge University Press.

Freedman, L. (2020) 'Strategy for a pandemic: the UK and COVID-19', *Survival*, 62(3): 25–76.

Good Law Project (2022) 'Revealed for the first time: full list of VIP Test and Trace firms given priority treatment', 7 September. Available at: https://goodlawproject.org/revealed-for-the-first-time-full-list-of-vip-test-and-trace-firms-given-priority-treatment/ (accessed 19 July 2022).

Greener, I. (2021) *Comparing health systems*, Bristol: Policy Press.

Hall, S. (1979) 'The great moving right show', *Marxism Today*, January: 14–20.

Hennessy, P. (1997) *Muddling through: power, politics and the quality of government in post-war Britain*, London: Phoenix.

Jarvis, L. (2022) 'Constructing the coronavirus crisis: narratives of time in British political discourse on COVID-19', *British Politics*, 17(1): 24–43.

Lalot, F., Davies, B. and Abrams, D. (2020) *Trust and cohesion in Britain during the 2020 COVID-19 pandemic across place, scale and time*, Canterbury: Centre for the Study of Group Processes, University of Kent.

Mance, H. (2016) 'Britain has had enough of experts, says Gove', *Financial Times*, 3 June.

Mathieu, E., Ritchie, H., Rodés-Guirao, L., Appel, C., Giattino, C., Hasell, J., Macdonald, B., Dattani, S., Beltekian, D., Ortiz-Ospina, E. and Roser, M. (2020) 'Coronavirus pandemic (COVID-19)', *Our World In Data*. Available at: https://ourworldindata.org/covid-deaths#licence (accessed 19 July 2023).

Morelock, J. (ed) (2018) *Critical theory and authoritarian populism*, London: University of Westminster Press.

Oppenheim, B., Gallivan, M., Madhav, N.K., Brown, N., Serhiyenko, V., Wolfe, N.D. and Ayscue, P. (2019) 'Assessing global preparedness for the next pandemic: development and application of an Epidemic Preparedness Index', *BMJ Global Health*, 4(1): e001157. doi: 10.1136/bmjgh-2018-001157

Sanders, K.B. (2020) 'British government communication during the 2020 COVID-19 pandemic: learning from high reliability organizations', *Church, Communication and Culture*, 5(3): 356–77.

Sridhar, D. (2020) 'This is what you should be demanding from your government to contain the virus', *The Guardian*, 4 May. Available at: www. theguardian.com/commentisfree/2020/may/04/eight-lessons-controll ing-coronavirus-east-asian-nations-pandemic-public-health (accessed 19 July 2023).

The Guardian (2020) 'The Guardian view on the UK's testing failure: much to learn from Germany', 2 April. Available at: www.theguardian.com/ commentisfree/2020/apr/02/the-guardian-view-on-the-uks-testing-fail ure-much-to-learn-from-germany (accessed 19 July 2023).

Trent, M., Seale, H., Chughtai, A.A., Salmon, D. and Raina MacIntyre, C. (2022) 'Trust in government, intention to vaccinate and COVID-19 vaccine hesitancy: a comparative survey of five large cities in the United States, United Kingdom, and Australia', *Vaccine*, 40(17): 2498–505.

Williams, G., Rajan, S. and Cylus, J. (2021) 'COVID-19 in the United Kingdom: how austerity and a loss of state capacity undermined the crisis response', in S.L. Greer, E.J. King, E. Massard da Fonseca and A. Peralta-Santos (eds) *Coronavirus politics: the comparative politics and policy of COVID-19*, Anne Arbor: University of Michigan Press, pp 215–34.

6

The governance of social policy under the Conservatives

Catherine Bochel and Hugh Bochel

Introduction

With the different emphases and approaches of successive governments to social policies from the 1980s onwards, it has become increasingly apparent that the means of policy formulation, implementation and evaluation can be as important as the policies themselves (Bochel and Bochel, 2018). The move away from the postwar preference for direct provision by the state, funded by general taxation, towards one for competition, markets and market-like mechanisms that started under the Thatcher governments, in particular, highlighted that the use of such approaches to deliver public services is likely to contribute to different outcomes, such as greater inequality, than universal provision by the state, at the same time as shifting responsibility away from the state and towards individuals and families.

As not only policies changed, but also the style and means of policy making and implementation altered, and the role of the state was reduced in many areas, the use of the term 'governance' could be seen as trying 'to make sense of the changing nature of the state' (Richards and Smith, 2002, p 14) and came to be associated, for many, with a shift in the role of the state from central command and control to a position where power and responsibility are spread across a wider variety of different actors and organisations at local, regional, national, transnational and global levels, resulting in a more fragmented and less coherent process of policy making and implementation.

The changing governance of social policy, 1979–2015

Arguably it was the changes made by the Thatcher governments, to policies and to the ways in which they were made and implemented, that encouraged many to reconsider the importance of different approaches, including for social policy. In particular, from 1988 there was a shift towards policy making strongly influenced by the neoliberal views of the New Right (for example, Rhodes, 1997; Williams, 2021), with a preference for a smaller state and a free market, and with greater competition and consumer choice being seen as ways through which self-interested, inefficient state bureaucracies (Niskanen, 1971) could be reduced and controlled. This, and the increased emphasis on efficiency, effectiveness and economy, saw a variety of changes being introduced that have continued to shape policy making and implementation. These included the functions of local authorities being reduced and removed, as well as the introduction of controls over their ability to raise income from local taxation, attempts to increase consumer choice and redress, and the more widespread use of macro-governance structures such as arm's-length bodies and agencies to undertake functions that had previously been undertaken directly by central and local government.

When Labour returned to power in 1997, there were, perhaps inevitably, both continuities and discontinuities with the Conservatives' approach. The former included emphasising the role of local authorities as enablers of services, the use of providers from across the public, private and not-for-profit sectors, and the widespread use of mechanisms of audit and inspection with the aim of improving quality and standards in services. At the same time, there were also very different and even radical departures in some areas, including the Human Rights Act 1988, which incorporated the European Convention on Human Rights into UK law, and devolution, which as Chapter 17 explores in greater depth, allowed for potentially greater policy divergence within the UK.

Labour also made some attempts to improve policy making processes in the belief that these would result in better policies – for example, with the encouragement of 'joined-up', 'evidence-based' and 'inclusive' approaches and a focus on coordination and cooperation (Bochel and Duncan, 2007). However, like the Conservatives, they retained a fondness for top-down approaches and central control, and, linked with the desire to extend consumer choice in public services, this saw extensive use of performance measures, league tables and mechanisms of audit and inspection, as well as the retention of market mechanisms in many areas.

Following the 2010 general election, with no party having a majority in the House of Commons, the Conservatives formed a coalition government with the Liberal Democrats. The Coalition government's decision to seek to lower the deficit by reducing public expenditure, rather than by increasing taxes, was also important in terms of policy making and implementation more generally, serving to facilitate a neoliberal approach in many areas of social policy (Taylor-Gooby, 2012), including market-like techniques within the National Health Service (NHS) and education. In addition, the protection of spending in some policy areas, most notably the NHS and the State Pension, as well as international aid, meant that others were harder hit and that cuts did not fall evenly across government departments, with areas such as benefits and housing being very significantly affected.

The governance of social policy under the Conservatives since 2015

As highlighted in Chapter 1, from 2015 there has been considerable political and governmental instability, with David Cameron standing down as Prime Minister following the 2016 Brexit referendum and his successor Theresa May struggling with Brexit and the loss of a majority at the 2017 general election. Boris Johnson, despite winning a very substantial majority in the House of Commons at the 2019 general election, was buffeted, initially by the COVID-19 pandemic and then by related and some unrelated issues about the moral and leadership qualities of the Prime Minister. In June 2022 a vote of no confidence in Johnson's leadership was held among Conservative MPs, and 41 per cent voted against him. That was followed by his resignation the following month. Johnson was followed by Liz Truss, who campaigned on the basis of smaller government, deregulation and tax cuts. Truss was rapidly forced to resign following a disastrous 'mini-budget', and she was then succeeded by Rishi Sunak. All of this meant considerable uncertainty over the direction of government, and even the progress of key plans and commitments set out in the 2015, 2017 and 2019 Conservative manifestos, as new leaders sought to establish their own policy agendas and to respond to new challenges.

Given these changes and other domestic and international pressures, it is perhaps unsurprising that during this period it is difficult to identify 'core' approaches, ideas or styles in the making and implementation of social policies, as might have been the case with, for example, the Thatcher and Blair governments. Despite this, and perhaps reflecting the challenges of governing over the previous years, in June 2021, in a relatively unnoticed policy paper, *Declaration on Government Reform* (Cabinet Office, 2021), published in the name of the Prime Minister and the Cabinet Secretary, the Cabinet Office set out wide-ranging aspirations for the civil service, modernisation and reform. Among the emphases were: high standards, leadership and transparency in public life; levelling up, to make opportunity more equal; and, in order to achieve these things, intentions such as moving more civil servants out of London, improving diversity and inclusion, reinvigorating the principle of departmental accountability, improving cross-government functions, making better use of data, more collaborative working between ministers and officials, and greater clarity over the roles, responsibilities and accountability of ministers and senior officials. Following this, in July 2022 Lord Maude was asked to lead a wide-ranging review of civil service governance and accountability. However, the extent of ongoing problems with political and civil service leadership were highlighted repeatedly, notably in relation to the COVID-19 pandemic and also by the resignation of the Deputy Prime Minister, Dominic Raab, in April 2023 following allegations of bullying

Given this lack of obvious common threads and underpinning ideas, the approach taken in the remainder of this chapter is therefore to examine a number of what might be seen as the main themes – sometimes related, sometimes rather disparate – and then to draw together some conclusions about what these can tell us in terms of identifying and analysing the key developments under these governments.

Austerity and public expenditure

Perhaps the most obvious influence on policy making for much of this period was the ongoing dominance of the austerity narrative and cuts in public expenditure, with their implications for the political dimensions outlined in Table 1.1 (including a smaller state, preference for provision by the private sector and civil society, lower levels of benefits and services, and accountability through the market and competition), although these became more fractured with other developments, including the 2017 and 2019 general elections and the impact of the COVID-19 pandemic.

At the 2015 general election, the Conservatives' manifesto promised to eliminate the deficit, to halt reductions in public expenditure for the next two years, after which it would grow in line with inflation, and to not increase Value Added Tax, National Insurance or Income Tax. However, the loss of a majority at the 2017 general election in the face of Jeremy Corbyn's anti-austerity agenda led to increasing questions over the government's commitment to austerity, and in October 2018, in her speech to the Conservative Party Conference, Theresa May announced that austerity was 'over', although there remained considerable doubt about spending plans in the context of Brexit and the commitment not to increase mainstream taxes.

At the 2019 general election, the Conservatives, then led by Johnson, won a substantial majority in the House of Commons, pledging not only to 'get Brexit done', but also to 'level up' the country. While it was far from clear what either of those meant in concrete policy terms, the latter appeared to imply some loosening of public spending. In addition, the Conservatives made a number of other promises that also suggested an increase in public expenditure, including to build 40 new hospitals, increase the number of nurses in England by 50,000 and maintain the commitment to the 'triple lock' on the State Pension. With the arrival of the COVID-19 pandemic in early 2020 (see Chapter 5), public spending plans were effectively abandoned for a period, as the government was forced to use public expenditure, and to a considerable extent public services, including local authorities, the NHS and the income support system, in tackling the pandemic and attempting to mitigate the effects of lockdowns and other ramifications of the pandemic for the economy and society. The three-year Spending Review due in 2020 was replaced by an annual review; then, as the immediate impact of the initial stages of the pandemic receded, the Autumn Budget and Spending Review 2021 set departmental budgets up to 2024–25. However, the Institute for Fiscal Studies (2021) argued that the decisions made for the 2021 Spending Review were largely unrelated to the pandemic and that the decision to increase taxes by about £40 billion, to settle at a level 2.7 per cent higher than in 2019–20, reflected the demands of the health care system, as well as areas such as justice and social care, which had been severely affected by the austerity of the previous decade. They therefore suggested that austerity was 'over but not undone', as increases in spending would not make up for the reductions over the period since 2010. The decisions of the short-lived Truss government, and then the Sunak government, also meant that for many areas of the welfare state austerity was likely to continue in various forms (see Chapter 2).

In England, the use of market-type mechanisms in areas such as health and education arguably reflected the pressures of austerity, but also the ongoing neoliberal ideological preferences of the Conservatives, at least until the onset of the COVID-19 pandemic, and thus the similarities with New Right ideas as highlighted in Table 1.1. When Johnson agreed to stand down as Prime Minister, the subsequent Conservative Party leadership contest saw considerable emphasis on tax cuts. However, while the mini-budget of Truss' first Chancellor, Kwasi Kwarteng was widely seen as radical, it was also an immediate failure, prompting his resignation and replacement by Jeremy Hunt and, shortly after, Truss' replacement by Sunak, who had only recently lost to her in a ballot of Conservative Party members. On taking office, Sunak argued that spending cuts and tax increases were needed to satisfy the financial markets.

Efficiency savings

From the 1980s, particularly under Conservative and Coalition governments, 'efficiency savings' associated with market-type approaches, such as commissioning and payment by results, were viewed as important ways of making public provision more efficient, increasing productivity and controlling public expenditure (for example, KPMG, 2010). From 2015 there was broad continuity, not least in the use of market-type mechanisms in many areas and the continued use of large private sector companies such as Serco and Capita to provide public services. This clearly contributed to reducing the role of the state in provision, increased marketisation and in some instances further reduced the role and responsibilities of local government. Critics highlighted that the government's willingness to spend large sums of money on private sector provision, often with a relative lack of scrutiny, did not of itself suggest great emphasis on efficiency.

The huge increase in government expenditure in response to the pandemic led to new challenges, as reflected in the Autumn Budget and Spending Review 2021, which, as already noted, returned to a multiyear cycle going up to 2024–25.

Given this context, it is perhaps unsurprising that there was little by way of innovative practice during this period. Indeed, in early 2021 it emerged that the government was planning to reverse reforms to the NHS made under the Coalition government that created general practitioner-led commissioning groups (see Chapter 7).

The National Audit Office suggested that the previous decade had seen departments 'having to plan to deliver more with less' (2021a, p 4), effectively as a result of austerity, and that might mean that they would need to think more creatively and radically to achieve further efficiency gains, but also that the pandemic had required government to operate in new ways and that there might, therefore, be an opportunity to reconsider previous conventions around what might be possible. Reflecting the work of the National Audit Office, the House of Commons Public Accounts Committee (2021) noted that the efficiency savings of around 5 per cent asked of government departments by the Autumn Budget and Spending Review 2021 followed many previous efficiency drives and it might, therefore, be challenging for them to achieve these new targets. The 2022 Autumn Statement nevertheless made clear that government departments would again be required to make further 'efficiency savings', not least to help balance the government's books, with the support of an Efficiency and Savings Review, although in March 2023 the Chancellor, Jeremy Hunt, talking to the House of Commons Treasury Select Committee, appeared to drop his previous insistence that pay offers for doctors, nurses and teachers would have to be funded by departments making efficiency savings.

Levelling up

'Levelling up' was an idea that largely emerged from commitments made by Boris Johnson, particularly around the time of the 2019 general election. While it was arguably difficult to discern exactly what 'localism' and the 'Big Society' had entailed under Cameron, other than rather piecemeal and partial measures (for example, Kisby, 2010; Bochel, 2016), this was even more challenging where levelling up was concerned, not least as Johnson himself never made it particularly apparent, but also as there was no clear attempt to drive the agenda across government. It could, perhaps be seen broadly as addressing long-standing regional economic disparities, although these can clearly be measured in a variety of different ways, such as gross domestic product (GDP) or GDP per capita, productivity, household incomes, employment, or unemployment and qualifications (for example, Harari et al, 2021), while Johnson also highlighted inequalities, such as in life expectancy (for example, Johnson, 2021).

While the government was slow to develop policies on levelling up, the 2020 Spending Review announced the Levelling Up Fund worth £4.8 billion, with

£4 billion to be spent in England and the remainder in Northern Ireland, Scotland and Wales. However, analysis showed that in the first allocation of awards, 61 of the 100 most deprived areas of England did not receive any funding (Centre for Inequality and Levelling Up, 2021). Analysis of other initiatives, such as the UK Community Renewal Fund and the Towns Fund, again showed that some of the wealthiest parts of England were allocated substantially more funding per capita than the poorest (McIntyre et al, 2022).

Perhaps the most significant publication associated with the idea was the White Paper *Levelling Up the United Kingdom*, which set out 12 'missions' under four objectives, with the latter being to:

a. boost productivity, pay, jobs and living standards by growing the private sector, especially in those places where they are lagging;
b. spread opportunities and improve public services, especially in those places where they are weakest;
c. restore a sense of community, local pride and belonging, especially in those places where they have been lost; and
d. empower local leaders and communities, especially in those places lacking local agency. (HM Government, 2022, xiv)

It included a commitment to further devolution deals within England. While there was some support for the broad aims of the White Paper, including from local politicians, there were also significant concerns about its delivery, including the lack of funding (for example, Institute for Fiscal Studies, 2022) and the lack of detail and indeed of significant policies (for example, Institute for Government, 2022a).

In the turmoil before his resignation, Johnson sacked the Levelling Up Secretary, Michael Gove. While Gove was then reinstated by Sunak, the future of the idea of levelling up remained uncertain. Nevertheless, levelling up had value for the Conservatives, particularly under Johnson. In particular, it helped provide a platform that enabled them to appeal to Labour voters in parts of England that were traditionally not Conservative voting. It also provided some justification for higher levels of public spending in some areas, whether separate from or maintaining increases associated with the pandemic. And, even if largely rhetorical, it encouraged some parts of government to consider, arguably more than recently under the Conservatives, parts of England away from London and the South East.

Arm's-length governance

Despite regular commitments by the political parties to reduce the number of arm's-length bodies (often referred to as quangos), their use has long been a significant part of government activity. The bulk of spending by these bodies goes through NHS England, the Education and Skills Funding Agency (to fund state schools in England) and HM Revenue and Customs (in the form of child benefits and tax credits). Many arm's-length bodies are very small, however, with more than two fifths having ten or fewer staff (Institute for Government, 2022b).

Their development was given significant impetus under the Thatcher governments, particularly with the creation of agencies to undertake roles previously carried out by the mainstream civil service, while the Labour governments of 1997 to 2010 also made considerable use of them. As a result, while the periods of Labour (from 1979 to 1997) and Conservative and Coalition (from 1997 to 2010) governments saw some reduction in the numbers of arm's-length bodies, the amount of expenditure through them increased significantly (for example, Flinders et al, 2014). Under the Coalition government, the Public Bodies Reform Programme reduced the number of organisations defined by the government as 'public bodies' by nearly 300, to 468, although a significant proportion of that was achieved by mergers rather than by abolition. Since 2015, while there has been some fall in the number of arm's-length bodies, the total spend through them has increased, largely as a result of spending on the NHS in England (Institute for Government, 2022b). In January 2021, the Public Bodies Reform Programme 2020 to 2025 was established by the Treasury and Cabinet Office in an attempt to ensure that public bodies were aligned to priority workstreams in line with the Declaration on Government Reform in 2021, but it remains too early to judge any impact from this.

During the COVID-19 pandemic, some bodies came under particular scrutiny, as with Ofqual over the grading of the GCSE (General Certificate of Secondary Education) and A levels (advanced level qualifications) in England in August 2020, resulting in the resignation of the chief executive, while in 2021 Public Health England was replaced by the UK Health Security Agency and the Office for Health Improvement and Disparities. In 2022 the energy regulator, Ofgem, also came in for considerable criticism for its approach to the consumer price cap in the context of the rapid rises in gas and electricity prices following the Russian invasion of Ukraine, while Ofwat was widely criticised that summer for allowing water companies in England to make large profits and payments to their executives when much of the country was in drought conditions and the scale of leaks in the water infrastructure remained significant.

There is also considerable use of arm's-length bodies by the devolved administrations and by local government (although there are some differences in the operating environments set by the different governments of the UK), and very similar issues to those discussed earlier exist. For example, in Scotland a report by the Accounts Commission (2018) on the use of what it termed 'arm's-length external organisations' by local authorities in

Scotland highlighted the benefits and the risks associated with such bodies, and its recommendations included the consideration of other options that might bring similar benefits, setting clear criteria for reviewing arm's-length external organisations, and considering appointments to their boards and oversight of performance, financial position and associated risks.

Evidence-informed policy

After the claims, perhaps frequently overstated by the government itself, over the use of evidence-based policy during the New Labour years, it was perhaps unsurprising that under consecutive Coalition and Conservative governments the emphasis on 'evidence' was rather diminished (for example, Bochel, 2016), particularly in the context of public expenditure cuts effectively driving policy in many areas (although see Cairney, 2019, on 'evidence-based policy making' and 'policy-based evidence'). During the early period of the COVID-19 pandemic, the government frequently claimed to be following the evidence and scientific advice, although the extent to which it did so, and the speed at which this happened, was not always clear (see Chapter 5). However, the pandemic did help highlight the role of the government's chief advisers, with the Chief Scientific Adviser, Sir Patrick Vallance, and Chief Medical Officer, Professor Chris Whitty, along with others, regularly appearing at 10 Downing Street press conferences.

From a fairly positive perspective, the What Works Centres and What Works Network continued to operate, largely in social policy fields, with the aim of ensuring that evidence informs strategic decision-making. The best known are probably those such as the National Institute for Health and Care Excellence, which continued to play an important role in providing guidance and advice on health and social care, and the Education Endowment Foundation, but others include the Centre for Ageing Better, the Centre for Homelessness Impact and the Youth Futures Foundation.

While there also remained an apparent recognition of the importance of evaluation as part of the policy process, the National Audit Office (2021b) found that since 2013 evaluation of government spending had been variable and inconsistent, despite the establishment of an Evaluation Task Force, and that government had been slow to address barriers to evaluation. This meant that in many policy areas, the government could not have confidence that its spending was making a difference.

Under Cameron, the government had placed considerable emphasis on Open Government Data, not least as part of an attempt to make services more accountable and efficient through consumer pressures (although see also Chapter 13 on the use of data in family policy), but under his successors, while there was no obvious rolling back on this, there were also no significant steps forward. The most recent Action Plan (Open Government Partnership,

2021) highlighted the importance of transparency, accountability and public participation, but there has been little evidence of the initiative informing policy making and evaluation.

One area where there did continue to be a variety of developments was behaviour change. From the late 1990s, under New Labour, and perhaps in particular under the Coalition, governments started to pay attention to the potential of 'nudging' citizens to behave in what they saw as more desirable ways, often because it was anticipated to be cheaper than providing services and also because such approaches tended to align with views that favour change in individuals' behaviour rather than public or state responsibility for dealing with problems (Thaler and Sunstain, 2008). Critics, however, have noted, for example, that nudging may be insufficient to change behaviour significantly or over the longer term, and that it can be seen as shifting responsibility. In addition, during the early stages of the COVID-19 pandemic, some claimed that 'nudge' thinking slowed the government's response in terms of closing schools and banning large gatherings, as a result of concerns that people would grow tired of social distancing measures (for example, Yates, 2020).

The work of The Behavioural Insight Team has continued since 2015, albeit as a freestanding unit rather than within the Cabinet Office, and behaviour change continues to be widely pursued, not only by the Westminster administration but also by the devolved administrations and in local government. In Scotland, for example, the government continued to support a variety of behaviour change initiatives, including in the NHS and in crime and justice, and there were recommendations for a charge on single-use disposable beverage containers. Similarly, in Wales behaviour change has been supported in areas from the NHS to climate change. At the level of local government, councils in England, Scotland and Wales have also sought to use behaviour change, perhaps most obviously around recycling and climate change.

Although perhaps somewhat tangential to evidence-informed policy making, the role of government advisers, while often contentious, came under particular scrutiny under Johnson, not least with the appointment of Dominic Cummings as Chief Adviser to Boris Johnson in 2019. Cummings' subsequent resignation and revelations about Johnson and the workings of his government arguably contributed significantly to Johnson's own resignation in 2022. More generally, the number of special advisers in Downing Street grew: while in 2013 there were 22 special advisers supporting the Prime Minister, by 2022 there were 43 (Cabinet Office, 2022).

Parliament

Parliament's role in the scrutiny of the legislation and work of governments is widely recognised, and in recent years there have increasingly been arguments that support its influence not only in those areas but also, at times, on policy. Given that key drivers of parliamentary influence over governments include the size of the majority in the House of Commons and the support for a prime minister on their own benches, it is not surprising that the outcomes of recent elections have meant that the role and influence of Parliament varied considerably.

The need to legislate for Brexit, particularly given the divisions within the Conservative Party, highlighted the challenges that can face even a government with a House of Commons majority in passing legislation on divisive subjects. That was exacerbated for the Conservatives in 2017, when after a poor campaign May remained in office with no majority and dependent on the Democratic Unionist Party in the House of Commons. That, the political difficulties of achieving any agreement on Brexit, and the amount of government and civil service activity focused on Brexit meant that there was relatively little attention paid by government to other policies or to how they were made and delivered. When May resigned and was succeeded by Boris Johnson, it appeared that a new phase was dawning and that with a large majority in the House of Commons, Johnson would be able to get his way on most issues. However, Brexit continued to demand considerable government resources and parliamentary time and attention, and from 2020 to 2022 the COVID-19 pandemic was clearly a major challenge, in terms of how the government and society should respond to it, but also because there were implications for how Parliament could, and indeed should, work. The potential importance of Parliament was highlighted again with the downfall of first Johnson and then Truss as Prime Minister, with the former having won a vote of confidence among Conservative MPs only a month before he was forced to announce that he would stand down, and the latter resigning only a short time after having been elected as leader by the wider membership of the Conservative Party.

Under Johnson's premiership, there were other changes that affected the role of Parliament. The Dissolution and Calling of Parliament Act 2022 repealed the Fixed-Term Parliaments Act 2011, effectively increasing the power of the prime minister by giving them greater freedom to choose the date of a general election. However, Conservative proposals to reduce the number of MPs were not progressed. The size of the House of Lords continued to grow, to more than 800 (with Johnson having created 86 new peers even before his resignation honours list), having previously fallen to 690 following Labour's reform of the House in 2000. This raises a variety of important questions, including about the powers of the prime minister, the number of peers who have not been particularly active in the House, the credibility of the House and indeed practical considerations such as physical space and support services.

In addition, in the summer of 2022 the Conservative government also introduced the Bill of Rights Bill, which would make major revisions to the parts of the human rights framework of the UK, including by reducing the power of UK judges where legislation may be incompatible with the European Convention on Human Rights and by empowering UK courts and Parliament to not comply with judgements of the European Court of Human Rights (see, for example, Law Society, 2022). The Bill was paused by Liz Truss, and although it was revived under Sunak, by the spring of 2023 there was no timetable for its further progress through Parliament.

Devolution and the Union

As discussed in more depth in Chapter 17, since 1997 the devolved administrations in Northern Ireland, Scotland and Wales have become increasingly important in relation to the governance of social policy, with consecutive reforms giving greater powers to Scotland and Wales in particular. Under the Coalition government, the Scotland Act 2012 transferred additional powers, including over additional elements of taxation and borrowing, to the Scottish Parliament and Government, and the Wales Act 2014 gave additional financial powers to the National Assembly, including over devolved taxes, and extended the borrowing powers of the Welsh Government. Following the referendum on Scottish independence in September 2014, the Scotland Act 2016 gave the Scottish Parliament and Government greater control over a variety of areas, such as Income Tax, including rates and bands, a range of social security benefits, including the housing elements of Universal Credit, and abortion. The following year, the Wales Act 2017 moved Wales from a conferred matters model to a reserved matters model, as with Scotland, and increased the powers of the National Assembly for Wales (which became Senedd Cymru/Welsh Parliament in 2020) and the Welsh Government, including over Income Tax, equalities, its electoral system and borrowing. Demands for a second independence referendum in Scotland continued, although when the Scottish Government sought the view of the Supreme Court on its power to hold a referendum without the approval of the UK government, the Court ruled that the Scottish Parliament did not have that power. That, together with the resignation of Nicola Sturgeon as First Minister in 2023 and her replacement by Humza Yousaf, meant that the future of the independence debate was less clear.

In Northern Ireland, by contrast, the difficulties and unwillingness of getting controversial legislation through the Northern Ireland Assembly were highlighted by the abortion issue. The Belfast High Court ruled in 2015 that Northern Ireland's abortion legislation was in breach of human rights law. However, in early 2017 the executive collapsed, and later that year, following a case in the UK Supreme Court, the UK government announced that women in Northern would be able to have free abortions in England. Following additional legal challenges in 2018 and 2019, the Westminster Parliament approved an amendment to the Northern Ireland (Executive Formation) Bill that said that if devolution was not restored by 21 October 2020, the UK government should decriminalise abortion in Northern Ireland. As devolution was not restored by that date, the laws changed. However, a judicial review in 2021 then found that the Northern Ireland Secretary had failed to comply with the duty to 'expeditiously' provide access to abortion services, and in May 2022 new regulations placed an obligation on the Northern Ireland Department of Health to commission and fund abortion services. The wider challenges associated with devolution in Northern Ireland, and the requirement to have cross-community agreement, were also highlighted in May 2022 when the Democratic Unionist Party blocked the creation of a new power-sharing administration in protest at post-Brexit rules in the Northern Ireland Protocol.

Within England, the main developments in 'devolution' were arguably those that had been introduced by the Coalition government (although, as noted earlier, the *Levelling Up* White Paper raised the prospect of further devolution deals), such as the coming into being of the new Mayor of Greater Manchester, a post held by Labour's Andy Burnham. While 'metro mayor' (or 'combined authority mayor') positions potentially had considerable powers over a range of public services (albeit with powers differing from one area to another), critics noted that they had only very limited powers to determine levels of funding through a Council Tax precept, and also that they frequently required the agreement of other members of their combined authorities, including over any Council Tax precept). The 2017 Conservative manifesto said that the Party would continue to support elected mayors for combined authorities for big cities, but not for rural areas. In 2019, Boris Johnson committed to a White Paper on English devolution, which in May 2021 the government said would become the *Levelling Up* White Paper, and this was published in February 2022 (see, for example, Sandford, 2022). While there was, therefore, relatively little in terms of real change in devolution in England over the period from 2015, in August 2022 it was announced that York and North Yorkshire would move to an elected Mayor in 2024, and there was also the prospect of a similar move for Hull and East Riding of Yorkshire.

However, during the COVID-19 pandemic, metro mayors, such as Andy Burnham in Greater Manchester, Steve Rotheram in the Liverpool City Region, and Sadiq Khan in London, frequently played a prominent role in negotiating with central government over local lockdowns and highlighting the value of local decision-making and the role that local government could play in helping tackle the pandemic. Although the mayors did not have responsibility for public health, which lies with councils, they were able to speak for their areas with a degree of authority and legitimacy, and, at times, to oppose central government policy.

Conclusion

As noted in Chapter 1, considering the dimensions of political approaches set out in Table 1.1, the period since 2015 has arguably seen some divergence between the Conservatives' broad ideological preferences and the decisions made by governments. It is clear that, by and large, the desired approaches included: a deregulatory approach; the use of the private sector (and to some extent the not-for-profit sector) to deliver services (and including the desires of Johnson and Truss, in particular, to reduce the size of the civil service to 2016 levels, despite the growth of responsibilities since then arising from Brexit and a backlog in many areas resulting from the COVID-19 pandemic); competition; low levels of benefits and public expenditure; and accountability through the market. However, a variety of challenges, as discussed throughout this chapter, meant that to a considerable extent the decisions by governments were frequently rather different, even if made rather reluctantly. For example, instances of regulatory problems, and indeed regulatory failure, were a constant presence during this period, while the COVID-19 pandemic and then the pressure on prices, and particularly energy prices during the war in Ukraine, forced government to intervene in the economy and society, increase public expenditure in some fields and make greater use of the public sector than they would have wished.

The shift from Cameron's 'Big Society' through May's 'burning injustices' to Johnson's 'levelling up' reflected the perceived value of not only rhetorical appeals to the electorate but also the need for Conservative leaders to be seen to be addressing ongoing socioeconomic inequalities, despite the fact that many of their policies, and indeed their chosen approaches to making and implementing policies, continued to maintain and exacerbate them. Truss' short-lived attempt to shake up government and the UK economy, however, highlighted the limits of prime ministerial and indeed governmental power. Her successor, Rishi Sunak, came to office presiding over a government that, facing major economic and other challenges, appeared to be seeking to emphasise technocratic competence across a range of policy areas. At the same time, as some Conservative MPs were pointing out towards the end of 2022 and early 2023, that meant it was unclear what the Party now 'stood for' and what the future direction of the government would be.

References

Accounts Commission (2018) *Councils' use of arm's-length organisations*, Edinburgh: Audit Scotland.

Bochel, C. (2016) 'The changing governance of social policy', in H. Bochel and M. Powell (eds) *The Coalition government and social policy*, Bristol: Policy Press, pp 53–77.

Bochel, H. and Duncan, S. (eds) (2007) *Making policy in theory and practice*, Bristol: Policy Press.

Bochel, C. and Bochel, H. (2018) *Making and implementing public policy*, Basingstoke: Palgrave.

Cabinet Office (2021) 'Declaration on government reform', *Gov.uk*, 15 June. Available at www.gov.uk/government/publications/declaration-on-gov ernment-reform/declaration-on-government-reform (accessed 6 July 2022).

Cabinet Office (2022) 'Special adviser data releases: numbers and costs, July 2022 (HMTL)', 15 July. Available at: www.gov.uk/government/publicati ons/special-adviser-data-releases-numbers-and-costs-july-2022/special-adviser-data-releases-numbers-and-costs-june-2022-html (accessed 14 July 2022).

Cairney, P. (2019) 'The UK government's imaginative use of evidence to make policy', *British Politics*, 14(1): 1–22.

Centre for Inequality and Levelling Up (2021) *Funding levelling up: the story so far*, London: University of West London.

Flinders, M., Dommett, K. and Tonkiss, K. (2014) 'Bonfires and barbecues: coalition governance and the politics of quango reform', *Contemporary British History*, 28(1): 56–80.

Harari, D., Hutton, G., Keep, M., Powell, A., Sandford, M. and Ward, M. (2021) *The levelling up agenda*, Debate pack. London: House of Commons Library. Available at: https://researchbriefings.files.parliament.uk/docume nts/CDP-2021-0086/CDP-2021-0086.pdf (accessed 19 August 2022).

HM Government (2022) *Levelling up the United Kingdom*, CP 604, London: HMSO.

Institute for Fiscal Studies (2021) 'Spring Budget 2021', 3 March. Available at: https://ifs.org.uk/collections/spring-budget-2021-0 (accessed 17 April 2023).

Institute for Fiscal Studies (2022) *An initial IFS response to the government's Levelling up White Paper*, London: Institute for Fiscal Studies.

Institute for Government (2022a) *The Levelling up White Paper: welcome ambition but underwhelming policies*, London: Institute for Government.

Institute for Government (2022b) *Whitehall Monitor 2022*, London: Institute for Government. Available at: www.instituteforgovernment.org.uk/sites/default/files/publications/whitehall-monitor-2022.pdf (accessed 17 April 2023).

Johnson, B. (2021) 'The Prime Minister's levelling up speech: 15 July 2021', *Gov.uk*, 15 July. Available at: www.gov.uk/government/speec hes/the-prime-ministers-levelling-up-speech-15-july-2021 (accessed 9 February 2022).

Kisby, B. (2010) 'The Big Society: power to the people?', *The Political Quarterly*, 81(4): 484–91.

KPMG (2010) *Payment for success – how to shift power from Whitehall to public service customers*, London: KPMG.

Law Society (2022) 'Human Rights Act reforms and the Bill of Rights Bill', 12 July. Available at: www.lawsociety.org.uk/topics/human-rights/human-rights-act-reforms (accessed 25 August 2022).

McIntyre, N., Duncan P. and Halliday, J. (2022) 'Levelling-up: some wealthy areas of England to see 10 times more funding than poorest', *The Guardian*, 2 February. Available at: www.theguardian.com/inequality/2022/feb/02/levelling-up-funding-inequality-exposed-by-guardian-research (accessed 9 February 2022).

National Audit Office (2021a) *Efficiency in government*, London: National Audit Office.

National Audit Office (2021b) *Evaluating government spending*, London: National Audit Office.

Niskanen, W. (1971) *Bureaucracy and representative government*, Chicago, IL: Aldine-Atherton.

Open Government Partnership (2021) *UK Open Government National Action Plan 2021–2023*. Available at: www.opengovpartnership.org/wp-content/uploads/2022/02/United-Kingdom_Action-Plan_2021-2023.pdf (accessed 17 April 2023).

Public Accounts Committee (2021) *Efficiency in government*, London: House of Commons.

Rhodes, R. (1997) *Understanding governance: policy networks, governance, reflexivity and accountability*, Buckingham: Open University Press.

Richards, D. and Smith, M.J. (2002) *Governance and public policy in the UK*, Oxford: Oxford University Press.

Sandford, M. (2022) *Devolution to local government in England*, London: House of Commons Library. Available at: https://researchbriefings.files.parliament.uk/documents/SN07029/SN07029.pdf (accessed 18 August 2022).

Taylor-Gooby, P. (2012) 'Root and branch restructuring to achieve major cuts: the social policy programme of the 2010 UK coalition government', *Social Policy and Administration*, 46(1): 61–82.

Thaler, R.H. and Sunstein, C.R. (2008) *Nudge: improving decisions about health, wealth and happiness*, New York: Penguin.

Williams, B. (2021) 'The "New Right" and its legacy for British conservatism', *Journal of Political Ideologies*. doi: 10.1080/13569317.2021.1979139

Yates, T. (2020) 'Why is the government relying on nudge theory to fight coronavirus?', *The Guardian*, 13 March. Available at: www.theguardian.com/commentisfree/2020/mar/13/why-is-the-government-relying-on-nudge-theory-to-tackle-coronavirus (accessed 21 June 2021).

7

Conservative health policy, 2015–23

Martin Powell

Introduction

In many ways, Conservative health policy after 2015 was 'more of the same', continuing from the second half of Coalition health policy, which had tried to row back from the domination of the Health and Social Care Act (HSCA) 2012 in the first half of Coalition health policy (Appleby et al, 2015; Ham et al, 2015; Baggott, 2016; Powell, 2019b). It is possible to point to three broad themes: first, a continuation of the journey from 'peak' marketisation towards integration, initially in a series of 'workarounds' which gradually became formalised; second, a gradual loosening of austerity under the Conservatives compared with the Coalition, although recent increases in expenditure tend still to be below the long-term historical increases in expenditure since 1948; and third, as promised in a public health White Paper, a radical shift in the way of tackling public health challenges and a 'new era for public health' (Department of Health, 2010, p 4; see also Baggott, 2016). A great deal of stress has been placed on the rhetoric of prevention, but the previous emphasis by the National Health Service (NHS) on prevention has never resulted in significant action (Powell, 2009). This theme may be generalised, as it will be claimed that health policy broadly saw a large 'implementation gap' between policy rhetoric and action.

The journey away from the HSCA 2012 arguably began with the NHS' *Five Year Forward View* (NHS England, 2014), which is generally associated with the newly appointed Chief Executive of NHS England, Simon Stevens, a former NHS manager, Blair advisor and then Executive Vice President of UnitedHealth, a US private health company. This plan claimed that it would bring about patient-centred, coordinated, integrated care focusing on prevention, out-of-hospital care and the integration of primary, secondary and community care. It argued for a 'radical upgrade on prevention and public health' (p 3), recognised 'emerging models' (p 16) and 'radical new care delivery options' (p 4) and stressed the importance of devolution, such as 'Devo Manc', in which the £6 billion health and social care budget for

Greater Manchester was to be taken over by the region's councils and health groups. Ham et al (2015) state that taking the longer-term view, the *Five Year Forward View* may well be seen by historians as one of the most important events in health policy under the Coalition government.

Conservative health policy, 2015–23

This section examines Conservative health policy in a broadly chronological order. It focuses on England, though, while the devolved nations followed rather different paths, their health systems exhibited similar problems (see Chapter 17 for a discussion of devolution). It does not, however, explore the COVID-19 pandemic in depth (see Chapter 5). The Conservatives won an unexpected majority at the May 2015 general election, having promised to protect and improve the NHS, including commitments to continue to increase spending and to keep the NHS free to use (Conservative Party, 2015). It pledged to:

- spend at least £8 billion over and above inflation by 2020 to fund and support the NHS's own action plan for the next five years;
- ensure [people] can see a GP [general practitioner] and receive the hospital care [they] need, 7 days a week by 2020, with a guarantee that everyone over 75 will get a same-day appointment if they need one;
- integrate health and social care, through [the] Better Care Fund;
- lead the world in fighting cancer and finding a cure for dementia. (p 37)

Unsurprisingly, the Queen's Speech stated that the government would 'secure the future' of the NHS by implementing the service's five-year plan, increasing the health budget, integrating health and social care and ensuring the NHS 'works on a seven-day basis'. Moreover, it promised to 'improve access to GPs and to mental health care' (Hansard, 2015).

There has been no shortage of documents under the Conservatives since 2015. However, as shown later, many of them provide rather vague (or non-'SMART' – specific, measurable, achievable, relevant, time-bound) actions or are 'policy retreads', repeating actions similar to previous documents. For example, when Theresa May became Prime Minister in July 2016 after the resignation of David Cameron, while her government failed to 'get Brexit done' (in the words of Prime Minister Johnson, who followed May), it got many health documents done.

Childhood Obesity: A Plan for Action noted that 'nearly a third of children aged 2 to 15 are overweight or obese' (HM Government, 2016, p 3). It aimed to 'significantly reduce England's rate of childhood obesity within

... ten years' (p 3). It stated that it would, as a first major step, introduce a soft drinks industry levy across the UK.

There has been a stress on leadership and 'people plans'. *Developing People – Improving Care* (National Improvement and Leadership Development Board, 2016) pointed to building leadership and improvement capability as key factors in ensuring the NHS could continue to deliver high-quality care and support for patients and citizens. The framework focuses on helping NHS and social care staff to develop critical capabilities in systems leadership, quality improvement methods, inclusive and compassionate leadership and talent management.

Sir Ron Kerr, former Chief Executive Officer of Guy's and St Thomas' NHS Foundation Trust, was asked by the Department of Health and Social Care to lead a short review exploring three of the key challenges faced by executive leaders across the NHS, namely: the expectations and support available for leaders; the alignment of performance expectations at the organisational and system level; and the level of administrative burden placed on executive leaders. He replied in the form of a letter to the Secretary of State, following in the footsteps of Roy Griffiths in 1983, but without the impact, as yet another 'management review' was commissioned in 2021 (discussed later). Kerr (2018) produced recommendations under themes of: support and leadership; a 'new deal'; alignment and expectations; and reducing the burden. However, in a microcosm of the wider health system, the letter pointed out that 'these issues have been looked at in the past and the findings will not be surprising to those working in the NHS' (p 2). Kerr argued, for example, that while the NHS should 'empower leaders to lead, encouraging them to celebrate their successes and learn from their mistakes', the reality was that 'a culture of blame and negativity continues[d] to pervade the NHS'(p 6).

In October 2017, the government appointed an independent body to review the Mental Health Act 1983 (amended in 2007), which regulates compulsory detention and treatment of persons with a mental disorder in England and Wales. It was charged with understanding: the rising rates of detention; the disproportionate numbers of Black and minority ethnic groups in the detained population; and investigating concerns that some processes in the Act are out of step with a modern mental health system. It reported in 2018 (Independent Review of the Mental Health Act 1983, 2018), as discussed later.

The Conservatives lost their House of Commons majority at the 2017 general election, partly due to a disastrous section in their manifesto on social care (see Chapter 12). On health care, the manifesto (Conservative Party, 2017) stated that the Party believed in the founding principles of the NHS and that the next Conservative government would: 'give the NHS the resources it needs'; support the NHS' 'own plan', the *Five Year*

Forward View; 'review the operation of the internal market'; and 'make non-legislative changes to remove barriers to the integration of care' (pp 66, 67). The Conservatives intended to 'introduce a new GP contract to help develop wider primary care services' and to 'support NHS dentistry to improve coverage and reform contracts so that we pay for better outcomes' (p 68). It promised '[e]xceptional standards of care, wherever, whenever' (p 66), arguing that '[o]utcomes in the NHS for most major conditions are considerably better than three, five or ten years ago' (p 68). However, it noted that the founding intention for the NHS 'to provide good levels of care to everyone, wherever they live ... had not yet been achieved' and claimed that the government would 'act to put this right' (p 68), with an ambition to provide 'exceptional care to patients whenever they need it' (p 69). It wanted 'England to be the first nation in the world to provide a truly seven-day healthcare service'; it would 'continue to help the NHS on its journey to being the safest healthcare system in the world'; and it would deliver the new promise in cancer services 'to give patients a definitive diagnosis within 28 days by 2020' (p 69). Finally, it stated that the Conservatives 'gave parity of esteem to the treatment of mental health in the National Health Service' (p 56), noting that 'since 2010 we have increased spending on mental health each year to a record £11.4 billion in 2016/17, with a further investment of £1 billion by 20/21' (p 57).

The minority government's Queens Speech (Hansard, 2017) announced 27 Bills and draft Bills. The only significant health element was a draft Bill that set out a framework to help improve patient safety in the NHS through establishing the Health Service Safety Investigation Body in statute, providing it with clear powers to conduct independent and impartial investigations into patient safety risks in the NHS in England.

Following an interim report in May 2018, the final report of the review of the Mental Health Act, *Modernising the Mental Health Act* (Independent Review of the Mental Health Act 1983, 2018), was published in December 2018, with over 150 recommendations, based on four principles: choice and autonomy; least restriction; therapeutic benefit; and the person as an individual (discussed later).

Matt Hancock was appointed Secretary of State for Health and Social Care in July 2018, replacing Jeremy Hunt, who had held the post for nearly six years, becoming the longest-serving custodian of the NHS. *Prevention Is Better than Cure*, published in November 2018, set out 'a vision for putting prevention at the heart of [the] nation's health', with a mission 'to improve healthy life expectancy' with a target of 'at least five extra years of healthy, independent life' by 2035, as well as 'closing the gap between the richest and poorest' (Secretary of State for Health and Social Care, 2018, p 4). It stated that the UK spent '60% of public funding for healthcare on cure and rehabilitation, and only 5% on prevention', which translated into '£97 billion a year on treating diseases, and only £8 billion on preventing them' (p 14). This was followed by a Green Paper on prevention in July 2019, *Advancing our Health: Prevention in the 2020s*, which stated that the 2020s would be 'the decade of proactive, predictive, and personalised prevention', when people would 'not be passive recipients of care', but 'co-creators of their own health' (Parliamentary Under Secretary of State for Public Health and Primary Care, 2019, p 4). The NHS would provide 'intelligent screening', 'intelligent health checks' and 'precision medicine' (see Parliamentary Under Secretary of State for Public Health and Primary Care, 2019, pp 16–19). While there had been 'good progress in moving towards a smoke-free society', with smoking rates in Great Britain halving in the 35 years before the report was published, giving 'one of the lowest rates in Europe' (p 25), the trend was going in the wrong direction for other areas, with, for instance, 'only a third of adults [having] a healthy weight (p 28). Between 1993 and 2019, 'rates of adult obesity [had] almost doubled (to 29%), and morbid obesity [had] quadrupled (to 4%)', with one in three children aged 10 to 11 overweight or obese (p 28). Continuing the themes of its childhood obesity strategy, the government said it would 'end the sale of energy drinks to children under the age of 16' (p 29) and would set out 'bold action' on issues such as clear food labelling. It also set an 'ambition to go "smoke-free" in England by 2030', including an 'ultimatum for industry to make smoked tobacco obsolete' by that year, 'with smokers quitting or moving to reduced risk products like e-cigarettes' (p 25). It noted that 'great progress' had been made in 'helping people to live longer lives', due to developments in public health and health care (p 6). But it also stated that 'these improvements in life expectancy were beginning to slow, and over 20% of years lived are expected to be spent in poor health (p 7). Moreover, it noted a 'clear social gradient to healthy life expectancy', with people in deprived areas not only tending to live shorter lives but also spending more of those years in poor health (p 7). The Green Paper claimed that it signalled a new approach for the health and care system, meaning that government, both local and national, would work with the system to 'put prevention at the centre of all ... decision-making' (p 5).

There was some familiar 'retread' content in the *NHS Long Term Plan* of January 2019 (NHS England, 2019d), which provided an ambitious ten-year vision for health care in England. It set out the 'realities' of funding, staffing, increasing inequalities and pressures from a growing and ageing population as its starting point (p 6). It pointed out the scale of the challenge. For example, global obesity rates had 'tripled since 1975', with the UK ranking 'among the worst in Europe' (p 36). In terms of kit, such as CT scanners, the UK was near the bottom of 34 OECD (Organisation for Economic Co-operation and Development) nations, having about a tenth of the scanners per million population compared with the world leader, Japan (p 60). However, it argued that the NHS would be able to tackle these issues because: there was 'a secure and improved funding path for the NHS, averaging 3.4% a year over the next five years, compared with 2.2% over the past five years' (p 6); there was wide consensus about the changes now needed; and work that kicked off after the *Five Year Forward View* was now beginning to bear fruit – 'almost everything in this Plan is already being implemented successfully somewhere in the NHS' (p 6). The government would 'boost out-of-hospital care, and finally dissolve the historic divide between primary and community health services' (p 13). The main mechanism for change would involve local NHS organisations focusing increasingly on population health – moving to Integrated Care Systems, growing out of the current network of Sustainability and Transformation Partnerships, everywhere by April 2021. The document stated that it was necessary to remove the counterproductive effect that general competition rules and powers can have on the integration of NHS care, even admitting that many of these powers had been introduced by the Coalition government:

> We propose to remove the Competition and Markets Authority's … duties, introduced by the 2012 Act, to intervene in NHS provider mergers, and its powers in relation to NHS pricing and NHS provider licence condition decisions. … We propose similarly dispensing with Monitor's [the independent regulator for NHS foundation trusts] 2012 Act competition roles, so that it could focus fully on NHS provider development and oversight. (NHS England, 2019b, p 113)

It was claimed that some improvements in these areas were necessarily framed as ten-year goals, given the timelines needed to expand capacity and grow the workforce. For example, the plan committed to 'dramatically improving cancer survival' by 2028, partly by 'increasing the proportion of cancers diagnosed early, from a half to three quarters' (p 44). There were other grand claims, such as the creation – for the first time since the NHS was set up in 1948 – of 'fully integrated community-based health care' (p 15). Other commitments appeared to be rather vague. For example, it was necessary to

> do more to develop and embed cultures of compassion, inclusion, and collaboration across the NHS. Building on the ambitions of *Developing People: Improving Care* we will work to support all parts of the NHS to create an inclusive and just culture that leads to outstanding staff engagement and patient care. (NHS England, 2019d, p 89)

The *Interim NHS People Plan* of June 2019 stated that 'more of the same will not be enough to deliver the promise of the *NHS Long Term Plan*' and that 'different people in different professions working in different ways' would be needed, transforming the way 'the entire workforce' works together (NHS England, 2019a, p 2). It would be necessary to address the 'cultural changes that are necessary to build a workforce that befits a world-class 21st century healthcare system' (p 2). It was also necessary to 'promote positive cultures, build a pipeline of compassionate and engaging leaders and make the NHS an agile, inclusive and modern employer ... to attract and retain the people' needed to deliver the NHS' plans (p 2).

The *Interim NHS People Plan* set out a number of themes: making the NHS the best place to work; improving the leadership culture; addressing urgent workforce shortages in nursing; delivering 21st-century care; and providing a new operating model for the workforce (NHS England, 2019a, pp 3–4). It went on to state that the NHS would

> develop a new offer ... setting out explicitly the support [that people] could expect from the NHS as a modern employer ... framed around the broad themes of creating a healthy, inclusive and compassionate culture, enabling great development and fulfilling careers, and ensuring everyone feels they have voice, control and influence. (NHS England, 2019a, p 10)

In a rare moment of reflection, it was claimed that the NHS made a start on this agenda in 2016, but suggested that 'while *Developing People – Improving Care* has made some impact, it has not led to the widespread culture change it set out to deliver' (p 14).

The *NHS Long Term Plan Implementation Framework* of June 2019 claimed that '[o]ver the next five and ten years the NHS [would] progressively increase its focus on prevention and ensure that inequalities reduction is at the centre of [its] plans' (NHS England, 2019b, p 5). Similarly, the *NHS Mental Health Implementation Plan 2019/20–2034/24*, published in July 2019, stated that 'the NHS Long Term Plan renewed [the] commitment to pursue the most ambitious transformation of mental health care England has ever known' (NHS England, 2019c, p 3). This included a 'commitment that mental health services [would] grow faster than the overall NHS budget, with a ringfenced investment worth at least £2.3 billion a year for mental health services by 2023/24' (p 5).

Boris Johnson replaced Theresa May as Prime Minister in July 2019. The Queen's Speech of October 2019 (Hansard, 2019a) announced that the government would bring forward measures to support and strengthen the NHS, introduce new laws to help implement the *NHS Long Term Plan*, establish an independent body to investigate serious health care incidents and continue work to reform the Mental Health Act. Moreover, it would bring forward proposals to reform adult social care in England to ensure dignity in old age (see also Chapter 12).

The Conservative manifesto for the 2019 general election contained a personal 'guarantee' by Johnson of '[e]xtra funding for the NHS, with 50,000 more nurses and 50 million more GP surgery appointments a year' (Conservative Party, 2019), but also a promise not to raise the rate of Income Tax, Value Added Tax or National Insurance (discussed later). It stated that 'this new One Nation Conservative Government is giving the NHS its biggest ever cash boost, with 20 hospital upgrades and 40 new hospitals, while delivering 50,000 more nurses and 6,000 more doctors and creating an extra 50 million general practice appointments a year' (p 2). It continued that the Conservatives were 'committed to reducing health inequality' and would 'invest in preventing disease as well as curing it' (p 10), and would 'treat mental health with the same urgency as physical health' (p 11). They would also 'improve NHS performance, using [the] record funding settlement to bring down operating waiting times, improve A&E [Accident and Emergency] performance and increase cancer survival rates' (p 11).

Speaking on the Downing Street steps the day after the 2019 election, with a large Conservative majority in the House of Commons, Johnson declared that he had received clear instructions from the British people that 'we should focus above all on the NHS' (quoted in Urban, 2021, p 12). He promised to 'fix the crisis in social care once and for all with a clear plan we have prepared' (Johnson, 2019; see also Chapter 12).

The Queen's Speech of December 2019 (Hansard, 2019b) focused on 'getting Brexit done'. However, it stated that steps would be taken to grow and support the NHS workforce and a new visa would ensure qualified doctors, nurses and health professionals have fast-track entry to the UK. Ministers would continue work to reform the Mental Health Act. Turning to social care (see Chapter 12), ministers would 'seek cross-party consensus on proposals for long term reform of social care, ensuring 'that the social care system provides everyone with the dignity and security they deserve and that no one who needs care has to sell their home to pay for it'. However, these plans were derailed by COVID-19 (see Chapter 5) and the government's focus on the battle with the pandemic.

We Are the NHS: People Plan 2020/21 claimed that action outlined in the *Interim NHS People Plan* was already being taken to increase the support and recognition for the workforce, but '[t]hen the start of COVID-19 changed everything' (NHS England, 2020, p 5). It went on to say that workload remained a pressing concern and that in order to address this, 'the NHS needs more people, working differently, in a compassionate and inclusive culture' (p 6). It focused on 'looking after our people', 'belonging in the NHS', 'new ways of working and delivering care' and 'growing for the future' (p 6), and 'highlighting existing and deep-rooted inequalities' (p 10).

As in previous periods, a number of reviews and inquiries reported, providing continuing information of the problems within the NHS. A review of independent medicines and medical devices safety (Cumberlege, 2020) investigated two medications (hormone pregnancy tests, such as Primodos, and the anti-epileptic drug sodium valproate) and one medical device (pelvic mesh implants). It pointed out that these are all taken or used by women who have suffered harm and were not listened to for decades. It stated that the system is not good enough at spotting trends in practice and outcomes that give rise to safety concerns. It also stated that as listening to patients was pivotal, one of its principal recommendations (of nine) was the appointment of an independent patient safety commissioner.

In January 2021, the White Paper *Reforming the Mental Health Act* (Secretary of State for Health and Social Care and the Lord Chancellor and Secretary of State for Justice, 2021) accepted the 'vast majority' of the recommendations of the 'landmark' Independent Review of 2018, discussed earlier. It was stated that this would result in an 'unprecedented transformation', 'delivering the most ambitious programme for the transformation of mental health care England has ever known' (p 8).

The White Paper *Integration and Innovation: Working Together to Improve Health and Social Care for All* (Secretary of State for Health and Social Care, 2021) set out the legislative proposals for a Health and Care Bill. It built on the proposals set out in the *NHS Long Term Plan* and on innovations that emerged during the COVID-19 pandemic. It focused on 'removing the barriers that stop the system from being truly integrated', such as 'much of the transactional bureaucracy' (p 6), and ensuring a system that would be 'more accountable and responsive to the people that work in it and the people that use it' (p 6). It noted that 'the founding principles of the NHS – taxpayer-funded healthcare available to all, cradle-to-grave, and free at the point of delivery – remain as relevant now as they were in 1948' (p 6).

The White Paper pointed to two forms of integration: 'integration within the NHS to remove some of the cumbersome boundaries to collaboration and to make working together an organising principle; and greater collaboration between the NHS and local government, as well as wider delivery partners' (p 10). This would 'require changes to both competition law as it was applied to the NHS in the HSCA 2012, and the system of procurement applied to the NHS by that legislation' (p 11). It noted 'the road to better coordination of health and care' (p 18) that began in 2014 with the *Five Year Forward View* was concerned with 'stripping out needless bureaucracy' (p 21; forgetting to point out that much of this was imposed by the HSCA 2012), clarifying 'the central role of collaboration in driving performance and quality in the system, rather than competition' (p 42), by repealing s 75 of the HSCA 2012. It argued that the NHS should be 'free to make decisions on how it organises itself without the involvement of the Competition and Markets Authority' (p 25). The proposals included 'formally bring[ing] together NHS England and NHS Improvement into a single legal organisation' (p 26); linked to ensuring that 'the Secretary of State for Health and Social Care has appropriate intervention powers with respect to relevant functions of NHS England' (p 26); making it 'easier for the Secretary of State to direct NHS England to take on specific public health functions' (p 29); putting 'the Healthcare Safety Investigation Branch … on a statutory footing (p 29); and establishing 'a statutory medical examiners system within the NHS' (p 29).

Sajid Javid replaced Matt Hancock as Health Secretary in June 2021. *Building Back Better: Our Plan for Health and Social Care* (Prime Minister, 2021), published in September 2021, set out '[o]ur plan for healthcare' ('[t]ackling the electives backlog'; '[p]utting the NHS on a sustainable footing'; and '[f]ocussing on prevention' – see pp 9–13) and '[o]ur plan for adult social care in England' ('[c]apping adult social care costs'; '[f]inancial assistance to people without substantial assets'; '[w]ider support for the social care system'; and '[i]mproving the integration of health and social care' – see pp 14–21), which would be funded by a new Health and Social Care Levy.

The Health and Social Care Levy allowed Johnson's 'oven-ready' plan to tackle social care to once and for all emerge from the slow cooker. The levy initially involved increasing National Insurance contributions – breaking a manifesto pledge not to raise taxation – before becoming a new hypothecated tax of 1.25 per cent (see Chapter 12). It was estimated that this would raise some £12 billion each year for health and social care. This resulted in a strange role reversal of Conservatives taxing more while Labour argued against the rise (even though former Labour Chancellor Gordon Brown had increased National Insurance to increase funding for the NHS).

Partly as a result of its perceived failures during the COVID-19 pandemic, Public Health England was replaced by the UK Health Security Agency and the Office for Health Promotion in October 2021. The Office for Health Improvement and Disparities was launched, charged with driving the prevention agenda and tackling health inequalities.

The Health and Care Act was passed in 2022 (on this, see, for example, Kings Fund, 2022). It is complex and wide-ranging, with seven parts and 187 clauses. However, at its heart is the formalisation of Integrated Care Systems, continuing the journey to replace competition with collaboration. In particular, it abolished Section 75 of the HSCA 2012, which, some had argued, opened up England's NHS to competition on an unprecedented scale by requiring commissioners to put virtually all services out to tender. However, critics of the 2022 Act pointed to the potential for private providers to hold seats on Integrated Care Boards and to the increased powers for ministers to get involved with operational matters, having previously argued that the 2012 Act reduced the powers of ministers (Roderick and Pollock, 2022). It also established a new independent body, the Health Service Safety Investigations Body. However, this continues the work of the Healthcare

Safety Investigations Branch, which became operational in April 2017 as part of NHS Improvement, in conducting high-level investigations into patient safety incidents in the NHS. It is unclear if this will make any significant difference, apart from a change of letterhead.

Continuing the theme of prevention, the Khan review (2022) set out measures to make the UK smoke-free by 2030. Another inquiry with findings relevant to the state of the NHS was the Ockenden review of Maternity Services at The Shrewsbury and Telford Hospital NHS Trust. This found a string of 'repeated failures' spanning a period of 20 years, including at least 304 cases where there was avoidable harm, with the trust failing to investigate, failing to learn and failing to improve (Ockenden, 2022, p x). In addition to the 27 'Local Actions for Learning' for the Trust, and seven 'Immediate and Essential Actions' for maternity services across England set out by an interim report, the final report added a further 64 Local Actions for Learning and 15 areas for Immediate and Essential Actions across England (Ockenden, 2022).

Yet another review of NHS management pointed to problems of 'institutional inadequacy in the way that leadership and management is trained, developed and valued' and an 'institutional instinct ... to look upwards to furnish the needs of the hierarchy rather than downwards to the needs of the service-user' (Messenger and Pollard, 2022, p 4). The review noted that it 'encountered too many reports to ignore of poor behavioural cultures and incidences of discrimination, bullying, blame cultures and responsibility avoidance' (p 4). It produced seven broad recommendations: 'targeted interventions on collaborative leadership and organisational values'; 'positive equality, diversity and inclusion ... action'; 'consistent management standards delivered through accredited training'; 'a simplified, standard appraisal system for the NHS'; 'a new career and talent management function for managers'; 'effective recruitment and development of non-executive directors'; and 'encouraging top talent into challenged parts of the system' (Messenger and Pollard, 2022).

In the chaos surrounding Boris Johnson stepping down as Prime Minister, Sajid Javid resigned as Secretary of State for Health and Social Care in July 2022, to be replaced by Steve Barclay. Barclay's brief initial tenure (he returned for a second spell – discussed later) saw the publication of the *Women's Health Strategy for England* (Secretary of State for Health and Social Care, 2022), which set out a ten-year strategy for improving the way the health and care system listens to women's voices and boosting health outcomes for women and girls. It also announced the appointment of a Women's Health Ambassador for England.

The new Prime Minister, Liz Truss, appointed Thérèse Coffey as Health Secretary. However, after Rishi Sunak replaced Truss (following the shortest tenure of any prime minister, at 44 days), Barclay was reappointed as Health Secretary. Another inquiry on maternity services, focused on East Kent (Kirkup, 2022), placed failures in East Kent over a period of a decade within a cycle of endlessly repeating supposedly one-off catastrophic failures. The report noted that had care been given to the nationally recognised standards, the outcome could have been different in 97 of the 202 cases (48 per cent of cases) assessed by the panel and in 45 of the 65 baby deaths (69 per cent of cases). In the Autumn Statement (Hansard, 2022), the Chancellor, Jeremy Hunt, stated that the NHS budget had been increased to record levels to deal with the pandemic, but he would increase it further by £3.3 billion in each of the next two years (with £4.7 billion for social care), resulting in a record £8 billion package for the health and care system. However, as he claimed that we want 'Scandinavian quality alongside Singaporean efficiency, and both better outcomes for citizens and better value for taxpayers', he asked former Labour Health Secretary Patricia Hewitt to advise on how to make sure the new Integrated Care Boards operate efficiently, with appropriate autonomy and accountability, and she reported in April 2023 (Hewitt, 2023). He took notice of the former Chair of the Health and Social Care Committee (himself) and addressed workforce issues by publishing an independently verified plan for the number of doctors, nurses and other professionals required in five, ten and fifteen years' time. However, he delayed the implementation of the social care cap (see Chapter 12), tellingly referred to as the 'Dilnot reforms' (an oven-ready plan from 2011) for two years, allocating the funding to allow local authorities to provide more care packages.

In the 75th year of the NHS in 2023, it seems that the service is 'gridlock' NHS (Care Quality Commission, 2022), with long waiting lists, long A&E waits, missed cancer targets, slow ambulance response times, many beds 'blocked', large staff shortages, a seemingly never-ending series of critical inquiries and a series of strikes by NHS staff, including nurses, ambulance workers and junior doctors.

Discussion

As we have seen, the Conservative governments have made many promises, but their impact appears rather limited, with clear problems in both health care and health (Care Quality Commission, 2022). While it has been said that the NHS has been in perpetual 'crisis' from its birth, the term seems to be used more often in recent years, with 'winter crises' now appearing throughout the year in a 'Narnia' fashion. The Collins Dictionary word of the year for 2022 was 'permacrisis', meaning an extended period of instability and insecurity, especially one resulting from a series of catastrophic events – this seems very apt in a discussion of the NHS.

One aspect of this sense of crisis can be seen in the continuing series of NHS scandals. The Mid-Staffordshire NHS Hospital Trust Inquiry is perhaps the largest and best known, but others have quickly followed, at places such as Winterbourne View, Morecambe Bay, Liverpool, Gosport (Powell, 2019a) and, more recently, at Nottingham, Essex, Cwm Taf and Shrewsbury and Telford (see, for example, Ockenden, 2022) and, most recently, East Kent. Urban (2021) provided a 'half-time analysis' on what the Johnson government had achieved. On health, the analysis stated that while the government delivered on its commitment to invest record sums into the health service, it was off-target on numerous other health-related pledges, with most of the manifesto pledges classed as 'at risk'. It acknowledged that some pledges had been directly affected by the pandemic, but noted that other pledges were off-target despite not being directly affected by the pandemic. The report tended to focus on health care, but turning to health, improvements in health, as assessed by ill health and life expectancy, had slowed markedly over the decade from 2010, and health inequalities were growing (Marmot et al, 2020). Moreover, COVID-19 acted as an amplifier of existing inequalities, with greater mortality in areas of higher deprivation (see Chapter 5).

The themes from the second half of the Coalition government broadly continued. First, policy has tended to stress integration rather than marketisation. Second, the NHS has received more money, although arguably not enough to deal with the huge backlog due to the pandemic. Third, a great deal of rhetorical stress has been placed on issues such as prevention and mental health, but it is more difficult to detect a similar level of policy impact on the ground. For example, the 'plan for action' on childhood obesity (HM Government, 2016) produced limited action and few positive outcomes. There appear to be few SMART targets, while many of those few SMART targets having been missed (Urban, 2021). There has been a stress on leadership (two reports), people plans (two reports) and many documents on mental health and prevention. However, there has also been a reliance on vague 'policy retreads' – for instance, concerning 'prevention' and 'culture change'.

In terms of the dimensions outlined in Table 1.1, it can be argued that in some ways the Conservatives followed the broad path of the Coalition: stressing deregulation and responsibilities (more than rights). However, there was a rhetorical stress on equality in the form of 'levelling up' (but with few concrete outcomes), some continuing moves away from competition towards integration, and an increase in expenditure both for the NHS and social security and employment protection during the COVID-19 pandemic. The public/private mix was a little more problematic. During the pandemic, the government issued many contracts to (unproven) private companies for personal protective equipment and

COVID-19 testing, ignoring help from 'little boat' laboratories, and put its faith in the central Public Health England rather than local authority public health teams. Finally, it is difficult to detect the extent to which the Cameron, May, Johnson, Truss and Sunak governments of 2015 onwards had similar approaches to health policy compared with each other and with the Coalition government. While they all claimed the 'One Nation Conservative' label to some degree, critics argued that labels such as 'neoliberal' were more appropriate. Similarly, it is difficult to detect any major differences between the brief periods of many different health secretaries. This is partly because manifestos and Queen's Speeches do not seem to be good guides to activity and outcomes. Some of the claims appeared ambitious even without COVID-19, with some now looking faintly ridiculous. In short, there appears to be a theme of overclaiming and underdelivering.

Conclusion

In some ways, Conservative health policy after 2015 is as simple as ABC: austerity, Brexit and COVID-19. Paton (2022) points to a slightly different '[t]oxic cocktail: a hangover from austerity, the pandemic, Brexit and barely sorted social care'. First, while there has been a gradual loosening of austerity under the Conservative governments compared with the Coalition government, increases in expenditure tend still to be below the long-term historical increases in expenditure since 1948. Second, Hervey et al (2021) considers that all forms of Brexit have overwhelmingly negative implications for health care and health within the UK (see also Chapter 4). Third, Marmot et al (2020) found that COVID-19 led to higher excess deaths than in other European countries and further revealed and amplified inequalities in health, with clear socioeconomic and ethnic inequalities in risk mortality (see also Chapter 5). Fourth, Johnson's 'oven-ready' social care package has been placed back in the fridge (see Chapter 12).

There has been a continuing attempt, begun by the Coalition government, to move from competition to integration, within a context of some small reduction in austerity before 'normal' policy was largely becalmed by the 'external shocks' of Brexit and COVID-19 (see Chapters 4 and 5). It may be argued that 'events' (external shocks, the extraordinary churn of prime ministers and health secretaries) were more important than 'ideology' and made 'normal' policy making problematic. Moreover, although the government produced many health documents, it is difficult to determine their impact. Despite any 'good intentions' (in relation to prevention, mental health and women's health), the state of the NHS continued to decline, overwhelmed by playing 'catch-up' after the pandemic and after years of austerity, significant workforce shortages and strike action. Even with record funding for the NHS, there does not appear to be much to celebrate on the NHS' 75th anniversary in 2023.

References

Appleby, J., Baird, B., Thompson, J. and Jabbal, J. (2015) *The NHS under the Coalition government. Part two: NHS performance*, London: King's Fund.

Baggott, R. (2016) 'Health policy', in H. Bochel and M. Powell (eds) *The Coalition government and social policy*, Bristol: Policy Press, pp 99–126.

Care Quality Commission (2022) *The state of health care and adult social care in England 2021/22*, London: CQC.

Conservative Party (2015) *Strong leadership, a clear economic plan, a brighter, more secure future. The Conservative Party Manifesto 2015*, London: Conservative Party.

Conservative Party (2017) *Forward together: our plan for a stronger Britain and a prosperous future. The Conservative and Unionist Party Manifesto 2017*, London: Conservative Party.

Conservative Party (2019) *Get Brexit done, unleash Britain's potential. The Conservative and Unionist Party manifesto 2019*, London: Conservative Party.

Cumberlege, J. (2020) *First do no harm: the report of the Independent Medicines and Medical Devices Safety Review*, London: HSMO.

Department of Health (2010) *Healthy lives, healthy people*, London: TSO.

Dilnot, A. (2011) *Fairer care funding*, London: Commission on Funding of Care and Support.

Ham, C., Baird, B., Gregory, S., Jabbal, J. and Alderwick, H. (2015) *The NHS under the Coalition government. Part one: NHS reform*, London: King's Fund.

Hansard, House of Commons (2015) Queen's Speech, Vol 596, col 31, 27 May.

Hansard, House of Commons (2017) Queen's Speech, Vol 626, col 34–36, 21 June.

Hansard, House of Commons (2019a) Queen's Speech, Vol 666, col 3, 14 October.

Hansard, House of Commons (2019b) Queen's Speech, Vol 669, col 31, 19 December.

Hansard, House of Commons (2022) *Autumn Statement*, Vol 722, col 844–93, 17 November.

Hervey, T., Antova, I., Flear, M.L, McHale, J.V., Speakman, E. and Wood, M. (2021) 'Health "Brexternalities": the Brexit effect on health and health care outside the United Kingdom', *Journal of Health Politics, Policy and Law*, 46(1): 177–203.

Hewitt, P. (2023) *The Hewitt Review: an independent review of Integrated Care Systems*, London: TSO.

HM Government (2016) *Childhood obesity: a plan for action*, London: HMSO.

Independent Review of the Mental Health Act 1983 (2018) *Modernising the Mental Health Act: increasing choice, reducing compulsion. Final report of the Independent Review of the Mental Health Act 1983* (Chair: S. Wesseley), London: Department of Health and Social Care.

Johnson, B. (2019) 'Boris Johnson's first speech as Prime Minister: 24 July 2019', *Gov.uk*, 24 July. Available at: www.gov.uk/government/speeches/boris-johnsons-first-speech-as-prime-minister-24-july-2019 (accessed 19 July 2023).

Kerr, R. (2018) *Empowering NHS leaders to lead*, London: Department of Health and Social Care.

Khan, J. (2022) *Making smoking obsolete: independent review into smokefree 2030 policies* (The Khan review), London: Office for Health Improvement and Disparities.

King's Fund (2022) 'The Health and Care Act: six key questions', 17 May. Available at: www.kingsfund.org.uk/publications/health-and-care-act-key-questions (accessed 19 July 2023).

Kirkup, B. (2022) *Reading the signals: maternity and neonatal services in East Kent – the report of the independent investigation*, London: Department of Health and Social Care.

Marmot, M., Allen, J., Goldblatt, P., Herd, E. and Morrison, J. (2020) *Build back fairer: the COVID-19 Marmot review. The pandemic, socioeconomic and health inequalities in England*, London: Institute of Health Equity.

Messenger, G. and Pollard, L. (2022) *Leadership for a collaborative and inclusive future*, London: TSO.

National Improvement and Leadership Development Board (2016) *Developing people – improving care*, London: NHS Improvement.

NHS England (2014) *Five year forward view*, London: NHS England.

NHS England (2019a) *Interim NHS people plan*, London: NHS England.

NHS England (2019b) *NHS long term plan implementation framework*, London: NHS England.

NHS England (2019c) *NHS mental health implementation plan 2019/20–2023/24*, London: NHS England.

NHS England (2019d) *The NHS long term plan*, London: NHS England.

NHS England (2020) *We are the NHS: people plan 2020/21 – action for us all*, London: NHS England.

Ockenden, D. (2022) *Findings, conclusions and essential actions from the Independent Review of Maternity Services at The Shrewsbury and Telford Hospital NHS Trust*, HC 1219, London: HMSO.

Parliamentary Under Secretary of State for Public Health and Primary Care (2019) *Advancing our health: prevention in the 2020s*, CP 110, London: TSO.

Paton, C. (2022) *NHS reform and health politics in the UK: revolution, counter-revolution and Covid crisis*, Basingstoke: Palgrave Macmillan.

Powell, M. (2009) 'Beveridge's giant of disease: from negative to positive welfare?', in K. Rummery, I. Greener and C. Holden (eds) *Social Policy Review 21*, Bristol: Policy Press, pp 67–86.

Powell, M. (2019a) 'Inquiries in the British National Health Service', *Political Quarterly*, 90(2): 180–4.

Powell, M. (2019b) 'The English National Health Service in a cold climate', in E. Heims and J. Rees (eds) *Social Policy Review 31*, Bristol: Policy Press, pp 7–28.

Prime Minister (2021) *Building back better: our plan for health and social care*, CP 506, London: TSO.

Roderick, P. and Pollock, A. (2022) 'Dismantling the National Health Service in England', *International Journal of Health Services*, 52(4): 470–9.

Secretary of State for Health and Social Care (2018) *Prevention is better than cure*, London: Department of Health and Social Care.

Secretary of State for Health and Social Care (2021) *Integration and innovation: working together to improve health and social care for all*, CP 381, London: TSO.

Secretary of State for Health and Social Care (2022) *Women's health strategy for England*, CP 736, London: TSO.

Secretary of State for Health and Social Care and the Lord Chancellor and Secretary of State for Justice (2021) *Reforming the Mental Health Act*, CP 355, London: TSO.

Urban, J. (2021) *The 2019 Conservative manifesto half-time analysis: what has the Johnson government achieved – and what is left to do?* London: Institute for Government.

8

The less things change: conservatism, COVID-19 and incoherence in education policy

Stephen J. Ball

Introduction

The field of education policy in England is organised and governed by sectors (preschool, compulsory, further education, higher education and adult), each of which has peculiar and specific characteristics. Nonetheless, across these sectors, certainly at present, it is possible to identify a set of recurring policy emphases. This chapter addresses education policy with a primary focus on the compulsory schooling sector. Even so, this is in no way a comprehensive account of compulsory education policy under the Conservatives; that is simply impossible – there is too much policy. Rather it uses the COVID-19 interregnum and the Schools Bill 2022 as moments in which a more general set of issues in relation to education policy played out – issues of governance and issues of inequality.

The 'story' of Conservative education policy from 2015 to 2023 can be told two ways. One highlights some underlying principles that have a 'history' in Conservative political thought; the other emphasises muddle and lack of direction. The chapter gives some consideration to each, and to some extent joins them up by drawing attention to the tensions (in political rationality) and the resulting incoherence (in practice) that arise. That is to say, there are clearly aspects of different political rationalities embedded in the making of Conservative education policy; and at the level of practice, these produce contradictions. However, most policy analysis work begins with an assumption, or brings to bear a perspective, of coherence or planned order, and in this sense the analysis often works to constitute the object of its concern. We lack the tools, and perhaps also the predilection, to address policy as incoherent or absurd.

The education policies of the Conservative governments of Cameron (2015–16), May (2016–19), Johnson (2019–22), Truss (2022) and Sunak (2022–) have exemplified and continued the main trends and tensions initiated by the Conservative administrations led by Margaret Thatcher

(1979–90). First, a neoconservative commitment to traditional and canonical principles and priorities – particularly as regards the school curriculum, a form of 'restorationism' – and concomitantly an assertion of central controls over more and more aspects of education practice. Education is peculiar and exceptional in regard to the importance of this assertive nostalgia. Second, a neoliberal commitment to competition and choice, and a general commodification and commercialisation of education, together with forms of devolution and a 'destatalisation' of provision through the recruitment of businesses and third sector actors to deliver education services, over and against the marginalisation of elected local authorities.

Put another way, this is the putting together of things that do not fit together – the making of policy from disparate, irreconcilable ideological elements that appeal to different parts of the Conservative Party and different sections of the voting public. The neoconservative emphasis rests on a peculiar combination of proscriptions and prescriptions based on ministerial whims and enthusiasms, the predilections of hand-picked experts and the deliberations of various working parties established by the Department for Education. As regards the curriculum, this boils down to a form of cultural restorationism and what I called, many years ago, the 'curriculum of the dead' (Ball, 1993). These prescriptions and proscriptions are part of a more general concentration of powers within the Department for Education and in the hands of the secretary of state. Ironically, Kenneth Baker, a former Conservative education secretary under Margaret Thatcher, attacked the provisions of the Schools Bill 2022 in the House of Lords, saying 'it increases the powers of the Secretary of State and the Department for Education in a way unprecedented since 1870' (Hansard, House of Lords, 2022). Baker himself, Secretary of State for Education in 1988, benefited from almost 150 new powers granted to him by the Education Reform Act 1988. As Fisher noted then: 'The purpose of the Act was not, however, primarily structural. It was driven by an intention to dictate to state schools what was to be taught and how it was to be assessed in an attempt to control from the centre and drive up standards' (2008, p 256). Curriculum restorationism was referenced in a set of hearings of the Education Select Committee, with Nadhim Zahawi (the then Secretary of State) in mid-2022, when the Committee chairman, Robert Halfon, asked what a 'knowledge-rich curriculum' means, complained that the ghosts of the traditionalists were plaguing the Department for Education, questioned why £4 million was being spent on Latin (almost as much as on addressing absenteeism) and asked why financial education, oracy and careers education were not more embedded in schools.

Steadily, since the Education Reform Act 1988, the responsibility for curriculum decision-making has been removed from teachers, while at the same time schools, including new sorts of schools, like academies and free schools, studio schools and university technical colleges, have been, supposedly, granted greater freedoms to determine their provision. In 2012, Michael Gove, a key figure in championing both tradition and equity in education policy, offered a neat semantic resolution of this dissonance. In a speech at Brighton College, a private school, he referred to the 'freedom to concentrate on what matters' (Gove, 2012), where 'what matters', what Apple (2000) calls 'official knowledge', is determined to a considerable extent by the secretary of state. The infusion of this policy mix with forms of 'equality talk', in its most recent iteration, 'levelling up' (Michael Gove was Secretary of State for Levelling Up, Housing and Communities until sacked by Boris Johnson in July 2022, and he was then reinstated by Rishi Sunak in October 2022), adds a further dimension of incoherence. Both diversity of provision and a 'knowledge-rich curriculum' are asserted to be factors in providing greater equality of opportunity to students. Both are articulated with a continuing focus on school performance and performance improvement, driven and measured in a regime of testing and examination, and league tables. This has been reiterated by every Conservative secretary of state since 2010. For example:

Pockets of excellence are fantastic and act as trailblazers for the system, but their impact will be marginal if we cannot find a way for the rest of the system to learn from their success. Because we're not asking schools to do any more than the best schools are already doing.

Our country can't afford a 2-tier education system with London streaking ahead and areas like Knowsley and Medway lagging behind. It's morally wrong and economically self-defeating. (Morgan, 2016)

[R]ight at the core of this government's ambition is building what the Prime Minister called a shared society, and that means driving social mobility for those from disadvantaged backgrounds and those just-managing families: breaking the link between a person's background and where they get to in life.

Our school-led system is driving improvement across England – nearly 1.8 million more children are now in good or outstanding schools than in 2010.

However, there are still 1 million of our children in schools that Ofsted has rated as not good enough and for them [–] that's the education they are getting. They are disproportionately located in areas of disadvantage. (Greening, 2017)

I am clear that we need to improve schools with a history of long-term underperformance. These are the schools which have been judged requires improvement or worse by Ofsted in their last three consecutive full inspections.

I want to bring these schools into strong multi-academy trusts, and I hope to be able to share more details in due course. I will of course consult fully with the sector before making these changes. (Williamson, 2021)

My job as Education Secretary is to make sure that every child, wherever they are from, has the same chance to get on in life. Everything I do, everything, is driven by a clear duty to make excellence the expectation, not the exception, for every child right across our nation.

And I need your help to go further. Standards in some areas of our country are still too low, so we need our best leaders and trusts (that means you) to drive change and level up opportunity. (Zahawi, 2022)

The rhetorics of equity, performance and autonomy are easily joined up in ministerial utterances, as shown in these quotations, but in terms of actual policy they do not translate easily into practice; teachers and school leaders are left to deal with the consequences. As Andrew Marr put it, referring to the Johnson government as a whole: 'we no longer have a government in the sense of a single national authority which knows in a general way what it is about and is taking the nation in a clear direction. We have, instead, a general paralysis – a mush – debilitating, exhausting shapelessness' (2022, p 14).

Within the plethora of Conservative education policies, this chapter takes two points of focus, two moments of policy – the Schools Bill 2022 and government responses to the COVID-19 crisis – as vehicles to explore the tensions adumbrated earlier. These moments are in turn cross-cut with and modified by specific preoccupations with the discourses of performance and equality.

The Schools Bill 2022

Key aspects of the tensions outlined earlier – market relations/devolved responsibilities/diverse providers/innovation, as against centralisation/traditionalism/prescription – are captured very clearly in the original version of the Schools Bill 2022 and the related announcement that launched a review of the relation between the Department for Education and academy trusts. Of the original Bill, the Department for Education (2022c) said:

The current regulatory framework is not fit for a multi-academy trust led system – as the Secretary of State said in his recent speech, 'the current system is in many ways, held together by rubber bands'.

What that means is that the system for regulating trusts hasn't kept pace with the expansion of the academy system. Every academy has a contract with the Department known as a 'funding agreement' – it outlines a set of requirements which academies must follow in order to carry on receiving Government funding. This means the rules individual academies are bound by are dependent on the terms of their funding agreements at the time they are set up. Because of this, there's a mixed picture in terms of the rules academies have to follow.

In June 2022, the Department for Education launched a review of how it works with academy trusts. The review was 'to look at the standards trusts are held to, and the thresholds at which the government uses its powers to intervene in rare cases of underperformance, helping minimise trust failure and retain parents' confidence'. It also announced that '[t]he government intends for all schools to be in or joining strong academy trusts by 2030' (Department for Education, 2022b). Explaining this further, Schools Minister Baroness Barran said:

> not every school is currently in a strong trust or has the option of joining one. Our three-pronged approach between the Schools White Paper, Schools Bill, and our new regulatory review, will change that. It will create a new, higher performing school system that parents love and gives every child every chance of success. (Department for Education, 2022b)

The Department for Education (2022b) claimed that the Bill would enable it to 'maximise academy trusts' innovation and reduce regulatory burdens' while also 'enforcing clear standards' and using 'new powers' to focus 'government action on preventing failure' and improving 'how intervention works'. This semantic fudge (attempting to resolve intervention, standards with innovation and reduced regulation) reflects two competing forms of governance and a response to an unacknowledged policy failure (that is, the failure of a devolved academy system to deliver across-the-board improvements in performance, and the closure and underperformance of specific trusts).

However, within days the Bill ran into difficulties in the House of Lords. As reported in *The Guardian*:

> Ministers have announced a U-turn on key elements of the government's schools bill, scrapping or amending clauses that would have given the Department for Education (DfE) greater control over 'virtually every aspect' of academy trusts in England. [...] Geoff Barton, the general secretary of the Association of School and College Leaders, said the bill 'was a ridiculous attempt to centralise power in

Whitehall over matters which are obviously much better decided by professional educators who know the needs of their schools and their pupils'. (Adams, 2022)

In December 2022, Gillian Keegan, then the fourth secretary of state to have served in six months, announced that given other legislative priorities the government would not be proceeding with the Bill.

Levelling up

The Schools Bill 2022 was also threaded through with a second level of irreconcilability, between a supposed commitment to greater equality in education (the focus of this being on a combination of geography and 'social disadvantage') and a levelling up of performance on the one hand, and the drive to improve performance overall on the other. This tension indicates the most obvious difference between Conservative education policy now (2016–23) and previously (1979–90). That is a rearticulation of policy through the rhetorics of fairness, equity and levelling up. This has been in part 'borrowed' from and inflected by the New Labour and Coalition governments' education policies. In the latter case, for example, the Liberal Democrats insisted on Pupil Premium payments to schools based on their social intake. New Labour gave emphasis to social inclusion and equality of opportunity, within a framework of social obligations rather than social rights, which rested on a very individualised version of inequality and its causes. In the run-up to the 2010 election, taking up this version of social equity, speeches by Conservative shadow ministers spoke repeatedly about poverty, educational inequality, inclusion, mobility, 'the education gap' and the intention of helping 'the very poorest' and 'making opportunity more equal'. In 2019, this was reiterated by Boris Johnson: 'I promised on my first day in Downing Street to make sure every child has equal opportunities to succeed – regardless of their background or where they live. Because I believe that talent and genius is evenly distributed but so often opportunity is not, and my job is to change this' (quoted in Ferguson, 2019).

This 'equality talk' remained in place as part of the Johnson government's levelling up agenda (see Chapter 1). The Department for Education (2022a) said:

Every person should have the same opportunity to make the most of their abilities and succeed in life. But, currently, too many people's chances of getting on in life are adversely affected by where they live. … In education, ability is evenly spread but opportunity is not. We need to ensure that all children are able to access excellent schools, progress to high quality technical and higher education, and go on into good jobs.

This agenda was enacted in a series of diverse programmes and initiatives aimed at ensuring 'a stronger school system, with every school able to access the support they need to improve' (Department for Education, 2022a), with the assumption being that school experience will compensate for and be unaffected by structural inequalities. For example, in February 2022 the Department for Education claimed: 'We've identified 55 'cold spots' of the country where school outcomes are the weakest to target intensive investment, support and action to level up – these areas include Suffolk, Isle of Wight and County Durham' (Department for Education, 2022a). Following up on this, the *Levelling Up* White Paper pledged the creation of a new 'National Academy' to 'support pupils from all backgrounds and areas to succeed at the very highest levels' (HM Government, 2022a, p xxl). The chapter returns to the question of the National Academy later on. It remains to be seen whether and to what extent the Sunak government will pursue the rhetorics of equity.

Coping with COVID-19: biopolitics, inequality and profit

The second point of focus for this chapter is COVID-19. The trends, dissonances and tensions in policy adumbrated earlier were played out in various ways in the COVID-19 interregnum of 2020–21. Thus, in general terms, we saw the government in firm biopolitical mode, at the same time harnessing and creating opportunities for private and third sector participation in the response to COVID-19 and its aftermath. This aftermath is marked by the stark (re)assertion of 'new' and 'old' inequalities. COVID-19 highlighted the continuing unevenness and multiple inequalities within the education system – with, despite a plethora of equity policies, an increasing performance gap (which began before COVID-19) between socially advantaged and disadvantaged students – and the role of specific socioeconomic factors, like digital exclusion, in exacerbating these inequalities. The Department for Education (2021) interim report on pupils' progress in the 2020 to 2021 academic year showed that much of the progress made in reducing the attainment gap for disadvantaged children over the previous decade was eradicated during the pandemic, and significant regional disparities were evident, with pupils in some parts of northern England losing twice as much learning as those in London.

The pandemic made very evident a particular form of government, what Foucault (2010, p 240) calls the '*étatisation du biologique*', meaning nationalisation of the biological, that was manifest in specific ways in relation to education, as for example in relation to the gaps and disparities noted earlier. Lorenzini's characterisation seems particularly apt. She says:

biopolitics is always a politics of *differential vulnerability*. Far from being a politics that erases social and racial inequalities by reminding us of our common belonging to the same biological species, it is a politics that structurally relies on the establishment of hierarchies in the value of lives, producing and multiplying vulnerability as a means of governing people. (Lorenzini, 2021, S43–S44)

Putting it another way, Judith Butler (2020) remarks on 'the rapidity with which radical inequality, nationalism, and capitalist exploitation find ways to reproduce and strengthen themselves within the pandemic zones'.

The outbreak of COVID-19 and state reactions to it made clear the ways in which human biology and life itself have become the subject of governance in contemporary political systems. It demonstrated the intrusiveness of regulation, expanding it from public and social matters to personal life and even the inside of the human body – for example, by the tight monitoring and enforcement of quarantine and self-isolation measures, promotion of apps tracking health, behaviour and movement, calls for certain groups to be isolated and proposals for the introduction of 'immunity passports'. The boundaries between the human body, the person as the object of regulation, and political power have become blurred.[1]

Thus, schools in all parts of the UK were closed to most children by the start of the week commencing Monday 23 March 2020. In England, schools remained open where necessary for vulnerable children and the children of critical workers. Schools remained closed to most pupils until the beginning of the autumn 2020 term – September in England and Wales, and August in Northern Ireland and Scotland. Schools in all four nations opened with the expectation of full attendance for the new 2020–21 school year. Then, during an address to the nation on 4 January 2021, Prime Minister Boris Johnson announced that primary schools, secondary schools and colleges in England would move to remote learning for most pupils until after the February half term, subject to review. Vulnerable pupils and critical workers' children could continue to attend face-to-face provision, and the Department for Education subsequently indicated that special schools and alternative provision would remain open. In England, pupils began returning to schools from 8 March 2021.

During 2020–21, the COVID-19 virus became the main preoccupation of education policy in many countries, at least as regards the number of policy texts issues by governments, even though children were not at school for considerable periods of time. In this biopolitical space of lockdown, edu-businesses acted swiftly to provide free education tools, 'position[ing] educational technology as an integral component of education globally, bringing private sector and commercial organisations into the centre of essential education services' (Williamson and Hogan, 2020, p 1). Google and

Microsoft, for example, in many countries, offered the G Suite for Education and Microsoft 365 Education platforms to school systems with no charge for a limited period (until September 2020), alongside an enormous variety of teaching and learning resources, as well as training on how to use their packages. In England, all of this activity fitted neatly into the government's existing edtech strategy, which was aimed at '[r]ealising the potential of technology in education', and was described as a strategy for education providers and the technology industry to help improve and increase the effective use of technology in education (Department for Education, 2019). The plan was to provide clarity on the challenges that educators face so as to catalyse business investment and drive demand, and to stimulate the edtech market by facilitating opportunities for buyers and sellers to meet, as well as to test products in the real world and build the evidence base on effectiveness of edtech products and services. COVID-19 speeded all of this up and provided for a huge rise in the number of new account holders for the platform providers and opportunities to develop brand loyalty. Since the start of the crisis, for example, the use of Google Classroom has grown 400 per cent.

Generally, in the period of lockdown there was a flourishing of initiatives from providers of educational materials and contents that were offered to schools, teachers and families as ready-to-use solutions to be uploaded onto platforms and learning management systems for use in remote teaching (see the Oak National Academy, discussed later). However, in April 2020, James Leonard, the UK Lead for Google for Education, claimed that England, compared to Northern Ireland, Scotland and Wales, was 'lagging behind from the start of COVID-19 crisis because it lacked a national edtech platform' (Gibbons, 2020). As reported in *TES magazine*, in his speech at the Westminster Education Forum on the future of edtech in England, 'Mr Leonard said a number of schools were "caught out in the rain" partly due to the "decentralised nature of the system"' (Gibbons, 2020). While Wales had already implemented a collection of online tools via Hwb, to ease the adoption of both G Suite and Office 365, and Scotland used Glow Connect and Northern Ireland used C2K Services for Schools, England was still unprepared. Leonard argued for 'an educator-designed and led' national platform for 'useful, secure and reliable resources', and the establishing of 'a unified super-fast broadband infrastructure implemented via Government investment, partnership with Telecom companies and building on existing super-fast networks or approaches', and he concluded that '[w]e need to capture the learning across the UK education system to design more resilience across the sector including digital approaches' (Leonard in Gibbons, 2020).

Within all of this, Google, Microsoft and the other donor companies presented themselves as saviours of education in a time of crisis. They merged business interests and humanitarian endeavours, perfectly enacting what Burns defines as 'the philanthro-capitalism of digital humanitarianism' (2019, p 1107). Outmanoeuvring many of their competitors, Google and Microsoft established themselves as key actors in the education policy process in England, partnering with government and its agencies of education reform to create the potential for systemic change.

However, while the introduction of remote learning brought many long-term benefits for platform and materials providers, it also exacerbated existing inequalities. An Education Endowment Foundation report concluded that: 'school closures are likely to reverse progress made to close the (achievement) gap in the last decade'; 'supporting effective remote learning will mitigate the extent to which the gap widens'; and 'sustained support will be needed to help disadvantaged pupils catch up' (2020, p 4). In particular, the move to remote learning highlighted the socially uneven access to the internet and digital poverty. The likelihood of having access to the internet from home increases along with income, such that in 2018 only 51 per cent of households earning between £6,000 and £10,000 had home internet access compared with 99 per cent of households with an income of over £40,001 (Office for National Statistics, 2019). The link between poverty and digital exclusion is clear: if you are poor, you have less chance of being online. Research done by the Sutton Trust during the period of school closure found that:

> 23% of pupils are reported to be taking part in live and recorded lessons online every day. However, pupils from middle class homes are much more likely to do so (30%), compared to working class pupils (16%). At private schools, 51% of primary and 57% of secondary students have accessed online lessons every day, more than twice as likely as their counterparts in state schools. 50% of teachers in private schools report they are receiving more than three quarters of work back, compared with 27% in the most advantaged state schools, and just 8% in the least advantaged state schools. (Cullinane and Montacute, 2020, p 1)

In February 2021, a blog post by the Institute of Fiscal Studies (Sibieta, 2021) noted that '[b]y the time the pandemic is over, most children across the UK will have missed over half a year of normal, in person schooling. That's likely to be more than 5% of their entire time in school.' It went on to say: 'The negative effects are also likely to extend beyond educational attainment. We are already seeing clear evidence of reductions in mental health among young people, with 27% of young women showing potential mental health problems.' The report also reiterated the unequal effects of school closures, saying '[t]he negative effects are over 50% larger for disadvantaged children'. It added that there is 'the clear possibility that the effects of lost learning could be neutralized for those from well-off families and the long-run negative effects could be concentrated among those from disadvantaged backgrounds'. In addition, a more general point is made:

> The long-run risks to the public finances are also severe. If 30–40 per cent of future lifetime earnings ends up as taxes, then lost earnings of £350 billion would mean over £100 billion less tax revenue over the long-run to spend on public services or paying down the debts we are currently accumulating. (Sibieta, 2021)

In response to such criticisms, the government argued: 'That's why we are launching the £1 billion Covid-19 catch-up plan that will lift outcomes for all pupils, with targeted support for those from disadvantaged backgrounds who are most at risk of falling behind because of this disruption' (Williamson, 2020). However, evidence thus far suggests the catch-up plan has had minimal impact on the performance gap. The COVID-19 pandemic exacerbated existing trends.

Policy and profit

This section looks at some of the ways in which businesses and third sector organisations have been able to 'profit' from the education policy responses to COVID-19 (see Ball, 2018, for a more general discussion of the commercialisation of education).

At the beginning of 2020, the UK government's response to the pandemic in England was overall shambolic and tardy (see Chapter 5). After the government's initial hope of avoiding it, a lockdown and working and studying from home policy for most children was launched, with (at least in policy/theory) schools and colleges switching to home online learning. However, many schools were unprepared to move lessons online, many teachers lacked the skills to deliver online teaching, and many children and their families experienced problems due to shortage of technical equipment or the absence of internet connection, or were unable to afford internet accounts – all of which had been signalled in the 2019 edtech strategy paper (Department for Education, 2019) as systemic problems. This situation stimulated a substantial investment from the state to enable the extension of remote education in the shortest time possible. On 24 April 2020, £105 million of funding was announced to enhance remote education: £85 million for laptops, tablets and 4G dongles; £14 million for technical support to schools; and £6 million to further support the demonstrator schools and colleges programme.

A national open access platform – Oak National Academy – was also established very quickly, led by a third sector organisation and academy sponsor, The Reach Foundation. The platform was built in just over two weeks in

April 2020; the Sutton Trust and education charity Teach First contributed by supplying a small communication team; Johnson Banks, a brand design agency, provided a captivating brand identity, an acorn falling as a metaphor of how education works: 'As it falls, it releases seeds and renews' (Johnson Banks, 2020); iPLM, a software firm, and Havas, a French public relations company, also provided services; Google offered technological support for free. Initially the government provided £4.84 million in funding for the initiative.

The plan was to keep the digital academy open throughout the following school year, envisaging a platform that could provide learning support both in school and at home in case of local lockdowns, or if children needed to shield or were ill, but there was no attempt to address the digital divide noted earlier. The creation of Oak National Academy is a particular example of what Peck and Theodore (2015) call 'fast policy'. That is to say, policy that is imbued with 'heightened immediacy, saliency, and indeed urgency' and which is played out and the brought to realisation within a 'compressed policymaking moment' (Peck and Theodore, 2015, p xvii).

In 2021, it was announced that Oak would stay open and free to use for at least the next two terms, after the Department for Education approved another grant worth £2.1 million. In August 2022, it was announced that Oak National Academy would become a public body, but would remain 'fully independent'. However, several organisations associated with it expressed concerns about the influence of government, with both the chief executive and board roles being subject to public appointment rules. This is another example of the tensions between devolved activities and more centralised control.

Alongside this, as noted previously, the government launched a national catch-up programme, with special provisions for disadvantaged students to address lost time for learning and the increasing performance gap; this included the National Tutoring Programme. A total of 32 organisations, including charities, a school partnership and private firms, were selected as 'Tuition Partners' by the Education Endowment Foundation, which received £76 million to run the initiative on behalf of government in its first year. Schools could choose between different providers and a variety of models, including face-to-face and online tutoring, and were able to book tutoring with Tuition Partners. Approximately 15,000 tutors were involved in the scheme.

As part of the second element of the programme, 188 'Academic Mentors', recruited and trained by Teach First, were given the mission 'to build a fair education for all'. Mentors were to provide intensive academic support to students most in need. In total, Teach First received £6.8 million from government to run this initiative.

In February 2021, the government announced the appointment of Sir Kevan Collins, Chief Executive of the Education Endowment Foundation, as Education Recovery Commissioner. It was announced that 'Sir Kevan will report directly to the Education Secretary and the Prime Minister, and will consult closely with parents, teachers and schools as part of his role' (Prime Minister's Office, 2021). However, in June 2021, Sir Kevan resigned in protest over what he described as the Prime Minister's scaled-down recovery plan, warning, that it '"does not come close" to meeting the needs of children whose education has been thrown into chaos by the pandemic' (Weale, 2021a).

Even before Sir Kevan's resignation, *The Guardian* had reported that one of the providers approved by the Education Endowment Foundation, Third Space Learning, was employing tutors in Sri Lanka as young as 17 and paid as little as £1.50 (425 Sri Lankan rupees) for each session of tuition (Weale, 2021b). When the programme was funded to continue for a second year, a £25 million contract for its delivery was awarded to the Dutch multinational human relations company Randstad, which has offices in 38 countries spread across five continents and an annual turnover of £17 billion.

Conclusion

Considering education policy trends in England between 1979 and 2023, there are many continuities and recurrences. These include neoliberal techniques such as the use of market forms, the disarticulation of the state system, the use of private companies and third sector organisations for delivery of state services (Ball, 2018a), the deregulation of teacher education and sidelining of the role of local authorities, and the use of performance management techniques to drive a 'standards' agenda (Ball, 2012). Thus, the Conservatives have pursued and expanded the academies and free schools programmes and introduced other new kinds of schools run by non-state providers. The ill-fated 2022 White Paper anticipated all schools becoming academies or free schools by 2030 (HM Government, 2022b). There was also, across New Labour and the Coalition and Conservative governments, a rhetorical political discourse with some similarities, focusing on equity and social justice. However, this translates differently into policy, with the Conservatives emphasising social mobility through mechanisms like grammar schools and 'traditional' practices in pedagogy and curriculum. These have been supplemented by programmes of character education and resilience, and de-emphasising structural factors of social disadvantage (neoconservative emphases). We can see trends and emphases but also U-turns, funding withdrawals, passing fads and knee-jerk reactions.

Alongside 'competition', 'freedom and diversity' and 'innovation', the educational apparatus is animated and inundated by a bewildering and reactive form of 'policy hyperactivity' – mostly aimed at raising performance and tying educational outcomes more directly to the needs of the economy and employment. Within this, edtech was given a particular priority, not just during the COVID-19 pandemic but also before, although the government announced the closure of the demonstrator schools programme in the summer of 2022.

The result of all this in terms of education policy overall is an incoherence and a set of stubborn contradictions (Ball, 2018b), both within policy itself and in terms of its outcomes in the education system. Schools are being expected to be both innovative and conservative, to deliver social mobility and social cohesion, to improve cognitive and noncognitive skills, to be collaborative and entrepreneurial. There is centralisation and fragmentation at the same time; there is deregulation, dissolution, deconcentration and the recruitment of non-state actors in all aspects of policy, and intervention, prescription and regulation at the same time. In the midst of this hyperactivity, policy begets policy as new 'solutions' are generated to respond to the failures, inadequacies and inefficacies of previous fixes. Schools must make sense of, respond to and enact (or not) a constant stream of initiatives, funding streams and programmes, alongside continually changing measures, indicators, targets and benchmarks, all of which contribute to increasing workloads (Sellen, 2016).

This mix of deconcentration and intervention begets ever more complex forms of segregation and inequality while delivering an impoverished curriculum to children who are increasingly stressed by the demands of performance, many of whom experience low levels of individual well-being, without any clear sense of purpose and value other than that which can be calculated from test scores and examination grades. The increased participation of businesses and third sector organisations as key actors in education policy and service delivery, and new expert voices and new public–private partnerships, are established as passage points for the design of the future of education. During her short-lived government, Liz Truss pitched herself as the 'education prime minister' with a plan that included replacing failing academies with 'a new wave of free schools' and improving maths and literacy standards (PA Media, 2022b). Rishi Sunak's Education Secretary, Gillian Keegan (appointed in October 2022), continued to focus on the same issues but was initially primarily occupied with the demands made by teachers for increased pay and the related strike actions.

The direction of policy over this period indicates both greater control of and greater diversification of provision – privatisation and marketisation – and further increases in inequality and overall reductions in expenditure in real terms (despite announced funding increases). There was a continuing emphasis on STEM (science, technology, engineering and mathematics) subjects and on tradition and nostalgia in forms of provision, such as grammar schools and apprenticeships, combining selection with vocational/academic divisions. Keegan also had to confront gender issues of various kinds and faced calls to revisit the question of school inspection grades in the light of the suicide of headteacher Ruth Perry in January 2023 (BBC News, 2023). Education policy is therefore perhaps not so much directionless as moving in different directions at the same time.

Note

1 Biopolitics generally refers to applying specific knowledge from statistics, demography, epidemiology and biology in order to govern individuals and groups. Foucault (2010) argues that biopolitical technology found its pure expression of power through medicine – which he calls a power/knowledge that can be applied to both the body and the population, and therefore has both disciplinary effects and regulatory effects.

References

Adams, R. (2022a) 'Nadhim Zahawi makes U-turn on schools bill after criticism', *The Guardian*, 30 June. Available at: www.theguardian.com/education/2022/jun/30/government-announces-u-turn-on-schools-bill-after-criticism (accessed 25 April 2023).

Apple, M. (2000) *Official knowledge: democratic education in a Conservative age*, New York: Routledge.

Ball, S.J. (1993) 'Education, Majorism and "the curriculum of the dead"', *Curriculum Studies*, 1(2): 195–214.

Ball, S.J. (2012) 'Performativity, commodification and commitment: an I-spy guide to the neoliberal university', *British Journal of Educational Studies*, 60(1): 17–28.

Ball, S.J. (2018a) 'Commericalising education: profiting from reform!', *Journal of Education Policy*, 33(5): 587–9.

Ball, S.J. (2018b) 'The tragedy of state education in England: reluctance, compromise and muddle—a system in disarray', *Journal of the British Academy*, 6: 207–38.

BBC News (2023) 'Halt Ofsted inspections after Ruth Perry's death, says sister', 21 April. Available at: www.bbc.com/news/education-65339944 (accessed 24 April 2023).

Burns, R. (2019) 'New frontiers of philanthro-capitalism: digital technologies and humanitarianism', *Antipode*, 51(4): 1101–22.

Butler, J. (2020) 'Capitalism has its limits', *Verso*, 30 March. Available at: www.versobooks.com/en-gb/blogs/news/4603-capitalism-has-its-limits (accessed 25 April 2022).

Cullinane, C. and Montacute, R. (2020) *Research brief, April 2020. COVID-19 and social mobility impact brief #1: school shutdown*, London: The Sutton Trust.

Department for Education (2019) *Realising the potential of technology in education: a strategy for education providers and the technology industry*, London: Department for Education.

Department for Education (2021) *Understanding progress in the 2020/21 academic year: complete findings from the spring term*, London: Department for Education.

Department for Education (2022a) 'How we are levelling up education all over the country', *The Education Hub*, 1 February. Available at: https://educationhub.blog.gov.uk/2022/02/01/how-we-are-levelling-up-education-all-over-the-country/ (accessed 25 April 2023).

Department for Education (2022b) 'Review launches to future proof role of academy trusts', *Gov.uk*, 29 June. Available at: www.gov.uk/government/news/review-launches-to-future-proof-role-of-academy-trusts (accessed 25 April 2022).

Department for Education (2022c) 'What the Schools Bill means for academies', *The Education Hub*, 24 June. Available at: https://educationhub.blog.gov.uk/2022/06/24/what-the-schools-bill-means-for-academies/ (accessed 25 April 2023).

Education Endowment Foundation (2020) *Impact of school closures on the attainment gap: rapid evidence assessment*, London: Education Endowment Foundation.

Ferguson, K. (2019) 'BOJO SCHOOLS BOOST Boris Johnson vows to give every child a "world class education" as he hands schools £2.6billion in funding', *The Sun*, 11 October. Available at: www.thesun.co.uk/news/10111000/boris-johnson-child-world-class-education/ (accessed 25 April 2022).

Fisher, T. (2008) 'The era of centralisation: the 1988 Education Reform Act and its consequences', *FORUM: for promoting 3–19 comprehensive education*, 50(2): 255–61.

Foucault, M. (2010) *Society must be defended: lectures at the Collège de France, 1975–76*, London: Penguin.

Gibbons, A. (2020) 'Google: England behind on edtech from start of crisis' *TES magazine*, 30 June.

Gove, M. (2012) 'Education Secretary Michael Gove's speech to Brighton College', *Gov.uk*, 10 May. Available at: www.gov.uk/government/speeches/education-secretary-michael-goves-speech-to-brighton-college (accessed 25 April 2022).

Greening, J. (2017) 'Justine Greening: education at the core of social mobility', *Gov.uk*, 18 January. Available at: www.gov.uk/government/speeches/justine-greening-education-at-the-core-of-social-mobility (accessed 25 April 2022).

Hansard, House of Lords (2022) 23 May, vol 822, col 689.

HM Government (2022a) *Levelling up the United Kingdom*, CP 604, London: HMSO.

HM Government (2022b) *Opportunity for all: strong schools with great teachers for your child*, CP 650, London: TSO.

Johnson Banks (2020) 'Oak National Academy: as the acorn falls'. Available at: www.johnsonbanks.co.uk/work/oak-national-academy (accessed 16 April 2022).

Lorenzini, D. (2021) 'Biopolitics in the time of Coronavirus', *Critical Inquiry*, 47(52): S40–S45.

Marr, A. (2022) 'Courts, rivers, teeth: No 10 has shed its responsibilities', *New Statesman*, 25 May.

Morgan, N. (2016) 'Nicky Morgan: educational excellence everywhere', *Gov.uk*, 17 March. Available at: www.gov.uk/government/speeches/nicky-morgan-educational-excellence-everywhere#:~:text=Our%20country%20can%27t%20afford,directing%20and%20driving%20from%20Whitehall (accessed 25 April 2022).

Office for National Statistics (2019) *Exploring the UK's digital divide*, London: Office for National Statistics.

PA Media (2022b) 'Liz Truss pitches herself as the "education prime minister"', *The Guardian*, 30 July. Available at: www.theguardian.com/polit ics/2022/jul/30/liz-truss-pitches-herself-as-the-education-prime-minister (accessed 26 April 2023).

Peck, J. and Theodore, N. (2015) *Fast policy: experimental statecraft at the thresholds of neoliberalism*, Minneapolis: University of Minnesota Press.

Peruzzo, F., Ball, S.J. and Grimaldi, E. (2022) 'Peopling the crowded education state: heterarchical spaces, edtech markets and new modes of governing during the COVID-19 pandemic', *International Journal of Educational Research*, 114(1): 1–13.

Prime Minister's Office (2021) 'New Commissioner appointed to oversee education catch-up', *Gov.uk*, 3 February. Available at: www.gov.uk/gov ernment/news/new-commissioner-appointed-to-oversee-education-catch-up (accessed 26 April 2022).

Sellen, P. (2016) *Teacher workload and professional development in England's secondary schools: insights from TALIS*, London: Education Policy Institute.

Sibieta, L. (2021) 'The crisis in lost learning calls for a massive national policy response', *Institute for Fiscal Studies*, 1 February, Available at https://ifs. org.uk/articles/crisis-lost-learning-calls-massive-national-policy-response (accessed 2 February 20212).

Weale, S. (2021a) 'Education recovery chief quits in English schools catch-up row', *The Guardian*, 2 June. Available at: www.theguardian.com/politics/2021/ jun/02/education-recovery-chief-kevan-collins-quit-english-schools-catch-up-row (accessed 26 April 2022).

Weale, S. (2021b) 'UK tutoring scheme uses under-18s in Sri Lanka paid as little as £1.57 an hour', *The Guardian*, 19 March. Available at: www.theg uardian.com/education/2021/mar/19/uk-tutoring-scheme-uses-sri-lan kan-under-18s-paid-as-little-as-157-an-hour (accessed 26 April 2022).

Williamson, B. and Hogan, A. (2020) *Commercialisation and privatisation in/of education in the context of Covid-19*, Brussels: Education International.

Williamson, G. (2020) 'Education Secretary's statement on coronavirus (COVID-19): 19 June 2020', *Gov.uk*, 22 June. Available at: www.gov.uk/government/speeches/education-secretarys-statement-on-coronavirus-covid-19-19-june-2020 (accessed 26 April 2022).

Williamson, G. (2021) 'Education Secretary speech to the Confederation of School Trusts', *Gov.uk*, 28 April. Available at: www.gov.uk/government/speeches/education-secretary-speech-to-the-confederation-of-school-trusts (accessed 25 April 2022).

Zahawi, N. (2022) 'Education Secretary addresses Confederation of School Trusts Annual Conference', *Gov.uk*, 16 June. Available at: www.gov.uk/government/speeches/education-secretary-addresses-confederation-of-school-trusts-annual-conference (accessed 25 April 2022).

9

Conservative housing policy in England

Peter Somerville

Introduction

Conservative housing policy is based on two key commitments: increasing home ownership (going back to the 1920s); and promoting a market in renting for those who cannot afford or prefer not to buy their own home (particularly since the 1980s). This chapter considers Conservative policies since 2015 on new housebuilding, changes in housing tenure, homelessness, housing conditions and 'levelling up'. It concludes that these policies have largely failed, or are very likely to fail, to meet their aims. In some cases, they seem irrelevant to meeting need or serving a public good.

Responsibility for housing in the UK is devolved to its constituent nations (Torrance, 2022), so for the sake of brevity, this chapter focuses on England.

300,000 new homes a year?

The total numbers of households in England rose by an average of around 200,000 a year in the 1950s and 1960s, 130,000 a year in the 1970s, 200,000 a year in the 1980s, and 110,000 a year in the 1990s. From 2000 to 2010–11 the numbers increased by a total of approximately 1.6 million (an average of around 160,000 a year), and from 2010–11 to 2020–21 they rose by approximately 2.1 million (an average of around 210,000 a year; Table 9.1). In comparison, housing completions in England averaged just over 114,000 a year from 2011 to 2014, and slightly over 159,000 a year from 2015 to 2021 (Table 9.2). Therefore, although housing completions have increased significantly since 2015, they are still sufficient only to meet the level of increased demand from 2000 to 2010, and they fall far short of meeting the increased demand from 2010 to 2020, which would require at least 210,000 new homes a year (and this takes no account of pent-up housing demand from earlier years, and indeed decades).

In their 2015 election manifesto, the Conservatives committed to delivering a million new homes by the end of 2020 (Conservative Party, 2015). In their 2017 election manifesto, they reaffirmed this commitment

Table 9.1: Trends in tenure, households in England (thousands)

Year	Owner-occupiers	Council tenants	Housing association tenants	Total social housing tenants	Private tenants	Total
1961	5,990			3,240	4,690	13,920
1971	8,060			4,640	3,240	15,940
1981	9,860			5,461	1,904	17,225
1991	13,050			4,435	1,824	19,309
2001	14,358			3,983	2,062	20,403
2010–11	14,450	1,835	1,992	3,826	3,617	21,893
2011–12	14,388	1,782	2,026	3,808	3,843	22,040
2012–13	14,337	1,684	2,000	3,684	3,956	21,977
2013–14	14,319	1,641	2,279	3,920	4,377	22,617
2014–15	14,324	1,639	2,272	3,912	4,278	22,514
2015–16	14,330	1,605	2,313	3,918	4,528	22,776
2016–17	14,444	1,566	2,381	3,947	4,692	23,083
2017–18	14,784	1,581	2,377	3,958	4,530	23,272
2018–19	15,018	1,591	2,372	3,963	4,552	23,534
2019–20	15,362	1,581	2,398	3,978	4,438	23,778
2020–21	15,540	1,570	2,414	3,984	4,434	23,958

Source: Adapted from Office for National Statistics (2022a)

Table 9.2: Housing completions, England

Housing completions	Private enterprise	Housing associations	Local authorities	Total
2011	85,890	25,950	2,230	114,030
2012	88,750	25,440	1,410	115,590
2013	87,010	21,600	840	109,450
2014	92,850	23,790	1,180	117,820
2015	110,700	30,130	1,660	142,480
2016	115,350	24,430	2,110	141,880
2017	133,460	27,290	1,750	162,470
2018	135,220	27,580	2,680	165,490
2019	143,690	32,000	2,190	177,880
2020	121,140	25,470	1,290	147,890
2021	142,590	31,290	1,610	175,480

Source: Adapted from Department for Levelling Up, Housing and Communities (2022c, Table 213)
Note: totals are not exactly equivalent due to rounding up.

and added a further commitment to 'deliver half a million more by the end of 2022' (Conservative Party, 2017, p 70). In their 2019 manifesto, they set a target of 300,000 new homes a year by the mid-2020s and 'at least 1 million more homes over the next Parliament' (Conservative Party, 2019, p 31), an average of 200,000 a year. However, by the end of 2020, only 795,610 homes had been completed, well short of the 2015 commitment, and the additional 2017 commitment of 500,000 over 2021 and 2022 was highly unlikely to have been met either, given that 175,480 homes were completed in 2021 and the figure for 2022 was likely to be similar. Even the commitment to deliver at least 200,000 new homes a year from 2020 is not yet being met.

Since 2015, government policies to reach these targets have included: starter homes or first homes; direct commissioning of housing by government; the Help to Buy scheme (started in 2013, extended to 2023); the long-standing Affordable Homes Programme; permitted development rights; and further planning reforms. Each of these is considered in this chapter (earlier failed policies such as the New Homes Bonus and the Community Right to Build (Somerville, 2016) have been quietly dropped or otherwise ceased to function). London is commonly treated separately from the rest of England because of its significantly greater housing pressures and higher house prices, and because of the strategic housing powers devolved to the Mayor of London (Brown, 2020).

Starter Homes/First Homes

Following a 2015 election manifesto commitment, the Housing and Planning Act 2016 provided for a 20 per cent discount on the market value of 200,000 new homes for first-time buyers under the age of 40, up to a maximum price of £250,000 outside London and £450,000 in London – this was known as the Starter Home initiative. A sum of £2.3 billion was earmarked to fund 60,000 of these homes, and £250 million was spent by mid-2018 on acquiring and preparing land for this purpose. However, the provision turned out to be unaffordable for most households, and, not surprisingly, the National Audit Office (2019, p 8) found that no houses had actually been built.

A new policy, called First Homes, replaced the failed Starter Home initiative. This was launched in 2021 and looks much the same as the original, applying to new homes priced up to £250,000 (£420,000 in London), but now on offer with at least 30 per cent discount, and is funded by developers as part of a planning agreement with local authorities. Eligible buyers are local people or key workers with annual household incomes of up to £80,000 (£90,000 in London), and the discount will be passed on to future buyers. However, in view of the continuing problem of unaffordability (Somerville, 2016), this policy is unlikely to be much more successful than its predecessor, and the number of households benefiting from the scheme is likely to be small.

Direct commissioning and 'accelerated construction'

In 2015, the government identified five pilot sites on which it planned to directly commission 13,000 new homes. Lack of progress on this policy by 2017 led to it being overtaken by the ironically named Accelerated Construction Programme (Wilson, 2021, p 29), in which the government worked with the construction industry to develop surplus public land. Funding for this was not made available until 2019. Work has since started on a number of sites, but so far the only completed scheme is for 550 homes in Northstowe.

Help to Buy

The policy of Help to Buy, initiated by the Coalition government in 2013, continues to be the government's key policy for increasing the amount of housing in England. As Somerville notes: 'Help to Buy ... is the only policy that can be shown to have achieved the Coalition's aim of increasing the number of available homes to buy' (2016, p 161). Help to Buy offers an equity loan in which the government lends up to 20 per cent of the value of a new build home (40 per cent in London), interest-free for the first five years, and enables people to buy with a minimum 5 per cent deposit.

Completions of Help to Buy secured through an equity loan have amounted to 355,634 from 2013 to 2021, peaking at over 50,000 a year in 2018 and 2019 (Department for Levelling Up, Housing and Communities, 2022b). These increased more or less in tandem with private sector completions as a whole and numbers of owner-occupiers from 2013 to 2019 (Ministry of Housing, Communities and Local Government, 2021a). However, it is not clear how many of these homes are additional to what would have been constructed without the loan provision or how the scheme might impact on house prices. Carozzi et al (2020) compared the situation at the border between London (40 per cent loan) and the rest of England (20 per cent loan) with the situation at the border between England (20 per cent loan) and Wales (no loan). They found that new build prices rose 6 per cent more within London than outside, but construction activity was not appreciably different. At the England/Wales border, however, they found significant increases in construction activity in England (sales rise of 8 per cent compared with Wales), but house prices did not rise more on England's side of the border. It appears, therefore, that Help to Buy results in additional homes outside London but not in London. In London in particular, where households are in greatest need of assistance to buy their own homes, the scheme produced no additional homes and inflated prices by more than the value of the government loan – that is, the scheme's value for money is negative. The only real winners in London seem to be property owners and developers. More generally, it could be that in an area where housing supply is not constrained, increased demand results in increased supply, whereas in an area where housing supply is constrained, increased demand results in higher prices.

Affordable Homes Programme

The Affordable Homes Programme (originally launched in 2011) is the main source of funding for new homes to buy or rent by households who would otherwise be at risk of losing out in the housing market. Total housing completions in England *outside* London under this policy amounted to 186,423 from 2011–12 to 2015–16 (Homes England, 2019) and 180,526 from 2016–17 to 2020–21 (Homes England, 2022). Therefore, despite significant changes in the nature of provision (such as a major shift from social rent to affordable rent from 2011 to 2016 and an increase in marketed provision since 2018), it is clear that the overall contribution to the total number of homes resulting from this provision has remained more or less the same over the whole decade, at around 36,000–37,000 homes a year. Consequently, it cannot be said that this programme has been responsible for the increased rate of completions since 2015, noted earlier. And this historical rate of completions under the Affordable Homes Programme is set to decline under the 2021–26 programme, since the goal is 130,000 new homes by 2026 (amounting to only 26,000 a year), and the level of funding works out at more or less the same as In 2016–21, at just over £7 billion (Elliott, 2020; Ministry of Housing, Communities and Local Government, 2020b).

The Greater London statistics show housing completions of 56,717 for the period 2011–12 to 2015–16 and 43,494 for 2016–17 to 2020–21 – that is, a *lower* rate of completions since 2015 (down from 11,372 a year to 8,699 a year; Greater London Authority, 2022). However, the £4 billion allocated to the Greater London Authority for 2021–26 looks generous compared to the £7 billion for the rest of the country (Ministry of Housing, Communities and Local Government, 2020b), which seems inconsistent with the 'levelling up' agenda (discussed later). The deal reached by the Mayor of London is expected to result in 79,000 starts over 2021–26, with over half of the first tranche of 29,456 homes being for social rent (Mayor of London, 2021). This is potentially a considerable improvement on earlier periods, not only in terms of numbers of affordable homes but also in the genuineness of their affordability (as socially rented).

Over the years, and despite an increasing variety of policies, it can be concluded that performance has so far failed to match the government's rhetoric on the provision of 'affordable' homes. The National Audit Office confirmed that the 2021 Affordable Homes Programme is not on course to meet its targets by 2026 and that its business case for this 'did not follow best practice' (2022, p 7).

Permitted development rights

Permitted development rights allow certain changes to a building without having to apply for planning permission. It is commonly believed that increasing such rights must lead to more homes being built or more existing buildings changed to residential use, with the downside being that the homes risk being of lower quality and/or detrimental to the area. The House of Lords Built Environment Committee noted: 'Nearly 73,000 new homes were added to the housing stock through change of use permitted development rights between 2015/16 and 2019/20. Of these, 64,798 (89%) were created through office to residential conversions' (2022, p 62).

However, the Royal Institution of Chartered Surveyors found that permitted development rights office-to-residential schemes were 'significantly worse' than those which had been through the full planning process in terms of space standards, lack of amenity space and lack of residential amenities (Clifford et al, 2018, p 5). The permitted change of use has also resulted in multimillion-pound losses for local authorities because of the loss of developer contributions for around 13,500 affordable homes through Section 106 agreements (Local Government Association, 2020) and loss of planning application fees (Clifford et al, 2018). Clifford et al (2020) report that only 22 per cent of the conversions met national space standards compared with 73 per cent of planning permission homes, and they were often considerably below those standards, with some dwellings having no windows at all. Following the latter report, the government required all habitable rooms of such housing to have adequate natural light (Clifford et al, 2020), but the space standards were still described by the lead researcher, in a press release, as 'appalling' (UCL, 2020). This does not sound like a viable way forward for meeting housing need.

Planning reforms

It is commonly believed that developers blame planners for what they see as unnecessary red tape and delays in getting their applications approved and work started on site, while planners accuse builders of profiteering, in particular from land banking (that is, holding onto land with planning permission on the assumption that it will increase in value so that they can make more profit). The truth, however, is often more complicated, with developers wanting to make profits as quickly as possible and planners trying to ensure that the development is fully appropriate and of the required standard.

The National Planning Policy Framework, introduced in 2012, provides a general presumption in favour of development. This framework, however, has been repeatedly amended by: extending the scope of permitted development rights in 2015; announcing measures in 2017 to ease housing development but not taking them further; introducing a new standard method of assessing housing need in 2018, changing that standard in 2020 (Ministry of Housing, Communities and Local Government, 2020a) and changing it again in 2021 (Barton and Grimwood, 2021); and proposing mandatory housing targets for local authorities to reach the national target of 300,000 more homes a year (Ministry of Housing, Communities and Local Government, 2020c) and then abandoning this mandate in December 2022 (see Wright, 2023).

This continual changing of policy makes effective local planning impossible. Research for the Campaign to Protect Rural England in 2020 found that only 30 per cent of local authorities had a local plan in place (Campaign to Protect Rural England, 2020). The House of Lords Built Environment Committee noted that '[w]hen the future of planning is uncertain, landowners are reluctant to sell land for development' – because they might want to wait to see if its value rises or they may be anxious about the type of development that might be permitted – 'developers are reluctant to submit plans that they may have to change later, and councils are hesitant about drafting or approving new local plans' –because they might result in more housing than they would like and/or in areas they regard as unsuitable (2022, p 48). So the government's persistent and increasing pressure for housing development appears to have had the opposite effect to what was intended.

Notwithstanding, the planning system is still working, with 90 per cent of applications being approved, and planners can hardly be blamed for 1.1 million homes with planning permission in the last decade still not being built (House of Lords Built Environment Committee, 2022, p 68). This also casts doubt on the common belief that '[i]nadequate land release is the principal hindrance to new home construction' (Lund, 2019, p 248). Some commentators have argued that the main reason for lack of housing development is England's system of land ownership, which rewards people simply for holding onto agricultural land (with exemption from Council Tax and Inheritance Tax, and subsidies based on the amount of land involved), whose value increases with planning permission and with increasing scarcity (Shrubsole, 2019; Hetherington, 2021). A land value tax is commonly proposed, not least by economists (Jessop, 2017), to stimulate new housing development (Hughes et al, 2020) and reduce the inequality between owners and non-owners of land, but this has never been Conservative policy.

An important cause of the failure to build enough housing is the collapse of new build in the public sector. From 1970 to 2008, the rate of private sector new housing completions fluctuated between 130,000 and 200,000 a year, falling below 100,000 a year from 2009 to 2015 (Lund, 2019) and then rising to nearly 144,000 in 2019 (Table 9.2). Public sector completions, however, plummeted from nearly 150,000 a year in the 1970s down to under 23,000 a year between 1998 and 2007 (Lund, 2019), and these have only recovered to around 34,000 in 2019 (Table 9.2). Arguably, therefore, building far fewer than 300,000 homes a year is due mainly to a failure of the public sector to provide enough investment in affordable housing.

Given this record of failure, it seems highly unlikely that a target of 300,000 new permanent homes a year will be built in England in the foreseeable future. Indeed, the concept of an overarching national target may be a mistake, given that in many areas of England housing completions are already higher than assessed housing need or homes planned for (House of Lords Built Environment Committee, 2022). Worth noting also is the estimate that 'under current policy, housing alone [specifically the 300,000 new homes target] would consume 113% of England's cumulative carbon budget for 2050' (zu Ermgassen et al, 2022).

Housing tenure

Discussions of housing policy tend to begin with a summary of historical changes in housing tenure (see Table 9.1). Traditionally dominated by private renting up to the First World War, this tenure declined from a peak of around 6.5 million households in 1953 to a trough of 1.7 million in 1988. After that, however, it recovered to reach a new peak of 4.7 million in 2016–17, from which it has fallen back slightly to 4.4 million in 2020–21. In contrast, owner-occupation increased year on year from 4.1 million in 1953 to a peak of 14.7 million in 2003, then averaging at that level until 2008–09. It then declined slightly to 14.3 million in 2012–13, but from 2015–16 rose again to 15.5 million in 2020–21 – the largest annual increases since the 1980s. Council housing rose from only a few thousand in the early 20th century to a peak of 5.5 million in 1981, then declining to 1.6 million by 2013–14, with little change since. Housing association homes have increased from only a few thousand in 1974 to 2.4 million in 2020–21.

Homeownership

As implied in the earlier discussion, the increase in homeownership since 2013–14 (Table 9.1) can be attributed to some extent to Help to Buy, but not entirely. It cannot be due to homeownership becoming more affordable generally, because it has not   the gap between incomes and house prices continues to grow in all regions in England, as does the gap between the most and least affordable local authority areas (Office for National Statistics, 2022b; for a useful historical account, see McMullan et al, 2021). The Right to Buy scheme continues to be important, encouraged by increased discounts from 2012, rising further in line with the Consumer Price Index since 2014, resulting in 18,100 sales in 2016–17, but declining to 15,288 in 2019–20 and further to 9,319 sales in 2020–21 (Department for Levelling Up, Housing and Communities, 2022d; for a useful review, see Eardley, 2022). This addition to owner-occupation looks small, however, when compared with that made by Help to Buy.

Much of the recent rise in homeownership, therefore, remains to be explained. Possible causes include continuing recovery from austerity, declining relative attraction of the private rented sector (see later discussion) and greater use of the 'bank of mum and dad'. It is a decisive reversal of the preceding slight decline in homeownership, which has been attributed to the rise of buy-to-let (Somerville, 2016).

Since at least the 1970s, many measures have been proposed that appear to make it easier to access owner-occupation but whose main effect is to increase demand, which results in higher house prices and make access more difficult. Governments of different colours have treated the issue superficially (for example, by providing subsidies or credit) and ended up in failure, with house prices rising too high relative to household incomes.

Council housing

The Coalition government ended with proposals to require local housing authorities to sell their more expensive housing and transfer the receipts to the Exchequer (Somerville, 2016) and to require higher-income council tenants to pay market rent (so-called 'pay to stay'). These anti-council housing policies were enshrined in the Conservatives' Housing and Planning Act 2016, along with proposals to make fixed-term tenancies mandatory for local authorities. All of these measures, however, ran counter to the Conservatives' long-held commitment to localism, residential stability and mixed communities. If implemented, they would have served to further residualise and stigmatise council tenants as a group (for a detailed assessment of the Housing and Planning Act 2016, see Bowie, 2017).

Following the Grenfell fire in 2017, the government appeared to have a change of heart and published a Green Paper in 2018 entitled *A New Deal for Social Housing* (Ministry of Housing, Communities and Local Government, 2018). In this, they promised to listen to tenants' views and not implement the Housing and Planning Act provisions that force councils to sell off their higher-value homes (p 59) or to have fixed-term tenancies instead of so-called 'lifetime' tenancies (at least not 'at this time' in the latter case;

p 65). 'Pay to stay' also seems to have been dropped off the agenda, as it depended on ending lifetime tenancies (strictly speaking, council tenants do not have lifetime tenancies, but periodic tenancies that are renewed on regular payment of rent, though they have some protection against eviction and basic tenancy rights originally conferred under the Housing Act 1980).

This Green Paper was followed, belatedly, by a White Paper, *The Charter for Social Housing Residents* (Ministry of Housing, Communities and Local Government, 2020d), and then the Social Housing (Regulation) Bill (Cromarty, 2023). These measures help to ensure the health and safety of people living in council and housing association housing by increasing responsibilities and powers for the regulator and for the Housing Ombudsman Service, requiring stronger resident engagement by landlords and reviewing the Decent Homes Standard. However, they have nothing to say about the ongoing disruption and destruction of council tenants' lives caused by so-called 'regeneration' in areas of London in particular (Watt, 2021), nor about climate change, nor about welfare reform – social housing is not even mentioned in the government's 2023 publication *Powering up Britain* (HM Government, 2023).

Housing associations

The key policy affecting housing associations is the seismic shift of new housing provision away from social rent and towards affordable rent from 2011 to 2017 (Homes England, 2019, p 9). This is in line with the government's primary aim to foster a more free housing market (Somerville, 2016). However, due to the increasing unaffordability of affordable rents (at 80 per cent of market rents) and the 1 per cent a year cut in social rents from 2016 to 2020, which damaged housing association new build plans, the number of new affordable rent completions peaked at 30,834 in 2014–15 and fell by more than half in succeeding years right up to 2021–22 (Homes England, 2022). As a result, the affordable renting programme is producing far fewer new homes than the old social renting programme did before 2011. Overall, new housing completions by housing associations since 2011 have fluctuated between just over 20,000 a year (in 2013) and just over 30,000 a year (in 2015, 2019 and 2021). Clearly, the *Strategic Plan 2018/19–2022/23* to 'accelerate' housebuilding (Homes England, 2018) has not yet borne fruit.

The so-called 'voluntary right to buy' is perhaps also worth mentioning. Extending the right to buy to housing associations was originally proposed back in the 1980s, but this was withdrawn because at that time the government wanted housing associations to become more like private landlords and also because it would have damaged the status of charitable housing associations. The idea was revived by the Coalition government, who wanted to introduce something similar to the right to buy for council tenants, but were persuaded to reach an agreement with the National Housing Federation (which represents housing associations) whereby housing associations would receive compensation for selling homes to tenants at a discount but would also provide one-for-one replacement homes within three years after the sale. Where their home was not eligible for sale, a tenant would have a right to move their discount to another property. The government has now signalled that it is ready to implement this policy, though some technical issues remain, such as on securing replacement homes and on the use of capital receipts from the sales (Wilson and Barton, 2022). It is difficult to predict how many homes are likely to be sold as a result.

Private rented sector

The historically unprecedented rise of private renting from 1988 to 2016 (Table 9.1 indicates the scale of this rise) has been attributed, first, to the liberating measures of the Housing Act 1988 (particularly, deregulation of renting and removal of security of tenure) and, second, to the rise of buy-to-let, with increasing numbers of people buying properties that come onto the market in order to let them to tenants (Somerville, 2016). Since this new type of purchaser is in competition with those seeking a home in which to live, it follows that the rise of buy-to-let will result in fewer homes being available for would-be owner-occupiers, and conversely, other things being equal, a fall in the numbers of buy-to-lets will be associated with a rise in owner-occupation. And this is what we find: after it peaked in 2003, owner-occupation remained relatively stable at 14.7 million to 14.8 million until the financial crash in 2008, after which it declined year on year to 14.3 million in 2013–14 (a period in which buy-to-let really took off), and since then it has increased year on year to 15.5 million in 2020–21 (Table 9.1). At the same time, after initial increases from its lowest point ever of 1.7 million in 1988 to just over 2 million in 1997, at which it remained until 2001, private renting began to rise again more steeply year on year to almost 4.7 million in 2016–17 (largely due to buy-to-let), before declining to around 4.4 million in 2020–21 (Table 9.1). The inverse relationship between owner-occupation and private renting seems unlikely to be a coincidence. Reducing subsidies to private landlords (which are massive; Somerville, 2016) might help to increase homeownership, but might also result in higher rents (which are already excessive).

The 'Renters' Reform' White Paper (Department for Levelling Up, Housing and Communities, 2022a) fulfils a Conservative 2019 manifesto commitment to repeal Section 21 of the Housing Act 1988, which allowed landlords to evict tenants without having to provide reasons (Wilson et al, 2022). They also pledged to: introduce a single Ombudsman and 'property portal' that all private landlords must join; crack down on criminal landlords;

ban blanket bans on renting to families with children or those in receipt of benefits; and give tenants the right to request a pet in their property, which the landlord must consider and cannot unreasonably refuse. At the time of writing (April 2023), the promised Renters' Reform Bill had not been introduced to Parliament.

Homelessness

Two government policies are notable on homelessness since 2015. The first was the Homelessness Reduction Act 2017, which primarily addressed statutory homelessness, meaning lacking in accommodation that is reasonably available to live in and being in priority need (primarily children, pregnant women and people deemed to be 'vulnerable'). This led to a significant reduction in the number of people assessed as threatened with homelessness (by 20 per cent from 2019–20 to 119,400 in 2020–21), although the number assessed as actually homeless rose by 7 per cent to 149,160 (Ministry of Housing, Communities and Local Government, 2021b, p 1). One positive impact of the Act has been 'the reorientation it has prompted towards a culture of personalised support rather than entitlement testing' (Watts et al, 2022, p 1), though it is recognised that funding remains insufficient, there are difficulties in staffing the service, the duties on public authorities are not strong or inclusive enough to solve the problem and wider government action is needed to effectively prevent homelessness, including via housing supply, access and regulatory reform and poverty reduction efforts (Fitzpatrick et al, 2019).

The second policy was the Everyone In initiative, which was launched in 2020 to tackle 'core homelessness' in response to the COVID-19 pandemic. Core homelessness includes

> people sleeping rough, staying in places not intended as residential accommodation (e.g. cars, tents, boats, sheds, etc.), living in homeless hostels, refuges and shelters, placed in unsuitable temporary accommodation (e.g. Bed and Breakfast hotels, Out of Area Placements, etc.), and sofa surfing (i.e., staying with non-family, on a short-term basis, in overcrowded conditions). (Watts et al, 2022, xxii)

Core homelessness in England increased year on year under the Conservative government from 187,018 in 2012 to 213,200 in 2019. In the Everyone In initiative, local authorities sought to move all those sleeping rough and in communal shelters into a safe place, ideally in self-contained accommodation. This initiative appears to have been remarkably successful in addressing core homelessness: it contacted 37,430 people sleeping rough or at risk of doing so or sleeping in communal shelters, moved them into hotel or similar accommodation, helped them avoid infections, hospital admissions, intensive care admissions and deaths (Watts et al, 2022), and transitioned 70 per cent of them into longer-term accommodation, defined as tenancies of at least six months, or supported housing (Watts et al, 2022). This resulted in a 5 per cent reduction in the number of core homeless households, to 203,400, in 2020 (Watts et al, 2002).

The government is committed to ending rough sleeping by 2024, but we have been here before, and there is clearly still a long way to go, with Watts et al (2022) forecasting that core homelessness will be one third higher in 2024 than in 2019, especially rough sleeping and sofa surfing. To reach its goal, the government needs to do more to prevent rough sleeping occurring in the first place and to secure more sustainable move-on options with the support of a package of welfare benefit policies, social housing lettings quotas targeting core homeless households, scaling up of the Housing First approach, and raising and indexing of the Local Housing Allowance (currently frozen at 30 per cent of market rents) (Watts et al, 2022).

Housing quality

Until recently, the Conservatives have never had a clear policy of their own on housing quality, even though the UK has some of the oldest and poorest housing conditions in Europe (Nicol et al, 2015). Since 2010, the government has maintained the previous Labour government's policy of achieving the Decent Homes Standard for all social rented homes (Department for Communities and Local Government, 2006). In 2015 it also launched a £2.5 billion flood defence programme, which by April 2022 resulted in protection for 314,000 homes (Department for Environment, Food and Rural Affairs, 2022) out of 5.2 million at risk in England (Environment Agency, 2009).

After the Grenfell tragedy in 2017, the government provided £400 million for local authorities and housing associations to remove and replace unsafe aluminium composite material cladding on those of their social residential buildings that were 18 metres or over in height (Ministry of Housing, Communities and Local Government, 2018). However, aluminium composite material is far from being the only dangerous cladding material, and up to 9,000 medium-rise blocks of flats have combustible facades dangerous enough to be deemed a 'life safety' risk.[1] It seems clear, therefore, that the government response to the fire falls far short of what is needed. The final report of the Grenfell inquiry will not be published before October 2023, but so far the inquiry has revealed the dysfunctional character of the building control system and the failure of government, at national and local levels, both before and after the tragedy, to regulate and enforce appropriately to ensure that the buildings we live in are safe. It seems that the ideologically based drive to minimise regulation, or even to do without it altogether, resulting inevitably in governance failure, has much to answer for (for an excoriating critique of government policy on improving homes, see Wakefield, 2021). The government hopes to improve things through its Social Housing (Regulation) Bill (Cromarty, 2023), but it is not clear how far this will reduce the likelihood of future Grenfell-type disasters.

The worst housing conditions have always been found in the private rented sector. The government has proposed to halve the number of non-decent rented homes by 2030 (HM Government, 2022), require privately rented homes to meet the Decent Homes Standard (Department for Levelling Up, Housing and Communities, 2022a) and increase the minimum standard for rental properties to energy performance certificate (EPC) level C by 2028 (HM Government, 2023). How this is all to be achieved remains unclear, and more is almost certainly required to address ongoing energy poverty and mitigate climate change. The government's Net Zero Strategy is particularly weak on the topic of energy efficiency (for a critique of the strategy and energy policy, see Somerville, 2020).

The failed Green Homes Grant scheme has been replaced by the Boiler Upgrade Scheme (mainly replacing gas boilers with heat pumps), but this has had only 14,000 applications since it started in May 2022 (HM Government, 2023), which is well short of the 600,000 installations a year by 2028 envisaged by the Net Zero Strategy. At this rate, it simply will not be possible to reduce greenhouse gas emissions from buildings to the extent expected by the strategy (see Teanby and Norton, 2022). The Committee on Climate Change calls only for a 2030 outcome where 'as many homes are at least EPC C as is practical' (2022, p 199), with no explanation of what might be practical and without recognising the problems with the EPC rating system (for example, it measures economic efficiency rather than energy efficiency). One can only hope that the Clean Heat Market Mechanism, launching in 2024, will help to achieve the extent of heat decarbonisation required. Meanwhile, other countries are moving ahead, such as France with its new Loi climat 2021 (République Française, 2021) and the Republic of Ireland with its National Retrofitting Scheme (Woodfield, 2022).

For social housing in particular, the Social Housing Decarbonisation Fund provided £61 million to retrofit 2,300 homes in 2021–22, has allocated a further £179 million for around 20,000 homes in 2022–23 (Department for Business, Energy and Industrial Strategy, 2022a) and is currently offering up to £800 million over three years, from 2023 to 2025 (Department for Business, Energy and Industrial Strategy, 2022b). However, this is still covering only a minority of socially rented homes and, as the Committee on Climate Change (2022) has noted (and many others since then), it will not be enough to meet the current and rising demand for energy and energy-saving measures (the government's support for domestic energy bills does not address the energy efficiency issue; see Green Finance Institute, 2022, for a plausible way forward for social housing).

In 2023, the government launched the Great British Insulation Scheme. This involves providing loft and cavity wall insulation for 300,000 least-efficient homes by March 2026, funded through the Energy Company Obligation. This is useful but hardly amounts to the mass retrofit programme that is needed, and the extent of emissions savings is unclear.

For new properties, in 2006 the New Labour government set a target of 2016 for zero carbon emissions, which the Coalition government initially confirmed in July 2010 but later abandoned in 2015 (Oldfield, 2015). Later, in 2019, the Conservative government set a Future Homes Standard, which it aims to implement fully in 2025 (Woodfield and Pullen, 2022). From June 2022, new homes must emit 30 per cent less carbon than before, with a target of 75–80 per cent less by 2025. The Future Homes proposal will go out to consultation in 2023, followed by legislation in 2024. This is good news, but it is not clear why the process could not have been started years earlier.

Levelling up?

'Levelling up' is the slogan associated with the Conservatives' victory in the 2019 general election (see Chapter 1), enshrined in the renaming of the traditional Ministry of Housing and Local Government as the Department for Levelling Up, Housing and Communities. It seems to be mainly about reducing the inequality among English regions, to ensure that the Conservatives retain the seats they gained in 2019 in the so-called 'red wall' of traditional Labour strongholds in the north of England.

The *Levelling Up* White Paper was published in February 2022 (HM Government, 2022). In terms of housing, it pledged to regenerate 20 towns and cities (mainly in Northern England and the Midlands) with an emphasis on 'assembling and remediating brownfield land and working with the private sector to bring about transformational developments combining housing, retail and business in sustainable, walkable, beautiful new neighbourhoods' (HM Government, 2022, p xxiv). The paper did not say what effect this might have on the housing stock (or indeed on reducing carbon emissions). The only evidence of housing policy in relation to levelling up the regions is this statement: 'We will scrap the 80/20 funding rule that focused investment in Greater London and instead invest in more homes in the North and Midlands to relieve pressure on the South East' (HM Government, 2022, p xxvi). This seems incompatible with existing policy on two counts: first, the government accepts that the need for new homes is greater in the South East (Department for Levelling Up, Housing and Communities, 2021; see also House of Lords Built Environment Committee, 2022, p 67); and, second, as noted earlier, the Affordable Homes Programme for 2021–26 provides £4 billion funding for

London and £7 billion for the rest of England, which is even more biased towards London than a 20/80 split. It also seems likely that London will get the lion's share of the £11 billion funding for local economic growth. As has been pointed out (Longlands, 2022), there is no credible strategy or objectives here, and the House of Commons Committee of Public Accounts (2022) have been very critical of the whole funding process. Needless to add, perhaps, the latest version of the Levelling Up and Regeneration Bill does not mandate a national target for new homes construction.

Conclusion

Conservative housing policy continues to be blighted by neoliberal ideology and blinkered short-term thinking – hence the number of failed and failing policies. There is a contradiction between its emphasis on multiple initiatives dictated from central government and its long-professed aim to give greater freedom to citizens. Its continual interference in housing markets is incompatible with its assumption that government needs to get out of the way as far as possible. It also seems to lack understanding that the interests of housing developers and local communities often do not coincide. Its continuing support for private property owners, both owner-occupiers and private landlords, is largely to the detriment of tenants, both private and social, and therefore reinforces and exacerbates social inequality.

Overall, Conservative housing policy may seem incoherent in a number of respects, but actually it is possible to discern a certain pragmatic consistency, which goes back historically to the Tories of the 18th century. This can be summarised as a defence of private property ownership and promotion of a free market in property dealing. This helps to explain the following themes (see Table 1.1): an emphasis on abolishing regulation that is seen to constrain this privilege and freedom; a concern about inequality only to the extent of helping the propertyless to become property owners (as with Right to Buy and Help to Buy – contrasted with the purely rhetorical character of the levelling up agenda); and an emphasis on private enterprise and control, low taxation and low public expenditure (except where it benefits private property owners).

A problem with this approach, however, is that it is not well suited to coping with market failures, such as the failure to provide enough affordable housing, and the government's responses to these failures have left much to be desired – and indeed have been inconsistent with their basic approach (for example, the setting of national housing targets appears to contradict their commitment to a bottom-up market-based approach). A more serious problem, of course, is that it tends to neglect the propertyless (tenants and homeless people) unless the problem becomes too visible to ignore, as with rough sleepers or the Grenfell tragedy or the cost of living crisis (or the climate crisis in the future, perhaps). Even then, the response has rarely been adequate, whether that be in terms of insulating homes or ensuring that they are safe for our future well-being.

Note
[1] *Private Eye* #1575, 17–30 June 2022.

References

Barton, C. and Grimwood, G.G. (2021) *Calculating housing need in the planning system (England)*, London: House of Commons Library. Available at: https://researchbriefings.files.parliament.uk/documents/CBP-9268/CBP-9268.pdf (accessed 9 September 2022).

Bowie, D. (2017) *Radical solutions to the housing supply crisis*, Bristol: Policy Press.

Brown, R. (2020) 'What housing and planning powers do London Mayors actually have?', *On London*, 9 January. Available at: www.onlondon.co.uk/richard-brown-what-housing-planning-powers-do-london-mayors-have/ (accessed 29 September 2022).

Campaign to Protect Rural England (2020) 'What's the plan? An analysis of local plan coverage cross England'. Available at: https://www.cpre.org.uk/wp-content/uploads/2020/05/Whats-the-plan-_Full-report_2020.pdf (accessed 3 August 2023).

Carozzi, F., Hilber, C.A.L. and Yu, X. (2020) *On the economic impacts of mortgage credit expansion policies: evidence from Help to Buy*, Centre for Economic Policy Discussion Paper No 1618, London: Centre for Economic Performance. Available at: https://cep.lse.ac.uk/pubs/download/dp1681.pdf (accessed 9 August 2022).

Clifford, B., Canelas, P., Ferm, J., Livingstone, N., Bibby, P., Brindley, P., Henneberry, J., McLean, A., Tubridy, D. and Dunning, R. (2018) *Extending permitted development rights in England: the implications for public authorities and communities*, London: Royal Institute of Chartered Surveyors. Available at: http://offlinehbpl.hbpl.co.uk/NewsAttachments/RLP/RICSExtendingPermittedDevelopmentRights.pdf (accessed 16 August 2022).

Clifford, B., Canelas, P., Ferm, J., Livingstone, N., Lord, A. and Dunning, R. (2020) *Research into the quality standard of homes delivered through change of use permitted development rights*, London: Ministry of Housing, Communities and Local Government.

Committee on Climate Change (2022) *Progress in reducing emissions: 2022 report to Parliament*, London: Committee on Climate Change. Available at: www.theccc.org.uk/publication/2022-progress-report-to-parliament/ (accessed 9 September 2022).

Conservative Party (2015) *Strong leadership, a clear economic plan, a brighter, more secure future. The Conservative Party manifesto 2015*, London: Conservative Party.

Conservative Party (2017) *Forward together: our plan for a stronger Britain and a prosperous future. The Conservative and Unionist Party Manifesto 2017*, London: Conservative Party. Available at: https://general-election-2010.co.uk/2017-general-election-manifestos/conservative-manifesto-2017.pdf (accessed 16 August 2022).

Conservative Party (2019) *Get Brexit done: unleash Britain's potential. The Conservative and Unionist Party Manifesto 2019*, London: Conservative Party. Available at: www.conservatives.com/our-plan/conservative-party-manifesto-2019 (accessed 9 August 2022).

Cromarty, H. (2023) *Social Housing (Regulation) Bill 2022–23: Progress of the Bill*, London: House of Commons Library. Available at: https://researchbriefings.files.parliament.uk/documents/CBP-9659/CBP-9659.pdf (accessed 4 April 2023).

Department for Business, Energy and Industrial Strategy (2022a) *Social Housing Decarbonisation Fund Wave 1: successful bids*, London: Department for Business, Energy and Industrial Strategy. Available at: www.gov.uk/government/publications/social-housing-decarbonisation-fund-wave-1-successful-bids (accessed 9 September 2022).

Department for Business, Energy and Industrial Strategy (2022b) *Social Housing Decarbonisation Fund Wave 2.1*, London: Department for Business, Energy and Industrial Strategy. Available at: www.gov.uk/government/publications/social-housing-decarbonisation-fund-wave-2#:~:text=The%20fund%20follows%20on%20from,around%201%2C200%20local%20jobs%20supported (accessed 9 September 2022).

Department for Communities and Local Government (2006) *A decent home: definition and guidance for implementation*, London: Department for Communities and Local Government. Available at: https://assets.publishing.service.gov.uk/government/uploads/system/uploads/attachment_data/file/7812/138355.pdf (accessed 29 September 2022).

Department for Environment, Food and Rural Affairs (2022) 'Over 314,000 homes better protected due to flood protection work', London: Department for Environment, Food and Rural Affairs. Available at: www.gov.uk/government/news/over-314000-homes-better-protected-due-to-flood-protection-work (accessed 17 August 2022).

Department for Levelling Up, Housing and Communities (2021) 'Housing and economic needs assessment'. Available at: https://www.gov.uk/guidance/housing-and-economic-development-needs-assessments (accessed 15 August 2022).

Department for Levelling Up, Housing and Communities (2022a) *A fairer private rented sector*, London: HMSO. Available at: https://assets.publishing.service.gov.uk/government/uploads/system/uploads/attachment_data/file/1083381/A_fairer_private_rented_sector_print.pdf (accessed 9 August 2022).

Department for Levelling Up, Housing and Communities (2022b) 'Help to Buy Tables. Table 1: Number of legal completions, and value of equity loans, England'. Available at: www.gov.uk/government/statistics/help-to-buy-equity-loan-scheme-data-to-31-march-2022 (accessed 16 August 2022).

Department for Levelling Up, Housing and Communities (2022c) 'Live tables on housing supply. Table 213: permanent dwellings started and completed, by tenure, England'. Available at: www.gov.uk/government/statistical-data-sets/live-tables-on-house-building (accessed 9 August 2022).

Department for Levelling Up, Housing and Communities (2022d) 'Social housing sales and demolitions 2020–21: Right to Buy sales'. Available at: www.gov.uk/government/statistics/social-housing-sales-and-demolitions-2020-21-england/social-housing-sales-and-demolitions-2020-21-right-to-buy-sales (accessed 17 August 22).

Eardley, F. (2022) *Right to Buy: past, present and future*, London: House of Lords Library. Available at: https://lordslibrary.parliament.uk/right-to-buy-past-present-and-future/ (accessed 17 August 2022).

Elliott, A. (2020) 'New Affordable Homes Programme – how does it compare?', London: Altair. Available at: https://altairltd.co.uk/2020/09/15/affordable-homes-programme-altair/ (accessed 17 August 2022).

Environment Agency (2009) *Flooding in England: a national assessment of flood risk*, Bristol: Environment Agency. Available at: https://assets.publishing.service.gov.uk/government/uploads/system/uploads/attachment_data/file/292928/geho0609bqds-e-e.pdf (accessed 17 August).

Fitzpatrick, S., Mackie, P. and Wood, J. (2019) *Homelessness prevention in the UK: policy briefing*, UK Collaborative Centre for Housing Evidence. Available at: https://housingevidence.ac.uk/wp-content/uploads/2019/07/Homelessness-Prevention-in-the-UK-Policy-Brief-July-2019-final.pdf (accessed 22 April 2022).

Greater London Authority (2022) *GLA housing starts and completions*, London: Greater London Authority. Available at: www.london.gov.uk/sites/default/files/affordable_housing_starts_and_completions_-_end_of_june_22.pdf (accessed 22 April 2023).

Green Finance Institute (2022) *Retrofitting social housing*, London: Green Finance Institute. Available at: www.greenfinanceinstitute.co.uk/wp-content/uploads/2022/10/GFI-RETROFITTING-SOCIAL-HOUSING-1.pdf (accessed 4 April 2023).

Hetherington, P. (2021) *Land renewed: reworking the countryside*, Bristol: Bristol University Press.

HM Government (2022) *Levelling up the United Kingdom*, London: HMSO.

HM Government (2023) *Powering up Britain*, London: HMSO. Available at: https://assets.publishing.service.gov.uk/government/uploads/system/uploads/attachment_data/file/1147340/powering-up-britain-joint-overview.pdf (accessed 4 April 2023).

Homes England (2018) *Strategic Plan 2018/19 – 2022/23*, London: Homes England. Available at: https://assets.publishing.service.gov.uk/government/uploads/system/uploads/attachment_data/file/752686/Homes_England_Strategic_Plan_AW_REV_150dpi_REV.pdf (accessed 15 August 2022).

Homes England (2019) Homes England *Housing Statistics: 1 April 2018–31 March 2019*, London: Homes England. Available at: https://assets.publishing.service.gov.uk/government/uploads/system/uploads/attachment_data/file/809580/Housing_Statistics_June_2019.pdf (accessed 9 August 2022).

Homes England (2022) *Housing Statistics: 1 April–31 March 2022*, London: Homes England. Available at: https://assets.publishing.service.gov.uk/government/uploads/system/uploads/attachment_data/file/1084880/Housing_Statistics_June_2022.pdf (accessed 9 August 2022).

House of Commons Committee of Public Accounts (2022) *Local economic growth*, London: House of Commons. Available at: https://committees.parliament.uk/publications/22483/documents/165800/default/ (accessed 15 August 2022).

House of Lords Built Environment Committee (2022) *Meeting housing demand*, HL Paper 132, London: House of Lords. Available at: https://committees.parliament.uk/publications/8354/documents/85292/default/ (accessed 9 August 2022).

Hughes, C., Sayce, S., Shepherd, E. and Wyatt, P. (2020) 'Implementing a land value tax: considerations on moving from theory to practice', *Land Use Policy*, 94: 104494. Available at https://centaur.reading.ac.uk/88754/ (accessed 29 September 2022).

Jessop, J. (2017) *Would a land value tax get Britain building?* London: Institute of Economic Affairs. Available at: https://iea.org.uk/would-a-land-value-tax-lvt-get-britain-building/ (accessed 29 September 2022).

Local Government Association (2020) 'Over 13,500 affordable homes lost through office conversions', *Local Government Association*, 11 January. Available at: www.local.gov.uk/about/news/lga-over-13500-affordable-homes-lost-through-office-conversions (accessed 16 August 2022).

Longlands, S. (2022) 'Can levelling up survive the collapse of Boris Johnson's government?', *New Statesman*, 7 July. Available at: www.newstatesman.com/spotlight/regional-development/2022/07/can-levelling-up-survive-boris-johnsons-government?mc_cid=f75712587f&mc_eid=afbb250 72a (accessed 15 August 2022).

Lund, B. (2019) *Housing in the United Kingdom: whose crisis?* Basingstoke: Palgrave Macmillan.

Mayor of London (2021) 'Mayor strikes deals for thousands of new council homes', 31 August. Available at: www.london.gov.uk/press-releases/mayoral/boroughs-set-to-build-thousands-of-council-homes (accessed 16 August 2022).

McMullan, L., Osborne, H., Blight, G. and Duncan, P. (2021) 'UK housing crisis: how did owning a home become unaffordable?', *The Guardian*, 31 March. Available at: www.theguardian.com/business/ng-interactive/2021/mar/31/uk-housing-crisis-how-did-owning-a-home-become-unafforda ble (accessed 17 August 2022).

Ministry of Housing, Communities and Local Government (2018) *A new deal for social housing*, London: Ministry of Housing, Communities and Local Government.

Ministry of Housing, Communities and Local Government (2020a) 'Changes to the current planning system', *Gov.uk*, 6 August. Available at: www.gov.uk/government/consultations/changes-to-the-current-planning-system (accessed 19 July 2023).

Ministry of Housing, Communities and Local Government (2020b) 'Jenrick unveils huge £12 billion boost for affordable homes' [press release]. Available at: www.gov.uk/government/news/jenrick-unveils-huge-12-bill ion-boost-for-affordable-homes (accessed 9 August 2022).

Ministry of Housing, Communities and Local Government (2020c) *Planning for the future*, London: Ministry of Housing, Communities and Local Government.

Ministry of Housing, Communities and Local Government (2020d) *The charter for social housing residents: social housing White Paper*, London: Ministry of Housing, Communities and Local Government. Available at: www.gov.uk/government/publications/the-charter-for-social-housing-residents-soc ial-housing-white-paper (accessed 4 April 2023).

Ministry of Housing, Communities and Local Government (2021a) *English Housing Survey: Home ownership, 2019–20*, London: Ministry of Housing, Communities and Local Government. Available at: https://assets.publish ing.service.gov.uk/government/uploads/system/uploads/attachment_data/file/1000040/EHS_19-20_Home_ownership_report.pdf (accessed 16 August 2022).

Ministry of Housing, Communities and Local Government (2021b) *Statutory homelessness annual report 2020–21, England*, London: Ministry of Housing, Communities and Local Government. Available at: https://assets.publish ing.service.gov.uk/government/uploads/system/uploads/attachment_data/file/1016146/Annual_Statutory_Homelessness_2020-21.pdf (accessed 9 September 2022).

National Audit Office (2019) *Investigation into starter homes*, London: National Audit Office. Available at: www.nao.org.uk/wp-content/uploads/2019/11/Investigation-into-starter-homes.pdf (accessed 16 August 2022).

National Audit Office (2022) *The Affordable Homes Programme since 2015*, London: National Audit Office. Available at: www.nao.org.uk/wp-cont ent/uploads/2022/09/The-Affordable-Homes-Programme-since-2015. pdf (accessed 4 April 2023).

Nicol, S., Roys, M., Ormandy, D. and Ezratty, V. (2015) *The cost of poor housing in the European Union*, London: BRE. Available at: www.bre.co.uk/ filelibrary/Briefing%20papers/92993_BRE_Poor-Housing_in_-Europe. pdf (accessed 29 September 2022).

Office for National Statistics (2022a) 'Dwelling stock by tenure, UK. Table FT1101 (S101): Trends in tenure'. Available at: www.ons.gov.uk/peopl epopulationandcommunity/housing/datasets/dwellingstockbytenureuk (accessed 9 September 2022).

Office for National Statistics (2022b) *Housing affordability in England and Wales*, London: Office for National Statistics. Available at: www.ons.gov. uk/peoplepopulationandcommunity/housing/bulletins/housingaffordabili tyinenglandandwales/2021#:~:text=Since%201997%2C%20housing%20af fordability%20has,prices%20increasing%20faster%20than%20earnings (accessed 17 August 2022).

Oldfield, P. (2015) 'UK scraps zero carbon homes plan', *The Guardian*, 10 July. Available at: www.theguardian.com/environment/2015/jul/10/uk-scr aps-zero-carbon-home-target (accessed 15 August 2022).

République Française (2021) *Loi du 22 août 2021 portant lutte contre le dérèglement climatique et renforcement de la résilience face à ses effets*. Available at: www-vie--publique-fr.translate.goog/loi/278460-loi-22-aout-2021-climat-et-resilience-convention-citoyenne-climat?_x_tr_sl=fr&_x_tr_tl= en&_x_tr_hl=en&_x_tr_pto=sc (accessed 15 August 2022).

Shrubsole, G. (2019) *Who owns England? How we lost our land and how to take it back*, London: William Collins.

Somerville, P. (2016) 'Conservative housing policy', in H. Bochel and M. Powell (eds) *The Coalition government and social policy*, Bristol: Policy Press.

Somerville, P. (2020) 'The continuing failure of UK climate change mitigation policy', *Critical Social Policy*, 41(4): 628–50.

Teanby, A. and Norton, E. (2022) 'Will the heat pump scheme turn out to be another flop?', *Landscope*, 10 August. Available at: www.savills.co.uk/ landing-pages/landscope/10-august-2022.aspx (accessed 4 April 2023).

Torrance, D. (2022) *Introduction to devolution in the UK*, London: House of Commons Library. Available at: https://researchbriefings.files.parliament. uk/documents/CBP-8599/CBP-8599.pdf (accessed 28 September 2022).

UCL (University College London) (2020) 'Government publishes UCL-led research on permitted development housing quality'. Available at: https://www. ucl.ac.uk/bartlett/planning/news/2020/jul/government-publishes-ucl-led-research-permitted-development-housing-quality (accessed 18 August 2022).

Wakefield, M. (2021) 'Britain's leaky homes make the energy crisis worse: why have governments not fixed them?', *The Guardian*, 28 September. Available at: www.theguardian.com/commentisfree/2021/sep/28/britain-homes-energy-crisis-governments-insulation-low-carbon-heating (accessed 29 September 2022).

Watt, P. (2021) *Estate regeneration and its discontents: public housing, place and inequality in London*, Bristol: Policy Press.

Watts, B., Bramley, G., Pawson, H., Young, G., Fitzpatrick, S. and McMordie, L. (2022) *The homelessness monitor: England 2022*, London: Crisis.

Wilson, E. and Barton, C. (2022) *Introducing a voluntary Right to Buy for housing association tenants in England*, London: House of Commons Library. Available at: https://researchbriefings.files.parliament.uk/documents/CBP-7224/CBP-7224.pdf (accessed 17 August 2022).

Wilson, W. (2021) *Stimulating housing supply - government initiatives (England)*, London: House of Commons Library. Available at: https://researchbriefings.files.parliament.uk/documents/SN06416/SN06416.pdf (accessed 4 April 2023).

Wilson, W., Barton, C. and Cromarty, H. (2022) *The end of 'no fault' section 21 evictions (England)*, London: House of Commons Library. Available at: https://researchbriefings.files.parliament.uk/documents/CBP-8658/CBP-8658.pdf (accessed 17 August 2022).

Woodfield, J. (2022) 'Ireland's retrofit ambitions lay down challenge for UK government', *Homebuilding & Renovating*, 10 March. Available at: www.homebuilding.co.uk/news/ireland-retrofit-scheme (accessed 30 July 2022).

Woodfield, J. and Pullen, T. (2022) 'Future Homes Standard: the complete guide to the new targets', *Homebuilding & Renovating*, 22 July. Available at: www.homebuilding.co.uk/advice/future-homes-standard (accessed 9 August 2022).

Wright, O. (2023) 'UK housing crisis: planning targets scrapped in "win for nimbys"', *The Times*, 7 April. Available at: www.thetimes.co.uk/article/uk-housing-supply-crisis-home-building-england-2023-v0wjkwl0j (accessed 13 April 2023).

zu Ermgassen, S.O.S.E., Drewniok, M.P., Bull, J.W., Corlet Walker, C.M., Mancini, M., Ryan-Collins, J. and Cabrera Serrenho, A. (2022) 'A home for all within planetary boundaries: pathways for meeting England's housing needs without transgressing national climate and biodiversity goals', *SocArXiv*. Available at: https://osf.io/5jxce/ (accessed 5 April 2023).

10

Social security policies under the Conservatives 2015–22: austerity, COVID-19 and the living cost crisis

Stephen McKay and Karen Rowlingson

Introduction

The period following 2015 represented a continuation of the key social security policies begun during the Coalition government of 2010–15. This phase was characterised by the reduction of protection for working-age individuals and simultaneous enhancement of support for older people. These patterns were largely set in place with the Welfare Reform Act 2012, continued via the Welfare Reform and Work Act 2016 (largely repealing the Child Poverty Act 2010). The social security response to the COVID-19 pandemic showed the potential for change, yet it also highlighted the significant gap between the situation at that time and such transformative measures during more normal times.

In the decade beginning 2010, the most influential reformer, particularly for benefits aimed at working-age recipients, was Iain Duncan Smith. Writing in 2013, he expressed concern about the economic viability of the welfare system. He stated that '[t]he welfare bill has become unsustainably expensive' and unveiled plans for what he described as 'the most far-reaching change that the welfare system has witnessed in generations' (Department for Work and Pensions, 2010, p 1). His response was the introduction of Universal Credit. This new system replaced several other benefits, which had somewhat inconsistent rules and procedures. While social security policy is not generally a devolved area of responsibility, Scotland in particular has made some different decisions in this space, with other innovations in Wales, such as piloting a basic income scheme for care leavers (see Chapter 17 for a fuller discussion of devolution).

A number of key strands may be identified during the period of the Coalition government (McKay and Rowlingson, 2016) and until the time of writing. Some of these have an even earlier origin, of course, dating back to the 1980s and evolving since then. We focus on three key patterns of reform – the different strategies according to age, austerity and private arrangements.

First, a significant split in approaches to benefits based solely on the age of recipients. There is an increasingly strong division between benefits for those of working age versus those benefits (pensions) for people of pensionable age. The main thrust of policy for working-age people has been to move the system on to a largely means-tested footing in the form of Universal Credit. In contrast, for individuals of pension age, policy reinforced the contributory aspect of support through the introduction of the new State Pension. This change reduced reliance on the means-tested Pension Credit. Furthermore, the government aimed to secure pensioners' living standards by introducing the 'triple lock' guarantee. This mechanism ensured consistent increases in pensions, thereby serving as a protective measure against any potential decline in living standards, including a 10.1 per cent increase in the State Pension in April 2023.

The second key strand of reform is that of restriction and cost-cutting – in other words, austerity. Various measures – both large-scale changes and more minor reforms – have been used to ensure that spending was contained where possible. In terms of financial savings, this is most clear in the five-year freeze in the cash value of most benefits for those of working age from 2015 to 2020. This meant, of course, that the spending power of those relying on those benefits was eroded over time. In addition, the introduction of a 'benefit cap' put an overall limit on the amounts of benefit that could be paid (with exemptions in the case of disability and those in paid work). The introduction of a highly controversial 'two-child limit' in the Summer Budget 2015 meant no specific payments for a third child (or more) in larger families. Under this heading of austerity, we may also include substantially renewed efforts to contain spending on disability-related benefits, the replacement of Disability Living Allowance with Personal Independence Payment in 2013 having failed to deliver the financial savings expected.

Third, there have been shifts towards more private schemes, especially in pension reforms. The most significant innovation is the introduction of the auto-enrolment system from 2012 onwards. This measure is intended to ensure that more individuals will have a supplementary non-state pension upon retirement, to enhance their state-provided pension benefits. Under new arrangements for child maintenance (or 'child support'), the statutory system primarily serves as a safety net, while private agreements are encouraged as the primary mechanism.

Party manifestos and departmental leadership

Manifesto commitments

Party manifestos present the ideas of political parties to the voting public in the lead-up to general elections. However, in terms of social security policies presented, the material has been relatively thin. The 2015 Conservative Party manifesto sought to position social security alongside policy on taxes and immigration, specifically 'Cutting your taxes, making welfare fairer and controlling immigration' (Conservative Party, 2015. This highlighted the plan to 'cap overall welfare spending, lower the amount of benefits that any household can receive to £23,000 and continue to roll out Universal Credit, to make work pay' (p 25). It was also declared that '[t]he days of something for nothing are over' (p 25), and there was a pledge to freeze working-age benefits for two years from April 2016. Separately, section 6, 'Dignity in your retirement', was more generous with promises to continue increasing the State Pension through the triple lock (increasing pensions by the highest of: inflation, earnings, or 2.5 per cent).

The text-heavy 2017 manifesto had relatively little to say about social security, emphasising there were 'no plans for further radical welfare reform' (Conservative Party, 2017, p 52), but that the long rollout of Universal Credit would continue. There was, therefore, nothing included here to tackle the 'burning [social] injustices' that May had highlighted in her first speech as Prime Minister in 2016 (see Chapter 1). In a small gesture at reducing pensioner spending, there were proposals to move from the triple lock on state pensions to only a double lock in 2020 (based on inflation or earnings, but without the guaranteed 2.5 per cent minimum) and to means-test Winter Fuel Payments – neither of which actually happened in the curtailed two-year Parliament which followed.

The 2019 manifesto, titled 'Get Brexit done', marked a return to full support of the triple lock mechanism on pensions and reiterated the Party's commitment to continue the Universal Credit rollout (Conservative Party, 2019, p 17). The manifesto also introduced the 'levelling up' agenda, aimed at addressing regional inequalities (see Chapter 1). While this approach was perhaps appealing to the Labour-held 'red wall' seats, it primarily focused on geographic disparities rather than individual economic inequality, making its exact application somewhat ambiguous. The manifesto took a strong stance against fraudulent activities, asserting the need to be 'sure **those who cheat the system by committing benefit fraud** are punished' (Conservative Party, 2019, p 17, emphasis in the original text). However, it lacked specific details on novel approaches to combat this issue beyond previously attempted measures. On a more optimistic note, the manifesto promised to essentially halt austerity measures by ending the long-standing freeze on benefits.

Departmental leadership: Secretaries of State

From 2015 to 2022, the Department for Work and Pensions experienced rapid turnover in leadership, with no fewer than nine different Secretaries of State at its helm. This period of instability was particularly marked during Theresa May's tenure (see Table 10.1), when none of the four Secretaries of State remained in their role for a full year. Despite this turnover, the policy

Table 10.1: Secretaries of State for Work and Pensions, 2010–22

# Incumbent	Spell	Prime Minister on appointment
1. Iain Duncan Smith	May 2010–March 2016	David Cameron
2. Stephen Crabb	March 2016–July 2016	
3. Damian Green	July 2016–June 2017	Theresa May
4. David Gauke	June 2017–January 2018	
5. Ester McVey	January 2018–November 2018	
6. Amber Rudd	November 2018–September 2019	
7. Thérèse Coffey	September 2019–September 2022	Boris Johnson
8. Chloe Smith	September 2022–October 2022	Liz Truss
9. Mel Stride	25 October 2022–	Rishi Sunak

direction initiated by the first Secretary of State during this period, Iain Duncan Smith, remained a prominent and potentially the most significant element of social security reform, specifically for those of working age. His introduction of Universal Credit became a cornerstone of the social security structure.

The frequent changes in leadership likely contributed to the relative dearth of substantial reform during this period. The complexities of the UK's social security system require considerable time for new ministers to fully understand and navigate, potentially hindering prompt policy transformation (Royston, 2017, provides a comprehensive discussion of these challenges).

Social security spending

The Department for Work and Pensions continues to be one of the largest spending government departments. Spending on 'welfare benefits' is more than £230 billion a year, and in 2021–22 represented more than 11 per cent of national income (see Figure 10.1). Measures taken during the pandemic – the main furlough and self-employment support packages – added 3.8 per cent to this total in 2020–21, falling to 1.1 per cent in 2022–23, in addition to specific increases in Universal Credit and in the numbers requiring such support.

Most spending is on older people, rather than those of working age – for 2022–23, spending on working-age welfare is expected to be 4.9 per cent of gross domestic product while spending on older people, predominantly through the contributory State Pension system, is rather higher at 6 per cent.

Policies: changes in working-age benefits

As discussed earlier, the key elements of policies towards those of working age have been attempts at cost containment plus continuing the much-extended

Figure 10.1: Social security spending (percentage of GDP), 2010–11 to 2022–23

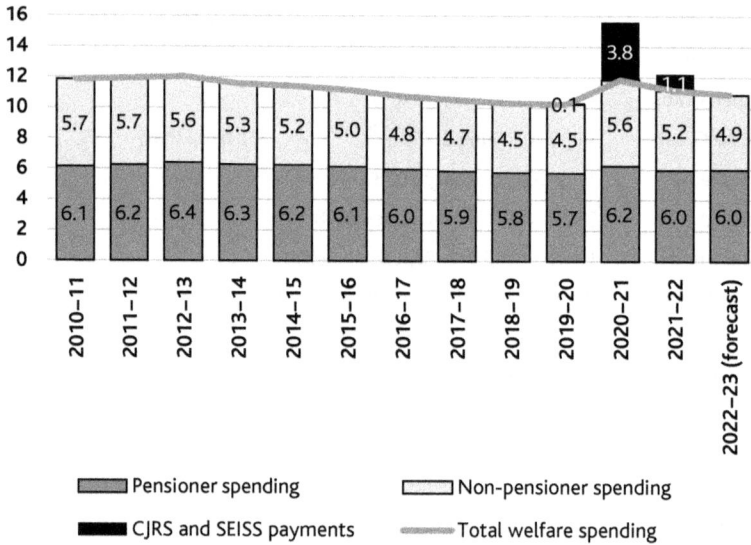

Note: CJRS refers to the Coronavirus Job Retention Scheme; SEISS refers to the Self-Employment Income Support Scheme.
Source: Office for Budget Responsibility welfare trends report (https://obr.uk/welfare-trends-rep ort-may-2022/)

introduction of Universal Credit. However, for much of the relevant period, the main policy was a freeze in the level of cash benefits, which we next describe.

Benefit levels: long frozen for those of working age

A key feature of social security benefits from 2015 was the freeze in benefits rates that lasted from April 2015 until March 2020. The customary approach of increasing benefits in line with inflation was abandoned – at least for those of working age. McKay and Rowlingson (2016) characterise the period from 2010 to 2015 as one of shredding the system for people of working age, while protecting older people. This judgement may be confirmed for the period since 2015, by the way in which benefit levels were frozen during 2015–20 for most recipients of working age, while the levels of State Pension and means-tested Pension Credit continued to increase ahead of inflation. Taking the period 2015–22 as a whole, the basic State Pension increased in value by 22 per cent and prices (as measured by the Consumer Prices Index) rose by 20 per cent, but rates of Income Support and Jobseeker's Allowance rose by only 5 per cent (see Table 10.2). These reforms were, of course,

Table 10.2: Rates of selected social security benefits (including state pensions), 2014–22

Year from April	Basic State Pension*	New State Pension	Pension Credit	Jobseeker's Allowance 25+	Income Support: 18–24**	Child Benefit	Consumer Prices Index***
2014	£113.10		£148.35	£72.40	£57.35	£20.50	100.10
2015	£115.95		£151.20	£73.10	£57.90	£20.70	99.90
2016	£119.30	£155.65	£155.60	£73.10	£57.90	£20.70	100.20
2017	£122.30	£159.55	£159.35	£73.10	£57.90	£20.70	102.90
2018	£125.95	£164.35	£163.00	£73.10	£57.90	£20.70	105.40
2019	£129.20	£168.60	£167.25	£73.10	£57.90	£20.70	107.60
2020	£134.25	£175.20	£173.75	£74.35	£58.90	£21.05	108.50
2021	£137.60	£179.60	£177.10	£74.70	£59.20	£21.15	110.10
2022	£141.85	£185.15	£182.60	£77.00	£61.05	£21.18	120.00
Change 2014–22	22%	NA	21%	5%	5%	2%	20%

Notes: *Basic State Pension for single persons aged under 80 with own National Insurance contribution.
**Income Support for single person aged 18–24.
***Consumer Prices Index 00: All items: 2015 = 100.
Figures in grey shading represent the benefits freeze for those benefits.
Source: DWP uprating announcements, various years

made in the light of the austerity policies of the government – though they were not applied to older people.

Hence, these differences reinforce the differential treatment of working-age jobseekers and those over State Pension age. They therefore seem to be primarily ideologically driven, either by the belief that jobseekers need more financial motivation to find work or by the belief that jobseekers are less deserving of support – ideas that can be traced back to the Poor Law.

Child Benefit for the first child rose by only 2 per cent in 2015–22. In 2013, it was decided that Child Benefit would be tapered away from families where the higher-paid person had earnings of between £50,000 and £60,000. These trigger points for reducing and eventually removing Child Benefit have not changed at all since then, capturing more families in this reduction as earnings levels increase in money terms.

As a result of this policy, the amount of income paid to those below State Pension age increasingly trails that of older people. In April 2015, the basic State Pension was roughly 1.6 times the level of the amount payable in contributory Jobseeker's Allowance to someone aged 25 or older while unemployed. By April 2022, the State Pension was almost 85 per cent greater than Jobseeker's Allowance. However, a new system, appropriately enough

Table 10.3: Rates of Universal Credit, 2014–22

Year from April (unless otherwise noted):	Universal Credit: under 25*	Weekly	Universal Credit: 25 to State Pension age**	Weekly
2014	£249.28	£57.53	£314.67	£72.62
2015	£251.77	£58.10	£317.82	£73.34
2016	£251.77	£58.10	£317.82	£73.34
2017	£251.77	£58.10	£317.82	£73.34
2018	£251.77	£58.10	£317.82	£73.34
2019	£251.77	£58.10	£317.82	£73.34
2020	£256.05	£59.09	£323.22	£74.59
2020 *with temporary Coronavirus pandemic increase*	£342.72	£79.09	£409.89	£94.59
2021 *with temporary Coronavirus pandemic increase*	£344.00	£79.38	£411.51	£94.96
From October 2021 rate announced by 2021 uprating order	£257.33	£59.38	£324.84	£74.96
2022	£265.31	£61.23	£334.91	£77.29
Change April 2015–April 2022	5%	5%	5%	5%

Note: *Universal Credit for single persons aged 18–24; **Universal Credit from age 25 until State Pension age.

Source: DWP uprating announcements, various years

called the 'new State Pension', meant that newly retiring pensioners with full contribution records would now have state payments some 2.4 times greater than Jobseeker's Allowance.

Likewise, rates of Universal Credit maintain a sizeable difference between those older and younger than 25 years of age (see Table 10.3). As we describe in the discussion that follows, Universal Credit became a mainstay of policy under COVID-19 with a temporary uplift. It was subject to the same benefits level freeze described above.

Universal Credit

A staple of Conservative policies in this period was the continued rollout of Universal Credit. Before the phased introduction of Universal Credit, being progressively rolled out nationwide since 2013, there was a stark division in the system of benefits between *out of work* means-tested benefits, such as Income Support, and certain tax credits paid for those *in work*, such as Working Tax Credit. At 16 hours of paid work per week, one set of benefits (such as Income Support) became largely replaced by the other (including

Working Tax Credit). At the same time, a few benefits (like Housing Benefit) were available both for workers and non-workers.

To replace this divided system, Universal Credit is a single benefit structure and set of rules designed to replace: Income Support, Housing Benefit, Working Tax Credit, Child Tax Credit and the non-contributory elements of both Jobseeker's Allowance and Employment and Support Allowance. It brought these together into a single system, removing some anomalies and inconsistencies of approach. The introduction of Universal Credit also brought in other changes that were significant departures from the past system, some of which were very important. For instance, claiming was to be online rather than in person, as part of a move to a digital system. There was also a shift from the previous patterns of weekly payments to instead having monthly payments, which would affect family budgeting. An additional change was to stop paying Housing Benefit (for rent) direct to landlords and instead pay rent to claimants (Northern Ireland excepted), which runs the risk of those in receipt incurring rent arrears but also gives greater financial responsibility to households. Such reforms were justified as making the experience of benefit receipt more like that of earned employment. Many of these individual changes caused controversy, even if the overall simplification of Universal Credit may be seen as a positive (for a dissenting view about the overall concept, see Millar and Bennett, 2017, and for concerns about encroaching conditionality, see Dwyer and Wright, 2014). The need to keep down costs meant that decisions regarding rules had to level down rather than level up where there were inconsistencies (for example, if one member of a couple was below pension age that meant a Universal Credit claim, which in the past might have been a Pension Credit claim, with higher rates).

Caps, limits and other austerity measures

The rollout of Universal Credit was on a less generous basis then initially envisaged, finally prompting the resignation of its main government architect, Iain Duncan Smith. However there were certainly other reforms that aimed at cost reduction. The summer 2015 Budget introduced the two-child limit, which meant that Universal Credit recipients would not receive additional amounts for any third or subsequent child. The amount of Housing Benefit (or other rental support within Universal Credit) was restricted to the bottom 30 per cent of local tenancies – a level that was then fixed over time, until the pandemic.

A key policy reform was the benefit cap. This legislated an upper limit on the amount of benefits that a person may receive. This was introduced in 2013 at rate of £26,000 (approximately average income, or £18,200 for single people). However this was sharply reduced in 2016, and it remains the case in 2022 that the most that may be claimed is £13,400 a year for single adults, and £20,000 for couples or single parents.[1] However, in a rare departure from austerity, the November 2022 Autumn Statement announced an inflation-linked increase in the value of the benefit cap. As with other austerity-led reforms, those older than State Pension age are not included in the benefit cap. Large-scale research has linked the process of capping benefits with reduced mental health and possibly increasing the effective distance from being in work (Reeves et al, 2022).

Disability benefits

In early 2022, the Work and Pensions Select Committee used its parliamentary powers to force the publication of a report about disabled people's experiences of the benefits system, which the Department for Work and Pensions had long been declining to publish (for details, see UK Parliament, 2021). The report found instances of unmet need, stating: 'Participants with limited financial resources beyond their health and disability benefits reported that they were often unable to meet essential day to day living costs' (National Centre for Social Research, 2022, p 22). In an oral evidence session with the then Secretary of State on 8 December 2021, there was also the following exchange:

Chair: According to a report from Disability News Service last week, 'After being shown the first draft of the report, DWP [Department for Work and Pensions] told NatCen [National Centre for Social Research] to reduce the number of references to "unmet needs"' and the final version 'had far fewer references to unmet needs'. Is that true?

Dr Thérèse Coffey: I am not aware of the sources of Disability News Service. (House of Commons Work and Pensions Committee, 2021, Q 135)

Benefit reforms over successive years have often been perceived as negatively affecting disabled people. As a result, research by the Social Security Advisory Committee found that '[o]ne of the principal themes was that the last decade had seen a deterioration in the relationship between DWP [Department for Work and Pensions] and disabled people which was hindering DWP's ability to improve its services or to meet its policy objectives' (2021, p 23).

Responses under COVID-19

The lockdowns resulting from the COVID-19 pandemic saw a massive increase in people claiming Universal Credit due to job losses and reductions in working hours. Hence, the Department for Work and Pensions was responsible for dealing with many more people than anticipated. Mostly they were able to respond to this additional demand thanks to the digital basis of Universal Credit. Government intervention also reduced the numbers of people needing to claim Universal Credit due to the introduction of the Coronavirus Job Retention Scheme (or 'furlough' scheme), which supported 11.7 million employments between March 2020 and September 2021. There was also support for the self-employed through the Self-Employment Income Support Scheme. As of 15 September 2021, the scheme had supported 2.9 million people. Adjustments to the social security safety net were also made, including the £1,000 per annum Universal Credit uplift (the £20 per week uplift), a realignment of Housing Benefit to increase support for rent payments and a relaxation of the Statutory Sick Pay rules. In addition, local authorities received extra funds to help vulnerable households with costs for essentials such as food, clothing and utilities and Council Tax bills.

The £20 uplift certainly increased the ability of those on means-tested benefits to attain a minimum income standard, although this looks like an admission of inadequacy in the standard rates to which we have now returned. The pressure of the pandemic also led to a temporary cessation of the regime of benefit sanctions.

The living cost crisis 2022–

As the country emerged from the pandemic and lockdowns in 2021, a new crisis loomed in 2022: the living cost crisis. This was sparked partly by the economic recovery (and the impact of Brexit), as demand for goods exceeded supply leading to general inflation, and then the war in Ukraine added to economic uncertainty and inflation, particularly in relation to energy. The government responded to the cost of living crisis in February 2022 with a £150 Council Tax rebate for those in Bands A to D (with Scotland and Wales introducing similar policies) and a £200 temporary rebate (to be repaid) on all electricity bills in the autumn. After further lobbying, the government announced in May 2022 that every household in the UK would get an energy bill discount of £400. Eight million households on means-tested benefits would also get £650 paid directly into their bank accounts in two lump sums – one in July, the other in the autumn. And there would be separate one-off payments of £300 to pensioner households and £150 to individuals receiving disability benefits. The emergency Household Support Fund, which is allocated by councils in England, was also be extended by £500 million to £1.5 billion, and the devolved governments received equivalent funding.

The short-lived 'plan for growth' (2022) and after

The arrival of Liz Truss as Prime Minister in September 2022 signalled a very significant (if ultimately short-lived) change in policy direction – though perhaps one with continued support in some ranks of the Conservatives. The new Chancellor of the Exchequer's (Kwasi Kwarteng's) fiscal event (or 'mini-budget' or financial statement) included a set of tax cuts worth around £45 billion. This level of tax giveaway represented a set of (uncosted) reforms unmatched in the previous 50 years, and apparently financed by a higher deficit rather than through any offsetting tax increases elsewhere. Analysis by the Resolution Foundation found that half the tax cuts were to the benefit of the relatively small number of very high earners: 'The result is that almost half (47 per cent) of the gains will go to the richest 5 per cent of households, compared to 12 per cent for the entire poorer half' (Bell et al, 2022, p 3).

The reorientation of this new package of reforms included the claim that, '[f]or too long in this country we have indulged in a fight over redistribution' (Kwarteng, Hansard, House of Commons, 2022). This brings to mind a similar phrase from a decade earlier in *Britannia unchained*, by Kwarteng, Truss and others, that the country should 'stop indulging in irrelevant debates about sharing the pie between manufacturing and services, the north and the south, women and men' (Kwarteng et al, 2012, p 2). One commentator called the interventions 'a naked exercise in redistributing wealth upwards' (Jacobs, 2022).

Measures relating to social security benefits were also announced at this time, echoing again the concern expressed in *Britannia unchained* that '[t]oo many people in Britain prefer a lie-in ... to hard work' (Kwarteng et al, 2012, p 5). Thus the government announced an increase in sanctions and additional requirements for job search and/or working longer hours for those receiving Universal Credit. Leaving aside the changes to fuel prices, benefiting all energy consumers, the mini-budget had nothing for those on out-of-work benefits.

In particular, the 2022 plan made an increase to the levels of earnings (called the 'administrative earnings threshold') at which Universal Credit recipients would not face pressure to increase earnings or working hours. Initially, 9 hours of work (at the National Living Wage) was sufficient. But this is increasing to 24 hours a week for couples and 15 hours for individual claimants. This means that about 120,000 more low-earning Universal Credit claimants will move from the Light Touch labour market regime to the Intensive Work Search labour market regime, and hence expected to actively search for work and attend weekly/fortnightly appointments. The 2022 Autumn Statement also provided for strengthening the Universal Credit sanctions regime to set, it seems, yet clearer work expectations. The other change announced was to increase the offer of support for those aged 50 or older who are long-term unemployed. This is against the background of evidence of more people over 50 leaving the labour market in the wake of the COVID-19 pandemic and lockdowns, despite rises in the number of known job vacancies in the economy.[2]

The mini-budget caused extensive panic in global markets and most of the key policy proposals in were abandoned by Truss, after removing the Chancellor. But this was insufficient to save Truss, who was replaced by Rishi Sunak in October 2022. His approach to social security in particular is yet to be fully elaborated: the subsequent Autumn Statement increased benefits (and the benefit cap, arguably long overdue) by inflation, but envisaged longer-term overall reductions in public spending.

Policies: changes in pensions and older-age benefits

As we have mentioned, the punitive measures affecting those of working age were not extended to those of State Pension age or older. Instead, older people's pensions were better protected and indeed guaranteed to increase compared to other groups. Maintenance of the triple lock in pensions was made despite austerity, although at the cost of continuing increases in older State Pension ages. One group (WASPI – Women Against State Pension Inequality) did try to slow or reverse such changes but, at the time of writing, without success. The biggest reform was the introduction of a new contributory pension at a more generous level than the prevailing arrangements.

The new State Pension

From April 2016, new pensioners received something called the 'new State Pension', rather than the existing state retirement pension that is paid to those reaching State Pension age before that date. Both pensions require that recipients have paid into the schemes, via National Insurance contributions, over a decent numbers of years when working. The older pension really had two sets of elements, one being paid at a flat rate and others depending on the level of past contributions (that is, earnings). By April 2016, this flat-rate element was worth £119.30 per week. However, there is also a means-tested benefit for older people, Pension Credit, for those without significant savings and whose incomes are below a set threshold. In April 2016, for a single person, that amount was £155.60 – in other words, older people with just the older basic State Pension as their income will generally be entitled to a means-tested addition to bring their income up to this level. Lower-income pensioners may also be eligible for Housing Benefit (if paying rent) and Council Tax Support.

However, in practice, many older people might also receive one or more of a number of earnings-related state pensions. These top up the basic pension and pay more to those who earned more during their working lifetimes – unless they decided to 'opt out' (contract out) into a non-state pension, such as an occupational pension or a private pension. The earnings-related pensions have changed considerably over time, encompassing the 1960s Graduated Retirement Benefit, the 1970s State Earnings-Related Pensions Scheme and the 2000s State Second Pension. These earnings-related additions meant that those earning more in the their working lifetimes, though not in a private pension, received an overall pension of more than the basic minimum. These pensions have generally been relatively complex and subject to little-understood legislative changes that generally eroded their value.

Nevertheless, older people often have above-average incomes. In 2020–21, the average single pensioner income (after housing costs) was £246 a week, and for pensioner couples was £511 per week. Overall 19 per cent of pensioners are in the bottom fifth of incomes, and 14 per cent are in the top fifth of incomes (Department for Work and Pensions, 2022).

The new State Pension essentially combines the existing basic State Pension with the average from the various earnings-related elements. As a result, there is a new flat-rate scheme, but paid at a higher level than the former pension, removing the series of state earnings-related schemes (and removing contracting out). At least, that is how the scheme will work when fully established, and those retiring for now may have elements from both schemes checked to ensure they do not lose out on any pre-existing rights. The new State Pension is sufficient to move pensioners above the level of the means-tested floor, Pension Credit – though generally not by much. In April 2022, the respective weekly figures for new State Pension and Pension Credit were £185.15 and £182.60, and tenants might still receive Housing Benefit in addition, on a means-tested basis. This overall reform will tend to benefit lower earners (as they receive more than they might have done from the state earnings-related supplements), but at the expense of those whose earnings might have made for a higher State Pension under the older system. Many middle and higher earners were, in any case, opted out of those top-ups and in private pensions, and hence less affected (though no longer having a financial gain from the ability to contract out of an element of National Insurance).

Non-state pensions and auto-enrolment

Another policy in force at the earlier part of the period (started in October 2012) but with ongoing effects was the introduction of 'automatic enrolment' into non-state pensions (McKay and Rowlingson, 2016). This meant that all workers (above a low earnings threshold) would be automatically joined into pensions. At first, this only affected those with larger employers, but now it affects all employees. In the longer term, this may somewhat increase pensioner incomes, with the new State Pension providing a floor, meaning that such pensions would not generally only be offsetting the means-tested benefit, Pension Credit.

Access to a private pension scheme does not, however, necessarily mean that people are contributing enough into it to meet their basic needs in retirement, and indeed the majority of workplace pensions managed by the biggest provider, Nest, were actually 'inactive' in 2022 (McKay et al, 2022).

State Pension ages

The Pensions Act 1995 signalled the process of equalising State Pension ages, which were then 65 for men and 60 for women. It was suggested that women's pension ages would start to rise in 2010, matching men's ages in 2020. However, given the perceived need to save costs, it was later felt necessary to also increase men's pensions ages, and this also affected the progress of equalisation of State Pension ages (it was speeded up). Women born in the 1950s experienced the sharpest increases in their State Pension ages, retiring when perhaps five or six years older than their sisters born in the 1940s.

It has been debated how much effective notice was provided to the women affected by the reforms, with the claim being made that many women continued to expect their state pension to start at age 60, oblivious to the reforms, and made their labour market plans accordingly, only to then experience a gap in their incomes of five years. This led to a significant campaign against those increases in pension age (Pemberton, 2017). However, this did not lead to any changes in the increases in State Pension ages.

Incomes and poverty

Levels of poverty since 2010 have generally been regarded as high. In November 2018, the United Nations Special Rapporteur on Extreme Poverty and Human Rights concluded his visit to the UK with a memorandum starkly describing actual and projected levels of child poverty: 'twenty-first century Britain is not just a disgrace, but a social calamity and an economic disaster, all rolled into one' (Alston, 2018, p 1).

Prior to the pandemic, income poverty affected one child in every four (25 per cent). However, measuring poverty is made difficult by the intervening period of the pandemic. This brought with it substantial state support, but of a temporary kind. At the time of writing, the most recent information relates to April 2020–March 2021, which is not necessarily representative of either the current situation or what is to follow. Indeed, Cribb et al (2022) note that the pandemic measures did largely offset earlier changes to means-tested benefits and tax credits, but were only in place temporarily. Those pandemic measures to social security acted to increase the incomes of those at the lower end of the distribution, to reduce levels of poverty and even to moderate levels of economic inequality. This shows that the right political action can have quite decisive effects, where there is the will (or perhaps the opportunity – like lockdowns) to make this possible. An analysis of social security reforms for the longer period, 2010–17, found the overall effects to be regressive (Reed, 2020). Moreover the effects were found to be particularly negative for households with children and for disabled people, as well as those on low incomes in general. While we are still awaiting good data on incomes following on from the lockdowns, it seems likely that the pre-existing rates of inequality will be persisting – albeit having largely plateaued in the 21st century.

Conclusion

The social security policies followed by the Conservative governments since 2015 show a considerable degree of continuity with those introduced under the Coalition. In particular, despite rhetoric to tackle 'burning [social] injustice' and to 'level up', there was a continuation, in practice, of relatively harsh constraints for those of working age against a more generous regime for those older than the State Pension age.

The inadequacy of benefit rates to maintain living standards was starkly exposed when millions of new claimants discovered firsthand the modesty of the benefits. To alleviate this, a temporary increase of £20 per week was introduced, but only for those newly registered or transitioned to Universal Credit – not those on older benefit schemes. In an unusual move for a New Right government, the COVID-19 response involved spending billions to subsidise wages, and 'mass handouts' were extended into 2022 and 2023 to help combat the cost of living crisis.

The end of this period witnessed an abrupt, though swiftly abandoned, turn to the extreme Right in terms of fiscal policy, with the Truss/Kwarteng plan for growth signalling greater deregulation, lower taxes and a disdain for analysis of distributional consequences of policies. Such radicalism was too much for the markets and now Sunak and his Chancellor, Jeremy Hunt, have rowed back from most of the tax-cutting fiscal plans. However, they retained greater work obligations for part-time claimants, further support for those over 50 who experience greater labour market disengagement, plus the depressingly tired refrain for harsher benefit sanctions for those found to be noncompliant.

Conversely, older individuals, bolstered by state and non-state pensions, have generally fared better. Their living standards have largely matched price increases. For future generations, the policy of auto-enrolment into Defined Contribution pensions should provide some income boost, albeit potentially modest, compared to the previous system – even if other trends (less secure pensions, lower homeownership) provide reasons for caution about future pensioner living standards.

The ongoing cost of living crisis (winter 2022–23) is incredibly challenging for many millions of people, and opinion polls suggest that the electorate may have lost patience with the Conservative government – though things could well change before the next general election (due by January 2025 at the very latest). A quick glance at Labour's approach to social security suggests a return to familiar New Labour ground, with a New Deal for Working People being the key focus rather than anything more radical. Whether any party has the appropriate response to avoid mass hardship given the scale of the crisis remains to be seen.

Notes

[1]   Amounts are about £3,000 a year higher for those living in London.
[2]   For information, see the Office for National Statistics' 'Labour market overview, UK' at: www.ons.gov.uk/employmentandlabourmarket/peopleinwork/employmentandem ployeetypes/bulletins/uklabourmarket/latest.

References

Alston, P. (2018) *Statement on visit to the United Kingdom, by Professor Philip Alston, United Nations Special Rapporteur on extreme poverty and human rights.* Available at: www.ohchr.org/sites/default/files/Documents/Issues/Pove rty/EOM_GB_16Nov2018.pdf (accessed 19 July 2023).

Bell, T., Broome, M., Cominetti, N., Corlett, A., Fry, E., Handscomb, K., Judge, L., Leslie, J., Murphy, L., Shah, K., Slaughter, H., Smith, J., Thwaites, G. and Try, L. (2022) *Blowing the budget: assessing the implications of the September 2022 fiscal statement*, London: Resolution Foundation. Available at: www.resolutionfoundation.org/app/uploads/2022/09/Blow ing-the-budget.pdf (accessed 19 July 2023).

Conservative Party (2015) *Strong leadership, a clear economic plan, a brighter, more secure future. The Conservative Party Manifesto 2015*, London: Conservative Party.

Conservative Party (2017) *Forward together: our plan for a stronger Britain and a prosperous future. The Conservative and Unionist Party Manifesto 2017*, London: Conservative Party.

Conservative Party (2019) *Get Brexit done: unleash Britain's potential. The Conservative and Unionist Party Manifesto 2019*, London: Conservative Party.

Cribb, J., Waters, T., Wernham, T. and Xu, X. (2022) *Living standards, poverty and inequality in the UK: 2022*, London: Institute for Fiscal Studies. Available at: https://ifs.org.uk/sites/default/files/output_url_files/R215-Living-standards-poverty-and-inequality-in-the-UK-2022.pdf (accessed 19 July 2023).

Department for Work and Pensions (2010) *Universal Credit: welfare that works*, London: The Stationery Office.

Department for Work and Pensions (2022) 'Pensioners' Incomes series: financial year 2020 to 2021', 31 March. Available at: www.gov.uk/government/statistics/pensioners-incomes-series-financial-year-2020-to-2021/pensioners-incomes-series-financial-year-2020-to-2021 (accessed 19 July 2023).

Dwyer, P. and Wright, S. (2014) 'Universal Credit, ubiquitous conditionality and its implications for social citizenship', *Journal of Poverty and Social Justice*, 22(1): 27–35.

Hansard, House of Commons (2022) *The growth plan*, vol 719, col 938, 23 September. Available at: https://hansard.parliament.uk/commons/2022-09-23/debates/6F82FA4B-DB6B-4E89-BA39-4ABEA1045ABF/TheGrowthPlan (accessed 19 July 2023).

House of Commons Work and Pensions Committee (2021) *Oral evidence: the work of the Secretary of State for Work and Pensions*, HC 514. Available at: https://committees.parliament.uk/oralevidence/3168/pdf/ (accessed 19 July 2023).

Jacobs, M. (2022) 'This "mini-budget" is a naked exercise in redistributing wealth upwards', *The Guardian*, 23 September. Available at: www.theguardian.com/commentisfree/2022/sep/23/mini-budget-redistributing-wealth-economy-liz-truss-kwasi-kwarteng (accessed 19 July 2023).

Kwarteng, K., Patel, P., Raab, D., Skidmore, C. and Truss, E. (2012) *Britannia unchained*, London: Palgrave Macmillan.

McKay, S. and Rowlingson, K. (2016) 'Social security under the Coalition and Conservatives: shredding the system for people of working age; privileging pensioners', in H. Bochel and M. Powell (eds) *The Coalition government and social policy: restructuring the welfare state*, Bristol: Policy Press, pp 179–200.

McKay, S., Rowlingson, K. and Atkinson, A. (2022) *Financial inclusion monitor 2022*, Birmingham: University of Birmingham.

Millar, J. and Bennett, F. (2017) 'Universal Credit: assumptions, contradictions and virtual reality', *Social Policy and Society*, 16(2): 169–82.

National Centre for Social Research (2022) *Uses of health and disability benefits*, Report for DWP ordered to be published by the Work and Pensions Select Committee. Available at: https://committees.parliament.uk/publications/8745/documents/88599/default/ (accessed 19 July 2023).

Pemberton, H. (2017) 'WASPI's is (mostly) a campaign for inequality', *The Political Quarterly*, 88(3): 510–16.

Reed, H. (2020) 'The distributional impact of tax and social security reforms in the UK from 2010 to 2017', *Social Policy and Society*, 19(3): 470–86.

Reeves, A., Fransham, M., Stewart, K. and Patrick, R. (2022) 'Does capping social security harm health? A natural experiment in the UK', *Social Policy & Administration*, 56(3): 345–59.

Royston, S. (2017) *Broken benefits: what's gone wrong with welfare reform*, Bristol: Policy Press.

Social Security Advisory Committee (2021) *How DWP involves disabled people when developing or evaluating programmes that affect them*, Occasional paper 25, London: Social Security Advisory Committee. Available at: www.gov. uk/government/publications/ssac-occasional-paper-25-how-dwp-invol ves-disabled-people-when-developing-or-evaluating-programmes-that-aff ect-them/how-dwp-involves-disabled-people-when-developing-or-eva luating-programmes-that-affect-them-occasional-paper-25 (accessed 19 July 2023).

UK Parliament (2021) 'Disabled people's experiences of the benefits system: Work and Pensions Secretary given "final chance" to publish report', 16 December. Available at: https://committees.parliament.uk/committee/ 164/work-and-pensions-committee/news/159956/disabled-peoples-expe riences-of-the-benefits-system-work-and-pensions-secretary-given-final- chance-to-publish-report/ (accessed 19 July 2023).

11

Labour market strategies and welfare policies: the Conservative record

Anne Daguerre and David Etherington

Introduction

The post-2015 period has been characterised by considerable government instability. Once David Cameron resigned from office after the 2016 Brexit referendum, Theresa May became Prime Minister. Forced to leave in July 2019, she was replaced by Boris Johnson. In December 2019 Boris Johnson secured an 80-seat majority in Parliament on the promise to 'get Brexit done', only to be ousted from office in July 2022 following a multitude of scandals. During the summer of 2022, Liz Truss, former Foreign Secretary, campaigned on a platform of deregulatory supply-side and tax cut reforms, and was handed the keys to Number 10 in early September. Newly appointed Chancellor Kwasi Kwarteng, co-author (with Liz Truss) of *Britannia Unchained* (2012), announced a mini-budget consisting of unfunded tax cuts on 23 September 2022. Hostile market reaction provoked the demise of first Kwarteng and then Truss, and the nomination of Rishi Sunak as leader of the Conservative Party and Prime Minister on 24 October 2022. With Sunak in charge, large parts of supply-side shock therapy policies were put to rest.

External shocks – the COVID-19 crisis, the war in Ukraine and the rising costs of food and energy – clearly considerably limited the ability of post-2019 Conservative governments to roll out a coherent programme (Peele, 2021), as noted throughout this book. In fact, there has been a pattern of stop and go between One Nation Toryism – a form of socially compassionate paternalism in the tradition of Disraeli – and a small state, low-tax vision promoted most clearly by the hard Brexiter European Research Group. This small state vision is incompatible with the 'levelling up' imperative formulated by Boris Johnson to appeal to red wall voters in the north of England and the Midlands.

Welfare and employment policies, which were prominent issues in the 2015 Conservative election manifesto (Conservative Party, 2015), did not define the politics of Conservative governments after the Brexit vote.

The Department for Work and Pensions continued to operate within the parameters of tight spending controls set by the Treasury and the Office for Budget Responsibility. On the whole, the residual safety net for working-age people was eroded, while spending on pensions was maintained. The 'triple lock' on pensions reflected the political choices of governments whose fate rested in the hands of a rapidly ageing population (although the triple lock was suspended in 2022–23). Comparatively more support was given to certain categories of the 'deserving' poor, in particular working families with only two children (the per child element in Universal Credit was limited to two children for new claims and births from 6 April 2017) at the expense of working-age adults without children and large families. In this regard, there was remarkable continuity between the Coalition government's policies and those of David Cameron, Theresa May and Boris Johnson post 2015. The three prime ministers each claimed to embrace a form of One Nation Toryism focused on reducing regional inequalities and promoting equality of opportunity through education and apprenticeships (see Chapter 1). During the COVID-19 crisis, Universal Credit was the main vehicle for getting additional money into the pockets of low-income households. Post COVID-19, the main issue for the Department for Work and Pensions was to get economically inactive individuals back into paid employment in the context of massive labour shortages. The department resumed its traditional 'work first' policy of getting economically inactive and unemployed people into low-paid work, quickly, to serve the interest of local employers (Etherington, 2020). The harsh conditionality, work first regime that had characterised the first years of the Coalition government, therefore, made a comeback in rhetoric and reality, as illustrated by the sharp rise in benefit sanctions in 2021–22 (Webster, 2022).

This chapter explores the trajectory of Conservative welfare and active labour market policies post 2015. It is divided into four sections. First, it shows that the overall trajectory is policy continuity, with successive governments implementing the rollout of Universal Credit. Second, it examines how external shocks seemed to change Conservative government thinking on welfare support and conditionality, at least for a while. The third section analyses welfare, skills and levelling up policies post COVID-19 and in the context of the cost of living crisis. The fourth section concludes the chapter.

Welfare reform and active labour market policies post 2015: an overall trajectory of continuity

A key aim of the Coalition government had been to simplify the benefit system and create a model which would make work pay, broadly in line with previous New Labour priorities (Daguerre and Etherington, 2016). This was the thinking behind the design of Universal Credit, which replaces the main means-tested benefits for those on low incomes, both in and out of work (Housing Benefit, Jobseeker's Allowance, Income Support, Employment and Support Allowance, tax credits), with a single benefit paid to the 'head of the household'. Universal Credit works by creating one household allowance (called a personal allowance). This personal allowance is paid in full if the household has no other income and any savings are less than £6,000 (the household will not receive Universal Credit if they have savings above £16,000). A key component is claimant commitment around work search requirements and the expanded use of benefit sanctions.

At the time of its introduction, in 2013, Universal Credit represented a major overhaul of the tax and benefit system. It aimed to smooth the transition into work and encourage work claimants to take on additional hours, through increased reward for the claimant being in work (Department for Work and Pensions, 2012). In addition, benefit payments paid monthly were supposed to nudge claimants towards monthly budgeting, which in turn was expected to encourage work behaviours (Department for Work and Pensions, 2016). The benefit is paid directly, in arrears, to claimants in exchange for commitment to find work, with a broad expectation that recipients will spend at least 35 hours a week searching for work, without considering any mitigating circumstances. Claimants must also manage their money just like a self-sufficient employee does, paying their bills and rent each month. Budgeting support and debt advice is available, when needed, for recipients who traditionally pay their bills fortnightly or weekly.

A host of serious design and operational flaws plagued the implementation of Universal Credit. Although the initial intention had been to support low-income people to make the transition into paid employment by enabling them to take on mini-jobs and expand their hours, it became more punitive than was originally intended. A portion of the blame for this was the chronic underfunding and benefit cuts imposed by then Chancellor George Osborne (Freud, 2021). In 2015, the Conservative manifesto pledged to cut expenditure on working-age benefits to the tune of £12 billion (Hobson, 2020). It stated:

> We will freeze working age benefits for two years from April 2016, with exemptions for disability and pensioner benefits – as at present – as well as maternity allowance, statutory maternity pay, statutory paternity pay, statutory adoption pay and statutory sick pay. [...] We will lower the maximum amount that a single household can claim in benefits each year from £26,000 to £23,000, so we reward work. (Conservative Party, 2015, p 28)

The last major reform to the tax and benefit system was the Welfare Reform and Work Act 2016. Some of the main measures outlined by Hobson are:

- Lowering the household benefit cap threshold from £26,000 for a family and £18,200 for a single person, to £23,000 in London (£15,410 for a single person) and £20,000 (£13,400 for a single person) elsewhere in the UK;
- A four-year benefits freeze applying to most working age benefits;
- Limiting support for children through Child Tax Credits and Universal Credit [the two-child cap)];
- The abolition of Employment and Support Allowance Work-Related Activity Component. (2020, p 18)

The cumulative impact of the scale of the benefit cuts (the household benefit cap, the four-year benefit freeze and the two-child limit for Child Tax Credit) cannot be underestimated. These cuts were widely criticised at the time, including by David Freud, one of the main architects of Universal Credit, and Iain Duncan Smith, Secretary of State for Work and Pensions from 2010 to 2016. Planned cuts to tax credits were partially reversed because of a revolt in the House of Lords (Hobson, 2020; Freud, 2021). But some reforms went ahead, notably the two-child limit post 2017, the benefit cap and cuts to Employment and Support Allowance. Iain Duncan Smith resigned in protest.

Following the referendum on the UK's membership of the European Union in June 2016, David Cameron immediately resigned and was replaced by Theresa May. The Brexit issue consumed the political energy of the May government, with little time for welfare reform, as the 2017 Conservative manifesto made clear: 'We have no plans for further radical welfare reform in this parliament and will continue the roll-out of Universal Credit, to ensure that it always pays to be in work' (Conservative Party, 2017, p 54). Between 2016 and 2019 leadership at the Department for Work and Pensions kept changing, but most of the work and pensions secretaries (Damian Green, Stephen Crabb, David Gauke and Amber Rudd), other than Esther McVey, embraced a form of One Nation Conservatism based on the imperative to 'protect the most vulnerable' (Hunt, 2022) and the language of a rights and responsibility contract between the state and benefit claimants (Daguerre, 2020).

When the Conservative Party lost its majority in the May 2017 general election, David Gauke took over, followed by Esther McVey (January to November 2018). McVey was positioned to the Right of the Party. In contrast to McVey, Amber Rudd (November 2018–September 2019), identified as a One Nation Conservative: Rudd became co-chair of the One Nation caucus of Conservative MPs in 2019. She made a series of conciliatory statements. For instance, she announced that three-year benefit sanctions were counterproductive and would be reduced to a maximum of six months (Daguerre, 2020). Part of the reason for Rudd's more conciliatory stance toward benefit sanctions was perhaps because she represented a marginal seat in Hastings, a deprived constituency in East Sussex. She also paused the migration of legacy benefit recipients to Universal Credit with the aim of 'piloting' the new benefit in Harrogate to test its implementation and 'iron out' its design faults. Rudd resigned in September 2019 and quit the Conservative Party following profound disagreements over Boris Johnson's Brexit policies. Johnson appointed libertarian and socially conservative Thérèse Coffey, as Work and Pensions Secretary (September 2019– September 2022).

There has been no major reform since the Welfare Reform and Work Act 2016. The Resolution Foundation, summarising the cumulative impact of welfare reform since 2013, concluded that the UK social security system had lost some of its automatic stabiliser functions because of cuts in the amount of financial support for those most in need (Gardiner, 2019). This was even though, on average, the new Universal Credit system was not less generous than the legacy benefits it sought to replace after a series of policy reversals post 2015, as austerity fatigue kicked in (Daguerre, 2020). Nevertheless, the overall picture was increased targeting, a more demanding job search regime for benefit claimants and less income support for working-age adults with or without dependent children and working-age people with chronic health conditions (Gardiner, 2019).

Welfare reform and labour market policies were not a priority for the premiership of Boris Johnson, despite its commitment to 'fairness in the workplace' and strengthening workers' rights post Brexit. On welfare reform, the 2019 manifesto stated:

> We will continue the roll-out of Universal Credit, which combines multiple benefits into one while building a clearer pathway from welfare into work. We have already acted to increase work allowances, a move worth £630 to working families with children, and those with disabilities, and we will do more to make sure that Universal Credit works for the most vulnerable. We will also end the benefit freeze, while making sure it pays to work more hours. (Conservative Party, 2019, p 17)

This was very much a continuity pledge, albeit with some modifications in terms of the value of the standard allowance and the end of the benefit freeze. But the COVID-19 crisis changed this attitude of not so benign neglect. Public health interventions that resulted in a series of national lockdowns since March 2020 represented a great exogenous shock and put the social security system under tremendous pressure (Harris et al, 2020). This was particularly the case for Universal Credit because of its crucial role in supporting people with low incomes or newly unemployed individuals who were not included in the Coronavirus Job Retention Scheme (Mackley, 2021).

The safety net during the COVID-19 crisis

Boris Johnson's Cabinet included a number of individuals positioned to the Right of the Conservative Party, not least Jacob Rees-Mogg, Thérèse Coffey and Rishi Sunak, the Chancellor. However, in response to the lockdown and the massive fall of employment predicted by the Office for Budget Responsibility, the priority for the Johnson government was to protect jobs. The Coronavirus Job Retention Scheme (known as the 'furlough' scheme), Chancellor Sunak's brainchild, paid furloughed employees 80 per cent of their wages during the first phase of the pandemic, with government support gradually reduced from 80 per cent to 70 per cent and then 60 per cent. The furlough scheme, particularly for a party imbued with a laissez-faire approach, was a bold experiment in a country that never had generous job protection schemes, supporting nine million jobs at the peak of the crisis and costing £69 billion to the Treasury (Pope and Shearer, 2021). While support was more generous for people at risk of losing their jobs (furloughed employees) than for Universal Credit recipients (Harris et al, 2020), Universal Credit coped with the crisis better than expected. The Department for Work and Pensions was praised for having dealt well with a sudden and massive increase in the number of Universal Credit claimants, from 3 million in March 2020 to 5.2 million in May 2020 (Mackley, 2021, p 12). Universal Credit had been enjoying 'its moment in the sun' thanks to the COVID-19 crisis (Timmins, 2020). The Select Committee on Work and Pensions stated in its June 2020 report that the Department for Work and Pensions 'should be commended for its rapid response to an unprecedented increase in claims. In particular, the extraordinary work of its front-line staff, whose efforts have led to most claimants receiving their first payment on time, deserves the highest praise' (Work and Pensions Committee, 2020, p 14, para 21). The department adapted quickly to the new situation, making a series of operational and administrative adjustments. New rules were adopted through statutory instruments, leading to a substantial relaxation of the administrative hurdles that characterise the delivery of Universal Credit. In their July 2020 review, Harris et al explained that 'political pressure to loosen the purse strings' resulted in increased generosity of entitlements (2020, p 58). Measures included: the increase in the standard allowance for all new claimants (but not those on legacy benefits); the suspension of the minimum income floor for self-employed individuals; the introduction of a nine-month 'grace period' for new claimants whose earnings in each of the 12 months prior to their claim were equivalent to at least 16 hours at the National Minimum Wage; and the restoration of the levels of the Local Housing Allowance to the 30th percentile for rents in local areas (Harris et al, 2020). It is important to note that these increases were temporary, with various sunset clauses, giving the government maximum flexibility as to when and how to revisit these measures. For instance, when questioned in Parliament in May 2020 about the persistence of the five-week wait for the first payment and the benefit cap, Thérèse Coffey declared: 'The fundamentals of universal credit do not change. The reason for the assessment period is to understand people's general income and use that as a basis, but that is where the advances come in: to help people who cannot make ends meet in between' (Hansard, 2020). In this exchange, Coffey made it clear that the principles of Universal Credit were not going to be substantially altered. She pointed instead to the ways in which the Department for Work and Pensions had adjusted to the increase in the volume of claims – an additional 1.2 million during the first lockdown; these included the redeployment of the department's 8,500 staff to claim processing, suspending work-related conditionality and face-to-face meetings, and overall streamlining the application process. The department received an estimated additional £7 billion to implement policy changes (Brewer and Handscomb, 2020, p 17).

The Department for Work and Pensions significantly reduced delays in payments, with 93 per cent of new Universal Credit claimants receiving their first full payments on time, compared to 85 per cent of payment timeliness prior to the pandemic (Mackley, 2021, p 9). The capacity to handle an unprecedented volume of claims was attributed to a large extent to the digital and automated structure of the system (Timmins, 2020).

How can we assess the Johnson government's response to the COVID-19 crisis? There are three aspects to addressing this question. First, there is a consensus in the economic literature (Brewer and Tasseva, 2021; Cribb et al, 2022) that the government did manage some poverty reduction, in both relative and absolute terms. Cribb et al summarise these antipoverty effects as follows:

> Indeed, the benefit giveaways were enough to return the working-age benefit system to (on average) something quite close to the 2011–12 system, at least for low-earning households. Together these patterns meant that income poverty fell, on both an absolute and a relative basis. This picture is quite different from the one seen over the past decade or so, where growth was strongest around the middle of the distribution thanks to rises in income from employment, while poorer households saw a substantial share of their employment income increases offset by reductions to the real value of benefits and tax credits. (2022, p 28)

Second, there has been a rise of what can be referred to as 'in-work poverty' – around two thirds (68 per cent) of working-age adults in poverty live in a household where at least one adult is in work. This is the highest figure since records of households below average income began in 1996–97, when the figure stood below 50 per cent (Joseph Rowntree Foundation, 2022).

People in workless households, living in a family with a disabled family member, in a household headed by a non-White person, in single-person households or in very large families are more at risk of experiencing deep poverty or even destitution (Schmuecker et al, 2022). This is why there is a disconnect between headline poverty figures and the deep poverty and destitution experienced by specific demographic groups and deprived local areas (Etherington et al, 2021). This deepening and worsening of poverty indicate an Americanisation of the safety net (Gingrich and King, 2019). In the US, deep poverty and destitution have risen because of cuts to single-parent family benefits in 1996 (Desmond, 2015; Edin and Shaefer, 2015).

Third, the government's emergency response entrenched a 'two-tier claimant hierarchy', establishing a distinction between people on legacy benefits (mainly workless households claiming disability benefits and working households where people had lost full-time work because of the pandemic (Meers, 2022). Indeed, the £20 uplift did not apply to legacy benefit claimants. Research undertaken by the Disability Benefits Consortium (2021) found that disabled people and those with long-term health conditions particularly suffered during the pandemic, with 78 per cent reporting being worse off as a result of increased basic costs such as food and fuel, 67 per cent struggling to eat a balanced diet and 46 per cent falling behind on bills and rent.

While conditionality was suspended during the height of the crisis, it made a gradual comeback as the economy started to reopen. In particular, the UK, like other Anglo-American countries (Australia and the US), experienced an extremely tight labour market (Duval et al, 2022). While unemployment fell – it is now back to pre-pandemic levels – economic inactivity continued to rise, 'peaking in December 2021-February 2022 at 8.89 million, nearly 450,000 more than in January-March 2020', with an economic inactivity rate at 21.7 per cent (Powell et al, 2022, p 4). In January–March 2022, redundancies were below pre-pandemic levels and job vacancies were at record highs. There was a clear need to help disadvantaged workers back into paid employment through increased support, which is the reason why the Department for Work and Pensions launched a series of active labour market schemes. However, the pandemic seems to have changed worker preferences, with workers being less willing to work in contact-intensive jobs and choosing to work in teleworking occupations (Duval et al, 2022, p 13). The reduction in immigration, especially European Union immigration post Brexit, could have played a contributing factor to the sharp rise in unfilled vacancies in contact-intensive occupations (Duval et al, 2022). A key factor behind the rise in economic inactivity, as identified by the Institute for Employment Studies, relates to fewer people returning to work who have long-term health conditions, with the number of people out of work due to long-term ill health who last worked at least three years ago up by more than 200 thousand since the pandemic. However, we also find an increase in those who left work 2–3 years ago due to ill health, with Long Covid almost certainly playing a part in this (and in particular in a growth of 30 thousand in the number who last worked 2–3 years ago and state that they are off work due to temporary illness). (2022, p 4)

The Institute for Employment Studies also imply that austerity is a factor in this because of the reduction of employment and health support for disabled people. The high cost of childcare (dues to the low level of subsidies) has disadvantaged women and families with children:

The growth in those looking after family and home is particularly worrying, as it is reversing a thirty-year trend of rising participation among parents and particularly lone parents. This may suggest that more people (particularly women) are finding it harder to combine work and caring, likely combined with rising costs and less availability of childcare and transport. (Institute for Employment Studies, 2022, p 5)

The return to harsh conditionality and the stalling of levelling up

As highlighted earlier, post COVID-19 the demand for labour exceeded labour supply, partially because of high economic inactivity, particularly among those aged 50 plus. In a context of tight labour markets, the priority for the Department for Work and Pensions was to get people into available jobs, as stated by Thérèse Coffey in her foreword to the department's annual report for 2021–22: 'With more than a million vacancies, we have continued to strengthen our focus on filling these posts *quickly* to fulfil people's potential and *ensure employers can access* the skills and talent they need for the future. (Department for Work and Pensions, 2022, p 2, emphasis added).

Coffey's foreword, while couched in a language of help and support, was in fact work first (Daguerre, 2015) in its pure form – under her leadership, the department's mission was to help employers find available labour quickly. This also tallied with her refusal to publish the department's report on benefit sanctions, which would have revealed their negative impact in terms of depriving claimants of their income (Butler, 2022).

Meanwhile, benefit sanctions increased. According to David Webster, in 2022 'the average number of monthly [Universal Credit] sanctions has reached over two and half times the average in the first three months before the pandemic' (2022, p 4).

Proceeding with the 'managed migration' of claimants to Universal Credit without the findings of the evaluation of the 'pilot' was also likely to increase claimant exposure to sanctions/loss of benefits. The migration meant moving 1.7 million claimants on legacy benefits onto Universal Credit. The initial attempt at migration (in 2017) was paused with a consultation on this organised by the Social Security Advisory Committee (2018). There were numerous protests and complaints from the welfare rights movement because of administration problems and claimants having their benefits stopped altogether or being significantly worse off financially due to the process.

On welfare, there has therefore been a shift to New Right policies post COVID-19, an inflexion that predated the (temporary) establishment of Liz Truss as leader of the Conservative Party in September 2022. This has continued under the fiscally conservative premiership of Rishi Sunak, partially as a response to financial pressures. Truss and Kwarteng's ideas on the matter can be found in *Britannia unchained* (Kwarteng et al, 2012). The fourth chapter of that book, entitled 'Work ethic', laments the 'massive rise in welfare dependency' and cites research from the Centre for Social Justice claiming that for too long work had not paid (Kwarteng et al, 2012, p 70). The chapter then quotes an article by Dunn (2010) concluding that the level of Jobseeker's Allowance is still encouraging the unemployed to be fussier about which jobs they are prepared to do. The only academic work cited is Dunn's article, which, by the author's own account, is not representative of the mainstream academic view and argues that people will always prefer work to life on benefits (see Dunn, 2013; Dunn et al, 2014; and the reply to Dunn by Marston, 2013). Although Sunak did not co-write *Britannia Unchained*, his stance on benefit claimants was as harsh, and arguably harsher, than that of Truss. At a husting in Belfast, Sunak promised to get much tougher on welfare and declared that benefit claimants should have to take on available jobs: 'If there are hours to do, if there's a job going, people should have to take the job, as opposed to just being able to stay on benefits.' He also stated during this husting: 'Right now, there are more people claiming unemployment benefit than there are job vacancies in the economy. Just think about that for a second. And that's happening under a Conservative government. That's clearly not right – something's gone wrong' (quoted in Bloom, 2022). The expectation that Universal Credit will solve labour inactivity and shortages via harsher conditionality was underpinned in the autumn 2022 spending plans and policy priorities. Jeremy Hunt's Autumn Statement provided little solace for benefit claimants and people on low incomes. There were provisions for addressing the cost of living crisis and a benefit increase in line with inflation (HM Government, 2022a). The cost of living support of a £900 top-up on benefits for 2022–23 was criticised as inadequate, with the Institute for Fiscal Studies commenting:

> we are set to see the largest fall in real household disposable income per head (4.3%) since the late 1940s. ... Average household income per head is due to be the same in 2027-28 as it was in 2018-19, and 31% below where it would have been if the pre-2008 trend had continued. (Adam et al, 2022)

In line with One Nation Conservatism, Cameron, May and Johnson each pledged to reduce territorial inequalities, especially the gap between north and south. May's government (2016–19) rolled-out a 'place agenda' to drive regional prosperity, making links with sectoral and local UK Industrial Strategy. However, this was scrapped by Johnson and replaced with a £4 billion Levelling Up Fund, announced in the November 2020 Spending Review. Political promises to reduce sociospatial inequalities were placed at the core of the Johnson government's levelling up agenda, with the White Paper (HM Government, 2022b) offering bold rhetoric and ambitions (Gray, 2022; Hudson, 2022; see also Chapter 1).

Green suggests that the main impacts of the COVID-19 crisis were that major increases in the claimant count placed excessive pressures on the employment and skills system. The increase in the propensity towards insecure and precarious work is one result, though this is also due to a decline in training. This exacerbates the structural problems of the labour market as the requirement for reskilling increases in the face of rising unemployment and the disadvantaged are locked out of this process (Green, cited by Etherington et al, 2023, p 12).

Furthermore, local government in the so-called 'left behind' areas has been the subject of long-term austerity measures through welfare reform and local government cuts, and this is likely to be a major source of tensions around this policy agenda (Gray and Barford, 2018; Etherington, 2020). Health inequalities, already a cause for concern, have been heightened due to the COVID-19 pandemic within the older industrial areas, where the numbers classified as economically inactive have increased (Beatty and Fothergill, 2022).

Conclusion

This chapter has told the story of the trajectory of Conservative welfare and labour market policies post 2015. There are six major messages from the analysis. First, the overall picture is continuity between the Coalition and post-2015 policies. The Conservatives went ahead with rolling out Universal Credit, albeit with a series of small adjustments to address some structural issues with design. Some form of softening up (especially on benefit sanctions) took place post 2015, but this was not enough to reverse the regressive trajectory of social welfare policies that had been set in motion since 2011–12.

Second, it took a major exogenous shock – the COVID-19 pandemic and the need to support low-income households because of repeated lockdowns – to initiate a major U-turn on Universal Credit. On average, the incomes of the poorer households were protected by the Treasury because of the increase in working-age benefits, especially the uplift – albeit temporary – in Universal Credit. There was therefore something of a shift away from a New Right low benefits and increased responsibilities approach (see Chapter 1).

Third, there has been a sharp divide between the 'deserving' and the 'undeserving' poor, with a deterrence policy consisting of making life on benefits as repellent and stigmatising as possible. It has become much more difficult to sustain large families on meagre benefits. This is poverty by design for large families and single working-age adults. The messages are stark and can be summarised as follows: (a) do not have children at the expense of the taxpayer and (b) for working-age adults without disabilities, not being in a form of paid employment is likely to lead to destitution. As a result, there has been a continued increase in deep poverty, especially for large families, who have come to rely on a network of charities and food banks given the purposeful inadequacy of social security.

Fourth, Universal Credit has become a policy instrument of choice and its utility has been demonstrated by the response by the Department for Work and Pensions to the COVID-19 crisis. However inadequate, Universal Credit is here to stay and is likely to be expanded again to respond to the crisis of living standards.

Fifth, disciplining the poor through benefit sanctions and in work conditionality is back in fashion in Conservative circles, again indicating a shift back to New Right discourses and policies, especially about economically inactive individuals and people with disabilities. This signals a return to a workfare logic that had been experimented with in the 1930s, at least in Britain (Cooper, 2022).

Sixth, the endorsement of One Nation Conservatism (as proclaimed, for example, by Boris Johnson in his foreword to the 2019 manifesto) was always more rhetorical than real, despite the various U-turns dictated by a wave of external shocks such as the COVID-19 crisis and rising inflation rates.

The biggest takeaway of this chapter is therefore that the UK welfare and benefit system, especially in England, has resumed a work first, benefit-sanction-oriented trajectory following a brief pause in welfare to work conditionality during the COVID-19 pandemic. As a result, welfare provision in the UK has become increasingly lean and mean, accentuating a story of decline in human capital investment in the poorest parts of the UK. In short, this seems to be the very opposite of levelling up.

References

Adam, S., Emmerson, C., Johnson, P., Joyce, R., Karjalainen, H., Levell, P., Stockton, I., Waters, T., Wernham, T., Xu, X. and Zaranko, B. (2022) 'Autumn Statement 2022 response', *Institute for Fiscal Studies*, 17 November. Available at: https://ifs.org.uk/articles/autumn-statement-2022-response (accessed 23 August 2022).

Beatty, C., Fothergill, S., Gore, T. and Leather D. (2022) *The Real Level of Unemployment 2022*, Sheffield: Centre for Regional Economic and Social Research, Sheffield Hallam University.

Bloom D. (2022) 'Next Prime Minister threatens benefits crackdown – as Sunak vows to be "much tougher"', *The Mirror*, 17 August. Available at: www.mirror.co.uk/news/politics/next-prime-minister-threatens-benefits-27765144 (accessed 19 July 2023).

Brewer, M. and Handscomb, K. (2020) *This time is different – Universal Credit's first recession: assessing the welfare system and its effect on living standards during the coronavirus epidemic*, London: Resolution Foundation.

Brewer, M. and Tasseva, I.V. (2021) 'Did the UK policy response to Covid-19 protect household incomes?', *The Journal of Economic Inequality*, 19(3): 433–58.

Butler, P. (2022) 'Report on effectiveness of benefit sanctions blocked by DWP', *The Guardian*, 30 January. Available at: www.theguardian.com/society/2022/jan/27/report-on-effectiveness-of-benefit-sanctions-blocked-by-dwp (accessed 27 April 2023).

Conservative Party (2015) *Strong leadership, a clear economic plan, a brighter, more secure future. The Conservative Party manifesto 2015*, London: Conservative Party. Available at: www.theresavilliers.co.uk/sites/www.theresavilliers.co.uk/files/conservativemanifesto2015.pdf (accessed 19 July 2023).

Conservative Party (2017) *Forward together: our plan for a stronger Britain and a prosperous future. The Conservative and Unionist Party Manifesto 2017*, London: Conservative Party. Available at: https://ucrel.lancs.ac.uk/wmatrix/ukmanifestos2017/localpdf/Conservatives.pdf (accessed 19 July 2023).

Conservative Party (2019) *Get Brexit done, unleash Britain's potential. The Conservative and Unionist Party Manifesto 2019*, London: Conservative Party. Available at: https://assets-global.website-files.com/5da42e2cae7ebd3f8bde353c/5dda924905da587992a064ba_Conservative%202019%20Manifesto.pdf (accessed 19 July 2023).

Cooper, M. (2022) 'The return of forced labour in the workfare state: enforced work for benefits in the UK in the 1930s and since 2010', *Journal of Poverty and Social Justice*, 30(3): 193–209.

Cribb, J., Waters, T., Wernham, T. and Xu, X. (2022) *Living standards, poverty, and inequality in the UK: 2022*, IFS Report R215, London: Institute for Fiscal Studies.

Daguerre, A. (2015) 'The unemployed and the moral case for benefit sanctions', *Journal of Social Security Law*, 22(3): 130–50.

Daguerre, A. (2020) 'Employment and labour market reforms: towards a residual safety net?', in H. Bochel and G. Daly (eds) *Social policy*, London: Routledge, pp 245–66.

Daguerre, A. and Etherington, D. (2016) 'Welfare and active labour market policies in the UK: the Coalition government approach', in H. Bochel and M. Powell (eds) *The Coalition government and social policy: restructuring the welfare state*, Bristol: Policy Press, pp 201–20.

Department for Work and Pensions (2012) *Universal Credit evaluation framework*, London: Department for Work and Pensions.

Department for Work and Pensions (2016) *Universal Credit evaluation framework*, London: Department for Work and Pensions.

Department for Work and Pensions (2022) *DWP annual report and accounts 2021–22*, London: Department for Work and Pensions.

Desmond M. (2015) 'Severe deprivation in America: an introduction', *RSF: The Russell Sage Foundation Journal of the Social Sciences*, 1(1): 1–11.

Disability Benefits Consortium (2021) *The Millions Missing Out*, London: Disability Benefits Consortium. Available at: https://disabilit ybenefitsconsortium.com/2021/08/26/test-post/ (accessed 19 July 2023).

Dunn, A. (2010) 'The "dole or drudgery" dilemma: education, the work ethic and unemployment', Social *Policy & Administration*, 44(1): 1–19.

Dunn, A. (2013) 'Activation workers' perceptions of their long-term unemployed clients' attitudes towards employment', *Journal of Social Policy*, 42(4): 799–817.

Dunn, A., Grasso, M.T. and Saunders, C. (2014) 'Unemployment and attitudes to work: asking the "right" question', *Work, Employment and Society*, 28(6): 904–25.

Duval, R.A., Ji, Y., Li, L., Oikonomou, M., Pizzinelli, C., Shibata, I., Sozzi, A. and Tavares, M. (2022) 'Labor market tightness in advanced economies', IMF Staff Discussion Note 001/2022, Washington, DC, International Monetary Fund.

Edin, K. and Shaefer, H.L. (2015) *$2.00 a day: living on almost nothing in America*, Boston: Houghton Mifflin Harcourt.

Etherington, D. (2020) *Austerity, welfare and work: exploring politics, geographies and inequalities*, Bristol: Policy Press.

Etherington, D., Jones, M., Harris, S. and Hubbard, S. (2021) *Post Covid-19 crisis and its impact on poverty and destitution in Stoke-on-Trent*, Stoke-on-Trent: Staffordshire University.

Etherington, D., Jones, M. and Telford, L. (2023) 'COVID crisis, austerity and the "Left Behind" city: Exploring poverty and destitution in Stoke-on-Trent', *Local Economy*, 37(8): 692–707.

Freud, D. (2021) *Clashing agendas: inside the welfare trap*, London: Nine Elms Books.

Gardiner, L. (2019) *The shifting shape of social security, charting the changing size and shape of the British welfare system*, London: Resolution Foundation.

Gingrich, J. and King, D. (2019) 'Americanising Brexit Britain's welfare state?', *The Political Quarterly*, 90(1): 89–98.

Gray, M. and Barford, A. (2018) 'The depth of the cuts: the uneven geography of local government austerity', *Cambridge Journal of Regions, Economy and Society*, 11(3): 541–63.

Gray, N. (2022) 'The UK Shared Prosperity Fund: what can we learn from government's plans to replace EU funds', London: IPPR. Available at: www.ippr.org/news-and-media/press-releases/exposed-the-gap-between-levelling-up-rhetoric-and-reality (accessed 12 December 2022).

Hansard (2020) 'Covid-19: DWP update', 4 May 2020, col 435. Available at: https://hansard.parliament.uk/commons/2020-05-04/debates/CEE2A 905-7589-40D0-B14C-219F12CCB242/Covid-19DWPUpdate (accessed 13 August 2021).

Harris, N., Fitzpatrick, C., Meers, J. and Simpson, M. (2020) 'Coronavirus and social security entitlement in the UK', *Journal Social Security Law*, 27(2): 55–84.

HM Government (2022a) 'Autumn Statement 2022: cost of living fact sheet', London: HM Treasury. Available at: www.gov.uk/government/publications/autumn-statement-2022-cost-of-living-support-factsheet (accessed 19 July 2023).

HM Government (2022b) *Levelling up: levelling up the United Kingdom*, London: HMSO.

Hobson, F. (2020) *The aims of ten years of welfare reform (2010–2020)*, Briefing paper 9090, London: House of Commons Library.

Hudson, R. (2022) '"Levelling up" in post-Brexit United Kingdom: economic realism or political opportunism?', *Local Economy*, 1(2): 50–65.

Hunt, J. (2022) 'The Autumn Statement 2022 speech', *Gov.uk*, 17 November. Available at: www.gov.uk/government/speeches/the-autumn-statement-2022-speech (accessed 12 December 2022).

Institute for Employment Studies (2022) *Labour market statistics November 2022*, Brighton: Institute for Employment Studies. Available at: www.employment-studies.co.uk/resource/labour-market-statistics-november-2022 (accessed 19 July 2023).

Joseph Rowntree Foundation (2022) *UK poverty 2022*, York: Joseph Rowntree Foundation. Available at: www.jrf.org.uk/report/uk-poverty-2022 (accessed 19 July 2023).

Kwarteng, K., Patel, P., Raab, D., Skidmore, C. and Truss, E. (2012) *Britannia unchained*, London: Palgrave Macmillan.

Mackley, A. (2021) *Coronavirus: Universal Credit during the crisis*, London: House of Commons Library.

Marston, G. (2013) 'On "Activation workers' perceptions"': a reply to Dunn', *Journal of Social Policy*, 42(4): 819–27.

Meers, J. (2022) 'Legacy benefits and the Universal Credit uplift: justified discrimination in the COVID-19 social security response', *Journal of Social Welfare and Family Law*, 44(2): 245–7.

Peele, G. (2021) 'Post Brexit and post-Covid: reflections on the contemporary Conservative Party', *The Political Quarterly*, 92(3): 404–11.

Pope, T. and Shearer, E. (2021) *The Coronavirus Job Retention Scheme: how successful has the furlough scheme been and what should happen next?* London: Institute for Government. Available at: www.instituteforgov ernment.org.uk/sites/default/files/publications/coronavirus-job-retent ion-scheme-success.pdf (accessed 1 November 2022).

Powell, A., Francis-Devine, B. and Clark, H. (2022) *Coronavirus: impact on the labour market*, London: House of Commons Library.

Schmuecker, K., Matejic, P., Bestwick, M. and Clark, T. (2022) *Going without: deepening poverty in the UK*, York: Joseph Rowntree Foundation. Available at: www.jrf.org.uk/report/going-without-deepening-poverty-uk (accessed 19 July 2023).

Social Security Advisory Committee (2018) *Report by the Social Security Advisory Committee under Sections 172(1) and Section 174(1) of the Social Security Administration Act 1992 and statement by the Secretary of State for Work and Pensions in accordance with Section 174(2) of that Act.* Available at: http://ass ets.publishing.service.gov.uk/government/uploads/system/uploads/atta chment_data/file/753714/draft-universal-credit-managed-migration-regu lations-2018-report.pdf (accessed 19 July 2023).

Timmins, N. (2020) 'Coronavirus is giving Universal Credit its moment in the sun', *Institute for Government*, 2 April. Available at: www.instituteforgov ernment.org.uk/blog/universal-credit-coronavirus (accessed 19 July 2023).

Webster, D. (2022) *Briefing: benefit sanctions statistics*. Available at: www. mostewartresearch.co.uk/wp-content/uploads/2022/09/22-08-Sancti ons-Stats-Briefing-D.Webster.pdf (accessed 27 April 2023).

Work and Pensions Select Committee (2020) *DWP's response to the coronavirus outbreak*, HC 178, London: House of Commons.

12

The Conservatives and adult social care

Jon Glasby

Introduction

As set out throughout this book, it can be difficult to locate recent Conservative governments, not least because of stark differences between stated aims and subsequent realities. There have also been a series of unprecedented international events, which might have caught any government by surprise. Faced with these challenges, the Conservatives' approach has largely been one of inaction: failing to address the very significant impacts of austerity and underdelivering on promises to reform long-term care funding. However, such inaction spans a number of governments: since the late 1990s there have been at least 12 adult social care White or Green Papers, reviews and strategy documents, with none of the funding proposals actually being implemented. While the latest version of these proposed reforms made it onto the statute books, it has since been delayed yet again (perhaps indefinitely), and it was in any case a pale imitation of the measures that were going to be introduced in 2014.

After summarising the legacy of the Coalition government (2010–15), this chapter turns to events under Conservative governments since 2015. Throughout, the approach includes an unusual mix of elements of traditional Conservative ideology, a pragmatic recognition of the difficulties of genuinely trying to resolve some of the very thorny issues at stake and some slightly odd twists and turns en route. In the early 2020s, there is no doubt that adult social care faces even more challenges than in 2010, with recent policy overpromising and underdelivering. While similar underlying themes may well exist across all four nations of the UK, the details in this chapter focus on England.

The Coalition government, 2010–15

In Bochel and Powell's (2016) edited collection, Glasby (2016) reviewed the Coalition's journey from 'initial neglect to the Care Act 2014'. While social care hardly featured in the 2010 Conservative manifesto or the

Coalition's *Programme for Government* (Cabinet Office, 2010; Conservative Party, 2010), a series of Liberal Democrat care services ministers developed and implemented the Care Act 2014. This modernised a series of previous statutes (which had grown up piecemeal over decades), seeking to deliver greater well-being and prevention, better information and advice, and a reformed system of long-term care funding. In particular, the aim was to ensure that people know the maximum they will need to pay if living in a care home and can better prepare for future care costs and avoid having to sell their homes. In the end, this was scuppered by a twofold process:

1. A decision to set the 'cap' (the maximum anyone pays towards care costs) at a rate which seemed too high to benefit enough people or to act as a meaningful incentive to prepare for future care costs. Throughout subsequent policies, the notion of a cap relates to the additional costs of being looked after arising out of frailty or disability, with charges still applying to the equivalent of living/housing costs for people living in a care home.
2. A subsequent decision to postpone the introduction of these funding reforms – initially for a set period of time, and later indefinitely.

As Glasby argues:

> In the end, what emerged was so underwhelming that it is difficult to avoid the conclusion that … this may have been a pragmatic attempt to be seen to be responding to a long-standing but contentious issue in a way that effectively kicks the topic into the long grass again. … Rather than this being an ideologically charged issue, most governments over time seem to have concluded that it is just too hard, and that being seen to be doing something about it without really doing something about it is the best way forward. (2016, p 232)

Elsewhere, there was also significant disappointment. Despite the laudable principles of the Care Act, these reforms were rendered almost meaningless by the impact of austerity. Over time, local government found itself facing greater unmet need, more self-funding, significant concerns about care quality, a growing financial/workforce crisis and increased pressures on staff, families and partner agencies (Glasby et al, 2020, pp 428–9). Other Coalition reforms were equally underwhelming. Despite pledging more integrated care, the 2012 Lansley reforms created a much more fragmented system. Despite promising a focus on prevention, this proved hard to achieve in practice, not least given the scale of the financial challenge facing local government. While the personalisation of adult social care remains a stated aim, there is a risk that the current system simply co-opts the new language, leading to a form of 'zombie' personalisation (Duffy, 2014) and little real change (for an overview of some of these issues, see Glasby, 2016; Glasby et al, 2020). Although these policies seemed similar at face value to themes pursued by New Labour, there were more underlying differences than might first be apparent. For example, several commentators wondered if the apparent commitment to 'integrated care' may have been more to do with deflecting criticism from the Coalition's health reforms than a genuine attempt to join up care. Similarly, support for prevention might be one way of arguing that councils are sufficiently resourced to deliver their commitments, if only they would stop being so crisis focused. It is also possible to be an advocate of personalisation through a commitment to citizenship and social justice – or from a neoliberal desire to roll back the boundaries of the welfare state. This was summed up as 'it ain't what you do, it's the way that you do it' (Glasby, 2016).

The Conservatives since 2015

Since 2015, it has become increasingly clear that 'it ain't just the way you do it, but also *what* you do'. Looking back, this has been a strange period, with sudden bursts of apparently significant activity followed by subsequent inaction and/or potential backtracking. Despite seeming to herald an end to austerity, for example, there has been some relatively minor stabilising of local authority budgets, but little to reverse the previous devastating cuts (and any new money has tended to be eaten up by broader changes, including increases in the National Minimum Wage, let alone current inflation; see Glasby et al, 2020). While Theresa May made reform of long-term care funding a more central feature of the 2017 election than is often the case, her proposals felt ill thought-through, contributing to a disastrous result and thereby making it even less likely that future governments would be brave enough to intervene. Although Boris Johnson's government seemed to follow up initial pledges to introduce funding reform, the measures which emerged felt a long way away from the promise to 'fix the crisis in social care once and for all with a clear plan we have prepared' (Johnson, 2019) – and they have since been delayed yet again. Moreover, despite the then Secretary of State for Health and Social Care claiming to have thrown a 'protective ring' around care homes during the pandemic (see also Chapter 5), others (such as the Public Accounts Committee, 2020) have been highly critical, leading to a subsequent successful legal challenge (Booth, 2022). Finally, despite pledging to introduce 'carers' leave' to support unpaid carers who might need flexibility at work due to sudden emergencies in their caring arrangements, the government's proposed Employment Bill was excluded from the 2022 Queen's Speech, much to the frustration of carers and their organisations (Carers UK, 2022).

Making sense of all this is difficult – not least because most governments would have been distracted by broader events (such as the ongoing ramifications of Brexit and the devastating impacts of COVID-19). However, underneath some of these twists and turns, there seems to be a mix of ideology (for example, a desire to protect inheritance and a tendency to fall back on narratives that focus on families providing care for each other) and pragmatism (focusing on the needs of the much more politically significant National Health Service – NHS – at the expense of adult social care).

In 2015, for example, the Conservative manifesto made little mention of the bulk of the social care system, but (very vaguely) committed to 'look after you when you grow older' (Conservative Party, 2015, p 65). In practice, this repeated previous commitments to capping residential care costs and allowing deferred payment schemes (where care costs are paid from someone's estate after they die – already widely used prior to 2015, and often, like some other payment mechanisms, labelled as a form of 'death tax' by anyone not actually in government at the time and looking to score cheap political points). This was intended to protect people from unlimited costs 'if they develop very serious care needs – such as dementia' (pp 65–6). As previously suggested, this commitment was not met, as mechanisms to cap care costs introduced as part of the previous Care Act were delayed and later abandoned.

In 2017, the manifesto was equally vague in its promise to deliver 'dignity and protection in old age through the right long-term solution for elderly care' (Conservative Party, 2017, p 62). Although what followed was essentially about how best to pay for care, it was framed in terms of traditional Conservative values of family, community and social solidarity:

> No grandparent wants to see their grandchildren worse off than they were, yet that is precisely the fear many older people now have. No son or daughter wants to see their parents poorly cared for or their hard-earned assets whittled away, yet that is the reality for too many old people in care. We will restore the contract between the generations. … This solidarity is a Conservative principle, growing out of family, community and nation – all things that Conservatives believe in and work to conserve. (Conservative Party, 2017, p 63)

While proposed changes were complicated, they essentially involved a 'floor' rather than a 'cap' (that is, people would always retain £100,000 of their capital, rather than having a maximum that they know in advance they might have to contribute). Crucially, the new charging regime would apply to care in a person's own home as well as in a care home, which was a major, albeit possibly not widely understood, change. Previously, people living in their own homes were assessed for potential charges on the basis of their savings/income. However, people in residential care are assessed on the basis of income, savings and the value of their property. This was therefore a significant departure from previous approaches, and it was difficult to tell where it had come from, whether it could ever actually work in practice or why anyone thought this was a good idea in the first place. When someone gets assessed as to how much tax they should pay, whether or not they should pay prescription charges or what they should contribute as part of a young person's student loans, it is usually based on their income (variously defined), not on what kind of house they own. Certainly, the proposal took the social care sector by surprise, and there seemed little evidence that this measure had been broadly debated and sense-checked in advance. In the event, it generated a significant negative reaction, and May was forced to backtrack only days later, pledging to also introduce a cap on care costs and claiming that this was always what was intended (BBC, 2017). Having seemed to completely misjudge the situation, it is possible that the government thought they would win the election relatively easily and could hurry through unpopular funding measures in a way that would not usually be possible. When this backfired so spectacularly, the fear was that no one else would touch social care with a barge pole, in case it proved equally fatal.

Despite this, Boris Johnson's (2019) first speech as Prime Minister was clear that:

> My job is to protect you … from the fear of having to sell your home to pay for the costs of care and so I am announcing now – on the steps of Downing Street – that we will fix the crisis in social care once and for all with a clear plan we have prepared to give every older person the dignity and security they deserve.

This was restated in the 2019 manifesto, which again appealed to traditional Conservative values:

> It is a basic, compassionate Conservative belief that we should care for those in need – helping those who cannot help themselves. […] We need to have a system to give every person the dignity and security they deserve. […] So we will build a cross-party consensus to bring forward an answer that solves the problem, commands the widest possible support, and stands the test of time. That consensus will consider a range of options but one condition we do make is that nobody should be forced to sell their home to pay for it. (Conservative Party, 2019, p 12)

Of course, the fact that the main action was to build 'cross-party consensus' suggests there may not have been a 'clear plan' after all.

Alongside this and some modest funding announcements, there was also a pledge to 'extend the entitlement to leave for unpaid carers, the majority of whom are women, to one week' (Conservative Party, 2019, p 12). In the event, this was to culminate in the introduction of the Health and Social Care Levy on National Insurance, mainly focused on funding for the NHS to tackle the COVID-19 backlog, but also including some funding for the long-awaited cap on care home costs. In one sense, this was highly unusual, in that a proposed funding reform might actually be implemented – and with a Conservative government raising taxes (albeit via National Insurance rather than general taxation). It also seemed to be a pledge to which Downing Street was very committed, despite apparent concerns from the Treasury (and, indeed, despite the Labour Party calling for the tax increase to be scrapped in order to reduce pressures on people's incomes during the cost of living crisis, as well as pointing out that National Insurance increases would hit low-paid care workers harder than the better off). This felt odd: a Conservative Prime Minister championing higher taxes and Labour portraying itself as a party of lower taxation (ignoring the fact that New Labour had previously been prepared to increase taxes, including National Insurance, in order to fund NHS reforms). Perhaps normal business was resumed during the subsequent Conservative leadership context, with the majority of candidates pledging tax cuts and Liz Truss in particular taking aim at the new levy (which was later abandoned).

Despite Johnson's pledge, the 2019 speech was followed by several years of inaction – prompting further suspicions there may not really have been a 'clear plan'. Moreover, when the practicalities were finally announced, the small print proved to be deeply disappointing. Not only was the level of the cap set in such a way as to benefit far fewer people than many had hoped, but the approach to people on lower incomes was much less generous than under the Care Act 2014 (with any care funding via a means test for people with less resources not counting towards the cap). While the government argued that this was fair (everyone pays up to the same maximum), many commemorators felt that this disproportionately benefitted the wealthy. Thus, Warren (2022a) illustrates how

> people with the same level of needs will reach the cap at different points. In one example, a wealthy person would reach the cap after 3 years and 4 months whereas someone with less wealth would take almost twice as long to do so – 6 years and 5 months – almost double the need for care before getting the same financial support as the wealthy person.

Given regional differences in property prices, this benefits wealthier people in the south at the expense of poorer people in the Midlands and the north (the mirror image of the government's 'levelling up' agenda). There has also been widespread concern that this disadvantages disabled people of working age, who tend to have fewer opportunities to earn the same as the general population and who are more likely to receive means-tested support en route to reaching the cap. As Warren (2022a) concludes:

> The Prime Minister guaranteed that no one needing care would have to sell their home to pay for it. The change the government is pursuing would mean this promise is broken for older people with lower levels of wealth and for those living in the North East, Yorkshire and the Midlands. It would also significantly reduce the benefits to working age adults. Whether you support the change comes down to whether you think this is fair.

An additional element of the proposals was that people paying for their own place in a care home will in future be able to ask their local authority to arrange their care, thereby benefiting from cheaper fees (at the moment, councils can pay anything up to 40 per cent less than self-funders). Quite how this will work in practice is currently unclear, given that so many councils and providers are already facing financial difficulties, with a number of providers only surviving because they cross-subsidise local authority-funded placements with the higher fees charged to self-funders. If this cross-subsidy ends, it is anyone's guess as to what happens next in the care home market. Interestingly, this element of the reforms was subsequently delayed, applying only to new care home entrants in the first instance and being phased in for existing residents over the next 18 months. More recently, in a scene that is depressingly familiar, these reforms were delayed until at least October 2025 (justified, as previously, by concerns about capacity to implement the new measures) – bringing the whole policy into doubt.

Throughout these debates, the focus seems to have been on the bits of adult social care that touch the NHS (such as care homes) and on services for older people rather than people of working age (who account for around half the adult social care budget). In one sense, this is understandable politically, given the popularity of the NHS compared to adult social care, and the fact that Conservative voters tend to be older. However, there remain significant challenges for people of working age, whether this be barriers to employment for disabled people, difficulties accessing mental health services or a series of horrific care scandals in long-stay hospitals for people with learning disabilities and/or autism (with examples such as Winterbourne View, Whorlton Hall and Cawston Park continuing a long and very sad history of abuse, and raising significant questions about the nature of current regulation and quality assurance). Despite the largely positive long-term narrative set out in the 2021 White

Paper *People at the heart of care* (Department of Health and Social Care, 2021), there was little detail to back up the long-term vision, and most of the proposed actions were already in train and/or previously found wanting (Alderwick, 2021; Bottery, 2021; Oliver, 2021). For the *Local Government Chronicle*, 'social care reform is about as "done" as a raw chicken' (Golding, 2022).

Nowhere is this focus on the NHS and on older people (rather than on social care and on people of working age) more apparent than in widespread criticisms of the government's response to COVID-19. While the challenges created by the pandemic were unprecedented within living memory, many people drawing on care and support or working in social care felt that the government's response spoke volumes about a long-standing failure to understand or value care. A key contribution to this debate came from a highly critical review by the Public Accounts Committee:

> Years of inattention, funding cuts and delayed reforms have been compounded by the Government's slow, inconsistent and, at times, negligent approach to giving the sector the support it needed during the pandemic. This is illustrated by the decision to discharge 25,000 patients from hospitals into care homes without making sure all were first tested for COVID-19, a decision that remained in force even after it became clear people could transfer the virus without ever having symptoms.
>
> Reflecting on the Government's response to the pandemic so far, we are also particularly concerned by its failure to provide adequate PPE [personal protective equipment] for the social care sector and testing to the millions of staff and volunteers who risked their lives to help us through the first peak of the crisis. [...]
>
> There are many lessons that the government must learn, not least giving adult social care equal support to the NHS and considering them as two parts of a single system, adequately funded and with clear accountability arrangements. (2020, p 3)

This was followed in 2022 by the results of a high-profile legal challenge in which '[g]overnment policies on discharging untested patients from hospital to care homes in England at the start of the Covid pandemic have been ruled unlawful' (BBC, 2022).

Having emerged from what appeared to be the worst of COVID-19, adult social care found itself facing massive financial, service and workforce pressures, exacerbated by the impact of Brexit on the ability to recruit migrant care workers, by a widespread sense of exhaustion and burn-out and by the knock-on effects of the cost of living crisis. As the Association of Directors of Adult Social Services (2022) has argued:

Despite staff working relentlessly over the last two years, levels of unmet need, undermet or wrongly met needs are increasing, and the situation is getting worse. The growing numbers of people needing care and the increasing complexity of their needs are far outstripping the capacity to meet them. [...]

Not only are people waiting longer for care assessments, reviews, care packages and personal budgets, but family carers are having to shoulder greater responsibility and are being asked to take paid or unpaid leave from work when care and support are not available for their family members.

Making the focus of resources on acute hospitals, without addressing care and support at home, means people deteriorate and even more will need hospital care.

In spite of these stark warnings, there is no sign that policy makers have appreciated the seriousness of the situation. During the first 2022 Conservative Party leadership contest, social care was hardly mentioned, and any brief references seemed inconsistent and poorly thought-through. Liz Truss, for example, was opposed to the Health and Social Care Levy (which was subsequently shelved), yet still wanted extra social care funding – without any sense of where this would come from. As the King's Fund set out in a letter to *The Times*:

Liz Truss's statement that 'funding needs to go into social care' ... appears to fall short of a commitment to the necessary (albeit limited) social care reforms announced by the government. ... If Rishi Sunak and Liz Truss want to drag health and social care services away from perma-crisis, they should commit themselves to the planned overhaul of social care funding, address staff shortages in the sector and provide the funding needed to ensure people can access good quality care when they need it. (Warren, 2022b)

In her first speech as Prime Minister, moreover, Truss recognised the importance of creating a society 'where everyone everywhere has the opportunities they deserve', but made no reference to the role of care and support in enabling such opportunities for older and disabled people. Of three stated priorities, one was to: 'Make sure that people can get doctors' appointments and the NHS services they need. We will put our health service on a firm footing' (HM Government, 2022b). However, this only referred to the NHS and doctors, with not even the now customary reference to 'health and social care' that most ministers make when talking about what are really NHS priorities. References to 'opportunities' also seemed reminiscent of early statements by Theresa May ('burning injustices') and Boris Johnson ('levelling up') – no doubt easier to state at the start of a premiership than to achieve in practice.

Later statements by Truss' (short-lived) Secretary of State for Health and Social Care pledged to prioritise the 'ABCD' of ambulances, backlog, care and doctors, but without any initial detail. Although a subsequent release, *Our Plan for Patients*, promised some short-term funding to facilitate hospital discharge and support the international recruitment of care workers (Department of Health and Social Care, 2022), these announcements were criticised for looking at social care through an NHS lens and failing to grasp the scale of the issues. There was also a suggestion that pledges might come from existing budgets, rather than representing new funding. As one commentator tweeted: 'The money is of course welcome and necessary but its short-term nature and limited focus on discharge means it offers no more than couple of stitches to the gaping wound that is the state of #socialcare at the moment' (Simon Bottery, King's Fund, 22 September 2022).

Nor was there any more detail at the 2022 Conservative Party conference, with the Secretary of State essentially repeating the 'ABCD' platitude and Truss (2022) expressing a desire to 'bolster social care so that everyone gets the care they need'. Quite what being 'bolstered' meant is unclear, but one of the only real concrete measures – the £500 million Adult Social Care Discharge Fund previously announced – was described by a leading public service journalist and chair of a national social care charity as 'plainly just the latest in a depressing annual series of panic bungs to help the sector stagger through the winter' (Brindle, 2022).

This seemed to be confirmed under Rishi Sunak's leadership, with the 2022 Autumn Statement delaying proposed social care charging reforms until at least October 2025 (HM Government, 2022a). While some new money was announced, this took the form of funds that would have been spent on reform, money linked specifically to hospital discharge, money that has to be divided between child and adult services, and increases in Council Tax – still a million miles away from the long-term funding settlement needed for adult social care to adequately plan ahead. Unfortunately, worse was to come in April 2023, when a new government action plan (Department of Health and Social Care, 2023) seemed to renege on many of the (already limited) funding pledges from the December 2021 White Paper, appearing to significantly reduce already very limited money for staff training and development and for housing-related support. For the Association of Directors of Adult Social Services (2023): 'This plan leaves the Government's vision for reform in tatters. It ducks the hard decisions and kicks the can down the road again until after the next election.' Other commentators were less kind (see Box 12.1).

Box 12.1 Response to the 2023 action plan

I have rarely felt the fury that I feel at today's @DHSCgovuk 'announcement' on social care. A massive retreat from what was already bare minimum first steps in long-term reform. (Sally Warren, King's Fund, via Twitter, 4 April 2023)

Fury but also weary at so many wonderful, dedicated people in #socialcare being taken for fools yet again. (David Brindle, former Public Services Editor of *The Guardian*, via Twitter, 4 April 2023)

A shabby, shameful episode in our long-standing failure to reform a vital public service that most of us will need at some point in our lives. (Richard Humphries, Senior Advisor, Health Foundation, via Twitter, 4 April 2023)

We need the thesaurus to find new ways to express profound disappointment. ... The oven ready plan has gone up in smoke. (Helen Buckingham, Nuffield Trust, via Twitter, 4 April 2023)

Just three days before, one commentator had mused on possible April Fool's Day stories:

1. Lord Lucan discovered living in Rochdale
2. Shergar wins 2.30 at Goodwood
3. Elvis to release comeback album
4. Social care reform back on the table (Simon Bottery, King's Fund, via Twitter, 1 April 2023)

Flashes of underpinning ideology?

While much of this might be the result of a government struggling to respond to a series of global challenges, there have also been ongoing flashes of underpinning ideology (many of which correspond to the key categories set out in Table 1.1 at the start of this book). Whenever government seems to lack answers to the challenges facing adult social care, a common response is to fall back on the importance of families providing care for each other ('responsibilities'). For example, in 2017, a government minister appeared to suggest to a select committee that families should play a greater role:

People have just as much of a duty to look after their elderly parents as they do to care for their own children, a health minister has said. [...]
'One of the things that has struck me is no one ever questions that we look after our children – that is obvious. No one says that is a caring responsibility, it is what we do,' he said.

'I think some of that logic and some of the way we think about that in terms the volume of numbers that we are seeing coming down the track will have to impinge on the way that we think about caring for our parents. Because it is a responsibility in terms of our life cycle which is similar.' (Asthana, 2017)

Also in 2017, in a blog post on *Conservative Home*, Morrison (2017) argued:

Each generation should recognise and accept this responsibility. Family members are the people who in most circumstances can supply tenderness, dignity, memories, and alleviate loneliness. When we are old, we will find little of this in the care of society – unless we can afford to pay a great deal. Enabling our families to care reduces that necessity except in extreme circumstances. Why are governments more willing to pay strangers, rather than family members, to care for us in our old age?

At the 2021 Conservative Party conference, Sajid Javid (2021) said:

The state was needed in this pandemic more than anytime in peacetime. But government shouldn't own all risks and responsibilities in life. We as citizens have to take some responsibility for our health too. We shouldn't always go first to the state. What kind of society would that be? Health – and social care – begins at home. Family first, then community, then the state.

While this might appeal to traditional Conservative 'family values', there is a risk that it could simply be a smokescreen for a reduction in publicly funded support, with families having little choice but to provide support for each other (perhaps harking back to Cameron's 'Big Society'). While lots of men provide unpaid care, this is also highly gendered (see Age UK, 2019, for an example of how shortcomings in adult social care disproportionately affect women). With this in mind, it was deeply frustrating when the Employment Bill (first pledged in 2019, and thought to be about to introduce carers' leave) was jettisoned from the 2022 Queen's Speech.[1] Quite why this happened is unclear, but some would see it as a decision to prioritise business over the needs of the workforce and unpaid carers.

Conclusion

Overall, Conservative approaches to adult social care remain difficult to characterise. Despite the passage of the Care Act 2014 (championed by Liberal Democrat care services ministers), most of the period witnessed a combination of underfunding, inaction, delay, U-turns, pledges not fulfilled and missed opportunities. Faced with series of other crises, respective governments seem to have concluded that most of the issues were simply too difficult, papering over the cracks, pushing any scope for meaningful change into the long grass and focusing instead on the more publicly/politically popular NHS. While this is far from unusual in adult social care (and under a range of governments), the 'lost decade' of 2010–20 feels a particularly stark example of this tendency. At particular moments in time, there have been unusual developments – such as Johnson's apparent willingness to press ahead with a cap on care costs funded by tax rises. However, the reality of subsequent policy details has seldom matched the initial rhetoric. Interspersed with a largely pragmatic response, moreover, have been occasional examples of traditional Conservative ideology around issues such as inheritance, the role of family, the needs of business, tax cuts and financial changes which might disproportionately benefit the better off (many of which map well onto the dimensions set out in Table 1.1: inequality, responsibilities, competition, markets and low/pragmatic spending).

Despite this depressing summary, it would be wrong to end without reflecting on grounds for optimism. Notwithstanding all the above, there are lots of examples of dedication and good practice across the country, with numerous positive developments, often happening bottom-up and under the radar. During the pandemic, there were stories of low-paid care workers temporarily leaving their families and moving into the care homes where they worked so that they could carry on looking after residents without the risk that they would infect them with COVID-19. At local level, thousands of people are working to develop new models of support, more firmly rooted in the realities of people's relationships and communities, and building on people's strengths and what matters to them (rather than identifying 'deficits' that services should be helping to overcome). These are often small, local projects, but national organisations such as the Social Care Institute for Excellence have been working to scale such approaches, exploring the way in which innovations spread, sharing good practice and working on ways to move beyond individual projects to create more 'assets-based places'.[2] In my own work, we have £15 million provided by the Economic and Social Research Council and the Health Foundation to design and deliver a UK-wide centre for implementing evidence in adult social care (IMPACT), working to support positive changes in the realities of local services and people's lives.[3] Elsewhere, the social movement #SocialCareFuture has been tireless in challenging the current framing of social care debates, setting out a positive vision of the lives and the society we are all trying to create: 'We all want to live in the place we call home with the people and things that we love, in communities where we look out for one another, doing the things that matter to us' (#SocialCareFuture, nd). In one sense, many people feel that the sector has never experienced such difficult times. Equally, lots of people are talking about social care in a way that never really happened before the pandemic, and just about everyone recognises that things need to be different in future. In Scotland, as an example, there is a new National Care Service being developed, and there are active discussions in Wales and some debates in England around scope for similar reforms. While these concepts are very different to the way in which the health service is organised, there remains a sense that if 1948 was the year of the NHS, perhaps now is the time for a new approach to adult social care. While there has probably never been a harder time in recent history to be involved in adult social care, perhaps there has also never been a better time – and perhaps both these statements could be true at once (almost irrespective of who is in government).

Notes

[1] See Carers UK, 'What are my rights as a working carer?' (www.carersuk.org/news-and-campaigns/campaigns/right-to-carers-leave) for more on this campaign. While a subsequent Bill received Royal Assent in 2023, the initial absence from the Queen's Speech was still seen as a major omission.

[2] See Social Care Institute for Excellence (www.scie.org.uk for further information on strengths-based working and their Innovation Network).

[3] See more on the IMPACT project at: https://impact.bham.ac.uk/.

References

Age UK (2019) *Breaking point: the social care burden on women*, London: Age UK.

Alderwick, H. (2021) *New vision for social care will feel like hollow words without the money to deliver it*, London: Health Foundation.

Association of Directors of Adult Social Services (2022) 'ADASS Waiting for care report May 2022: more than half a million are waiting for social care', 13 May. Available at: www.adass.org.uk/waiting-for-care-adass-report-may-2022 (accessed 19 July 2023).

Association of Directors of Adult Social Services (2023) 'Press release: adult social care reform announcement response', 4 April. Available at: www.adass.org.uk/adass-response-to-adult-social-care-reform (accessed 19 July 2023).

Asthana, A. (2017) 'Take care of your elderly mothers and fathers, says Tory minister', *The Guardian*, 31 January. Available at: www.theguardian.com/society/2017/jan/31/take-care-of-your-elderly-mothers-and-fathers-says-tory-minister (accessed 19 July 2023).

BBC (2017) 'General election: Theresa May denies social care U-turn', 22 May. Available at: www.bbc.co.uk/news/election-2017-40001221.amp (accessed 19 July 2023).

BBC (2022) 'Covid: discharging untested patients to care homes "unlawful"', 27 April. Available at: www.bbc.co.uk/news/uk-england-61227709 (accessed 19 July 2023).

Bochel, H. and Powell, M. (eds) (2016) *The Coalition government and social policy*, Bristol: Policy Press.

Booth, R. (2022) 'Covid care home discharge policy was unlawful, says court', *The Guardian*, 27 April. Available at: www.theguardian.com/world/ 2022/apr/27/covid-discharging-untested-patients-into-care-homes-was-unlawful-says-court (accessed 19 July 2023).

Bottery, S. (2021) *The social care White Paper: not wrong, just not moving far enough in the right direction*, London: King's Fund.

Brindle, D. (2022) 'Government's new social care strategy "nowhere near a breakthrough"', *Social Care Today*, 7 October. Available at: https://soc ialcare.today/2022/10/07/opinion-governments-new-social-care-strat egy-nowhere-near-a-breakthrough/ (accessed 19 July 2023).

Cabinet Office (2010) *The Coalition: our programme for government*, London: Cabinet Office.

Carers UK (2022) 'Commenting on today's Queen's Speech, Helen Walker, Chief Executive of Carers UK said', Press release, 10 May. Available at: www.carersuk.org/news-and-campaigns/news/commenting-on-today-s-queen-s-speech-helen-walker-chief-executive-of-carers-uk-said (accessed 19 July 2023).

Conservative Party (2010) *Invitation to join the government of Britain. The Conservative manifesto 2010*, London: Conservative Party.

Conservative Party (2015) *Strong leadership: a clear economic plan, a brighter, more secure future*, London: Conservative Party.

Conservative Party (2017) *Forward together: our plan for a stronger Britain and a prosperous future*, London: Conservative Party.

Conservative Party (2019) *Get Brexit done: unleash Britain's potential*, London: Conservative Party.

Department of Health and Social Care (2021) *People at the heart of care: adult social care reform White Paper*, London: HMSO.

Department of Health and Social Care (2022) 'Our plan for patients', *Gov.uk*, 22 September. Available at: www.gov.uk/government/publications/our-plan-for-patients/our-plan-for-patients?s=03#care (accessed 19 July 2023).

Department of Health and Social Care (2023) 'Next steps to put people at the heart of care', *Gov.uk*, 4 April. Available at: www.gov.uk/governm ent/publications/adult-social-care-system-reform-next-steps-to-put-peo ple-at-the-heart-of-care/next-steps-to-put-people-at-the-heart-of-care (accessed 19 July 2023).

Duffy, S. (2014) 'After personalisation', in C. Needham and J. Glasby (eds) *Debates in personalisation*, Bristol: Policy Press, pp 167–84.

Glasby, J. (2016) '"It ain't what you do, it's the way that you do it": adult social care under the Coalition', in H. Bochel and M. Powell (eds) *The Coalition government and social policy*, Bristol: Policy Press, pp 221–41.

Glasby, J. (2021) 'Adult social care in England: more disappointment, delay, and distraction', *British Medical Journal*, 374: 2242. doi: https://doi.org/10.1136/bmj.n2242

Glasby, J. and Needham, C. (2020) 'The neglect of adult social care during COVID-19', *British Medical Journal*, 370: 3103. doi: https://doi.org/10.1136/bmj.m3103

Glasby, J., Zhang, Y., Bennett, M. and Hall, P. (2020) 'A lost decade? A renewed case for adult social care reform in England', *Journal of Social Policy*, 50(2): 406–37.

Golding, N. (2022) 'It's time for candour about social care not being "fixed"', *Local Government Chronicle*, 19 May. Available at: www.lgcplus.com/politics/lgc-briefing/its-time-for-candour-about-social-care-not-being-fixed-19-05-2022/ (accessed 19 July 2023).

HM Government (2021) *Build back better: our plan for health and social care*, CP 506, London: HMSO. Available at: https://assets.publishing.service.gov.uk/government/uploads/system/uploads/attachment_data/file/1015736/Build_Back_Better-_Our_Plan_for_Health_and_Social_Care.pdf (accessed 19 July 2023).

HM Government (2022a) 'Autumn Statement 2022 HTML', *Gov.uk*, 17 November. Available at: www.gov.uk/government/publications/autumn-statement-2022-documents/autumn-statement-2022-html (accessed 19 July 2023).

HM Government (2022b) 'Prime Minister Liz Truss's statement: 6 September 2022'. *Gov.uk*, 6 September. Available at: www.gov.uk/government/speeches/prime-minister-liz-trusss-statement-6-september-2022 (accessed 19 July 2023).

Javid, S. (2021) 'Sajid Javid's speech to Conservative Party conference' *Conservatives*, 5 October. Available at: www.conservatives.com/news/2021/sajid-javid-s-speech-to-conservative-party-conference (accessed 19 July 2023).

Johnson, B. (2019) 'Boris Johnson's first speech as Prime Minister: 24 July 2019'. *Gov.uk*, 24 July. Available at: www.gov.uk/government/speeches/boris-johnsons-first-speech-as-prime-minister-24-july-2019 (accessed 19 July 2023).

Morrison, L. (2017) '"Social care" should really become "family care"', *Conservative Home*, 13 May. Available at: www.conservativehome.com/platform/2017/05/loanna-morrison-social-care-should-really-become-family-care.html (accessed 19 July 2023).

Oliver, D. (2021) 'The social care White Paper provides few solutions to an urgent crisis', *British Medical Journal*, 376: o107. doi: https://doi.org/10.1136/bmj.o107 (accessed 19 July 2023).

Public Accounts Committee (2020) *Readying the NHS and social care for the COVID-19 peak*, London: House of Commons.

#SocialCareFuture (nd) 'Living in the place we call home – key themes'. Available at: https://socialcarefuture.org.uk/living-in-the-place-we-call-home-summary-of-key-themes/ (accessed 19 July 2023).

Sturrock, D. and Talloch, C. (2022) *Does the cap fit? Analysing the government's proposed amendment to the English social care charging system*, London: Institute for Fiscal Studies/Health Foundation.

Truss, L. (2022) 'Prime Minister Liz Truss's speech to Conservative Party conference 2022', *Conservatives*, 5 October. Available at: www.conservatives.com/news/2022/prime-minister-liz-truss-s-speech-to-conservative-party-conference-2022 (accessed 19 July 2023).

Warren, S. (2022a) 'The cap on care costs: what does the government proposal mean?' *King's Fund*, 4 March. Available at: www.kingsfund.org.uk/blog/2022/03/cap-care-costs-what-does-government-proposal-mean (accessed 19 July 2023).

Warren, S. (2022b) Letter to *The Times*, 17 August.

13

The Conservatives, family policy and the data revolution

Val Gillies and Rosalind Edwards

Introduction

The 2016 Brexit referendum and subsequent other tumultuous events have dominated policy-centred debates and governing rationales. Constitutional crises, internecine feuds and the COVID-19 pandemic have seen off four successive Conservative prime ministers in six years and directed attention away from concerns that occupied administrations of the past. In particular, the focus on family and the responsibilisation of parenting that was prominent in the David Cameron era has faded away. Most notably, when Theresa May took power, she substituted the previous administration's promise of a 'better future for hard-working families' for the assertion that she was 'working hard for hard-working people'. Her successor Boris Johnson's own 'complex' family relationships turned family policy into a minefield for his government and foreclosed any Cameron-style moralising on the subject. Following Liz Truss' short-lived premiership, her successor, Rishi Sunak, was initially preoccupied with the economy, with no direct mention of family policy, but threatened effects for families through austerity impositions and mention of a revised childcare system.

However, it would be a mistake to view the post-Brexit years as a family policy vacuum. As has long been understood, families are governed beyond and between overt policies, by political rationalities and technologies tied to shifting bodies of expertise and knowledge (Rose and Millar, 2010). More recent Conservative administrations have moved away from an overt family-centric rhetoric and agenda, other than quietly continuing the Supporting Families Programme (previously Troubled Families Programme – TFP), as discussed later. However, a lack of rhetoric and debate masks substantial developments in operational governance techniques, the effects of which have led to a significant reshaping of state–family relationships. Core to this new trajectory is the deployment of advanced ICT technology to amass and analyse citizen data, with the intention of solving ingrained social problems through holding more information and maximising public efficiency. This approach grew out of a prior technocratic preoccupation with evidence-based policy and evolved into what van Veenstra and Kotterink (2017) term 'data-driven policy making', with ambitions for digital-centred governance extending far into the policy realms of health, education, policing and immigration. The functionality and success of these plans though are in themselves largely dependent on the extensive data profiling of families through the mass collection and analysis of service records, case notes and database entries.

The resulting changes to family governance techniques are outlined in digital strategy documents rather than in political speeches and government policy papers, and reveal a marked turn towards digital surveillance (or 'dataveillance') to categorise, target and regulate children and parents. This centring of family data first emerged as a trend during the early period of Coalition government and has travelled a swift trajectory towards automation and algorithmic governance, characterised by the incorporation of 'big data' harvesting and mining, machine learning and predictive analytics into a range of policy practices. As a consequence, state–family relations are now increasingly mediated and shaped through online portals and dashboards.

In this chapter, we show how this commitment to data-driven policy making and the new mode of digital governance that is shaping state relations with families came to dominate Conservative visions for a stable future and how it was pursued through a privatised style of social investment. The 'troubled families' targeted by the Cameron administration were translated into digital data points and monetised, monitored and nudged as part of a 'digital revolution' (Cabinet Office, 2017). We begin by drawing out the phased development of this techno-social imaginary across the Cameron, May and Johnson administrations, and demonstrating how a commitment to tackle ingrained social ills through 'gripping' and 'turning around' dysfunctional, antisocial families morphed into data-led decisions and interventions, with serious consequences for those targeted. We show how rather than better managing families' needs, these data practices seek to calculate and pre-empt future risks, positioning disadvantaged and marginalised families in particular in a pre-dysfunctional and pre-criminal space before transgression or culpability has occurred.

Troubled families and the turn to data

When the Coalition government came to power in 2010, they inherited a social investment-centred policy infrastructure from the previous Labour administration. Blair's 'third way' philosophy had positioned children and families as holding the key to the future success and prosperity of late capitalism. New Labour operationalised this conviction through a front-loading of state spending on 'human capital development', investing in nursery entitlement, Sure Start centres, tax credits for families and a network of child welfare and parenting support organisations (Gillies et al, 2017), bolstered by a rhetoric of evidenced family policy making. A similar policy framework was implemented across much of the European Union, reflecting a widespread faith that early social investment in human capital would promote future economic growth and social stability (Jenson, 2010). After winning the 2010 election, the incoming Conservative-led Coalition retained the progressive-sounding narrative of investment in children, but crucially they withdrew most of the financial scaffolding sustaining it.

The extent to which the Conservative Party bought into the principle of a family-centred investment state is debateable, but initially at least Coalition family policy appeared to represent a point of convergence between Liberal Democratic and Conservative policy agendas. David Cameron and his Liberal Democrat deputy, Nick Clegg, were apparently united in their concern to increase intergenerational social mobility. But significantly, this agenda was pursued alongside a programme of austerity cuts. New Labour's social investment spending was branded ineffective, profligate and unaffordable in the wake of an economic crisis. A commitment to responsibilising and upskilling parents remained in place, but services and provisions were replaced by attempts to more precisely target the most 'dysfunctional' and/or needy families (Edwards and Gillies, 2016).

At the same time, an extensive reform of the social security system was initiated with the aim of rolling all benefit payments into one means-tested Universal Credit benefit with conditionality and sanctions that worked to inculcate the values and behaviour of a traditional family unit (Anderson, 2020; Bennett, 2021). A 'two-child benefit cap' was introduced to discourage parents from having more children than they could support, and households were required to make a joint claim and, following paid employment remuneration practice, to receive the allowance each month in one bank account. Furthermore, couples had to nominate one parent, most likely to be female according to equality impact assessments (Department for Work and Pensions, 2011), to be a 'lead carer', vulnerable to being pulled into employment-related conditionalities if the household income were to fall below a fixed threshold.

This disciplining of poor families was pursued aggressively through the introduction of the TFP, one of the Coalition's most prominent and expensive policy agendas (Crossley, 2018). Launched in 2012 after a period of rioting and disorder in England, the TFP was officially tasked with 'mending our broken society' and tackling 'a culture of disruption and irresponsibility that cascades down through generations' (Cameron, 2011). Heavy on moral rhetoric and recycled tropes of the underclass and 'problem families', the programme outlived Cameron's premiership, even though it fell well short of its stated objectives. Despite the scathing results of an independent evaluation suggesting the programme made no meaningful difference to the lives of the families it targeted (Day et al, 2016), the Cameron government expanded the remit and funding for the TFP to encompass families with health care problems or 'children in need'. As discussed later, under the Johnson administration the programme was renamed Supporting Families, and its aims were yoked to a vaguely articulated pledge to 'level up' society (see Chapter 1), with additional funding provided to improve local authority use of education, health, benefits, policing and other administrative records to support 'vulnerable' families (Ministry of Housing, Communities and Local Government, 2021a). The tying together of support and data in family-focused policy says more about the strategic significance of the programme as a gateway to service transformation than any faith in its perceived efficacy. As Redden et al (2020) note, the TFP was a driving force for the turn to data in children's services and the restructuring of state–family relationships this entailed.

From its inception, the structure of the TFP was inchoate and difficult to distinguish from the family support work that was already being undertaken by family services. The gap between the political rhetoric justifying the programme's administration and its practical implementation was vast (Crossley, 2018). In practice the TFP operated more as a local authority funding stream than a discrete family intervention programme, but its impact on the structure and delivery of family services, and on state–family relationships more generally, has been significant. More specifically, the TFP has operated to accelerate an administrative 'datafication' of households with family behaviours and circumstances being translated into digital data points in order to analyse, monitor, predict and pre-empt their behaviour. Family policy becomes driven by a logic in which families are regarded as data, and data is regarded as enabling knowledge about families and the ability to predict their future (Edwards and Ugwudike, 2023).

As we described elsewhere in assessing Coalition government family policy (Edwards and Gillies, 2016), lying beneath the TFP's pledge to tackle 'problem families' was a new payment-by-results system that allocated funding to local authorities by the Department for Communities and Local Government on the basis of an audit trail (Crossley, 2018). This new funding stream was offered in the context of swingeing austerity cuts to children's services and represented a significant resource for cash-strapped local authorities. But regions chasing the TFP funds were forced into an unprecedented collection, linking and processing of data on local families to produce the digital trails demanded by central government. This required investment in a whole new data infrastructure. The administrative data caches required to identify and track 'troubled families' were originally held within separate, often incompatible, central and local government repositories, as well as by independent services and charities. Each database enforced their own data protection protocols, and few local authorities had the requisite in-house technological resources to effectively manage the new data demands being placed on them.

The introduction of the TFP and its payment-by-results framework forced local authorities to 'innovate' at speed, supported by a wide range of government funding streams and quangos (Gillies et al, 2021). Signalling a further shift in state–family relations, most councils participating in the TFP turned to private companies specialising in 'data solutions'. They were guided by the government's 'digital marketplace', a procurement hub set up to promote access to around 3,000 data analytics companies, many offering products and services specially tailored towards family intervention (Edwards et al, 2021, p 270). Companies designed bespoke dashboards allowing local authorities to manage the TFP requirements, merging together family datasets that were previously stored in incompatible formats in order to maximise payment-by-results funds while promising to pinpoint which families are likely to meet or fail particular criteria.

In effect, the Cameron administration paved the way for a data-led governance of families operating through the financialisation of intervention projects and routine involvement of private industry and investors. The funding structure underpinning the TFP and its digital surveillance mechanisms constituted more than administrative technicalities for effective, targeted delivery of family policy. As Grimshaw (2013) argues, the austerity era and the reforms it imposed were largely centred on moving the UK from 'liberal collectivism' to a neoliberal 'market society'. The data-dependent payment-by-results framework and the audit-heavy bureaucracy it demanded opened the door to family interventions shaped by the data science industry, as local authorities were forced to upgrade their information technology (IT) capacity or contract out the labour-intensive work of targeting, measuring and evidencing change (Edwards et al, 2021). As we will show, with the Conservative governments that followed, family policy shifted to embrace what Morozov (2013) terms 'technological solutionism' – the idea that social problems can be fixed through the application of digital technologies. In the following sections, we demonstrate how family policy was unobtrusively digitised under the May administration and subsequently tied to a broader logic of algorithmic governance under Johnson's succession.

Theresa May: the digital transformation

Theresa May's short administration oversaw significant changes to frameworks of governance and service provision affecting families. In 2017, May's government set out a plan to 'transform the relationship between citizens and the state' by drawing on the 'tools, techniques, technology and approaches of the internet age' (Cabinet Office, 2017, p 6). The *Government Transformation Strategy* styled itself as 'the most ambitious programme of change of any government anywhere in the world', promising the digitisation of the state and the use of data as an enabler of services (Cabinet Office, 2017, p 4). The strategy heralded an extensive reorganisation of government infrastructure and notably a re-engineering of welfare state delivery. The first major government service to become internet-only was Universal Credit, the social security benefit system supporting the poorest families in the country. Access to benefits became contingent on claimants' ability to navigate complex automated online systems, further marginalising the most disadvantaged (Alston, 2018).

Moreover, electronic applications left a trackable digital trail that could be accessed to help meet the data needs of the TFP. Families claiming benefits – one of the TFP criteria for family intervention – were easily identified and checked against other TFP criteria, and their progress toward the specified behaviour targets set for the family by the TPP could be monitored. This digital turn in governance was justified largely on the basis of efficient and targeted delivery of family intervention. It was argued that state services would be streamlined and costs cut (Cabinet Office, 2017). In practice though, the digital-by-default rollout came to rely heavily on expensive private sector-provided IT resources and expertise, leaving the government lacking oversight and control (Public Accounts Committee, 2021). Having been incentivised by central government to invest in digital infrastructure to access TFP revenue, many local authorities upgraded and extended the range of tools and services to encompass data on the local family population generally (Gillies et al, 2021). As illustrated later, in relation to Insight Bristol and Xantura OneView, digital dashboards and surveillance products offering 'holistic' profiles of families as a whole and individual household members often have the capacity to categorise particular family characteristics, behaviours or social associations as 'risky' to support decision-making by any social workers and other professionals that might subsequently encounter the family.

As such, the TFP helped pave the way for a radically altered state–family relationship, with the routine collection, monitoring and storage of data extending out to encompass households across the country. While the governing of poor families has always revolved around the recording, categorisation and coding of their lives and relationships (Horsley et al, 2020), digital technology has massively extended the reach of this surveillance and transformed the way that families can be understood and targeted by government agencies and professionals. As Keddell (2019) points out, troublesome behaviour and parenting are reified as objectively knowable through data about sets of characteristics and aspects of behaviour, turning difficulties into estimable risks. The focus is shifted from actualities to potentialities through an anticipatory foregrounding of risk and probability (Rouvroy, 2013). Rather than attempting to understand and reform the drivers of negative outcomes, efforts are directed towards identifying data points as predispositions and targeting behaviours accordingly. In the process, families' struggles are interpreted through an individualistic lens, with the behaviour of parents and their children abstracted from their social and structural context, often with the aim of meeting datafied targets. This concern with predicting future risk in families also sees the fusing together of social policy with criminal justice as children and families become increasingly known to the state through a numerical calculation and ranked scoring of their propensity to misconduct (Edwards and Ugwudike, 2023).

Data-driven governance is built upon the processes, logics and technologies of the private sector (Dencik et al, 2019). The datafication of families in policy has worked to further embed and accelerate the financialisation of public policy by facilitating social impact bonds (SIBs) as a transactional model of welfare, with family policy areas as a target for this (Gillies et al, 2017). SIBs are designed to generate a surplus for an upfront capital investment in a public intervention or service on the basis that a set of predetermined goals are met. Initially launched as part of Cameron's Big Society agenda, they were further embedded by May as part of her vision for a 'shared society' (May, 2017). The Life Chances Fund, launched in 2016 by the Department for Digital, Culture, Media and Sport, allocated a budget of £80 million for SIBs in priority areas such as children's services, the early years and young people.

The Life Chances Fund has facilitated the financing of a range of interventions for at-risk families by social enterprises and other companies. Upfront capital payments from investors have, for example, been used to cover intensive targeted therapeutic work with families to address behavioural and emotional issues in children. Performance measures are not publicly divulged, but the expectation is that if they are met, local or central government will pay the investment back with a return on the investment (for examples, see the report by Hameed et al, 2021). In the field of family policy, SIBs operate as a Conservative reworking of social investment models, commodifying family services that had previously received direct government funds. Alongside little evidence for their effectiveness (Huckfield, 2020; Sinclair et al, 2021), the SIBs private investments impose a significant burden on welfare providers while reducing their flexibility to meet families' needs (Edmiston and Nicholls, 2018). They do, however, further a broader Conservative mission to privatise family support provision and other public and social services, resonating with the emerging techno-solutionist logic that came to propel much of the subsequent government's approach to policy making.

Boris Johnson: supporting families from 'seeing rooms'

Overt references to family policy were muted during the Johnson premiership, but the ramping up of solutionist data-driven policy making continued the framing of state–family relations. In the early months of Johnson's administration, his controversial Chief Adviser Dominic Cummings pushed forward a technocratic imaginary of 'smart governance'. He proposed a centralised policy model that harnessed the power of big data and technology to improve decision making and thereby solve a wide range of engrained social problems. Having called an early general election, Johnson had reclaimed rhetoric around 'working families' and promised to support them in his manifesto, but after a resounding victory this dissipated in the face of the practicalities of leaving the European Union, a global pandemic and Cummings' provocative reforms to state structures. Cummings' vision was of 'hub and spoke' governance with decision-making managed at the centre by data scientists, mathematicians, physicists and other 'super-talented weirdos' from panoptic 'seeing rooms' equipped with live data streams (Cummings, 2019, 2020). Key to this approach was faith in the capacity of data analytics to calculate risks and pre-empt social problems before they have yet manifested. Machine learning techniques applied to large datasets are used to identify the likelihood of future events based on patterns identified in historical data. Within this general model then, real-time data about families would be collated and subject to instant algorithmic analysis, driving policy making and responsive family service interventions.

Cummings' position at the centre of power was relatively short, but having gained ground under May's administration, belief in the capacity of datafication and automation to depoliticise policy decisions and deliver family support and other efficiencies retained considerable momentum. The Johnson government focused attention on achieving greater integration of artificial intelligence (AI) into policy frameworks and public delivery, with implications for family support. The public sector was positioned as a 'buyer', with the government helping services 'to evaluate suppliers, then confidently and responsibly procuring AI technologies for the benefit of citizens' (Department for Digital, Culture, Media and Sport, 2021). This was followed by plans to accelerate the use of transformative technologies, including in the delivery of family support services.

As the initial shock of the COVID-19 pandemic receded, public concern focused on the impact of extended lockdowns and school closures on children. In response, then Chancellor Rishi Sunak introduced a Start for Life offer in the 2021 Spending Review and promised to direct £300 million to fund family support projects. Start for Life was positioned predominantly as a health initiative, with responsibility for family support shifting away from a social-investment-centred emphasis on education to a more explicit focus on 'growing up well'. Parenting programmes were to be targeted at improving perinatal mental health and breastfeeding support, and a new Family Hubs system was introduced to 'transform' the way universal services are delivered.

Some read the Family Hubs proposal as an attempt to revive the Sure Start network of children's centres introduced by New Labour in the late 1990s (Simpson, 2022), encouraged by then Minister for Children and Families Will Quince describing Family Hubs as 'Sure Start plus plus plus' (Hill, 2021). Unlike the wide-ranging provision introduced as part of Sure Start, however, the Family Hubs project delivered relatively modest changes to service delivery models, bringing together already established resources to create centralised access points for services and support. Most family hubs operate from the few remaining children centres, while many exist only as virtual spaces signposting parents towards services. Crucially, this focus on meeting the needs of families was tied to the digitisation and sharing of personal child health records (commonly referred to as the 'red book'). Family hubs were supported by various funding streams including Growing up Well, a fund set up by the Department for Education to assist selected local authorities to 'develop digital and data products that will support the practical implementation of family hubs' (Knott, 2021), sharing digital information and referrals across education, health and social care.

The family hubs model is also linked to a further extension and development of the Supporting Families programme. Criteria for inclusion in Supporting Families were widened substantially from the previous 'troubled' indicators of worklessness, crime, truancy and high service cost to encompass almost any family relying on non-statutory state services. The programme's objectives shifted from 'turning around' families to become about building 'strong multi-agency local partnerships in every area, and mature local and national data systems, which enable partners to identify families in need of extra help, target services more effectively and track family level outcomes over the long term' (Ministry of Housing, Communities and Local Government, 2021b). Supporting Families also received £7.9 million to fund a children and families Data Accelerator Fund. The purpose of this was both to improve the efficiency of the technology that pools together and stores information on families and to develop more sophisticated data practices to identify, target and address family problems.

Beneath the policy claims and euphemisms, the practical implementation of this data-centric policy trend is obfuscated. Despite government claims of encouraging public sector transparency about the use of algorithmic tools (Central Digital and Data Office, 2022), there is a striking lack of transparency about how local authorities in England and Wales are deploying highly sophisticated digital tools to shape and inform their engagement with families. It takes freedom of information requests to reveal the collection and 'warehousing' of administrative data by councils and increasing use of AI to automatically classify, flag and target families (Dencik et al, 2019; Gillies et al, 2021). These vast quantities of accumulated administrative data are also being used to search (or 'mine') for identifiable patterns or correlations with the intention of generating predictive algorithms to guide decision-making and practices (generally known as 'predictive analytics'). Freedom of information requests also reveal that more pioneering local authorities are being supported to extend their consumption of family data beyond the confines of administrative databases (Gillies et al, 2021). A significant minority of local authorities have upgraded to 'data lake' systems that scrape, capture, link and store a wide range of information types and formats beyond their own administration records, including credit records, phone calls, images and social media posts.

These technologies are used in a variety of different ways depending on the local authority. For example, Low Income Family Trackers developed by the company Policy in Practice are now widely used to monitor disadvantaged households. The trackers process large amounts of merged household data to categorise, rank, score and 'flag' families predicted to be at risk of committing fraud, or falling into debt, homelessness, ill health or future mistreatment of children. These risk flags and predictions are treated as factual projections of future family problems. Flagged families have been targeted for proactive and anticipatory intervention ranging from simple advice to referrals to healthy eating campaigns, or even social services and the police. Xantura's OneView package, for example, processes both administrative records and informal data scraped from the internet and claims to identify, predict and model a whole range of family problem issues, including, in addition to those already mentioned, anger problems, dangerous dogs, a history of unsafe sex and even risks associated with COVID-19 (see EY and Xantura's COVID-19 analysis project briefing, cited in Big Brother Watch, 2021).

Governing risk in families

The policy turn to data is largely detached from moral arguments and justifications in relation to family lives. Instead, complex social issues are reduced to common sense problems and explained through a simple logic of risks and solutions. As Morozov (2013) argues, such technological solutionism offers a retreat from the realm of value, normalising and concealing power structures and taken-for-granted meanings in the process.

While presented as an apolitical commitment to delivering 'what works', the UK trajectory towards dataveillance, automation and techno-social management of families marks a substantial shift in policy in terms of how families are viewed and related to by the state. The commitment to early years intervention and social mobility of the Cameron era have faded, with rationales for data innovation focusing on the pre-emption of problems rather than the maximisation of children's future potential. References to 'early intervention' remain, but are used to emphasise the importance of harm prevention rather than childhood investment. For example, the Family

Hubs policy announcement carries a whole section on the significance of early childhood but centres only on reducing the risk of mental ill health in later life (Department of Health and Social Care and Department for Education, 2022). Data-led family intervention projects stress the importance of 'acting early', but the age of children targeted has moved significantly upwards and away from the previous policy preoccupation with under fives. Instead, predictive analytics projects tend to target children over ten years old, marking a growing alignment of family policy with crime reduction and prevention agendas (Gillies et al, 2021; Edwards and Ugwudike, 2023). The predictive analytic models currently in use are predominantly designed to prevent gang activity, county lines, sex trafficking, antisocial behaviour, domestic violence, homelessness and fraud.

In many cases, data warehouses/lakes are run collaboratively between local authorities and regional police forces. In Bristol, for example, the County Council's data analytics vehicle, Insight Bristol, is based in and run from a police station. Insight Bristol operates as an interagency data warehouse and analytics hub centred around the Think Family database operated by Avon and Somerset Police. It draws in data from over 35 sources including undisclosed privately operated databases (see Bristol City Council, nd). Predictions are made to target the families of children who are calculated to be at risk of 'criminal exploitation', 'sexual exploitation', becoming violent and/or NEET (not in education, employment or training). Similar projects, either directly or indirectly funded by central government, are running in a wide variety of English local authorities, including London boroughs, Essex, Kent and Dorset. There is little evidence that targeted individuals receive any substantial extra services or support. It seems that they are merely 'flagged' as high risk to inform and shape the practices of any professionals they might come into contact with in the future, with the potential effect of lowering thresholds for subsequent child protection or police investigation (Gillies et al, 2021). In practice then, this centring of risk generates a pre-criminal lens through which flagged families are judged and disciplined.

Child protection services are another area targeted for digital innovation, with the aim being to automatically risk-profile families and identify children at risk from abuse or neglect. Algorithmically driven social care scoring systems have been trialled in a number of local authorities and continue to be deployed despite their track record in overlooking the majority of at-risk children and young people (Clayton et al, 2020). This underwhelming performance has done little to dent government ambition; rather it is assumed to highlight the need for more comprehensive data and better modelling. Meanwhile concerns are growing about the impact on targeted families and the potential for such technologies to generate inaccurate and discriminatory categorisations. While evidence supporting the benefits of AI in this context is thin, profiling and risk scoring have been found to amplify inaccurate and discriminatory categorisations and to punish the most vulnerable families in societies (Eubanks, 2017; Vannier-Ducasse, 2021; Redden et al, 2022). The predictive variables and categorisations used turn in on themselves, perpetuating and reproducing gendered, classed and racialised family stereotypes and inequalities. Feedback loops become baked into the conduct of family policy where, for example, Black children are over-represented among children in need and in care, and thus Black parents are more likely to be flagged as risky by algorithms (Keddell, 2019; Roe and Rehill, 2021). Thus, not all families are datafied equally or in even ways in data-driven family policy making. This can have drastic consequences, including criminalisation, the loss of benefits and even the removal of children from their families (Glaberson, 2019). More broadly, dataveillance places poor families under a constant shadow of suspicion and subjects them to decisions and outcomes without explanation or justification.

A constant across the various Conservative administrations has been the positioning of poor families as dysfunctional and disordered. However, efforts to responsibilise 'troubled' households have receded. Rather than attempting to reform and re-educate disadvantaged parents, entitlements, sanctions and interventions are increasingly accessed and enforced via automated portals. Contemporary datafied modes of family regulation move beyond attempts to discipline and subjectivise through shame, stigma and threats, towards a management of problematised groups at scale without the knowledge or understanding of the targeted individuals. Families cannot easily see the digital categorisations that identify them and are unable to engage with or challenge them. The effect has been to redraw boundaries between families and the state largely without the knowledge and consent of those impacted.

Conclusion

In this chapter, we have shown how a lack of clearly articulated family policy from the May administration onwards has belied a very substantial change in state–family relationships. We have detailed how a quietly enacted turn to digital innovation has resulted in widespread datafication of families and a shift to management of families and family services via digital surveillance and predictive interventions. This emerging data regime marks a substantial change from previous efforts to safeguard the 'normal' development of children; instead, it works to identify and manage broad indicators of risk. Family relationships remain a key site for state intervention, but the aim and focus has shifted away from narratives of investment towards attenuation and control at the level of broad, stratified populations, largely though the policing and punishing of poor families. This data-centric approach has been characterised by deeper and faster privatisation, with public–private partnerships driving and capitalising on digital innovation in family services. Data analytic companies are operating largely outside of public knowledge and scrutiny, and well beyond traditional expectations of transparency and accountability.

As Rishi Sunak embarked upon office as the fifth Conservative prime minister in six years, there was no indication of the implications for direction for family policy. The pursuit of austerity cuts to public services threatened by his administration would inevitably impact heavily and disproportionately on the poorest families in society. Meanwhile, the implicit digital governance of family problems seems set to continue. Sunak has been long been a prominent supporter of data innovation, having argued during his campaign for leadership of the Conservative Party for greater use of AI in the classroom to reduce the workload of teachers (Morrison, 2022). He also set out plans to make Britain a 'science and tech superpower', declaring that 'science and innovation will be at the heart of my government' (Sunak, 2022). The Secretary of State for Digital, Culture and Media and Sport has also announced plans to ramp up data reform, replacing the General Data Protection Regulation with 'bespoke' business and consumer-friendly legislation (Donelan, 2022).

But while efforts may remain focused on the datafication, surveillance and control of poor families in the short term, this technological approach is expensive and poses risks to public trust (Edwards et al, 2021) and its utility remains dubious. The turn to digital innovation and predictive analytics has not brought about any evidencable improvements for families and has instead coincided with rising rates of poverty and violent crime (Clark, 2022; Office for National Statistics, 2022). It remains to be seen how long this techno-social imaginary will sustain in the current context of an energy crisis, soaring inflation, economic stagnation and industrial unrest.

References

Alston, P. (2018) *Statement on visit to the United Kingdom by Professor Philip Alston, United Nations Special Rapporteur on extreme poverty and human rights.* Available at: www.ohchr.org/sites/default/files/Documents/Issues/Pove rty/EOM_GB_16Nov2018.pdf (accessed 16 May 2022).

Anderson, K (2020) 'Universal Credit, gender and unpaid childcare: mothers' accounts of the new welfare conditionality regime', *Critical Social Policy*, 40(3): 430–49.

Bennett, F. (2021) 'How government sees couples on Universal Credit: a critical gender perspective', *Journal of Poverty and Social Justice*, 29(1): 3–20.

Big Brother Watch (2021) 'Poverty panopticon: the hidden algorithms shaping Britain's welfare state', London: Big Brother Watch. Available at: https://bigbrotherwatch.org.uk/wp-content/uploads/2021/07/Pove rty-Panopticon.pdf (accessed 15 May 2022).

Bristol City Council (nd) 'Insight Bristol and the Think Family database'. Available at: www.bristol.gov.uk/council-and-mayor/policies-plans-and-strategies/social-care-and-health/insight-bristol-and-the-think-family-database (accessed 19 July 2023).

Cabinet Office (2017) *Government transformation strategy*, London: Cabinet Office. Available at: https://assets.publishing.service.gov.uk/government/uploads/system/uploads/attachment_data/file/590199/Government_Transformation_Strategy.pdf (accessed 15 May 2022).

Cameron, D. (2011) 'Troubled families speech', *Gov.uk*, 15 December. Available at: www.gov.uk/government/speeches/troubled-families-speech (accessed 19 July 2023).

Central Digital and Data Office (2022) 'Algorithmic transparency reports', *Gov.uk*. Available at: www.gov.uk/government/collections/algorithmic-transparency-standard (accessed 16 May 2023).

Clark, D. (2022) 'Poverty in the UK - Statistics & Facts', *Statista*, 8 May. Available at: www.statista.com/topics/3809/poverty-in-the-uk/#topicHeader__wrapper (accessed 15 May 2022).

Clayton, V., Sanders, M., Schoenwald, E., Surkis, L. and Gibbons, D. (2020) *Machine learning in children's services: summary report*, London: What Works for Children's Social Care. Available at: https://whatworks-csc.org.uk/wp-content/uploads/WWCSC_technical-_report_machine_learning_in_childrens_services_does_it_work_Sep_2020.pdf (accessed 15 May 2022).

Crossley, S. (2018) *Troublemakers: the construction of 'troubled families' as a social problem*, Bristol: Policy Press.

Cummings, D. (2019) 'On the referendum #33: high performance government, "cognitive technologies", Michael Nielsen, Bret Victor, & "Seeing Rooms"', *Dominic Cummings's Blog*, 26 June. Available at: https://dominiccummings.com/2019/06/26/on-the-referendum-33-high-performance-government-cognitive-technologies-michael-nielsen-bret-victor-seeing-rooms/ (accessed 16 May 2022).

Cummings, D. (2020) 'Two hands are a lot – we're hiring data scientists, project managers, policy experts, assorted weirdos…', *Dominic Cummings's Blog*, 2 January. Available at: https://dominiccummings.com/2020/01/02/two-hands-are-a-lot-were-hiring-data-scientists-project-managers-policy-experts-assorted-weirdos/ (accessed 15 May 2022).

Day, L., Bryson, C., White, C., Purdon, S., Bewley, H., Sala, L.K. and Portes, J. (2016) *National evaluation of the Troubled Families Programme: final synthesis report*, London: Department for Communities and Local Government.

Dencik, L., Redden, J., Hintz, H. and Warne, H. (2019) 'The "golden view": data-driven governance in the scoring society', *Internet Policy Review*, 8(2). Available at: https://policyreview.info/articles/analysis/golden-view-data-driven-governance-scoring-society (accessed 15 May 2022).

Department for Digital Culture, Media and Sport (2021) 'Data: a new direction - government response to consultation', *Gov.uk*, 23 June. Available at: www.gov.uk/government/consultations/data-a-new-direction/outc ome/data-a-new-direction-government-response-to-consultation#execut ive-summary (accessed 15 May 2022).

Department for Work and Pensions (2011) *Conditionality, sanctions and hardship: equality impact assessment*, London: Department for Work and Pensions.

Department of Health and Social Care and Department for Education (2022) *Family Hubs and Start for Life programme guide*, London: Department of Health and Social Care and Department for Education. Available at: https:// assets.publishing.service.gov.uk/government/uploads/system/uploads/atta chment_data/file/1096786/Family_Hubs_and_Start_for_Life_programm e_guide.pdf (accessed 15 May 2023).

Donelan, M. (2022) 'CPC22: our plan for digital infrastructure, culture, media and sport', Speech to the Conservative Party conference, *Lewes Conservatives*, 3 October. Available at: www.lewesconservatives.com/news/ cpc22-our-plan-digital-infrastructure-culture-media-and-sport (accessed 15 May 2023).

Edmiston, D. and Nicholls, A. (2018) 'Social impact bonds: The role of private capital in outcome-based commissioning', *Journal of Social Policy*, 47(1): 57–76.

Edwards, R. and Gillies, V. (2016) 'Family policy: the mods and the rockers', in H. Bochel and M. Powell (eds) *The Coalition government and social policy: restructuring the welfare state*, Bristol: Policy Press.

Edwards, R. and Ugwudike, P. (2023) *Governing families: problematising technologies in social welfare and justice systems*, Abingdon: Routledge.

Edwards, R., Gillies, V. and Gorin, S. (2021) 'Problem-solving for problem-solving: data analytics to identify families for service intervention', *Critical Social Policy*, 42(1): 265–84.

Eubanks, V. (2017) *Automating inequality: how high-tech tools profile, police and punish the poor*, New York: St Martin's Press.

Gillies, V., Edwards, V. and Horsley, N. (2017) *Challenging the politics of early intervention: who's 'saving' children and why?* Bristol: Policy Press.

Gillies, V. and Gardiner, B. with Edwards, R. and Goring, S. (2021) *Freedom of information requests on the use of data analytics in children's services: generating transparency*, Working paper. Available at: https://generic.wordpress.soton. ac.uk/parentdata/wp-content/uploads/sites/394/2021/10/FoI-Respon ses-working-paper.pdf (accessed 16 May 2022).

Glaberson, S.K. (2019) 'Coding over the cracks: predictive analytics and child protection', *Fordham Urban Law Journal*, 46(2): 307–63.

Grimshaw, D. (2013) 'Austerity, privatization and levelling down: public sector reforms in the United Kingdom', in D. Vaughan-Whitehead (ed) *Public sector shock: the impact of policy retrenchment in Europe*, Cheltenham: Edward Elgar.

Hameed, T., Macdonald, J., Shiva, M. and Carter, E. (2021) *The use of social impact bonds in children's social care: a comparative analysis of project justifications and design considerations in the Life Chances Fund*, London: Department for Digital, Culture, Media and Sport. Available at: https://assets.publishing. service.gov.uk/government/uploads/system/uploads/attachment_data/ file/1003329/Main_report_20210629_TH.pdf (accessed 15 April 2023).

Hill, J. (2021) 'Minister says family hubs should be "Sure Start plus plus plus"', *Local Government Chronicle*, 4 November. Available at: www.lgcp lus.com/services/children/minister-says-family-hubs-should-be-sure-start-plus-plus-plus-04-11-2021/ (accessed 15 May 2022).

Horsley, N., Gillies, V. and Edwards, R. (2020) 'We've got a file on you: problematising families in poverty in four periods of austerity', *Journal of Poverty and Social Justice*, 28(2): 227–44.

Huckfield, L. (2020) 'The mythology of the social impact bond: a critical assessment from a concerned observer', *Historical Social Research*, 45(3): 161–83.

Jenson, J. (2010) 'The social investment perspective in Europe and Latin America', *Global Social Policy*, 10(1): 59–84.

Keddell, E. (2019) 'Algorithmic justice in child protection: statistical fairness, social justice and the implications from practice', *Social Sciences*, 8(10): 281. Available at: www.mdpi.com/2076-0760/8/10/281 (accessed 16 May 2022).

Knott, J. (2021) 'Government seeks three more councils for family hubs project', *Local Government Chronicle*, 11 August. Available at: www.lgcplus. com/services/children/government-seeks-three-more-councils-for-fam ily-hubs-project-11-08-2021/ (accessed 16 May 2022).

May, T. (2017) 'The shared society: Prime Minister's speech at the Charity Commission annual meeting', London: Cabinet Office. Available at: www. gov.uk/government/speeches/the-shared-society-prime-ministers-spe ech-at-the-charity-commission-annual-meeting (accessed 15 May 2022).

Ministry of Housing, Communities and Local Government (2021a) 'Next phase of £165 million programme for vulnerable families launched', *Gov. uk*, 9 January. Available at: www.gov.uk/government/news/next-phase-of-165-million-programme-for-vulnerable-families-launched#:~:text= The%20research%20showed%20that%20a,the%20role%20that%20keywork ers%20play (accessed 15 May 2022).

Ministry of Housing, Communities and Local Government (2021b) 'Supporting families - 2021–22 and beyond', *Gov.uk*, 16 March. Available at: www.gov.uk/government/publications/supporting-families-2021-to-2022-and-beyond/supporting-families-2021-22-and-beyond (accessed 15 May 2022).

Morozov, E. (2013) *To save everything, click here: the folly of technological solutionism*, New York: Public Affairs.

Morrison, R. (2022) 'Rishi Sunak wants more AI in classrooms but it's no substitute for teachers', *Techmonitor*, 10 August. Available at: https://tech monitor.ai/technology/ai-and-automation/rishi-sunak-ai-classrooms-teachers-education (accessed 15 May 2023).

Office for National Statistics (2022) 'Crime in England and Wales: year ending March 2022', *Office for National Statistics*, 21 July. Available at: www. ons.gov.uk/peoplepopulationandcommunity/crimeandjustice/bulletins/ crimeinenglandandwales/yearendingmarch2022 (accessed 15 May 2022).

Public Accounts Committee (2021) *Challenges in implementing digital change*, HC 637, London: House of Commons. Available at: https://committees. parliament.uk/publications/8146/documents/83439/default/ (accessed 16 May 2022).

Redden, J., Dencik, L. and Warne, H. (2020) 'Datafied child welfare services: unpacking politics, economics and power', *Policy Studies*, 41(5): 507–26.

Redden, J., Brand, J., Sander, I. and Warne, H. (2022) *Automating public services: learning from cancelled systems*, Dunfermline: Carnegie UK. Available at: https://d1ssu070pg2v9i.cloudfront.net/pex/pex_carnegie2021/2022/ 09/21101838/Automating-Public-Services-Learning-from-Cancelled-Syst ems-Final-Full-Report.pdf (accessed 15 May 2023).

Roe, A. and Rehill, J. (2021) 'Unequal chances? Ethnic disproportionality in child welfare and family justice', *Family Law*, 6 May. Available at: www. familylaw.co.uk/news_and_comment/unequal-chances-ethnic-disproporti onality-in-child-welfare-family-justice (accessed 15 May 2023).

Rose, N. and Miller, P. (2010) 'Political power beyond the state: problematics of government', *British Journal of Sociology*, 61(s1): 271–303.

Rouvroy, A. (2013) 'The end(s) of critique: data behaviourism verses due process', in M. Hildebrandt and K. de Vries (eds) *Privacy, due process and the computational turn: the philosophy of law meets the philosophy of technology*, London: Routledge, pp 143–68.

Simpson, J. (2022) 'Family hubs a "pale imitation" of Sure Start Centres, Labour says', *Children and Young People Now*, 15 February. Available at: www.cypnow.co.uk/news/article/family-hubs-a-pale-imitation-of-sure-start-centres-labour-says (accessed 16 May 2022).

Sinclair, S., McHugh, N. and Roy, M.J. (2021) 'Social innovation, financialisation and commodification: a critique of social impact bonds', *Journal of Economic Policy Reform*, 24(1): 11–27.

Sunak, R. (2022) 'Rishi Sunak: I will make UK a science and technology superpower', press release, *Ready for Rishi*, 23 August. Available at: www. ready4rishi.com/science_technology_superpower_press_release (accessed 15 May 2023).

Vannier Ducasse, H. (2021) 'Predictive risk modelling and the mistaken equation of socio–economic disadvantage with risk of maltreatment', *British Journal of Social Work*, 51(6): 3153–171.

van Veenstra, A.F. and Kotterink, B. (2017) 'Data-driven policy making: the policy lab approach', *Electronic Participation: Lecture Notes in Computer Science*, 10429. Available at: https://doi.org/10.1007/978-3-319-64322-9_9 (accessed 19 July 2023).

14

Troubling social policy during turbulent times: children and UK Conservative governments since 2015

Harriet Churchill

Introduction

This chapter reviews developments in social policy and state support for children and teenagers overseen by Conservative governments in the UK from 2015 to 2022 during a period of persistent economic problems, exceptional social policy challenges and increasing political instability (see Chapter 1). The chapter considers three main features of these social policies. First, it foregrounds analysis of the ways social policy agendas and reforms have constructed and addressed childhood disadvantage and child welfare as priority public issues and matters for government concern. Second, it considers government agendas and reforms in these areas, primarily in terms of rights to, and developments in, cash support, state welfare, parental support and, broadly defined, 'early help' and community social services. Third, given the focus of this volume, the chapter examines policy goals and reforms pursued by recent Conservative governments. In the chapter, therefore, some discussions concern UK-wide policies (for example related to fiscal, social security and employment policies) and others are about more England-specific policies (for example, related to public and social services).

The chapter initially reflects on the Conservative–Liberal Democrat government of 2010–15. It highlights the ways in which this period established key tenets of contemporary Conservative Party approaches to social and children's policies, such as austerity, targeted social investment and early intervention, localism, de-bureaucratisation and marketisation. It then turns to review the subsequent continuities, changes and implications of the Conservatives' agenda as it developed and shifted under successive prime ministers and as it was impacted by, and adapted to, ongoing public spending constraints, systemic economic problems, Brexit and the COVID-19 pandemic. The chapter highlights the ongoing significance in recent years of the Conservatives' welfare state cutbacks, social mobility reforms and child welfare reforms, and, in the context of the pandemic and economic problems, several child-orientated and family-focused crisis interventions. Ideologically, several camps of Conservative and Liberal thinking have influenced the Conservatives' policy approach (Page, 2015; see also Chapter 1), alongside greater interest in 'the new welfare paradigm of investing in children', particularly the more narrowly conceived profitable social investment approach (Lister, 2008). The chapter argues that while aspects of the Conservatives' 'modern progressive approach' have their merits, overall recent UK government social and children's policy reforms have been characterised by severe contradictions and shortcomings. There has been significant retrenchment in state support for young people, which has contributed to heightened childhood risks and inequalities. With rising levels of need, widening inequalities and overstretched services prominent features of the post-pandemic context, a more comprehensive and coherent child-centred approach is urgently needed.

'The days of big government are over'

The financial crisis from 2007 to 2008 led to heightened government debts and subsequent decisions to introduce public spending constraints and welfare state austerity. In the UK, the Conservative-Liberal Democrat Coalition government pursued a social policy agenda framed by 'a conviction that the days of big government are over' (HM Government, 2010, p 7) which incorporated the pursuit of a 'radical deficit reduction plan' as an immediate policy priority (HM Government, 2010, p 15). However, additional key policies were to 'maintain the goal of ending child poverty by 2020' and to 'protect poorer and vulnerable groups' (HM Government, 2010, p 19). On the part of the Liberal Democrats, these latter policy goals reflected commitments to social liberalism and children's rights (Liberal Democrat Party, 2010, pp 8–9). On the part of the Conservatives, their agenda was framed as post-Thatcherite social conservativism – a modern free market yet One Nation and compassionate Conservativism (Page, 2015). This emphasised the Conservatives' economic recovery policies, which combined market-led economic recovery, public spending cuts and pro-employment support, and which, they argued, would produce economic and social benefits for all, including future generations (Page, 2015). Added to this, compassionate Conservativism incorporated pledges to maintain the social safety net for those in need and to adopt modern family and childhood policies, including improved support for working parents and targeted social investment to boost children's life chances (Page, 2015; Churchill, 2016). By the end of the Coalition era, public spending, as a proportion of gross domestic product, had fallen by 6 per cent (Crawford and Johnson, 2015). However, challenging claims of social liberalism, One Nation and compassionate Conservativism, the Coalition's public spending cuts disproportionately reduced social rights and provisions for lower-income groups, families and children.

Three trends were significant. First, austerity measures directly reduced cash benefits provided to children, teenagers and families via reduced support for disadvantaged youth (for example, withdrawal of Child Trust Funds and the Educational Maintenance Allowance); abandonment of a universal right to Child Benefit, and reductions in the value of family benefits (such as freezes to, and reductions in, Child Benefit and family tax credits rates) (Churchill, 2016). Second, austerity measures reduced working-age welfare benefits and tax credits, which disproportionately impacted on low-income families with children. These included reduced entitlements to, and rates of, welfare benefits and tax credits; reduced help with childcare costs; reduced help with housing costs; and the introduction of the benefits cap. Analysis of the distributional impacts of the Coalition's cutbacks in family and welfare benefits found families with children suffered greater income losses than single-person or pensioner households (Browne, 2015). Tucker (2017, p 19) calculated that benefits cuts introduced under the Coalition led couple-headed and lone-parent family households to lose on average £1,200 and £500 a year, respectively, while other household types lost on average £250 or less. Moreover, the poorest 10 per cent of family households with children saw greater proportional loss in income compared to better-off family households (Tucker, 2017, p 21). Third, central government funding for state-funded and -provided services for children, youth and families saw major cutbacks. This included major reductions in central government funding for local authorities in England, which provide an array of local family, youth and children's services. For example, analysis of official spending data (adjusted for inflation) related to the Coalition's early intervention grant for 2010–11 to 2012–13 and subsequent equivalent local authority funding for 2012–13 to 2014–15 found this funding source for children's centres, youth services and family support services fell by 24 per cent from 2010–11 to 2014–15 (Action for Children et al, 2016, p 3).

Beyond these cutbacks, the Coalition's Child Poverty Strategy (HM Government, 2011) introduced significant reforms, drawing on the Conservatives' 'pathways to poverty' discourse (family breakdown, educational failure, worklessness, addiction and crime, and problem debt and housing; see Centre for Social Justice, 2007) and the Liberal Democrats' social mobility policies (Bochel and Powell, 2016; Churchill, 2016). The former narrowly and disparagingly framed child poverty as driven by 'educational failure, worklessness, family breakdown, severe debt and substance misuse' (HM Government, 2011, p 63). Cutbacks in benefits and tax credits were deemed key solutions, as they tackled 'the culture of worklessness and dependency that does harm to individuals, families and communities' (Department for

Work and Pensions, 2010, p 118). In addition, the Coalition: (a) gradually introduced Universal Credit as a new integrated approach to working-age benefits, incorporating stricter welfare-to-work conditions and substantial in-work support; (b) pursued a wide-ranging academisation and schools reform agenda; and (c) introduced the Troubled Families Programme to 'turn around the lives of troubled families' (Department for Communities and Local Government, 2012, p 10) deemed to place high demands on public spending due to problems framed in terms of anti-social behaviour, welfare dependency, educational failure and parenting problems (see also Chapter 13). Drawing on the Liberal Democrats' social mobility, anti-poverty and family policies, the Coalition also introduced: (a) a reduced tax burden for low earners; (b) part-time subsidised childcare for disadvantaged two-year-olds; (c) Pupil Premium funding for schools to support to disadvantaged pupils; (d) Early Years Pupil Premium funding for childcare providers to support disadvantaged three- to four-year-olds; and (e) Shared Parental Leave, allowing couples to share maternity leave and pay entitlements.

Another strand of reforms reconfigured local services for children and families in England, influenced by the Coalition's public services reform agenda to reduce costs and improve service outcomes via spending constraints, de-bureaucratisation, outsourcing and localism (Bochel and Powell, 2016). Resonating with the 'pathways to poverty' discourse discussed earlier, this agenda sought 'to break the cycle of deprivation and dysfunction from generation to generation' (Allen, 2011, p ix). The role of central government was reconfigured away from partnerships for child well-being towards supporting local authorities to improve cost-effectiveness via greater focus on those most in need; local authority autonomy, devolved budgets and innovation; reduced bureaucratic demands on professionals and services; cost-reducing and outcomes-focused outsourcing to the voluntary and private sectors; and initiatives to support evidence-based early intervention programmes and targeted service models (Purcell, 2020). Children's centres, youth services and family services were encouraged to better target their resources. Social workers were encouraged to improve child welfare practice via reduced administrative burdens, sharper focus on child-centred multi-agency working, and greater use of statutory social care placements and adoption. Alongside government agendas, the Munro (2011) review of child protection was highly influential in promoting developments in local authorities' early help strategies. However, Munro's (2011) call to better promote child welfare via increased funding for, and entitlements to, early help support and services were marginalised, and the broader context for local authorities was characterised by substantial cutbacks in funding, rising levels of needs and increasing demands on services. Purcell argues that the Coalition promoted localism in part 'to avoid close association with the implications of austerity and welfare reform' and to enable the government to blame 'local leaders for closures of services' and the performance of children's social care (2020, p 179).

'A plan for a better future … a plan for every stage of your life'

With opinion polls in 2015 predicting otherwise, the majority government win for the Conservatives, under the continued leadership of David Cameron, was both surprising and slim. It was in fact their Coalition partner, the Liberal Democrats, that suffered major electoral losses. However, to manage internal Conservative Party conflicts over European Union (EU) membership and the political threat from the United Kingdom Independence Party, the Conservatives' pledged to hold a referendum on EU membership. This was held in June 2016 and resulted in the decision for the UK to leave the EU, based on a 52 per cent majority vote. Following one year in office, and having campaigned for 'Remain', the referendum provoked Cameron's resignation as Prime Minister and the appointment of Theresa May as the new Conservative Party leader and Prime Minister in July 2016. Nevertheless, during its short term, the 2015–16 Cameron government took forward proposals floated by and policies established under the Coalition which had much significance for children and families. It framed its social policy agenda as supporting key phases of the life course, adopting 'a plan for every stage of your life' with pledges to promote 'the best start in life', pursue school reforms to enable young people to develop needed skills, and provide improved support to families (Conservative Party, 2015, p 1).

A new phase in the Conservatives' deficit reduction plan was swiftly introduced, taking forward a policy to reduce welfare spending by another £13 billion by 2020. With pensions protected, this policy meant further cuts to working-age and family benefits, which included: from April 2016, reduced work allowances for Universal Credit claimants and a four-year freeze on benefit rates for most working-age benefits, Child Benefit and Local Housing Allowance; from November 2016, a reduction in the benefits cap to £20,000 per annum for family households outside London and £23,000 per annum for those in London; and from April 2017, a two-child limit restricting eligibility for new claimants of Child Tax Credit, Housing Benefit and the child element of Universal Credit, the withdrawal of the family element of tax credits for new claims, and the withdrawal of the housing element of Universal Credit for most 18- to 21-year-olds. Reforms and cutbacks in disability benefits accompanied these measures.

Analysing the cumulative effects of the welfare and benefit system changes and cuts introduced by the Coalition and the 2015–16 Conservative government, Tucker (2017) found that family households with children saw greater losses in income than other households. For example, accounting for welfare benefits and tax credit changes (but omitting Universal Credit reforms), she estimated that in early 2017 compared to May 2010, lone-parent family households were on average £1,940 worse off (an annual household income loss of around 10 per cent) and couple households with children were on average £2,080 worse off (an annual household income loss of 6 per cent) due to welfare and tax credit cuts. In comparison, while pensioner households and working-age households without children also suffered income losses, these were on average all below £500 a year (annual household income losses of around 2–3 per cent). Further, this new phase of cutbacks targeted the new Universal Credit system, reducing its potential to support low-earning parents and reinforcing the benefit poverty traps it claimed to reduce. Tucker's analysis of the impact of these cuts pointed to: downward pressures on the household incomes of poorer families, lone-parent families, larger families, families with preschool children, families affected by disability and low-earning working parents; and upward pressures on child poverty rates.

The scale of the benefit cuts courted fierce opposition, including among Conservatives. Iain Duncan Smith, the Secretary of State for Work and Pensions, famously resigned in March 2016, calling into question the government's One Nation credentials and citing welfare benefit cuts as unfair in the context of increased pensions, less austerity and tax cuts for better-off groups. Opposition also led to a government U-turn on some proposed tax credits cuts for families. However, overall, the government's rebuttal to criticisms of its poverty-increasing benefit cuts was to emphasise the poverty-reducing goals of its pro-employment and 'life chances' reforms. As part of this agenda, the government introduced policies which sought to enhance family incomes via reduced taxation for lower earners, the new National Living Wage and further investment in childcare, particularly via 30 hours a week, 38 weeks a year, of subsidised childcare for lower-earning parents with three- and four-year-olds from September 2017. However, young workers under 25 missed out on the National Living Wage, the introduction of the childcare reforms was some way off, and local authorities warned of severe funding pressures inhibiting the childcare reforms. Further, analysis of the overall distributional effects of the range of taxation and benefits changes introduced under this government found that, on average, household incomes suffered more losses than gains and poorer households and families with children suffered the most losses (Browne, 2015).

In this context, the Conservatives stepped up efforts to reframe the child poverty debate and emphasise the role of parental responsibilities. Their 2015 election manifesto reiterated their 'root causes of poverty' discourse (Conservative Party, 2015, p 28), and the Welfare Reform and Work Act 2016 took forward plans to revise the Child Poverty Act 2010 and repeal its 2020 child poverty reduction targets. These were replaced with alternative measures related to life chances (namely, rates of workless family households with children and educational attainment at age 16). The Conservatives declared they would pursue a new life chances strategy to tackle the 'paucity of opportunity' among 'those left behind' (Cameron, 2016). The new policy phase was framed as addressing the pathways to poverty listed earlier and, in particular, addressing how they 'combine ... reinforce each other ... manifest themselves throughout someone's life' and generate 'the opportunity gap' (Cameron, 2016). Reforms under way were reframed as 'life chances policies', including the welfare-to-work measures, pro-employment measures, school system reforms, pupil premiums, the Troubled Families Programme and early intervention reforms. Further pledges were made to increase investment in early years and parenting interventions and tackle 'toxic stress' in early childhood, associated with harmful parenting, abuse, neglect and witnessing domestic violence (Cameron, 2016). A dominant discourse within the new 'life chances' approach was that of the profitable social investment approach to breaking cycles of disadvantage and dysfunction (Lister, 2008). This emphasises investing in evidence-based and targeted childhood and family interventions as prominent mechanisms to address behavioural causes of social problems, enhance human capital and social mobility, and promote responsible citizenship. This approach is also aligned with a dominant construction of childhood as preparation for adulthood, curtailment of social rights associated with welfare dependency, marginal engagement with holistic child well-being policies and limited consideration of children's rights (Lister, 2008). In line with these policy logics, the Conservatives' life chances agenda at this point paid little attention to poverty risks, and social inequalities related to lower earning capabilities and precarious employment, the disadvantages people and families faced related to disability, worsening mental health and health inequality trends, the demands of caring roles, the gendered patterns of parental responsibilities, or levels of societal discrimination. There was also indifference to the stresses placed on children and families arising from benefit cuts and living costs, and to the risks posed by reductions to support services. Studies, however, reported central government funding for local early intervention and family support services fell by 55 per cent from 2010–11 to 2015–16, while local authority spending fell by 31 per cent (Action for Children et al, 2016, p 5). Further, local authority spending on Sure Start children's centres (which serve families with preschool children) fell by 48 per cent (Action for Children et al, 2016, p 9).

'We will govern in the interests of ordinary, working families'

In several ways, the Conservative government under Theresa May sought to reclaim a One Nation Conservative agenda and distance itself from the more divisive and regressive neoliberal sentiments of the previous era

(Williams, 2017; Bochel and Powell, 2018; see also Chapter 1). On taking office, May famously pledged to tackle 'burning injustices' which inhibited equal opportunity and the pressures faced by hard-working families who are 'just about' managing (May, 2016). May (2017) characterised this social reform agenda as balancing 'rights', 'responsibilities' and 'fairness' alongside moving beyond the narrow focus of helping 'the very poorest' to supporting those 'who feel that the system is stacked against them'. Then, in the hope of strengthening the Conservatives' parliamentary majority and her own position in the Brexit negotiations, May called an early general election in June 2017. The Conservative Party (2017) manifesto likewise emphasised One Nation Conservativism with its declaration to 'govern in the interests of ordinary, working families' (Conservative Party, 2017, p 7) and provided further details of the new social reform agenda. Of significance for children, the agenda did not constitute a radical new departure, but sought to introduce progressive incremental reforms while implementing the planned benefit cuts. The main proposals included increased funding for schools, reduced tax burdens for low-earning parents, investment in child and youth mental health services, and measures to address domestic abuse. However, the election result saw the Conservatives gain the most seats but not secure an overall majority. To form a government, the Conservatives formed a coalition with the Northern Irish and conservative Democratic Unionist Party. Two years of fraught Brexit negotiations and political conflict followed, culminating in mid-2019 with Parliament rejecting the negotiated Brexit deal, the resignation of Theresa May and end of her government.

During this period, several significant developments for children and young people were introduced, but these were marked by contradictions, delay and shortcomings. There was some easing of austerity and the degree to which this targeted young people. For example, the planned cuts to Housing Benefit for 18- to 24-year-olds were scrapped, and the 'end of austerity' was declared (May, 2018). However, although lower earners were favoured in taxation reforms, the government implemented cutbacks in welfare benefits and Universal Credit despite the mounting evidence that benefit rates and the Universal Credit system, especially the latter's punitive use of a delayed first payment and welfare-to-work sanctions, were contributing to increases in severe child poverty and food bank use (Joseph Rowntree Foundation – JRF, 2021). There was additional investment and improved support for disadvantaged pupils and those with special educational needs, but a new schools funding framework meant that overall schools spending flatlined from 2014–15 to 2018–19 and spending per pupil fell (Lupton and Obolenskaya, 2021, p 18). Further, according to the official Department for Education measure, the 'educational attainment gap' widened from 2017 to 2019 (Lupton and Obolenskaya, 2021, p 45). A proposed review of children's centres and the life chances strategy did not materialise.

In May 2017, the Chair of the Social Mobility Commission resigned amidst severe criticism of the deprioritisation of social mobility issues and indifference to increasing rates of child poverty. This was followed by further high-level calls for the government to 'address the burning social injustices which [May] insisted ... would be her main priority' (cited in Purcell, 2020, p 124). Three further developments of note proceeded. In July 2018, a ministerial group was established to review children's development and outcomes among those under two years old, and the support and services they and their families received. While the renewed attention to early childhood concerns was welcomed and significant, calls for a new more ambitious national strategy to improve child and youth well-being and prospects across the age ranges were rejected, and the losses families with preschool children had suffered in the context of austerity measures were muted issues. In December 2018, the government published the Green Paper *Transforming Children and Young People's Mental Health* (Department of Health and Department for Education, 2018) with proposals for developments in school-based and community-based mental health initiatives and teams, and new targets to reduce waiting times for specialist child and adolescent mental health services. Experts in this area praised these priorities but also criticised what was deemed an inadequate commitment to additional funding and a limited analysis of the causes of increasing mental health problems among children and young people (Newlove-Delgado et al, 2021). In January 2019, the Domestic Abuse Bill was introduced, proposing new broader definitions of, and duties to tackle, domestic abuse. Yet this area had likewise experienced significant funding cuts since 2010, with one study indicating local authorities reported a 28 per cent reduction in funding available for domestic abuse services from 2010 to 2016 (Williams, 2017, p 9).

'Every child should have the same opportunity'

In mid-2019, Jeremy Hunt, former Health Secretary and Remain supporter, and Boris Johnson, former Foreign Secretary and leading Brexit campaigner, battled it out to be the third Conservative Party leader and Prime Minister since 2015. Johnson won the contest with fervent promises to 'deliver Brexit' and 'unite the country' (Johnson, 2019). He called an early election to strengthen his position, resulting in a major victory for the Conservatives, who secured their best result in decades and a substantial parliamentary majority. Following the period of fraught Brexit negotiations under Theresa May, a large part of Boris Johnson's and the Conservatives' appeal at this time were pledges to swiftly and decisively 'get Brexit done' with an 'oven-ready' deal (Conservative Party, 2019, p 3). In addition, the Conservatives' rhetoric positioned Boris Johnson as distinctively committed to Brexit, 'the people's decision', in contrast to anti-Brexit opposition parties and

Conservative colleagues (Conservative Party, 2019, p 5). Further, the failure to 'get Brexit done' under Theresa May was portrayed as causing systemic economic problems and thwarting the government's social mobility agenda. The Conservatives (2019, p 7) pledged to 'get Brexit done' so it can 'unleash Britain's potential', promising a new One Nation post-Brexit world of renewed stability, investment, opportunity and prosperity.

In terms of significance for children and young people, this agenda did not indicate a radical new approach, but it did repackage dominant themes in new ways and signal increases in public spending. Echoing earlier social mobility and life chances policies, it was stated that 'Conservatives believe passionately that every child should have the same opportunity to ... make the most of their lives' (Conservative Party, 2019, p 2). Cast as financed by funding that would previously have gone to the EU, the Conservatives pledged to 'level up' socioeconomic opportunities and give 'every child, in every part of the country' a chance, via measures such as its Shared Prosperity Fund for regional development and increases in funding for schools (Conservative Party, 2019, p 13). The emphasis on reducing child poverty via parental employment would be developed with increased investment in childcare, increases in the National Living Wage and pledges to not raise taxes. Further, additional developments took forward the Conservatives' policies for vulnerable children and families including improvements to the Troubled Families Programme, measures to 'champion' Family Hubs, a review of the care system, implementation of the Domestic Abuse Bill and introduction of new legislation on online harms (Conservative Party, 2019). Conversely, concerns about increasing child poverty rates and prominent child welfare risks were given little recognition.

In early 2020, following fraught political struggles, the new Conservative government fulfilled its pledge and secured the Brexit agreement and transition deal with the EU (see Chapter 4). Before much progress could be made on their social policy agenda, however, the COVID-19 pandemic emerged and rapidly developed (see Chapter 5). By the end of March 2020, the UK and devolved governments had adopted unprecedented public health measures. England effectively saw three periods of national lockdown (March to June 2020, October to December 2020, and January to March 2021), whereby social contact outside of households was highly restricted and, beyond those classified as essential services, all workplaces, schools, businesses, public buildings and services were closed and where possible their activities and interactions digitalised. The first lockdown phase was particularly chaotic as the situation evolved and measures were put in place, while later lockdowns saw the impacts and pressures of the pandemic and the public health measures accumulate. The lives of children and youths were profoundly impacted by major changes and uncertainties, and intermittent periods of lockdown and 'opening up'. Parents were faced with heightened demands, including overseeing home education and working from home. Social interaction became highly dependent on, and facilitated by, internet access and digital media and devices. Young people with heightened health risks, who were young carers or whose primary carers had heightened health risks, faced exceptional anxieties and persistent social contact restrictions. While public health restrictions eased from mid-July 2021 and the national vaccine programme was swiftly rolled out, rates of COVID-19 infections and ill health remained substantial during 2022.

A prominent social welfare charity stated the Conservative Government 'took bold and compassionate action' and measures during the pandemic (JRF, 2022b, p 2). These sought to protect jobs, businesses and incomes, and to provide social support in the context of lockdowns, public health risks and demands on the National Health Service and other essential services. Many parents working in sectors that had been closed and scaled back benefited from the Coronavirus Job Retention Scheme, which provided employers with up to 80 per cent of staff wages. The public health context led to the suspension of welfare-to-work and debt repayments rules in the benefits system. Claimants also received more support, mainly via the increase of £20 a week in the basic rate for Universal Credit and Working Tax Credit as well as increases in housing support. Greater numbers of parents claimed Universal Credit during this period: claimants rose from 3 million in March 2020 to 5.8 million in November 2020 (JRF, 2021).

In addition, local authorities received additional funding to provide support for children and families experiencing hardship. Although often following media and sector pressure, the government provided several strands of funding for charities and local authorities to provide food parcels and vouchers to children and families in need. Welfare as well as educational support was provided by schools. Parents whose children were in receipt of free school meals and in food poverty were eligible to access supermarket vouchers and food packages. A major area of concern was support for children and parents with respect to engaging with, and maintaining, school learning at home. This placed exceptional demands on parents and households, and many children and young people faced challenges and difficulties. A mixed picture of support for schools and support for children and families emerged. Two significant initiatives were: the Department for Education's Get Help with Technology scheme, which enabled schools, further education settings and local authorities to provide technology support (such as laptops, tablets, 4G wireless routers and internet access) to disadvantaged children and young people; and funding for schools to develop digital education platforms. However, while the Department for Education reported providing 1.3 million laptops and devices to disadvantaged children and young people by June 2021, many local authorities and schools reported high levels of digital exclusion and issues with internet access and digital literacy (Department for Education, 2021; see also Chapter 8).

Other shortcomings in the support provided meant that many vulnerable children and parents lost out. Examples include the omission of legacy welfare and disability benefits from the £20 uplift; enduring detrimental impact on family incomes from the benefit cap, first Universal Credit payment delays and the two-child limit; and delays and discrepancies in securing educational and welfare support via schools. Local authorities faced challenges in ensuring children and families most in need were aware and able to access local welfare support (JRF, 2022a). Further, there was major criticism that the government prematurely sought to remove temporary support measures in the context of enduring high needs, placing children at risk. High-profile campaigns secured extensions to food support schemes during school holidays, and the £20 uplift in benefits to October 2021. However, the latter was then withdrawn even though the child-centred case for retaining the uplift as inflation and living costs rose was substantial (JRF, 2022a).

Other policy initiatives progressed, with the Troubled Families Programme securing additional funding in 2020–21 and providing a key part of the local response to COVID-19 by supporting families and children in high need and 'pioneering remote and virtual ways of supporting families and carrying out safe home visits' (Ministry of Housing, Communities and Local Government, 2021). These services adopted creative approaches to engaging families, such as including messages and advice for families and children in food parcels and setting up local helplines for parents and domestic abuse victims. Since March 2021, renamed the Supporting Families programme, the scheme has continued to receive annual funding to support families with issues such as children's return to, and attendance at, school as well as parental employment, mental health support and domestic abuse interventions.

Child welfare concerns were significant during the height of the public health measures. The Domestic Abuse Act was passed into legislation in April 2021, and its measures include a new broader statutory definition of domestic abuse and new duties and powers for local authorities and the police to better protect victims of abuse and their children. More investment in services and prevention initiatives is needed though, given the rates of domestic abuse reports and pressures on services before, during and since the pandemic.

In July 2020, the agenda to review early years services and support was progressed with a major review into early years health led by Andrea Leadsom MP. This was followed in 2021 by *The Best Start for Life* report, which called for more joined-up support for families with children under two years old, particularly through developing children's centres into family hubs providing a wider range of community-based and community-orientated support and services for families with children, and via improved and integrated online and in-person support and services (Department of Health and Social Care, 2021). In January 2021, the Department for Education also established an independent review of outcomes among children in care, to propose reforms in this area; and in May 2021, it introduced the Online Safety Bill, which promised to better address child welfare risks arising from social media and harmful content that children and young people access online.

As the UK emerged from the height of pandemic, the government pursued an education recovery plan (Department for Education, 2021) and other measures to support children to catch up on lost learning (see also Chapter 8). However, many reports highlighted inadequate attention to, and lack of measures to address, the increased educational inequalities which have emerged from the pandemic and the scale of child well-being concerns (for example, Fancourt et al, 2022). New frameworks for child-orientated reforms have also been provided by the 'levelling up' strategy (HM Government, 2022), the Leadsom-led review mentioned earlier and *The Independent Review of Children's Social Care* (MacAlister, 2022). Levelling up provided the latest reiteration of the Conservatives' social mobility and life chances policies, and underscored the role of incremental childcare, schools, pro-employment and family hub reforms. However, progress in these areas has been slow, with the programme of additional investment in family hubs, for example, progressing in those local authorities which secure funding based on competitive bids. The *Independent Review of Children's Social Care* (MacAlister, 2022) took forward the Conservatives' agenda to review children's social care reform. At the time of writing (spring 2023), some additional investment and reforms have partly taken forward its recommendations, but the advocated 'radical policy reset' in favour of greater early help and family support is yet to materialise. Limited developments were partly due to the political instability that marked the summer and autumn of 2022, which saw revelations of parties in Downing Street provoke the resignation of Boris Johnson, a lengthy Conservative Party and government leadership contest involving Liz Truss and Rishi Sunak, a calamitous short spell as Prime Minister for Liz Truss and the replacement of her leadership with Rishi Sunak as Prime Minister. The wider context also continued to be tumultuous, with economic and political problems intensifying in the context of rapid increases in inflation, a proliferating cost of living crisis and the fallout from Russia's invasion of Ukraine. All of these things arguably contributed to and enabled a relative lack of government action on children and youth policy.

Conclusion

The social and children's policy agendas of recent UK Conservative governments led by David Cameron (2015–16), Theresa May (2016–19) and Boris Johnson (2019–22) shared many similarities, but also reflected some differences and contended with a variety of major challenges. Reflecting aspects of similarity, this chapter has highlighted the ongoing significance of neoliberal and neoconservative approaches to welfare state cutbacks and reforms, social mobility policies and child welfare reforms. Over the period, these features of Conservative government agendas and reforms have been criticised as highly contradictory and limited as austerity measures became increasingly regressive in their disproportionate emphasis on reduced state support for poorer groups and younger citizens, a trend that pandemic measures and 'post-austerity' policies did not reverse. Aligned with neoliberal politics, these developments were accompanied by discursive strategies which emphasised behavioural explanations for disadvantage and child welfare concerns to reinforce and legitimate the decisive shirt towards reduced social rights for children and families and greater personal and parental responsibilities for social and child welfare. In addition, the reforms pursued reflected greater interest across the political spectrum in active social policies and profitable social investment (Lister, 2008). Adopting neoliberal and One Nation Conservative perspectives, these orientations informed the Conservatives' pro-employment, targeted support, evidence-based and early intervention reforms.

These agendas built on reforms introduced by the Coalition and incorporated incremental developments in support and services for working parents, preschool children and children in need. While providing valuable additional support, however, they were based on policy logics that adhered to limited and behavioural conceptions of social disadvantage and child welfare risks. Counter to these shifts, however, the devolved administrations beyond England have often utilised their powers to resist austerity measures and cutbacks in social rights for children and families. The Scottish Government has used its enhanced powers in social security policy to pursue an extensive child poverty strategy, reinstate national targets for reducing child poverty rates, expand social protections for low-income families and strengthen children's rights (JRF, 2022a). The administrations in Wales and Northern Ireland have also introduced measures to mitigate benefits cuts for children and families, and pursued introduced broader, more holistic child poverty, child well-being and children's rights strategies (Rogers, 2019). With rising levels of need, widening inequalities and overstretched services prominent features of the post-pandemic context, wider UK adoption and development of these more comprehensive and coherent child-centred approaches to social policy are urgently needed.

References

Action for Children, National Children's Bureau and The Children's Society (2016) *Losing in the long run: trends in early intervention funding*, London: Action for Children.

Allen, G. (2011) *Early intervention: the next steps*, London: Department for Education.

Bochel, H. and Powell, M. (2016) 'The transformation of the welfare state? The Conservative–Liberal Democrat Coalition government and social policy', in H. Bochel and M. Powell (eds) *The Coalition government and social policy*, Bristol: Policy Press, pp 1–26.

Bochel, H. and Powell, M. (2018) 'Whatever happened to compassionate Conservatism under the Coalition government?', *British Politics*, 13(2): 146–70.

Browne, J. (2015) 'The impact of proposed tax, benefit and minimum wage reforms on household income and work incentives', *Institute for Fiscal Studies*, 19 November. Available at: www.ifs.org.uk/publications/8054 (accessed 10 October 2022).

Cameron, D. (2016) 'Prime Minister's speech on life chances', *Gov.uk*, 11 January. Available at: gov.uk/government/speeches/prime-ministers-speech-on-life-chances (accessed 15 September 2022).

Centre for Social Justice (2007) *Breakthrough Britain*, London: Centre for Social Justice.

Churchill, H. (2016) 'One step forward, two steps back: children, young people and the Conservative-Liberal Democrat Coalition', in H. Bochel and M. Powell (eds) *The Coalition government and social policy*, Bristol: Policy Press, pp 265–84.

Conservative Party (2015) *Strong leadership, a clear economic plan, a brighter, more secure future. The Conservative Party manifesto 2015*, London: Conservative Party.

Conservative Party (2017) *Forward together: our plan for a stronger Britain and a prosperous future. The Conservative and Unionist Party Manifesto 2017*, London: Conservative Party.

Conservative Party (2019) *Get Brexit done, unleash Britain's potential. The Conservative and Unionist Party manifesto 2019*, London: Conservative Party.

Crawford, R. and Johnson, P. (2015) 'The UK Coalition government's record, and challenges for the future', *Institute for Fiscal Studies*, 15 September. Available at: https://ifs.org.uk/articles/uk-coalition-governments-record-and-challenges-future (accessed 10 October 2022).

Department for Communities and Local Government (2012) *The Troubled Families Programme: financial framework for the Troubled Families Programme's payment by results scheme for local authorities*, London: Department for Communities and Local Government.

Department for Education (2021) 'Guidance: education recovery support', *Gov.uk*, 13 April. Available at: www.gov.uk/government/publications/education-recovery-support/education-recovery-support--2 (accessed 10 October 2022).

Department for Work and Pensions (2010) *21st century welfare*, London: The Stationery Office.

Department of Health and Department for Education (2018) *Transforming children and young people's mental health*, London: HMSO.

Department of Health and Social Care (2021) *The best start for life: a vision for the 1,001 critical days*, London: Department of Health and Social Care. Available at: www.gov.uk/government/publications/the-best-start-for-life-a-vision-for-the-1001-critical-days (accessed 1 October 2022).

Fancourt, D., Steptoe, A. and Bradbury, A. (2022) *Tracking the psychological and social consequences of the COVID-19 pandemic across the UK population: findings, impact, and recommendations from the COVID-19 social study (March 2020 – April 2022)*, London: University College London.

HM Government (2010) *The Coalition: our programme for government*, London: Cabinet Office.

HM Government (2011) *A new approach to child poverty: tackling the causes of disadvantage and transforming families' lives*, London: The Stationary Office.

HM Government (2022) *Levelling up the United Kingdom*, London: HMSO.

Johnson, B. (2019) 'Boris Johnson's first speech as Tory party leader', *PoliticsHome*, 23 July. Available at: www.politicshome.com/news/arti cle/read-in-full-boris-johnsons-first-speech-as-tory-leader (accessed 20 October 2022).

JRF (Joseph Rowntree Foundation) (2021) *Poverty and inequality in the UK*, York: JRF.

JRF (Joseph Rowntree Foundation) (2022a) *Going without: deepening poverty in the UK*, York: JRF.

JRF (2022b) 'Keep the lifeline: why the government should keep the £20 uplift to Universal Credit'. Briefing. Available at: https://www.jrf.org. uk/file/57351/download?token=QXtofzdL&filetype=briefing (accessed 1st August 2023).

Liberal Democrat Party (2010) *Change that works for you: building a fairer Britain*, London: Liberal Democrat Party.

Lister, R. (2008) 'Investing in childhood and children: a new welfare policy paradigm and its implications', in C. Saraceno and A. Liera (eds) *Childhood: changing contexts*, Stamford, CA: Emerald Group Publishing, pp 383–408.

Lupton, R. and Obdenskaya, P. (2021) 'Compulsory education from May 2015 to pre-COVID 2020', in P. Vizard and J. Hills (eds) *The Conservative governments' record on social policy from May 2015 to pre-COVID 2020: policies, spending and outcomes*, London: Centre for Analysis of Social Exclusion, LSE, pp 130–7.

MacAlister, J. (2022) *The independent review of children's social care: final report*, London: The Independent Review of Children's Social Care.

May, T. (2016) 'Statement from the new Prime Minister Theresa May', *Gov. uk*, 13 July. Available at: www.gov.uk/government/speeches/statement-from the new-prime-minister-theresa-may (accessed 15 February 2022).

May, T. (2017) 'The shared society', *Gov.uk*, 8 January. Available at: www.gov.uk/government/speeches/the-shared-society-article-by-theresa-may (accessed 20 October 2022).

May, T. (2018) 'Theresa May's full speech to 2018 Conservative Conference' [video], *BBC*, 3 October. Available at: www.bbc.co.uk/news/av/uk-polit ics-45733093/theresa-may-s-full-speech-to-2018-conservative-conference (accessed 20 October 2022).

Ministry of Housing, Communities and Local Government (2021a) *Improving families' lives: annual report of the Troubled Families Programme 2020 to 2021*, *Gov.uk*, 29 March. Available at: www.gov.uk/government/publications/improving-families-lives-annual-report-of-the-troubled-families-progra mme-2020-to-2021/improving-families-lives-annual-report-of-the-troub led-families-programme-2020-to-2021 (accessed 15 April 2022).

Munro, E. (2011) *The Munro review of child protection: final report. A child-centred system*, London: Department for Education. Available at: https:// assets.publishing.service.gov.uk/government/uploads/system/uploads/atta chment_data/file/175391/Munro-Review.pdf (accessed 15 October 2022).

Newlove-Delgado, T., McManus, S., Sadler, K., Thandi, S., Vizard, T., Cartwright, C. and Ford, T. (2021) 'Child mental health in England before and during the COVID-19 lockdown', *Lancet Psychiatry*, 8(5): 353–4.

Page, R. (2015) *Clear blue water? The Conservative Party and the welfare state since 1940*, Bristol: Policy Press.

Purcell, C. (2020) *The politics of children's services reform: re-examining two decades of policy change*, Bristol: Policy Press.

Rogers, M. (2019) *Devolution and child poverty policies: a four nations perspective*, London: British Academy. Available at: www.thebritishacademy.ac.uk/publications/childhood-devolution-and-child-poverty-policies-four-nati ons-perspective/ (accessed 1 September 2022).

Tucker, J. (2017) *The austerity generation*, London: Child Poverty Action Group. Available at: https://cpag.org.uk/sites/default/files/files/Auster ity%20Generation%20FINAL.pdf (accessed 1 September 2022).

Williams, B. (2017) 'Tory ideology and social policy under Theresa May: current and future directions', *Renewal*, 25(3–4): 128–37.

15

Conservative criminal justice: a strange rediscovery of 'law and order' politics

Peter Squires

Introduction

Despite winning three consecutive elections, in 2015, in 2017 (albeit short of a majority in the House of Commons) and in 2019, the Conservative governments of these years experienced increasingly troubled times. Each pillar of the Party's 'traditional appeal' – stable government, sound finance and law and order – came under sustained challenge. In this chapter, the latter theme, Conservative law and order and criminal justice policies, are subjected to particular scrutiny, although powerful conflicting influences played across all three themes.

A number of momentous events undoubtedly played their destabilising parts here, including Brexit and its long-drawn-out aftermath, the COVID-19 pandemic, the Russian invasion of Ukraine and the ensuing rapid escalation in energy prices, triggering, in turn, the highest inflation rates for 40 years and the cost of living crisis. But the Conservative Party also underwent a crisis, largely of its own making, resulting in a rapid turnover of leaders – prime ministers – five of whom eventually came to hold the reins of power during the eight years after 2015. Such a rapid turnover of leaders, in part reflecting factional tendencies within the Conservative Party (Guiney, 2022), including, for England and Wales, five home secretaries and seven secretaries of state for justice, inevitably had their impact upon the consistency of policy making across a wide range of areas of government, especially the criminal justice system.

As has been noted previously (Squires, 2016), while the Conservative-led Coalition government had pursued a number of consistent penal policy goals, centred on delivering austerity, managerialism and the outsourcing of criminal justice services (Skinns, 2016), the much-vaunted 'rehabilitation revolution' (later styled 'transforming rehabilitation') barely got off the ground. Less than four years into the newly outsourced community supervision arrangements, and following critical reports from both within

Westminster (National Audit Office, 2019) and partner nongovernmental organisations and policy experts (Plummer, 2018; Annison, 2019), David Gauke, the fourth justice secretary in four years, announced a major policy U-turn, bringing rehabilitation services back within the national Probation Service (Schofield and Johnstone, 2019). Rather worse was to follow as events took over and the relative clarity of the Coalition's policies turned into the more limited and pragmatic criminal justice ambitions of the administration coming to power in 2015, followed by the unrestrained overpromise of the Johnson administration elected in 2019. Yet, despite his dramatic electoral victory, with more traditional law and order values now front and centre, Johnson's fall from power was, at least in part, shaped by his leadership's failure to live within the COVID-19 restrictions (and the police powers these entailed) intended for everyone else. In the process, he became the first prime minister to incur criminal penalties while in office.

How the leader of a political party that had always represented itself as the party of law and order (Loader, 2020) came to be a law breaker is also the story of several profound political changes reflected in the UK after Brexit, shifts in the balance of power within the Conservative Party reflected in two manifestos (2015 and 2019) and the perceived problems they were intended to address.

The 2015 Conservative manifesto

For the party of law and order, the manifesto had surprisingly little to say about crime until page 58, and even then the highlighted commitments were largely 'continuation projects': 'finishing the job of police reform', 'reforming the prison system' and 'supporting victims', 'prioritising violence against women and girls' (VAWG) and, finally, in a step towards the Brexit agenda, 'scrapping the Human Rights Act' to streamline the deportation of foreign criminals. Reflecting the claim that (with the exception of a 35 per cent increase in reports of cybercrime (Office for National Statistics, 2021), recorded crime had fallen over a number of years 'by more than a fifth' (Conservative Party, 2015, p 58), the issue no longer exerted its familiar pull (Morgan and Smith, 2017). As Skinns (2016, p 24) notes, only 9 per cent of respondents to an Ipsos MORI poll in 2015 felt that crime was the most important issue facing the country. However, the manifesto also spoke of a new technological era for crime prevention, law enforcement and investigative techniques, capitalising on crime science to enhance public safety. The new programme, the *Modern Crime Prevention Strategy* was launched by Theresa May, then Home Secretary, in 2016 (Home Office, 2016b).

The new strategy emphasised targeting what it called the 'drivers' of serious crime, referring to 'opportunity', 'character', 'profit', 'drugs' and 'alcohol' as key factors. Chapter 4, however, focused on the effectiveness of the criminal justice system itself in suppressing crime trends. Unfortunately, in the wake of the Coalition's austerity measures (policing cuts, reductions in the number of police officers, including the abandonment of the 'national neighbourhood policing strategy' as 'unaffordable'; Williams and Squires, 2021, pp 222–3) and spending cuts for the Courts Service and the criminal justice system as a whole, evidence was accumulating that the criminal justice system was becoming rather less effective.

To take a few prominent examples, after 2015 police 'sanction detections' (cases cleared up) in respect of gun crime offences began to fall, and by 2021 they were down by a third (Allen and Burton, 2022). Over the same period, the proportion of knife violence offences cleared up fell by a half (Williams and Squires, 2021). In the case of VAWG, despite a tripling in reported sexual violence cases and widespread references to 'an epidemic of violent and abusive offending against women and girls' (HM Inspectorate of Constabulary and Fire Rescue Services – HMICFRS, 2021, p 1), the Crown Prosecution Service (2018) reported a 60 per cent significant fall off in rape prosecutions even as offence reports increased (Barr and Topping, 2021). In 2022, the National Police Chiefs' Council attributed falling clear-up rates to austerity measures and significant reductions in police and civilian staff (Syal and Dodd, 2022). By the end of 2020, the average length of time between the commission of an offence and its completion in the Crown Courts grew to a record 708 days (Clark, 2022), while the backlog of cases awaiting trial had grown by a third since 2017, to a record 60,000 (Casciani, 2021). Spending cuts to the Courts Service and Legal Aid were also responsible. By early 2022, concern was growing regarding the increasingly long delays facing rape prosecutions, – in many cases, over three years (Murray, 2022). The recent pandemic had played its part, but cuts to the Crown Prosecution Service, Courts Service and a shortage of suitable judges compounded these problems.

This catalogue of issues, notwithstanding the bland promises of the 2015 manifesto, pointed to a criminal justice system struggling to cope. This was so in two senses. First, austerity measures had seriously impacted the simple operational effectiveness of criminal justice agencies. Second, cuts in wider service provision, such as community health, youth services, local authority housing and social services meant that more social problems (undoubtedly 'drivers of crime') were piling up at the feet of the police. Yet policing experienced a combined loss of some 28,000 (police officers and police community support officers, or approximately 21 per cent of police staff) leading to a debate about how far policing cuts were implicated in street crime increases.

The 2019 Conservative manifesto

By 2019, with Boris Johnson as Conservative leader, although with the Brexit negotiation process still underway, the manifesto turned to embrace more populist Tory themes. Guiney (2022) argues that in order to better understand the evolution of recent Conservative law and order strategy, we need an analysis reaching beyond a simple two-dimensional 'more-or-less-punitive' account. In particular, he suggests that we need to pay more attention to the internal ideological rifts within contemporary conservatism. The manifesto covered a good deal of ground, but with each new proposal, it became clearer that its organising principle lay less in the kind of evidenced analysis reflected in the *Modern Crime Prevention Strategy* of 2016, and more in the deployment of a kind of Conservative populism that might play well to both a Conservative electorate and disillusioned Labour voters, the 'left behind' in the collapsing 'red wall' of former Labour strongholds (Cutts et al, 2020).

In this sense, the manifesto's organising theme was primarily ideological. It entailed an attempt to reset Conservative politics and resolve problems that the austerity measures of the preceding administration had often exacerbated. In terms of Andrew Gamble's (1988) original formulation, the manifesto marked something of a shift back to 'strong state conservatism' and its grasp of law and order and away from both the low-tax neoliberalism of the Coalition as well as the more recent 'more for less' austerity modernism, or 'smarter' justice (Morgan and Smith, 2017).

Strong on rhetorical principle, in true Johnsonian style the 2019 manifesto returned to the core themes of Conservative law and order: backing the police and strengthening their powers, standing up for the 'law-abiding majority', tougher sentencing and safeguarding the boundaries of nationhood via, for example, the deportation of foreign nationals guilty of crimes (Conservative Party, 2019, p 17). Although the entire document was prefaced by a section titled 'Get Brexit done', making the country safer and cutting crime were given early prominence in a section titled 'We will focus on your priorities' (see Conservative Party, 2019, pp 17–22). Law and order had regained its place in the Conservative worldview, albeit subsumed within the Brexit-inflected notion of 'taking back control' by tackling crime and taking control of our own laws. The central commitment in this package, involved 'backing our police' by 'putting 20,000 more officers on the streets, and giving them the powers to tackle crime' (Conservative Party, 2019, p 17). Yet, like many of the commitments in the document, the proposals on police numbers went little further than aiming to restore police strength to what it had been prior to the cuts and austerity measures of five years earlier. Conservative support for the police also extended to restoring police powers of stop and search and further rolling out the deployment of tasers. Both proposals, later becoming central features of Johnson's *Beating Crime Plan*, entailed considerable controversy.

The same might be said for a raft of further, more specific, proposals which followed; these included a commitment towards a reinvestment in national youth services, heavily hit by cuts, to the tune of £500 million. Many doubted that the new initiatives would make up for the accumulated loss of youth service provision over the preceding decade (Thapar, 2021, p 257). Eighteen new Violence Reduction Units were planned for 18 cities across the country. They were the 'flagship' elements of a new *Serious Violence Strategy*, launched in 2018 (Home Office, 2018) and tasked with delivering sustainable solutions to weapon-involved gang and youth violence. The *Serious Violence Strategy* was almost entirely focused around youth and gang violence. Tackling VAWG only slipped into the manifesto at the end of a long list of catch-all commitments on page 19 (referred to later). This marks a surprising oversight given that VAWG had been a rising national and international priority (Home Office, 2012, 2016a; World Health Organisation, 2012, 2021), a central feature of police thematic inspections (HM Inspectorate of Constabulary – HMIC, 2015) and an increasing priority for police and criminal justice agencies' operational management (HMICFRS, 2021), about which evidence had been accumulating for some time (Fulu et al, 2014). The number of sexual offences recorded had been rising fast, although only 1.4 per cent of rape cases reported to the police in 2019–20 resulted in a suspect being charged (HMICFRS, 2021). Furthermore, rates of case attrition were continuing to rise while the proportion of reported rapes resulting in conviction had fallen dramatically after 2016. Finally, new offences relating to aspects of predatory male behaviour – stalking, harassment, drink spiking, upskirting (voyeurism), 'revenge porn' and unwanted touching – were raising new concerns, culminating in the night-time economy being described as a hostile environment for many women (HMICFRS, 2021; Office for National Statistics, 2021).

While many of the policy proposals were rooted in the underlying populist Conservative philosophy reflected in the manifesto, the developing VAWG strategy was rather different, although featuring only fleetingly in the manifesto. Instead, the strategy emerged 'institutionally' as part of the regular review process of criminal justice agencies and inspectorates. Here, Kingdon's (2002) 'multiple streams' model of policy development provides a framework for understanding the prioritisation of VAWG, reflecting the conjunction of separate policy flows across a series of governments. So, for example, the growing priority given to addressing domestic and intimate violence in respect of a core Conservative value, the family (HMIC, 2015), combined with major policy initiatives on 'serious violence' and 'victims and vulnerability', prompting a major new emphasis on violence against women. Almost two years after the 2019 election, the kidnap, rape and murder of Sarah Everard by a serving police officer reinforced concerns about women's safety at night (Home Office, 2021c) and raised serious questions about police performance (End Violence against Women Coalition, 2021; Davis, 2022).

Further initiatives followed, a successful pilot project – Operation Vigilant was developed in 2021 by Thames Valley Police, involving teams of covert and uniformed police officers observing and, when they encountered incidents of predatory male behaviour, intervening (Magill and Squires, 2022). The deployed officers were trained in specialist behaviour awareness techniques and tasked with identifying potential sexual predators. By mid-2022, 15 other police forces had plans for rolling out the operation. Reviewing the achievements in this area by mid-2021, the Home Office claimed that 'huge strides' had been made in tackling VAWG (2021c, p 9). Increased penalties had been introduced for stalking and harassment, and automatic early release from prison for violent and sexual offenders had been abolished. Taken as a whole, there is a strong case for arguing that in the field of VAWG, the policies and strategies of the government elected in 2019 were in many respects especially consistent, positive and successful. Given that, it might appear all the more ironic that VAWG featured so peripherally in the 2019 manifesto. On the other hand, as we have suggested, the manifesto was primarily a potent ideological 'call to arms', and 'success' lay in energising the electoral base around conventional values and populist ideological principles rather than championing an end to gender inequalities in criminal victimisation.

Yet aside from an ideological commitment to diverse ways of 'taking back control', the one area of seeming policy coherence in the manifesto involved measures to revive both confidence and community cohesion in towns and cities – eventually feeding into the 'levelling up' agenda. However, the causes of the decline of towns and cities were adjudged to be primarily moral and behavioural rather than economic. Something was 'holding back' and 'letting down' our great towns and cities. The problem, above all, was perceived to be crime, disorder and antisocial behaviour: 'Too many communities feel let down. Violent crime and antisocial behaviour are ignored amid a backdrop of boarded-up department stores, shops and pubs' (Conservative Party, 2019, p 26). Rather than economic regeneration, the manifesto proposed a cultural makeover, safer shopping streets, the revival of youth clubs and renewed civic infrastructure, such as libraries and social clubs. First, however, came more police and police community support officers, investment in CCTV (closed-circuit television) systems and community wardens, retaking control. Control remained uppermost in a catalogue of disparate commitments towards the end of the 'law and order' section of the manifesto, intended to placate middle England: tackling unauthorised traveller camps and seizing vehicles, countering serious and organised crime, combating terrorism and extremism, toughening community sentences and expanding electronic tagging while cracking down on cybercrime. Many such proposals later found their way into the *Beating Crime Plan* (Home Office, 2021a). Addressing such 'localist' crime and disorder agendas was to be facilitated by strengthening the accountability of Police and Crime Commissioners, in a very practical way playing to the Conservative law and order agenda by upgrading the salience of 'governing through crime' at the local level.

Given the preponderance of law and order solutions proposed for the UK's array of social and economic problems, there was little surprise in the manifesto's promise of 10,000 additional prison places. Conservative rhetoric on law and order has generally prioritised locking people up. Reviewing evidence that prison sentences are now much longer than in the recent past, the Prison Reform Trust (2022b) notes that public support for longer sentences appears to be a virtually bottomless pit (Roberts et al, 2022). The 2019 manifesto clearly reflected this sentiment, treating locking people up as an end in itself, but paying little attention to the experience of imprisonment or its effectiveness in cutting crime. Indeed, the only reference to the experience of imprisonment by inmates was an isolated promise to maintain the UK ban on prisoners voting while incarcerated, an ideological gesture to the Tory gallery and a calculated snub to Europe and the European Court of Human Rights (Johnston, 2020). Following the election, the then Justice Secretary, Dominic Raab, clashed repeatedly with the Parole Board over suggested changes to the parole system (Prison Reform Trust, 2022a).

The prison population of England and Wales hovered just above the 82,000 mark in 2015, falling slightly by 2020. In Scotland, the average daily population remains around 8,000 and in Northern Ireland, around 1,500. Projections in each of the three jurisdictions suggest these totals will increase, and on present trends the numbers of older prisoners will continue to increase. The proportion serving 'life' sentences, currently around 12 per cent of the total, is predicted to grow, as will the racial disproportion of the prison population, in part a consequence of the increasing number of life sentences (including joint enterprise life sentences) imposed on allegedly gang-involved young people (Hulley et al, 2019). As Wright et al (2017) argue, the acute psychological challenges arising from these conditions of incarceration, overcrowding compounded by prison staffing reductions of around a third (another consequence of government austerity measures; Vize, 2020), have had a dramatic impact on prison conditions and the ability to run rehabilitative and educational programmes. As a consequence, assaults on prison staff grew by 42 per cent in 2016 (Munzinger, 2016), prison staff deployed violence against prisoners more frequently (Savage, 2021) and more prisoners were engaging in self-harming activities (Portal, 2019). A series of Prison Inspectorate reports had begun to describe prison conditions as 'the most disturbing ever seen' (Bulman, 2018).

Two years after the election, the government began to fill some of the gaps regarding its prisons policy by releasing a *Prisons Strategy* White Paper (Ministry of Justice, 2021b), belatedly addressing some of the troubling issues its more public-facing manifesto appeal had overlooked. The promised 10,000 additional prison places had now increased to 20,000, supplemented by 5,000 additional staff in a ten-year vision committing an additional £200 million new investment per year by 2024–25, towards improving the prison system which the Ministry of Justice described as the 'biggest prison-building programme in more than 100 years' (2021a, p 3). Despite these commitments, the Howard League for Penal Reform described the strategy as both confused and contradictory, failing to reconcile the differences between its declared political aspirations, increasing the prison population to 100,000 and the practical and logistical consequences of this growth:

> the new strategy comes across as counterproductive and counterintuitive. It fails to recognise the real source of problems in the prison estate: an ever-growing prison population. ... The White Paper represents a doubling down on the commitment to lock up more people for longer, while aspiring to improve the system. Fundamentally, it can't do both. (Coomber, 2021)

A related area of the 'taking back control' agenda concerned foreign criminals, sometimes pejoratively associated with concerns relating to terrorism (Zedner, 2019). The half dozen years after 2015 saw a significant escalation of domestic terror incidents, events bracketed by the murder of two MPs, Jo Cox in 2016 and David Amess in 2021, although involving strikingly different circumstances and perpetrators. In between were a number of vehicle attacks, bombings (including the Manchester Arena bombing, which killed 22 people), attempted bombings and rampage knife attacks.

The Conservative solution to foreign criminal risks has essentially been very simple: ban them or deport them once they have served their sentences. Nevertheless, even discussing deportation of foreign offenders, rather fundamental contradictions quickly become apparent. For example, despite the huge political significance vested in the 'removal of foreign criminals' (Conservative Party, 2019, p 18), relatively little progress has been made in actually reducing the numbers of foreign nationals in British prisons. Similarly, the number of foreign offenders (both European Union and non-European Union) deported on completion of a prison sentence has been falling, arising from a combination of cuts and delays impacting the adjudication processes as well as the courts' reluctance to further erode the rights of refugees and ex-offenders. Critics have tended to regard these measures in the broader light of the government's xenophobic 'hostile environment' policies, pursued during Theresa May's premiership (Griffiths and Yeo, 2021; see also Fekete, 2020). They provide an illustration of the 'enemy penology' idea (Fekete and Webber, 2010), or what has come to be called 'crimmigration control' – the criminalisation of immigration control, reinforcing a populist misconception that immigration and crime are largely the same thing (Aliverti, 2013; Griffiths, 2017; Bowling and

Westenra, 2020). Such points are clearly related to the doubling of reports of racially motivated hate crime during 2015 to 2019, although some of this increase is attributed to improvements in crime recording by the police (Booth, 2019). The 'Windrush scandal' (O'Nions, 2020a, 2020b; Williams, 2020), during which Black British citizens were unlawfully deported to the Caribbean,[1] closely paralleled the 'hostile environment' claims made during the Brexit referendum and were later echoed, as we have seen, once again in the Conservative manifesto.[2] Persisting with the toxic deportation narrative, Boris Johnson argued in the House of Commons in 2020 that a flight returning alleged former offenders to Jamaica should go ahead even though there seemed genuine doubts about the supposed criminal records of some of the men scheduled for deportation (Merrick, 2020).

In light of these developments, the manifesto's wider prescription for reform of the immigration system falls into place. After all, 'the vote to leave the EU was, among other things, a vote to take back control of our borders' (Conservative Party, 2019, p 20). The solution, spelled out in the manifesto was, yet again, to 'get Brexit done' while adopting an 'Australian-style points-based immigration system', which could reduce overall immigration numbers, especially low-skilled immigrants, while still attracting the *right kind* of immigrant and with the signal virtue of ensuring that 'the British people are always in control' (Conservative Party, 2019, p 20). As many commentators have noted, language and narratives such as this, in the wake of Brexit, directly conjured up the illusory racist anachronism of 'Empire 2.0' (Olusoga, 2017; Sanghera, 2021), creating further tension around issues of race, empire and 'wokeness'.

Yet, as the fragile inflatable boats overfilled with refugees and migrants crossed the English Channel in ever-increasing numbers between 2021 and 2022, the then Home Secretary, Priti Patel, unveiled a scheme, part of the *New Plan for Immigration* (Home Office, 2021b), to relocate migrants to Rwanda as a 'deterrent' (Dathan, 2022). The plan, premised on the notion that it would help undermine the power of criminal gangs and people traffickers, was condemned by the Refugee Council (2022) as inhumane, costly, counterproductive and, above all, likely to expose migrants and refugees to even greater risks. A related proposal involved the transfer of UK Border Control responsibilities to detachments of the Albanian police, intended to fast-track removals. The strategy reflected rising European concerns about the scale of Albanian 'economic' migration and the activities of Albanian crime gangs and criminal traffickers (of people, drugs and firearms) across Western Europe and into the UK (United Nations Office of Drugs and Crime, 2019; Syal, 2022). The UK border proposals, however, were criticised as contrary to international law (Dathan, 2022). With the number of migrant crossings passing the 40,000 mark (with only the November weather suppressing the numbers), many aspects of the new border control policies were facing serious legal challenges and concerted criticism (Taylor, 2022). As a migrant reception centre in Dover was firebombed, local councils voiced increasing reluctance to accept more refugees, even as charities and nongovernmental organisations criticised the poor standards and overcrowding in the available accommodation. The new Home Secretary, Suella Braverman, announced a fresh 'deal' with the French, costing £63 million per year, involving new surveillance technologies, British police 'embedded' with their French counterparts for the first time, and joint funding arrangements for a French immigration detention centre (Seddon and Casciani, 2022). Policing and deterrence, as the subsequent Illegal Migration Bill rather confirmed, were to remain the core UK responses to the refugee and migration crisis, prompting enormous criticism that irregular migration would become thoroughly criminalised and 'warnings that the proposed legislation would break the UN [United Nations] Charter and the European convention on human rights' (Sherwood and Savage, 2023).

Conclusion

So far, this tale of two manifestos has described a transition from an election in 2015 which downplayed both law and order and political ideology to another in 2019 in which a ramped-up commitment to law, order and 'taking control' sat at the centre of an ideologically revitalised post-Brexit conservatism fronted by Boris Johnson. In many respects, however, the 'control' aspired to in 2019 had, in many cases, largely been lost as a direct consequence of the austerity measures pursued by the Conservative-led Coalition government elected in 2010 and the Cameron/May/Johnson governments which followed. Whether the issue was crime, violence or police effectiveness, the operation of the prison system and offender rehabilitation, the smooth operation of the criminal justice system and the courts, an effective and fair immigration system or urban regeneration and community safety, governing through law and order, or tough conservativism, was now projected as a solution.

We have certainly been here before for, as has been said of an earlier Conservative government, there are two ways that governments put crime on the agenda: 'first, by articulating concerns about crime in a way that resonates with the electorate; and, second, by inadvertently producing the circumstances in which crime flourished', while previous Conservative policies have 'had a certain self-fulfilling aspect to them: the social and economic changes they unleashed ... had the net result of demanding a more punitive response to crime' (Farrall and Hay, 2010, p 566). As Loader (2020) might argue, if inequality is a profoundly destabilising influence, it may be debateable just how 'inadvertent' Conservative policies have been in their unleashing of crime and disorder.

Elected in December 2019 but still grappling with the supposedly 'oven-ready' Brexit deal, the Johnson government finally awoke to the COVID-19 pandemic in early 2020 (Calvert and Arbuthnot, 2021; see also Chapter 5). Already ideologically attuned to seeing social problems from a law and order perspective, the resource-strapped National Health Service and a poorly coordinated public health strategy quickly determined the government's adoption of a lockdown/containment strategy prioritising law enforcement, which treated the public as the virus (Fatsis and Lamb, 2022). A fear of infection rates outrunning health and hospital resources led to lockdown and social distancing restrictions intended to protect the state from the people, policing the public rather than protecting them, treating the pandemic as a public order crisis, replete with an array of enforcement powers, rather than a health emergency. In the first two months of the pandemic restrictions, over 14,000 fines and penalty notices were issued (Dearden, 2020). Although many of the 'lockdown' powers lapsed after two years, in March 2022, the resort to 'exceptional powers' in crisis circumstances prioritised law and order over health in a way that was not unfamiliar. The particular irony of the lockdown restrictions lay in the contribution they made to Johnson's own downfall as Prime Minister. Having introduced the social distancing regulations, he and a number of his senior colleagues and advisors then went on to contravene them in dramatic fashion ('Partygate'), and Johnson became the first prime minister to incur criminal penalties while in office. The BBC reported that a total of 126 fixed penalty notices had been issued in respect of breaches of social distancing rules in Downing Street (BBC News, 2022; Gray Report, 2022, p 2).

In other respects, the periods of lockdown during 2020–21 contributed to an 8 per cent reduction in recorded crime, although lockdown periods coincided with a 10 per cent increase in recorded domestic violence and, as noted earlier, a 35 per cent increase in reports of online crime, or cybercrime (Office for National Statistics, 2021). The augmentation of police powers to enforce lockdown conditions during the pandemic raised many issues regarding sweeping powers and police discretion which have hardly yet been resolved. Lockdown restrictions intersected with two further 'exceptional' series of events in the UK. The Black Lives Matter protests originating in the US, following the unlawful police killings of African American men, became an international phenomenon during 2020. Although it was recognised that Black and minority ethnic individuals were disproportionately susceptible to COVID-19 infections and complications – that COVID-19 was itself a Black Lives Matter issue – Tier 4 lockdown restrictions became part of the very mechanisms by which protests were discouraged, discredited and policed (Mason, 2020).[3] In very similar fashion, the silent vigil held following the rape and murder of Sarah Everard in March 2020 was also impacted by restrictions. The police sought to prohibit the original planned vigil, threatening arrests and fines. A more spontaneous vigil then followed at Clapham Common, which the police, prompting considerable outrage, chose to forcefully disrupt, manhandling and arresting women for breaking lockdown rules and trampling the floral tributes displayed. Fully two years after the original arrests, Crown Prosecution Service lawyers confirmed they were 'discontinuing' police efforts to criminally convict the arrested women as this was 'not in the public interest' (Townsend, 2022).

As has been argued before (Hall et al, 1978), 'exceptional police powers' drafted in crisis situations, have a habit of becoming 'normalised' responses to more routine problems, protests and disorders. A government addicted to law and order solutions and frustrated by protests (Black Lives Matter, Extinction Rebellion, Stop Oil and Insulate Britain, among others) drew on the sheer utility of recent restrictions, incorporating extensive new powers to curtail political protests into the Police, Crime, Sentencing and Courts Act 2022. A wide range of organisations, prominent among them Liberty, condemned the new legislation as a threat to democracy, dissent and civil rights: 'the new criminal justice legislation risks stifling dissent, criminalising ... marginalised communities ... [through] even more disproportionate policing [...] and the expansion of stop and search ... [I]t is shocking that this executive has chosen now to launch such a broad assault on our rights under the guise of safer communities' (Liberty, 2021). The Association of Police and Crime Commissioners and several former police chiefs voiced their agreement (Dearden, 2021; Dodd and Grierson, 2021). The new measures marked a dramatic about turn from the HMICs embrace of nurturing democracy by facilitating peaceful protest through policing by 'consent' of just over a decade earlier (HMIC, 2009).

Johnson was eventually forced to resign in 2022 and, following a protracted leadership election in which Conservative Party members rejected the leadership preferences of Conservative MPs, Liz Truss moved into 10 Downing Street – although not for long. During her leadership campaign, *The Sun* newspaper had been moved to complain that with the primary focus being on the imminent cost of living crisis, there had been relatively little on law and order in the leadership debate. Taking up this challenge, Truss had hastily recycled a few populist elements from the earlier *Beating Crime Plan* of 2021. In what was described as a 'back to basics' agenda, police were to be given new (20 per cent) crime reduction targets and chief officers of 'failing' forces were to be closely scrutinised. The 20,000 'uplift' officers, a cheque cashed twice already in the 2019 manifesto and the 2021 plan, was once more recycled, and police leaderships were encouraged to get back to 'real policing'. For their part, police leaders seemed unconvinced: 'soundbite-friendly' crime targets could do more harm than good, 'back to basics' often meant doing more that was popular but ineffective (Lewis, 2022), while the 'extra officers' would only take police overall numbers back to those of

2010. Rather like her predecessor, Truss, the 'continuity candidate', had pitched her meaningless overpromise on crime control to middle England (Dodd, 2022).

However, as former Chancellor Rishi Sunak, Truss' rival for Downing Street, had predicted, Truss' economic and fiscal strategy failed. Within days of her 'mini-budget', amidst rising interest rates, economic turmoil and collapsing confidence in sterling, the Bank of England was forced to intervene and Truss began to roll back elements of her economic and fiscal policy. In the meantime, the Party gathered in Birmingham for its annual conference, where, understandably, economic and fiscal policy took centre stage and law and order questions barely surfaced. Within 15 days of her first Leader's speech to conference, her entire strategy in tatters, Truss had resigned. Replacing her, Sunak garnered criticism for reinstating the recently resigned Suella Braverman as Home Secretary as the migrant crisis deepened. The flaw Loader (2020) had identified in Conservative crime control strategy had become even clearer: inequality and disorder provide a poor foundation for criminal justice.

As 2022 drew towards its end, law and order underwent a slight return to the headlines when the Home Secretary refloated the 'back to basics' script, which itself drew upon the *Beating Crime Plan* of 2021. Facing criticism from Conservative MPs in recently won former red wall constituencies that the ambitious levelling up agenda appeared to have been forgotten, the government sought to offer reassurances on police performance and community safety. Braverman repeated that she expected police forces to cut crime by 20 per cent. The timing was unfortunate as *The Observer* published the results of police force inspections revealing that half of 29 English police forces inspected during 2022 were already failing to meet Home Office standards for investigating crime and responding to the public (Jayanetti and Townsend, 2022). It was a deeply inauspicious outcome for a 'party of law and order'.

Notes

[1] A sequence of events which directly implicated then Prime Minister Theresa May and led to the resignation of Home Secretary Amber Rudd.

[2] On page 19, the manifesto asserted that 'a vote to leave the EU was a vote to take control of our borders' and yet, seemingly without irony, a mere three pages later it noted 'we will tackle prejudice, racism and discrimination' (Conservative Party, 2019, p 22).

[3] The Tier 4 COVID-19 restrictions stated that a person could only leave home if they had a 'reasonable excuse' to do so, and that a person may not participate in a 'gathering' that takes place outdoors and consists of more than two people, and to which no exception applies.

References

Aliverti, A. (2013) *Crimes of mobility: criminal law and the regulation of immigration*, London: Routledge.

Allen, G. and Burton, M. (2022) *Firearms crime statistics: England and Wales*, London: House of Commons Library.

Annison, H. (2019) 'Transforming rehabilitation as a policy disaster: unbalanced policy making and probation reform', *Probation Journal*, 66(1): 43–59.

Barr, C. and Topping, A. (2021) 'Rape: why have prosecutions fallen so dramatically in a decade?', *The Guardian*, 17 June. Available at: www.theg uardian.com/society/2021/jun/17/why-have-prosecutions-fallen-so-dramatically-in-a-decade (accessed 19 July 2023).

BBC News (2022) 'Downing Street parties: what Covid rules were broken?', 25 May. Available at: www.bbc.co.uk/news/uk-politics-59577129 (accessed 27 April 2023).

Booth, R. (2019) 'Racism rising since Brexit vote, nationwide study reveals', *The Guardian*, 20 May. Available at: www.theguardian.com/world/2019/may/20/racism-on-the-rise-since-brexit-vote-nationwide-study-reveals (accessed 19 July 2023).

Bowling, B. and Westenra, S. (2020) '"A really hostile environment": adiaphorization, global policing and the crimmigration control system', *Theoretical Criminology*, 24(2): 163–83.

Bulman, M. (2018) 'Prison conditions "most disturbing ever seen" with staff now accustomed to jails not fit for 21st century, says watchdog', *The Independent*, 20 September.

Calvert, J. and Arbuthnot, G. (2021) *Failures of state: the inside story of Britain's battle with coronavirus*, London: HarperCollins.

Casciani, D. (2021) 'Criminal prosecution delays hit record 708 days', *BBC News*, 20 January. Available at: www.bbc.co.uk/news/uk-60071691 (accessed 25 April 2023).

Clark, D. (2022) 'Number of days between offence and court conclusion in England and Wales 2010–2021', *Statista*, 6 April. Available at: www.stati sta.com/statistics/1102428/court-waiting-times-in-england-and-wales/ (accessed 25 April 2023).

Conservative Party (2015) *Strong leadership, a clear economic plan, a brighter, more secure future. The Conservative Party manifesto 2015*, London: Conservative Party.

Conservative Party (2019) *Get Brexit done, unleash Britain's potential. The Conservative and Unionist Party manifesto 2019*, London: Conservative Party.

Coomber, A. (2021) 'The Prisons Strategy White Paper', *Howard League for Penal Reform*, 10 December. Available at: https://howardleague.org/blog/the-prisons-strategy-white-paper/ (accessed 23 April 2023).

Crown Prosecution Service (2018) *Violence against women and girls report 2018–2019*, London: Crown Prosecution Service.

Cutts, D., Goodwin, M., Heath, O. and Surridge, P. (2020) 'Brexit, the 2019 general election and the realignment of British politics', *Political Quarterly*, 91(1): 7–23.

Dathan, M. (2022) 'Priti Patel pushed on with Rwanda scheme despite slavery warning', *The Times*, 31 August.

Davis, M. (2022) 'Sarah Everard's murder was a "watershed moment for women's safety which has been wasted"', *The Independent*, 27 February.

Dearden, L. (2020) 'All prosecutions under new Coronavirus Act unlawful, review finds', *The Independent*, 15 May.

Dearden, L. (2021) 'New protest powers go too far and are not needed, police commissioners say', *The Independent*, 16 March.

Dodd, V. (2022) 'Police Chief: Truss's crime proposal are meaningless', *The Guardian*, 3 September. Available at: www.theguardian.com/uk-news/2022/sep/02/liz-truss-law-and-order-policies-meaningless-says-police-chief (accessed 19 July 2023).

Dodd, V. and Grierson, J. (2021) 'Protest laws move UK towards paramilitary policing, says former chief', *The Guardian*, 28 March. Available at: www.theguardian.com/uk-news/2021/mar/28/protest-laws-move-uk-towards-paramilitary-policing-says-former-chief (accessed 19 July 2023).

End Violence Against Women Coalition (2021) 'Almost half of women have less trust in police following Sarah Everard murder', 18 November. Available at www.endviolenceagainstwomen.org.uk/almost-half-of-women-have-less-trust-in-police-following-sarah-everard-murder/ (accessed 26 April 2023).

Farrall, S. and Hay, C. (2010) 'Not so tough on crime? Why weren't the Thatcher governments more radical in transforming the criminal justice system?', *British Journal of Criminology*, 50(3): 550–69.

Fatsis, L. and Lamb, M. (2022) *Policing the pandemic: how public health becomes public order*, Bristol, Policy Press.

Fekete, L. (2020) 'Reclaiming the fight against racism in the UK', *Race and Class*, 61(4): 87–95.

Fekete, L. and Webber, F. (2010) 'Foreign nationals, enemy penology and the criminal justice system', *Race and Class*, 51(4): 1–25.

Fulu, E., Kerr-Wilson, A. and Lang J. (2014) *What works to prevent violence against women and girls? Evidence review of interventions to prevent violence against women and girls*, London: Department for International Development. Available at: https://assets.publishing.service.gov.uk/media/57a089a8ed915d3cfd00037c/What_Works_Inception_Report_June_2014_AnnexF_WG23_paper_prevention_interventions.pdf (accessed 24 April 2023).

Gamble, A. (1988) *The free economy and the strong state: the politics of Thatcherism*, Basingstoke: Palgrave Macmillan.

Gray, S. (2022) *Findings of Second Permanent Secretary's investigation into alleged gatherings on government premises during Covid restrictions*, London: Cabinet Office.

Griffiths, M. (2017) 'Foreign, criminal: doubly damned modern British folk-devil', *Citizenship Studies*, 21(5): 527–46.

Griffiths, M. and Yeo, C. (2021) 'The UK's hostile environment: deputising immigration control', *Critical Social Policy*, 41(4): 521–44.

Guiney, T. (2022) 'Ideologies, power and the politics of punishment: the case of the British Conservative Party', *British Journal of Criminology*, 62(5): 1158–74.

Hall, S. (1980) *Drifting into a 'law and order' society*, Cobden Trust Human Rights Day Lecture, London: Cobden Trust.

Hall, S., Roberts, B., Jefferson, T. and Critcher, C. (1978) *Policing the crisis: mugging the state and law and order*, London: Hutchinson.

HMIC (HM Inspectorate of Constabulary) (2009) *Adapting to protest – nurturing the British model of policing*, London: HMIC.

HMIC (HM Inspectorate of Constabulary) (2015) *Increasingly everyone's business: a progress report on the police response to domestic abuse*, London: HMIC.

HMICFRS (HM Inspectorate of Constabulary and Fire Rescue Services) (2021) *Police response to violence against women and girls: final inspection report*, London: HMICFRS, Justice Inspectorates.

Home Office (2012) *Call to end violence against women and girls: taking action – the next chapter*, London: Home Office.

Home Office (2016a) *Ending violence against women and girls: strategy 2016–2020*, London: Home Office.

Home Office (2016b) *Modern crime prevention strategy*, London: Home Office.

Home Office (2018) *Serious violence strategy*, London: Home Office.

Home Office (2021a) *Beating crime plan*, London: Home Office.

Home Office (2021b) *New plan for immigration. Consultation on the new plan for immigration: government response*, London: Home Office.

Home Office (2021c) *Tackling violence against women and girls*, London: Home Office.

Hulley, S., Crewe, B. and Wright, S. (2019) 'Making sense of "joint enterprise" for murder: legal legitimacy or instrumental acquiescence?', *British Journal of Criminology*, 59(6): 1328–46.

Jayanetti, C. and Townsend, M. (2022) 'Revealed: half of police forces fail to meet standards in crime investigations', *The Observer*, 27 November. Available at: www.theguardian.com/uk-news/2022/nov/26/revealed-half-of-english-police-forces-fail-to-meet-standards-in-investigations (accessed 19 July 2023).

Johnston, N. (2020) *Prisoners' voting rights: developments since May 2015*, London: House of Commons Library.

Kingdon, J. (2002) *Agendas, alternatives, and public policies*, New York: Longman.

Lewis, R. (2022) 'Truss's arbitrary crime targets could do more harm than good', *The Guardian*, 3 September.

Liberty (2021) 'Policing Bill threatens protest rights', 9 March. Available at: www.libertyhumanrights.org.uk/issue/policing-bill-threatens-protest-rights/ (accessed 27 April 2023).

Loader, I. (2020) 'Crime, order and the two faces of Conservatism: an encounter with criminology's other', *British Journal of Criminology*, 60(5): 1181–200.

Magill, C. and Squires, P. (2022) *Independent evaluation of Thames Valley Police: Project Vigilant*: Brighton: Thames Valley Police and the University of Brighton.

Mason, R. (2020) 'Black Lives Matter protests risk spreading Covid-19, says Hancock', *The Guardian*, 7 June. Available at: www.theguardian.com/world/2020/jun/07/black-lives-matter-protests-risk-spreading-covid19-says-matt-hancock (accessed 19 July 2023).

McCandless, R., Feist, A., Allan, J. and Morgan, N. (2016) *Do initiatives involving substantial increases in stop and search reduce crime? Assessing the impact of Operation Blunt 2*, London: Home Office. Available at: www.gov.uk/government/publications/do-initiatives-involving-substantial-increases-in-stop-and-search-reduce-crime-assessing-the-impact-of-operation-blunt-2 (accessed 15 May 2022).

Merrick, R. (2020) 'Boris Johnson insists first deportation of Caribbean nationals since Windrush scandal must go ahead', *The Independent*, 5 February. Available at: www.independent.co.uk/news/uk/politics/boris-johnson-deport-caribbean-flight-windrush-scandal-immigration-a9319336.html (accessed 19 July 2023).

Ministry of Justice (2021a) 'New prison strategy to rehabilitate offenders and cut crime', press release, 7 December, London: Ministry of Justice.

Ministry of Justice (2021b) *Prisons strategy White Paper*, London: Ministry of Justice.

Morgan, R. and Smith, D.J. (2017) 'Delivering more with less: austerity and the politics of law and order', in A. Liebling, S. Maruna and L. McAra (eds) *The Oxford handbook of criminology*, Oxford: Oxford University Press, pp 138–62.

Munzinger, H. (2016) 'Fewer prison officers and more assaults: How prison staffing has changed', *The Guardian*, 18 November 18. Available at: www.theguardian.com/society/datablog/2016/nov/18/fewer-prison-officers-and-more-assaults-how-uk-prison-staffing-has-changed (accessed 19 July 2023).

Murray, J. (2022) '1,000 days between rape offence and case completion, data shows', *The Guardian*, 31 January. Available at: www.theguardian.com/society/2022/jan/31/1000-days-between-offence-and-case-completion-in-uk-data-shows (accessed 19 July 2023).

National Audit Office (2019) *Transforming rehabilitation: progress review*, London: National Audit Office.

Office for National Statistics (2021) 'Sexual offences in England and Wales overview: year ending March 2020'. Available at: www.ons.gov.uk/peoplepopulationandcommunity/crimeandjustice/bulletins/sexualoffencesinenglandandwalesoverview/march2020 (accessed 25 April 2023).

Olusoga, D. (2017) 'Empire 2.0 is dangerous nostalgia for something that never existed', *The Guardian*, 19 March. Available at: www.theguardian. com/commentisfree/2017/mar/19/empire-20-is-dangerous-nostalgia-for-something-that-never-existed (accessed 19 July 2023).

O'Nions, H. (2020a) '"Fat cat" lawyers and "illegal" migrants: the impact of intersecting hostilities and toxic narratives on access to justice', *Journal of Social Welfare and Family Law*, 42(3): 319–40.

O'Nions, H. (2020b) 'No place called home. The banishment of "foreign criminals" in the public interest: a wrong without redress', *Laws*, 9(4): 26. doi: https://doi.org/10.3390/laws9040026

Plummer, J. (2018) 'Transforming rehabilitation has failed, says report', *Third Sector*, 5 May. Available at: www.thirdsector.co.uk/transforming-reh abilitation-failed-says-report/management/article/1463968 (accessed 26 April 2023).

Portal, G. (2019) 'How dangerous are prisons in England and Wales', *BBC News*, 13 August. Available at: www.bbc.co.uk/news/uk-49324718 (accessed 27 April 2023).

Prison Reform Trust (2022a) 'Parole Board: Dominic Raab making an "already difficult job close to impossible"', 26 August. Available at: https:// prisonreformtrust.org.uk/parole-board-dominic-raab-making-an-already-difficult-job-close-to-impossible/ (accessed 24 April 2023).

Prison Reform Trust (2022b) *Prison: the facts – summer 2022*, London: Prison Reform Trust.

Refugee Council (2022) 'Sending asylum seekers to Rwanda: Refugee Council response', press release, 14 April. Available at: www.refugeecoun cil.org.uk/latest/news/sending-asylum-seekers-to-rwanda-refugee-coun cil-repsonse/ (accessed 27 April 2022).

Roberts, J.V., Bild, J., Pina-Sánchez, J. and Hough, M. (2022) *Public knowledge of sentencing practice and trends*, London: Sentencing Academy.

Sanghera, S. (2021) *Empireland: how imperialism has shaped modern Britain*, London: Penguin Books.

Savage, M. (2021) 'Deep crisis in British prisons as use of force against inmates doubles', *The Observer*, 3 January.

Schofield, K. and Johnstone, R. (2019) 'Ministry of Justice to scrap probation reforms that failed after "breakneck speed" implementation', *Civil Service World*, 16 May. Available at: www.civilserviceworld.com/professions/ article/ministry-of-justice-to-scrap-probation-reforms-that-failed-after-breakneck-speed-implementation (accessed 19 July 2023).

Seddon, P. and Casciani, D. (2022) 'UK strikes revised deal with France on Channel migrants', *BBC News*, 14 November. Available at: www.bbc. co.uk/news/uk-politics-63615653 (accessed 24 April 2023).

Sherwood, H. and Savage, M. (2023) 'Illegal Migration Bill is "Cruelty without purpose" says Archbishop of York', *The Observer*, 12 March.

Skinns, D. (2016) *Coalition government penal policy 2010–2015: austerity, outsourcing and punishment*, Basingstoke: Palgrave Macmillan.

Squires, P. (2016) 'The Coalition and criminal justice', in H. Bochel and M. Powell (eds) *The Coalition government and social policy*, Bristol: Policy Press, pp 285–308.

Syal, R. (2022) 'Rise in Albanian asylum seekers may be down to criminal gangs', *The Guardian*, 25 August. Available at: www.theguardian.com/uk-news/2022/aug/25/rise-in-albanian-asylum-seekers-may-be-down-to-criminal-gangs (accessed 19 July 2023).

Syal, R. and Dodd, V. (2022) 'Police chiefs blame Tory cuts for a fall in detection and charge rates', *The Guardian*, 31 August. Available at: www.theguardian.com/uk-news/2022/aug/31/police-chiefs-blame-tory-cuts-for-fall-in-detection-and-charge-rates (accessed 19 July 2023).

Taylor, D. (2022) 'Home Office planning new deportation flight to Rwanda', *The Guardian*, 25 August. Available at: www.theguardian.com/uk-news/2022/aug/25/home-office-planning-new-deportation-flight-rwanda (accessed 19 July 2023).

Thapar, C. (2021) *Cut short: youth violence, loss and hope in the city*, London: Penguin.

Townsend, M. (2022) 'Sarah Everard: MET forced to halt "absurd" convictions over vigil', *The Guardian*, 13 August. Available at: www.theguardian.com/uk-news/2022/aug/13/sarah-everard-met-forced-to-halt-absurd-convictions-over-vigil#:~:text=Prosecutors%20have%20dramatically%20halted%20attempts,blow%20for%20Britain%27s%20biggest%20force (accessed 19 July 2023).

United Nations Office of Drugs and Crime (2019) *UNODC Regional Programme for South Eastern Europe: 2020–2023*, United Nations Office of Drugs and Crime.

Vize, R. (2020) 'England and Wales' disgraceful prisons expose ministers' refusal to learn from mistakes', *The Guardian*, 18 September. Available at: www.theguardian.com/society/2020/sep/18/england-wales-disgraceful-prisons-ministers-refusal-learn-mistakes (accessed 19 July 2023).

Williams, E. and Squires, P. (2021) *Rethinking knife crime: policing, violence and moral panic*, Basingstoke: Palgrave Macmillan.

Williams, W. (2020) *Windrush: lessons learned review*, London: House of Commons.

World Health Organization (2012) *Understanding and addressing violence against women: overview*, Geneva, World Health Organization.

World Health Organization (2021) 'Violence against women', 9 March. Available at www.who.int/news-room/fact-sheets/detail/violence-against-women (accessed 25 April 2023).

Wright, S., Crewe, B. and Hulley, S. (2017) 'Suppression, denial, sublimation: defending against the initial pains of very long life sentences', *Theoretical Criminology*, 21(2): 225–46.

Zedner, L. (2019) 'The hostile border: crimmigration, counter-terrorism or crossing the line on rights?', *New Criminal Law Review*, 22(3): 318–45.

16

Equalities and the Conservatives: the widening of social divisions?

Kirstein Rummery

Introduction

The Conservative government inherited the Coalition government's response to the private sector financial crisis of 2007 to 2008, as fiscal stimulus approaches to solving the crisis raised the budget deficit to 11.6 per cent in 2010 (Office for National Statistics – ONS, 2010). Over half of the cuts to government expenditure were to social security and local government – despite this sector making up only 27 per cent of total government expenditure – resulting in disabled people (8 per cent of the population) bearing 29 per cent of the costs of the cuts (Duffy, 2013). It is estimated that the 21 per cent of the female population living in poverty during that time bore the burden of 39 per cent of the spending cuts, and as 20 per cent of their income came from social security and tax benefits (compared to 10 per cent of men's income), £22 billion of the £26 billion cuts were borne by women (Hills, 2015). Black and Asian households in the lowest fifth of incomes experienced the largest drop in living standards due to austerity – around 20 per cent (Women's Budget Group and Runnymede Trust, 2017). The majority Conservative administration therefore inherited a sharply divided society where existing inequalities had widened considerably due to Coalition policies.

This chapter examines the Conservatives' record, focusing on social divisions of race, gender and disability. It assesses how these policies contributed to the unequal outcomes suffered by these groups under COVID-19 and discusses what can be learned to ameliorate inequality in a post-COVID-19 social policy landscape.

Race

Concerned about the persistent nature of racial inequality and associated social costs (Cabinet Office, 2017), in 2020 then Prime Minister Boris Johnson commissioned the Sewell report, which published in March 2021 (Commission on Race and Ethnic Disparities, 2021). Using data collected by the Cabinet Office's Race and Disparity Unit, it drew together disparate strands of data on ethnicity-based inequalities across different issues and sectors. It found that:

> The word mistrust was repeated often as some witnesses from the police service, mental health, education and health services felt that the system was not on their side. [...] The data also revealed many instances of success among minority communities. These have often been ignored or have been seen to be of little interest (to the media). (Commission on Race and Ethnic Disparities, 2021, p 6)

The tendency to merge the experiences of Black and Minority Ethnic (BAME) communities together when looking at inequalities masks variations within that population. In education, for example, children from Indian, Bangladeshi and African backgrounds outperformed children from White British and Black Caribbean backgrounds in England and Wales at GCSE (General Certificate of Secondary Education) level throughout the 2017 and 2019 Conservative administrations (Department for Education, 2019). Simplistic policies to 'close the attainment gap' that do not take intra-ethnicity differences into account therefore lead to misleading success rates.

The intersection between ethnicity and class in educational outcomes is important. Taking eligibility for free school meals (provided for children in families in receipt of a low-income welfare benefit) as a measure of deprivation, White British children have the biggest attainment gap compared to their non-free school meals peers than any other ethnic group (Department for Education, 2019). Poverty therefore has a bigger impact on attainment for White people than for any other ethnic group, although Black Caribbean children not on free school meals underperform all other ethnicities in that group (Centre for Social Justice – CSJ, 2020).

When looking at employment, the Commission on Race and Ethnic Disparities found that unemployment differences have been declining and that

> [t]he pay gap, meaning the difference between the median hourly earnings of all ethnic minority (not including White minority) groups and White groups, is at its lowest level since 2012 at 2.3%. Employees from the White Irish, Indian and Chinese ethnic groups on average have higher hourly earnings than the White British ethnic group. (Commission on Race and Ethnic Disparities, 2022, p 105)

However, this is a somewhat optimistic account. ONS figures indicate that in 2019 (the last year before the pandemic), White British employment rates (percentage of 16- to 65-year-olds in paid employment) were at 76 per cent compared to 56 per cent for Pakistani/Bangladeshi British and 67 per cent for Black British. Only Indian British working-age adults were achieving employment rates close to parity with White British adults (ONS, 2019). Moreover, 4 per cent of economically active White and Indian British workers were unemployed in 2019, compared to 9 per cent of Black British and 8 per cent of Pakistani/Bangladeshi British workers. These disparities exist even when factors such as region, health, dependents and education are controlled for (Li and Heath, 2020).

Using ONS (2020b) figures, the Commission reported that:

> The hourly median pay gap between all minorities and the White British ethnic group has shrunk to 2.3%, its smallest level since 2012 when it was 5.1%. This headline figure hides some large variations: the Pakistani ethnic group earned 16% less on average than the White British group, the Bangladeshi ethnic group 15% less, and the Black African group 8% less. Meanwhile the White Irish (41%), Chinese (23%) and Indian (16%) ethnic groups earned more on average than the White British group. (Commission on Race and Ethnic Disparities, 2022, p 110)

Working with the same data, the CSJ (2020) found that the biggest pay disparities were not between White and non-White groups, but within ethnic minority groups: 'whilst Indian British employees saw their wages rise from just under £12 [per hour] in 2012 to £13.50 in 2018, Bangladeshi British employees saw theirs rise from just over £8 to £9.50 in the same period' (CSJ, 2020, p 39). Occupational segregation accounts for some of the disparity: Pakistani, African and Bangladeshi British workers are more likely than others to be in semi-routine, casualised work than other groups. But even when factors such as the composition of work are considered, there is still a sharp earnings difference between White British and other groups, particularly in the 30–55 age group (Department for Education, 2019).

The Commission optimistically concluded that '[t]he gravitational force of dominant narratives tends to point our attention in negative directions, such as racist abuse on social media, and away from positive ones' (Commission on Race and Ethnic Disparities, 2021, p 29), asserting that the everyday lives of people are not defined by race (see also Adekoya, 2021) and that '[t]he evidence shows that geography, family influence, socio-economic background, culture and religion have more significant impact on life chances than the existence of racism' (Commission on Race and Ethnic Disparities, 2021, p 8). However, looking at largely the same data, the CSJ suggested more pessimistically that:

> so many of the problems around ethnic disparities are yet to be properly explained. For instance, evidence suggests that significant wage gaps

persist between many of Britain's ethnic groups, even after controlling for compositional factors. It is also the case that, despite students from ethnic minority backgrounds (on average) having higher educational attainment by age 16, and getting into university at higher proportions, this has tended not to translate into higher educational achievement and more equitable job market prospects. (2020, pp 8–9)

About 75 per cent of people in BAME groups voted 'Remain' in the 2016 referendum on leaving the European Union, in contrast to 47 per cent of White people. The predicted negative economic impacts of Brexit are difficult to assess due to the COVID-19 pandemic, but given the inequalities discussed, McIntosh et al (2018) concludes that BAME communities are likely to find themselves in a triple bind: socioeconomically worse off than White people, blamed for economic insecurity and cultural change, and a target for a rise in hate crimes as a result of being visible minorities.

The Commission set out an upbeat agenda to address inequality, focusing on building trust, fairness, agency and inclusivity in communities – linked to Prime Minister Johnson's 'levelling up' agenda. It asserts that it is not the substantive inequalities that are the problem; rather, changing attitudes and relationships between communities is the key, and society needs a 'further burst of momentum to the story of our country's progress to a successful multicultural community – a beacon to the rest of Europe and the world' (Commission on Race and Ethnic Disparities, 2021, p 8). The evidence, however, suggests that the Conservatives have come nowhere near achieving this multicultural vision, particularly for Black African, Caribbean, Pakistani and Bangladeshi Britons.

Gender

According to welfare conditionality, which requires benefit claimants to act in a way that fulfils eligibility conditions for receipt of a benefit, receiving benefits is not a social right. The Conservative administrations continued the shift towards incentivising paid work through welfare conditionality that had characterised previous administrations, most notably in the continued rollout of Universal Credit as a replacement for means-tested benefits, due to be completed in 2023. The shift to Universal Credit has a particular impact on women – for example, in their role as parents and primary carers of children. Benefits for child-related costs, even when means-tested, have always been paid to the main carer of the child, most often the mother. Now couples with children must nominate a 'responsible carer', and the majority are women (Department for Work and Pensions, 2015). The responsible carer is included in the calculation for their family's entitlement to Universal Credit. Responsible carers must undertake mandatory work preparation and job searching, or be sanctioned, impacting on the whole family's benefit status (Millar and Bennett, 2017). Andersen (2020) argues that this is the first time coupled mothers have been subject to welfare conditionality linked with severe sanctions, and this marks a substantive shift both in the rhetoric and reality of the state's relationship to mothers.

For women not dependent on the state for their income, the situation is hardly reassuring. The median gender pay gap is currently 18.4 per cent, but this masks substantial inequality between groups of women: 73 per cent of part-time workers are women, and part-time workers on average earn 35 per cent less per hour than full-time workers. Disabled women earn 6.1 per cent less than non-disabled women, and the pay gap is widest (40 per cent) at retirement age (ONS, 2021). Employment gaps due to motherhood and caring are an important part of the gender pay gap, as is occupational segregation (both horizontal and vertical). The Women and Equalities Select Committee (2016) found that the causes of the gender pay gap are complex and varied. Direct discrimination plays a part in women's lower wages, particularly for older women who entered the labour market on less equal terms to men and who may face dual discrimination on the grounds of age and gender.

Although the pay gap is 13 per cent lower than it was in the mid-1990s, that is mainly due to women's improved educational attainment (particularly the rise in numbers of women graduates) and a relative stagnation in male wages rather than proactive policy interventions to elicit structural change (Bennett, 2021). Mandatory gender pay gap reporting for organisations with over 250 employees is one of the few gender-related policies instigated by the Conservative administration in 2017. Analysis by Blundell (2021) shows that this led to a 1.6 per cent increase in women's wages, in part due to employers' actions to attract and retain women employees, rather than substantive structural change around occupational segregation, childcare or caring policies. Moreover, the duty to publish headline figures does 'not give employers sufficient information to identify the causes of the gender pay gap within their organisation. Nor will they be detailed enough to identify causes of unequal pay, or enable women to identify a comparator or make equal pay claims' (Fawcett Society, 2018, p 31).

Changes to the eligibility for Statutory Maternity Pay, Statutory Paternity Pay, Statutory Shared Parental Pay and Maternity Allowance have led to greater take-up, but this does not alter the fact that these benefits are paid at a flat rate and so do not address wages lost, or give parents a living wage while caring for young children. The Fawcett Society (2018) argues that these benefits, along with Carers Allowance, should be set at National Living Wage level, to reflect the fact that childcare and caring for disabled/ older relatives is work and to address women's poverty more generally. No such changes to policies have been advocated by the 2017 Conservative administration, or in any of the 'building back' proposals after COVID-19.

Research carried out by the Trades Union Congress (2016) found that 52 per cent of women had experienced some form of sexual harassment, with over 10 per cent reporting unwanted touching and sexual advances. Moreover, in 2008, 7.1 per cent of the Crown Prosecution Service caseload was taken up by violence against women and girls (VAWG), and by 2017 that had risen to 19.3 per cent (Crown Prosecution Service, 2017). The 2015 Conservative administration introduced new offences for coercive behaviour, revenge porn and upskirting, raised the maximum penalties for stalking and harassment, ended automatic early release of sexual offenders from prison and introduced new orders to prevent stalking, sexual harm and female genital mutilation.

Tackling Violence Against Women and Girls (Home Office, 2021) promised £43 million in the 2021–22 Spending Review to tackle VAWG (see also Chapter 15). Most provisions concern perpetrators and victims after the fact. The focus on perpetrators (called, revealingly, Pursuing Perpetrators) sets out interventions through the criminal justice system aimed at deterrence, funding for rehabilitation to prevent reoffending, removing the culture of 'getting away with it' and investment to identify serial sex offenders.

Alongside concerns about VAWG, the 2019–20 Crime Survey for England and Wales estimated that 2.3 million adults (70 per cent women) experienced domestic abuse that year. One in four women experience domestic abuse in their lifetime, compared to one in seven men. However, only one in five victims report their abuse to the police (ONS, 2020a). The Domestic Abuse Act 2021 created a statutory definition of domestic abuse that includes physical or sexual abuse, violent or threatening behaviour, controlling or coercive behaviour, economic abuse and psychological, emotional or other abuse (s 1). It broadened the concept of victim to include children related to perpetrators or victims who see, hear or experience the effect of the abuse (s 3). It also recognised the intersectional nature of abuse – for example, involving religion, female genital mutilation, honour-based crimes and crimes against people with disabilities and LGBT people. It established a Domestic Abuse Commissioner position and introduced new protection orders preventing perpetrators from contacting victims and mandating modifications to change offending behaviour.

There has been no comprehensive sectoral assessment of the impact of Brexit on different equality groups. The equality analysis the government produced for the European Union (Withdrawal) Bill 2017 anticipated little or no adverse impact, due to existing protections under UK law mirroring European Union directives and law. However, the negative impact on the economy is likely to disproportionately affect women, who tend to have lower incomes.

In terms of political representation, in 2017, 32 per cent of elected Members of Parliament (MPs) were women. Women made up 21 per cent of Conservative MPs, 45 per cent of Labour MPs, 33 per cent of Liberal Democrat MPs and 24 per cent of Scottish National Party MPs. The 2019 general election saw a slight rise in women's political representation overall. At Westminster, women currently make up 24 per cent of the Conservative MPs, 52 per cent of Labour MPs, 67 per cent of Liberal Democrat MPs and 36 per cent of Scottish National Party MPs. The Conservatives (and Liberal Democrats) explicitly do not use any proactive mechanisms to increase women's representation. Given their history of electoral success, the most effective measure they could instigate to improve representation would be to increase the number of women selected to run as candidates.

In the devolved parliaments, women currently make up 45 per cent of the Scottish Parliament, 43 per cent of the National Assembly for Wales and 36 per cent of the Northern Ireland Assembly. Local councils see even lower rates of representation by women: just 34 per cent of the 4,980 councillors elected in May 2021 were women. Here the Conservatives' electoral success also hinders the representation of women – they won the most seats but only 25 per cent of their elected councillors were women, in contrast to near parity for Labour (49 per cent) and a high percentage for the Green Party (43 per cent). The May 2022 Scottish local elections also returned 34 per cent women councillors. Women made up 41 per cent of the Scottish National Party councillors, 32 per cent of Labour councillors, 21 per cent of Conservative councillors, 33 per cent of Liberal Democrat councillors and 45 per cent of Scottish Greens councillors. Here, both the Labour and the Scottish National Party could improve political representation at a local level by increasing the number of women selected. However, incumbency somewhat weakens this being a successful strategy in the short to medium term.

Overall, the picture for women's equality under the Conservative administrations is discouraging. The biggest focus has been on reform of VAWG legislation, but this has focused on new and tougher sentences for perpetrators and improving services for survivors, rather than prevention. Women relying on Universal Credit for their income have been hit hard by the extension of conditionality underlying this benefit, and women's political participation appears to have made only slight improvements, largely down to proactive actions from those parties winning power in the devolved parliaments.

Disability

Around 21 per cent of the UK population is disabled – that is, they have 'a physical or mental impairment … [that] has a substantial and long-term adverse effect on [their] ability to carry out normal day-to-day activities' (Equality Act 2010). This means that around one fifth of the electorate are disabled. Given that 45 per cent of people over 65 are disabled, and over 80 per cent of eligible voters over 65 do vote (compared to 50 per cent of 18–24 year olds), this demographic should in theory be targeted by political parties attempting to gain power (British Election Survey, 2021), although disabled people tend to be less likely to vote than non-disabled people (Atkinson et al, 2017). Evans (2022) found that despite spending on disability remaining a popular priority among the electorate, there were few measures in election manifestos aimed specifically at disabled people. The 2015 Conservative manifesto contained specific pledges on reducing the disability employment gap, and the 2017 included promises to tackle disability discrimination, based on efforts targeted at individuals rather than substantive structural change.

The Conservatives inherited policy changes (largely driven by themselves during the Coalition government) which had already impacted on disabled people's lives. Welfare conditionality had changed the status of thousands of disabled people previously considered unable to work and placed mandatory work search conditions on benefits. Cuts to the Employment and Support Allowance for the Work Related Activity Group (those deemed capable of finding work with assistance) affected over 400,000 disabled people. Moreover, the process of the Work Capability assessment negatively affected the health of 78 per cent of claimants, according to claimants' responses, while 87 per cent of advisers said the assessment process had a negative impact on claimants' health (Hardest Hit, 2012).

Dwyer et al (2018) found that welfare conditionality did very little to facilitate the transition into paid work and, in many cases, caused such exacerbation to illness and impairment that claimants faced additional barriers in searching for paid work. Benefit sanctions were shown to have no positive effect:

> benefit sanctions routinely trigger profoundly negative personal, financial and health impacts that are likely to move disabled people further away from the paid labour market.
>
> Personalised, negotiated packages of support can help disabled people to overcome the barriers they face and help facilitate entry into work. However, much of the mandatory training and job search support on offer to disabled people is of poor quality and is largely ineffective in enabling them to enter and sustain paid employment. (Dwyer et al, 2018, p 1)

During the 2017–19 administration, over half a million disabled people lost their Disability Living Allowance in the transition to Personal Independence Payments. This was introduced with the explicit aim of saving over £2 billion, rather than increasing disabled people's independence. It was in fact counterproductive: 65 per cent of working claimants who lost Disability Living Allowance in the move to Personal Independence Payments found they were unable to continue working.

The Conservatives also cut social care funding introduced by the preceding Coalition government. An ambitious plan to create a National Care Service (HM Government, 2010), ending the postcode lottery of cash-strapped local councils being responsible for social care, was shelved. A service that was already on the brink of collapse by 2019 was deemed no longer sustainable amid service cuts, workforce concerns and several large-scale social care providers falling into bankruptcy (House of Lords, 2019). The Dilnot review (2011) had already found that private sector insurers were unwilling to risk involvement with social care funding, making market solutions to the funding crisis untenable. The Conservative government put forward several proposals, including an extension to means-testing for home care to include the value of the home (the so-called 'dementia tax' that was unpopular in the 2017 election), which were then largely abandoned (Jarrett, 2019; see also Chapter 12).

In 2015, the House of Lords appointed an ad hoc committee to consider the impact on disabled people of the Equality Act 2010 (which had combined disability with other areas of discrimination such as gender and race). It reported that the Act

> ignores a crucial distinction between disability and the other protected characteristics. For the other protected characteristics, with the possible exception of pregnancy and maternity, equality of opportunity is largely achieved by equality of treatment. For disabled people, equality of opportunity, to the extent that it is achievable, often requires different treatment. (House of Lords Select Committee on the Equality Act 2010 and Disability, 2016, p 21)

Advocacy for disabled people's people rights was judged to have been harmed by the formation of the Equality and Human Rights Commission and the dissolution of the Disability Rights Commission in 2010. The government responded with a robust defence of the status quo:

> This Government is committed to ensuring that everyone can live their lives free from discrimination and harassment, including disabled people. Disability discrimination legislation has been in place since 1995, when the then Conservative Government passed a landmark piece of legislation, the Disability Discrimination Act. This Act was the first domestic Act on the issue of disability discrimination, prior to which it was legal to discriminate and exclude on the basis of disability. The 1995 Act was subsequently incorporated, with the support of the

Conservative Party, into the Equality Act in 2010. We believe strongly therefore that the Equality Act 2010, and all our programmes that impact upon the lives of disabled people, act as tangible protections of disabled people's rights. As the Post-Legislative Scrutiny Memorandum on the Equality Act 2010 (CM 9101—July 2015) shows, the Equality Act has essentially preserved and taken forward the protections in the Disability Discrimination Act 1995. (Government Equalities Office, 2016, p 2)

Along with the devolved Equalities Commissions, the Equality and Human Rights Commission was invited to critique the government's record on disability rights considering the United Nations Convention on the Rights of Persons with Disabilities (CRPD). In their 2017 submission to the United Nations, they stated:

the UK and devolved governments have not taken all the appropriate steps to progress implementation of the CRPD and have introduced some retrogressive measures that have had a significant negative effect on disabled people. [...] Social security reforms introduced by successive UK governments since 2010 are having a particularly negative, disproportionate and cumulative impact on the rights to independent living and an adequate standard of living for disabled people. (UK Independent Mechanism 2017, pp 4, 47)

In the past, the European Union has also acted as an important vehicle for protecting disabled people's rights. The Employment Equality Framework Directive of 2000 was far more wide-ranging than the UK's Disability Discrimination Act 1995 in terms of coverage of small firms and extended rights to include indirect discrimination. Travel protection for disabled people, medicines regulation, health coverage and access issues are also covered by European Union regulations and were not well negotiated to protect disabled citizens' rights in the European Union (Withdrawal) Act 2018. As with other areas, the socioeconomic impact of Brexit on disabled people is difficult to assess in the light of the COVID-19 pandemic. Concerns about the economic fallout on women due to their overrepresentation among people living in poverty and relying on state income apply even more so to disabled people. They face a double impact as recovery from COVID-19 and post Brexit changes play out.

The differential impact of COVID-19

It was clear early in the pandemic that there was a differential morbidity and mortality impact by race: 13.6 per cent of admissions for COVID-19 in the first wave (to April 2020) were Black people, compared to 2.7 per cent of admissions for viral pneumonia in the same period in 2017. Overall, COVID-19 death rates among the Black Caribbean population were three times that of the White population, and the differences were even starker when age, population density and overall health were considered (Platt and Warwick, 2020). Platt and Warwick (2020) also found that only 1 per cent of White British working-age men were in an occupational sector that completely shut down, whereas over 29 per cent of Bangladeshi British working-age men were in these sectors, meaning they experienced a disproportionate effect on family finances and well-being throughout and beyond the pandemic.

Clearly, there is no correlation between Conservative policies and the disproportionate effect the virus had physically on different groups. However, some factors were open to policy intervention. The clustering of workers by ethnicity in front-facing, high-risk, low-paid occupations, and in overcrowded housing, are factors that have long been known to be responsible for differential education, income and work outcomes for different ethnicities. More could have been done in the two Conservative administrations leading up to the pandemic to address inequalities and mitigate against those same factors turning so starkly into higher death rates.

Although more men died from COVID-19 – there was an almost 18 per cent difference in the total number of COVID-19-related deaths for men (63,700) and women (53,300) between March 2020 and January 2021 in England and Wales – women's well-being overall was more negatively affected (ONS, 2022). A consistently greater number of women than men were furloughed between 1 July and 31 December 2020. On 1 July 2020, there were 2.9 million women on furlough, compared with 2.7 million men. By 31 October 2020, the number of women on furlough was 1.2 million compared with 1.1 million men. Between 31 October and 30 November 2020, the number on furlough increased to 1.9 million for women and 1.8 million for men (HM Revenue and Customs, 2021).

The move towards working from home affected men and women roughly equally. However, what they did at home differed markedly:

The amount of time women spent on unpaid household work fell from an average of 3 hours and 8 minutes per day during 2014 to 2015 to an average of 2 hours and 43 minutes per day during September and early October 2020. The amount of time men spent on unpaid household work increased from an average of 1 hour and 45 minutes per day during 2014 to 2015, to 1 hour and 58 minutes per day during the end of March and April 2020, before reducing to 1 hour and 40 minutes per day during September and early October. At the beginning of the UK's first lockdown in March 2020, women spent 55% more time than men on unpaid childcare. However, this difference is smaller than in September and October 2020, when women spent 99% more time on unpaid childcare than men. Additionally, a significantly greater proportion of women (67%) than men (52%) homeschooled a school-age child in late January and early February (13 January and 7 February 2021). In April and early May 2020, around one in three women (34%) reported that their well-being was negatively affected by homeschooling a school age child compared with only one in five men (20%). By late January and early February 2021, it was taking a greater toll on both women (53%) and men (45%). (ONS, 2022)

The impact of COVID-19 on people's mental health was also gendered, with women being 1.3 times more likely to report loneliness and 4 times more likely to report anxiety or depression than men. Men were significantly more likely to report being not at all worried about the effect of the pandemic on their lives (ONS, 2022).

It is easier to argue that the differential impact of COVID-19 by gender was both foreseeable and preventable if policy changes had taken place in the Conservative administrations that preceded it. Women's over-representation among those undertaking childcare and care of older/disabled family can explain both the differential impact of furlough/homeworking and the mental health impact of the pandemic. The availability and affordability of quality childcare and social care has been known to be a factor in gender equality in both the workplace and the home for some time (Rummery, 2021). The continuing reliance on a breadwinner model of welfare despite divergence from that across other welfare regimes (Guiliani, 2022) and underinvestment in public social care (Glasby et al, 2021) led inevitably to increased impact of the pandemic on women.

Perhaps the most direct result of the differential impact of COVID-19 could be seen in the experiences of disabled people. It was understood from quite early on that the highest risk of morbidity and mortality from the disease was for the over 65s, of whom 45 per cent were disabled (Harrison et al, 2020). The living circumstances of many disabled people meant they were in close proximity with others, not least due to ongoing personal care needs, and were unable to self-isolate to reduce their risk of transmission (Dickinson et al, 2020; Glynn et al, 2020). In addition, the obligation on local authorities to assess disabled people's needs was suspended under COVID-19 regulations, meaning that despite increased spending, important safeguards and basic levels of care were not met.

As with women, it was not just COVID-19 itself but the nature of government policy prior to the pandemic, and its policy responses to the pandemic, that had a disproportionate effect on disabled people. Surveys carried out by disabled people's organisations early in the pandemic found overwhelming evidence that underinvestment in social care services, inequality and poverty seriously restricted disabled people's ability to protect themselves during the pandemic (Inclusion London, 2020; Inclusion Scotland 2020). This resulted in high levels of distress, social isolation and lack of access to food, medication and social care. Moreover, disabled people died in far higher rates than any other group: 47 per cent of deaths from COVID-19 in the general population in the first wave were of people over 85, yet just 4 per cent of COVID-19 deaths in adults with intellectual disabilities were over 85 (Scottish Government, 2021). Over 50 per cent of people with intellectual disabilities who contracted COVID-19 did so from staff in care homes, and 27 per cent contracted it in hospital (Heslop et al, 2021).

Bambra and colleagues (2020) note that while COVID-19 did not cause inequalities, it had the effect of dramatically exposing them. The poverty, inequality, lack of work, income and inappropriate housing that led to the differential impact of the pandemic on disabled people cannot be ignored. Shakespeare et al studied the experiences of 69 disabled people and 28 support organisations during the first year of the pandemic and concluded that

> [t]he reestablishment of social supports and services, including day centres and other activities, is urgently needed to support disabled people, particularly people with learning disabilities and people with autism. COVID-19-safe alternatives need to be developed and health and social care funders and providers must work with disabled people and their organisations to develop new ways of delivering support. The withdrawal of these services has had a detrimental impact on these individuals and put intense pressure on their families and other support networks. (2021, p 114)

Conclusion

Conservative policy has served to reinforce and widen inequalities rather than narrowing them. This is largely due to a seemingly ideological disdain for structural reform. Acknowledging the deep-seated reasons for inequality experienced due to race, sex and disability would entail a significant shift in perspective from the individual to the social. Policy objectives have always been individualised – for example, to get more people into work, to punish VAWG offenders and to enable individual disabled people to access work. With paid work being one of the most successful ways to lift people out of poverty, retaining punitive measures demonstrated to be counterproductive and not addressing the barriers to work faced by many in terms of childcare, care services, education and the nature of work itself is responsible for enduring inequalities.

Brexit and COVID-19 served to highlight, rather than cause, inequalities. We know the world of work is changing post COVID-19. Remote working – long campaigned for by disabled people and women as being more accessible and amenable to care and childcare arrangements – has become the norm in many sectors. However, the long-standing problems with the funding and delivery of social care which were thrown into sharp relief by COVID-19 will not be solved without a fundamental rethink of those services. I have argued elsewhere that a universal care service taken out of the control of local authorities would make a significant difference to the inequality experienced by women (as both formal and informal carers) and disabled people (Rummery, 2021).

References

Adekoya, R. (2021) *Biracial Britain: a different way of looking at* race, London: Little, Brown.

Andersen, K. (2020) 'Universal Credit, gender and unpaid childcare: mothers' accounts of the new welfare conditionality regime', *Critical Social Policy*, 40(3): 430–49.

Atkinson, V., Aaberg, R. and Darnolf, S. (2017) 'Disability rights and election observation: increasing access to the political process', *Nordic Journal of Human Rights*, 35(4): 375–91.

Bennett, F. (2021) 'Gendered economic inequalities: a social policy perspective', *The IFS Deaton Review*, 6 December. Available at: https://ifs. org.uk/inequality/gendered-economic-inequalities (accessed 19 July 2023).

British Election Survey (2021) 'Age and voting behaviour at the 2019 general election', *British Election Study*, 27 January. Available at: www.britishelecti onstudy.com/bes-findings/age-and-voting-behaviour-at-the-2019-gene ral-election/#.YxS4N9PMI2w (accessed 19 July 2023).

Bambra, C., Riordan, R., Ford, J. and Matthews, F. (2020) 'The COVID-19 pandemic and health inequalities', *Journal of Epidemiology and Community Health*, 74(11): 964–8.

Blundell, J. (2021) *Wage responses to gender pay gap reporting requirements*, London: Centre for Economic Performance. Available at: https://cep.lse. ac.uk/pubs/download/dp1750.pdf (accessed 19 July 2023).

Cabinet Office (2017) *Race disparity audit – summary findings from the Ethnicity Facts and Figures website*, London: Cabinet Office. Available at: www.ethnic ity-facts-figures.service.gov.uk/static/race-disparity-audit-summary-findi ngs.pdf (accessed 22 May 2022).

Centre for Social Justice (2020) 'Facing the facts: ethnicity and disadvantage in Britain'. Available at: https://www.centreforsocialjustice.org.uk/wp-content/uploads/2020/11/CSJJ8513-Ethnicity-Poverty-Report-FINAL. pdf (accessed 31 July 2023).

Commission on Race and Ethnic Disparities (2021) *Commission on Race and Ethnic Disparities: the report* (Chair: Tony Sewell), London: HM Government. Available at: https://assets.publishing.service.gov.uk/government/uploads/ system/uploads/attachment_data/file/974507/20210331_-_CRED_Repo rt_-_FINAL_-_Web_Accessible.pdf (accessed 19 July 2023).

Crown Prosecution Service (2017) *Violence against women and girls crime report 2016–2017*, London: Crown Prosecution Service.

Department for Education (2019) *Graduate outcomes (LEO): outcomes in 2016 to 2017*, London: Department for Education.

Department for Work and Pensions (2015) *Welfare Reform and Work Bill: impact assessment of the change in conditionality for responsible carers on Universal Credit*, London: Department for Work and Pensions.

Dickinson, H., Carey, G. and Kavanagh, A.M. (2020) 'Personalisation and pandemic: an unforeseen collision course?', *Disability and Society*, 35(6): 1012–17.

Dilnot, A. (2011) *Fairer care funding*, London: Commission on Funding of Care and Support.

Duffy, S. (2013) *A fair society? How the cuts target disabled people*, London: Centre for Welfare reform. Available at: www.centreforwelfarereform.org/uploads/attachment/354/a-fair-society.pdf (accessed 22 May 2022).

Dwyer, P., Jones, K., McNeill, J., Scullion, L. and Stewart, A.B.R. (2018) *Final findings: disabled people*, York: University of York. Available at: www.welfareconditionality.ac.uk/wp-content/uploads/2018/05/40414-Disabled-people-web.pdf (accessed 19 July 2023).

Evans, E. (2022) 'Disability policy and UK political parties: absent, present or absent-present citizens?', *Disability & Society*. doi: 10.1080/09687599.2022.2045191

Fawcett Society (2018) *Sex discrimination law review*, London: Fawcett Society. Available at www.fawcettsociety.org.uk/Handlers/Download.ashx?IDMF=e473a103-28c1-4a6c-aa43-5099d34c0116 (accessed 19 July 2023).

Giuliani, G.A. (2022) 'The family policy positions of conservative parties: a farewell to the male-breadwinner family model?', *European Journal of Political Research*, 61: 678–98.

Glasby, J., Zhang, Y., Bennett, M. and Hall, P. (2021) 'A lost decade? A renewed case for adult social care reform in England', *Journal of Social Policy*, 50(2): 406–37.

Glynn, J.R., Fielding, K. and Shakespeare, T. (2020) 'COVID-19: excess all cause mortality in domiciliary care', *British Medical Journal*, 370: m2751. doi: https://doi.org/10.1136/bmj.m2751

Government Equalities Office (2016) *Government response to the House of Lords Select Committee report on the Equality Act 2010: the impact on disabled people*, London: Government Equalities Office.

Hardest Hit (2012) *The tipping point: the human and economic costs of cutting disabled people's support*, London: Hardest Hit. Available at: https://thehardesthit.files.wordpress.com/2012/10/the_tipping_point_oct_2012.pdf (accessed 19 July 2023).

Harrison, S.L., Fazio-Eynullayeva, E., Lane, D.A., Underhill, P. and Lip, G.Y.H. (2020) 'Comorbidities associated with mortality in 31,461 adults with COVID-19 in the United States: a federated electronic medical record analysis', *PLoS Medicine*, 17(9): e1003321. doi: https://doi.org/10.1371/journal.pmed.1003321

Heslop, P., Byrne, V., Calkin, R., Huxor, A., Sadoo, A. and Sullivan, B. (2021) 'Deaths of people with intellectual disabilities: analysis of deaths in England from COVID-19 and other causes', *Journal of Applied Research in Intellectual Disabilities*, 34(6): 1630–40.

Hills, J. (2015) *The Coalition's record on cash transfers, poverty and inequality 2010–2015*, London: LSE. Available at: http://sticerd.lse.ac.uk/dps/case/spcc/WP11.pdf (accessed 1 May 2022).

HM Government (2010) *Building the National Care Service*, London: TSO. Available at: www.gov.uk/government/publications/building-the-natio nal-care-service (accessed 19 July 2023).

HM Revenue and Customs (2021) 'Coronavirus Job Retention Scheme statistics: January 2021', *Gov.uk*, 28 January. Available at: www.gov.uk/gov ernment/statistics/coronavirus-job-retention-scheme-statistics-january-2021/coronavirus-job-retention-scheme-statistics-january-2021 (accessed 19 July 2023).

Home Office (2021) *Tackling violence against women and girls*, London: Home Office.

House of Lords Economic Affairs Committee (2019) *Social care funding: time to end a national scandal*, London: House of Lords. Available at: https://publications.parliament.uk/pa/ld201719/ldselect/ldeconaf/392/392.pdf (accessed 19 July 2023).

House of Lords Select Committee on the Equality Act 2010 and Disability (2016) *Equality Act 2010: the impact on disabled people*, London: House of Lords.

Inclusion London (2020) 'Abandoned, forgotten and ignored. The impact of the coronavirus pandemic on disabled people: interim report'. Available at: https://www.inclusionlondon.org.uk/wp-content/uploads/2020/06/Abandoned-Forgotten-and-Ignored-Final-1.pdf (accessed 31 July 2023).

Inclusion Scotland (2020) 'Rights at risk: COVID-19, disabled people and emergency planning in Scotland'. Available at: https://inclusionscotland. org/wp-content/uploads/2021/05/Rights-At-Risk-Main-Report.pdf (accessed 31 July 2023).

Jarrett, T. (2019) *Adult social care: the Government's ongoing policy review and anticipated Green Paper (England)*, London: House of Commons Library.

Li, Y. and Heath, A. (2020) 'Persisting disadvantages: a study of labour market dynamics of ethnic unemployment and earnings in the UK (2009–2015)', *Journal of Ethnic and Migration Studies*, 46(5): 857–78.

McIntosh, K., Mirza, R. and Ali, I.S. (2018) *Brexit for BAME Britain: investigating the impact*, Race on the Agenda Briefing Paper, London: ROTA.

Millar, J. and Bennett, F. (2017) 'Universal Credit: assumptions, contradictions and virtual reality', *Social Policy and Society*, 16(2): 169–82.

ONS (Office of National Statistics) (2010) *Pocket Databank*, London: ONS.

ONS (Office of National Statistics) (2019) *Pocket Databank*, London: ONS.

ONS (Office for National Statistics) (2020a) 'Domestic abuse victim characteristics, England and Wales: year ending March 2020', 25 November. Available at: www.ons.gov.uk/peoplepopulationandcommunity/crimeand justice/articles/domesticabusevictimcharacteristicsenglandandwales/year endingmarch2020 (accessed 19 July 2023).

ONS (Office for National Statistics) (2020b) 'Ethnicity pay gaps: 2019', 12 October. Available at: www.ons.gov.uk/employmentandlabourmarket/ peopleinwork/earningsandworkinghours/articles/ethnicitypaygapsingreat britain/2019 (accessed 19 July 2023).

ONS (Office for National Statistics) (2021) *Annual Survey of Hours and Earnings 2021*, London: ONS.

ONS (Office for National Statistics) (2022) *Coronavirus and the social impacts on Great Britain*, London: ONS.

Platt, L. and Warwick, R. (2020) *Are some ethnic groups more vulnerable to COVID-19 than others*, London: Institute for Fiscal Studies.

Rummery, K. (2021) 'Gender equality and the governance of long-term care policy: new comparative models and paradigms', *Journal of International and Comparative Social Policy*, 37(1): 16–33.

Scottish Government (2021) 'Coronavirus (COVID-19) – disabled people: health, social and economic harms – research report'. Available at: https://www.gov.scot/publications/covid-19-disabled-people-scotl and-health-social-economic-harms/pages/8/ (accessed 14 August 2023).

Shakespeare, T., Watson, N., Brunner, R., Cullingworth, J.B., Hameed, S., Scherer, N., Pearson, C. and Reichenberger, V. (2021) 'Disabled people in Britain and the impact of the COVID-19 pandemic', *Social Policy & Administration*, 56(1): 103–17.

Trades Union Congress (2016) *Still just a bit of banter? Sexual harassment in the workplace in 2016*, London: Trades Union Congress.

UK Independent Mechanism (2017) *Disability Rights in the UK: updated submission to the UN Committee on the Rights of Persons with Disabilities in advance of the public examination of the UK's implementation of the UN CRPD*, London: Equality and Human Rights Commission.

Women's Budget Group and Runnymede Trust (2017) *Intersecting inequalities: the impact of austerity on Black and minority ethnic women in the UK*, London: Women's Budget Group and Runnymede Trust.

Women and Equalities Select Committee (2016) *Gender pay gap inquiry: conclusion and recommendations*, London: House of Commons. Available at: www.parliament.uk/business/committees/committees-a-z/commons-select/women-and-equalities-committee/inquiries/parliament-2015/gender-pay-gap-15-16/ (accessed 19 July 2023).

17

The Conservative governments, devolution and social policy

Ann Marie Gray

Introduction

Review of social policies in the devolved countries of the UK during the Conservative–Liberal Democratic Coalition government at Westminster (2010–15) indicates a clear shift towards a social democratic approach in Scotland and Wales, with growing divergence from key UK government social policies (for example, Birrell and Gray, 2016). In Northern Ireland (NI), the mandatory power-sharing arrangements made it more difficult to discern a distinct political approach.

In the period since 2015, politics and social policy in the UK have been dominated by two major influences, Brexit and the COVID-19 pandemic, as well as the most serious cost of living crisis for several decades. These have brought into sharp focus the increasing tensions between the UK government and each of the devolved parliaments.

Changes to constitutional and financial powers

Both the Scottish Parliament and the National Assembly for Wales (now called Senedd Cymru/Welsh Parliament) gained significantly expanded powers in the period since 2014. In the wake of the 2014 Scottish independence referendum, the Smith Commission was established to take forward the commitments made by the pro-Union parties regarding further devolution of powers to the Scottish Parliament. Pillar 2 of the 'Smith Commission Agreement' is 'delivering prosperity, a healthy economy, jobs, and social justice' (Smith Commission, 2014, p 12). The commission recommended devolution of significant areas of social security responsibility so that, for example, while the State Pension and the National Minimum Wage would remain reserved to Westminster, a wide range of benefits for carers, disabled people and those who are ill, plus benefits which comprised the Regulated Social Fund (including the Cold Weather Payment, Sure Start Maternity Grants, Winter Fuel Payment and Discretionary Housing Payments) should be devolved. Universal Credit was to remain a reserved benefit administered and delivered by the Department for Work and Pensions, but the Scottish Government would have the power to change the frequency of Universal Credit payments, vary the existing plans for single-household payments and the housing costs element of Universal Credit, and pay landlords direct for housing costs in Scotland.

Wales has gone through various stages of constitutional change since devolution. In the period since 2015, this included the recognition of the Welsh Assembly as a parliament following the Senned and Elections (Wales) Act 2020. In the early days of devolution in Wales, First Minister Rhodri Morgan, keen to show the Welsh Government was taking a different approach to the New Labour focus on choice and competition, advocated a more 'citizen-centred' approach and referred to 'clear red water' between Cardiff and Westminster (Birrell, 2009, p 184). The ability of the Welsh Government to achieve this was limited by a more restricted devolution settlement than in Scotland or NI. The Silk Commission (Commission on Devolution in Wales, 2014) concluded that the devolution settlement created uncertainty over legislative competencies and advocated a move from a conferred model to a reserved model of devolution. The UK governments under Cameron and May progressed this and the Wales Act 2017 moved the Welsh Assembly from the conferred powers model to the reserved powers model, meaning that, similar to Scotland and NI, it could legislate on any matter not expressly reserved to the UK Parliament. It also provided for new powers over a number of areas, including elections and equal opportunities. In 2019, the Welsh Government called for a 'new constitutional settlement' in the relationship between the four UK nations, whereby the UK Parliament should not legislate on devolved matters without the consent of the relevant devolved legislature (Welsh Government, 2019). Under the provisions of the Government of Wales (Devolved Powers) Bill put forward in 2022, the UK government is not able to change the devolved powers of the Welsh Parliament without the support of at least two thirds of the parliament's members. The constitutional powers of the Welsh Government are under the spotlight again with the establishment of the Independent Commission on the Constitutional Future of Wales in July 2021 (Welsh Government, 2021a). Due to provide recommendations by the end of 2023, the commission has two broad objectives: to consider and develop options for fundamental reform of the constitutional structures of the UK, in which Wales remains an integral part; and to consider and develop all progressive principal options to strengthen Welsh democracy and deliver improvements for the people of Wales.

Devolution in NI since 1998 has been marked by volatility and instability, and the devolved institutions have collapsed several times. Whereas many of the threats to the working of government in NI have related to constitutional and conflict legacy issues, the collapse of the institutions in January 2017 was precipitated by a more 'ordinary' political scandal in the form of the mismanagement of the Renewable Heat Incentive scheme (referred to as the 'RHI scandal'), which had cost the Northern Ireland Executive £480 million (Coghlin et al, 2020). The resumption of devolved government in January 2020 following the *New Decade, New Approach* agreement (Northern Ireland Office, 2020) was relatively short-lived. In February 2022, the Democratic Unionist Party (DUP) First Minister Paul Givan resigned in opposition to the Ireland/Northern Ireland Protocol, triggering another collapse of the institutions.

Conservative governments, Brexit and devolution

The overall majority vote in the 2016 referendum in favour of the UK leaving the European Union (EU) masked differences across the four jurisdictions, with majorities voting Remain in Scotland and in NI and majorities voting Leave in England and Wales. In NI, the two parties in power, the DUP and Sinn Féin, took opposing positions, with the DUP firmly aligning itself to the Leave campaign in Britain. While the Welsh Government was pro Remain, there was a majority vote in Wales to leave the EU. Tensions between the UK government and the Scottish and Welsh governments had been very much in evidence in the run-up to the referendum (Scottish Parliament, 2016; Zolle, 2016). The more limited expression of concern by the Northern Ireland Executive was a result of the deep political cleavages between the two main parties, although there was consensus on the need to avoid a 'hard' border with the Republic of Ireland, protection of labour mobility, energy and agri-food trade (Birrell and Gray, 2017).

Control by the Westminster governments under May and Johnson over the EU withdrawal negotiations that followed the referendum saw little scope for involvement of the devolved governments despite the establishment in 2016 of the Joint Ministerial Committee for that purpose (House of Lords, 2017). UK government claims that Brexit would enhance the powers of the devolved governments (May, 2017) were not shared by devolved administrations in Scotland and Wales, and proposed measures in the first draft of the EU (Withdrawal Agreement) Bill to bring powers directly back to Westminster were seen as a power grab (see Sturgeon and Jones, 2017).

Brexit was always going to have particular consequences for NI given the land border with the Republic of Ireland, and it resulted in a paradigm shift not just in relations within NI but also between the UK and Irish governments. Theresa May's failure to gain support for a Bill which included a 'backstop', essentially an insurance policy which would mean that the border between the north and south of Ireland would remain open whatever the outcome of the negotiations (Phinnemore, 2018), resulted in her resignation in June 2019. Boris Johnson's negotiation of a new protocol placed NI in a very distinct legal position. In order to ensure that there would be no checks on the island of Ireland, NI remained aligned with the single market regulations in areas such as regulation of goods and environmental regulation. The Northern Ireland Protocol resulted in a customs and regulatory border between GB and NI in the Irish Sea, which has been a source of continuing controversy, and the opposition to it by Unionist parties in NI, particularly the DUP, contributed to the collapse of the political institutions in NI. Early in Rishi Sunak's premiership, the UK and the EU published a new agreement, *The Windsor Framework* (HM Government, 2023), to replace the Northern Ireland Protocol. Designed to make trade between NI and the rest of the UK easier, it was welcomed by most NI parties. However, the DUP voted against key aspects of the deal and, at the time of writing, has not re-entered the Northern Ireland Assembly.

Also contentious was the passing of the United Kingdom Internal Market Act 2020, which governs the internal trading relationship between the countries of the UK. Under this legislation, UK ministers have powers to provide financial assistance to any part of the UK for purposes of promoting economic development, providing infrastructure and supporting education and training (Sargeant and Stojanovic, 2020). This means that the UK government can spend money directly in devolved policy areas without consent, essentially bypassing the devolved administrations (Part 6 of the Internal Market Act). This will be largely done through the UK Shared Prosperity Fund, established to replace the funding from EU structural funds (discussed later).

Social policy: further divergence under Conservative governments

The tendency towards greater autonomy in social policy making for the devolved countries of the UK, particularly Wales and Scotland, since 2015 has clashed with some centralisation of powers under Conservative governments, as discussed later in the chapter. However, in all of the devolved jurisdictions, although to a lesser extent in NI, there continues to be evidence of policy innovation and divergence. The extent to which this has resulted in more positive outcomes is difficult to discern, particularly given the context of the COVID-19 pandemic. Earlier assessments (Rummery and McAngus, 2015; Cairney et al, 2016) noted that the rhetoric that Scotland was delivering more socially just policies did not bear empirical scrutiny and that there was little evidence that policy making differences have produced major differences in policy outcomes. Since then, extension of devolved powers has enabled the Scottish Government to introduce policies with more discernible long-term outcomes. For example, analysis by the Institute for Fiscal Studies has concluded that the Scottish

Government has used its devolved tax and benefit powers to craft a more progressive system than is in place in the rest of the UK. On average, taxes are higher for high-income households and benefits are more generous for low-income households (Adam and Phillips, 2021).

An area which has had a consistently strong focus from Scottish governments since 2015 is education. In the election to the Scottish Parliament in May 2016, the Scottish National Party (SNP) won the most seats (63 of 129) but did not have an overall majority, so Nicola Sturgeon formed a minority SNP government. A key focus of the SNP manifesto for the election had been the attainment gap in education: 'Ensuring educational excellence for all and closing the gap in attainment between young people in our most and least deprived communities will be the defining mission of the SNP in the next parliament' (SNP, 2016, p 8). The Scottish Attainment Challenge had been launched in 2015 to provide extra resources to schools in areas of high deprivation. Funded by a number of programmes, including Pupil Equity Funding, a total of £750 million was spent in the five years to 2021. Most of this went directly to schools, based on the number of pupils eligible for free school meals. The amount of funding is to increase to £1 billion over the five years from 2021 to 2026 (Audit Scotland, 2021). Outcome data shows that although some improvement occurred across most areas of attainment measures at national level, progress was limited and the poverty-related attainment gap remains wide (Audit Scotland, 2021; Education, Children and Young People Committee, 2022).

The newly devolved competences following the Smith Commission provided further opportunity for the Scottish Government to show that it had a different vision for social policy than that pertaining in England (Simpson et al, 2019), and this has been illustrated most specifically with regard to social security policy. Developments relating to poverty and social security policies are situated within a broader context of social justice (Scottish Government, 2016, p 3), with a commitment from the Scottish Government that social security would be delivered in a more humane way (Simpson, 2022). The Child Poverty (Scotland) Act 2017 reintroduced statutory targets and reporting that had been abandoned by the Westminster government. The Act requires the Scottish Government to ensure less than 18 per cent of children are living in poverty by 2023–24, moving to less than 10 per cent by 2030.

The Social Security (Scotland) Act 2018 established a new devolved social security system in Scotland, firmly positioned it as a public service and located it within a set of eight principles which recognised social security as a human right and essential to the realisation of other human rights (O'Cinneide, 2019). Respect for the dignity of individuals was to be at the heart of the Scottish social security system, and it was to advance equality and nondiscrimination. Most of the newly devolved social security powers relate to disability, child and carer benefits, including a Scottish Child Payment (for under 16s), Child Winter Heating Assistance and a Young Carer Grant (Kidner, 2022).

The devolved system of social security necessitated governance changes: a Cabinet Secretary for Social Security and Older People and a Social Security Committee in the Scottish Parliament; a new Scottish Government Social Security Directorate; a new social security agency, Social Security Scotland; and an independent scrutiny body, the Scottish Commission on Social Security. A social security charter was developed using a coproduction method with social security claimants (Social Security Scotland, 2019), which was seen as integral to ensuring dignity and respect. A statutory Poverty and Inequality Commission was established to advise Scottish ministers; an advisory nondepartmental public body with specific duties in regard to the Child Poverty (Scotland) Act 2017, including monitoring and scrutinising progress on poverty and inequality reduction.

Childcare has been a long-standing gap in welfare state provision in the UK, and none of the four countries has comprehensive provision, particularly for one- and two-year-olds (De Henau, 2022). The greatest progress can be seen in Scotland and Wales, with more limited provision in England and much less in NI, which offers the most restricted system and the least support for childcare, concentrating its focus on early years education. A long-awaited NI childcare strategy has not appeared. In September 2022, the Minister for Education indicated that the Northern Ireland Executive would publish a childcare strategy with costed options to be ready for March 2023. A core component of this is a new proposal to offer every child in their preschool year a minimum of 22.5 hours of preschool education per week (Department of Education (NI), 2022). Scotland has adopted a more holistic, integrated approach to funding with initiatives that blend both early education and childcare for working parents (Pascal et al, 2021). The extension of universal childcare in Scotland to 30 hours a week in term time from 2021 (or 1,140 hours a year – up from 600) for all three- and four-year-olds and eligible two-year-olds means it is significantly more expansive than is the case in England, where the equivalent hours are only offered to parents working 16 plus hours per week. The programme for government in Wales (Welsh Government, 2016), covering the period 2016–21, contained a commitment to a much more generous system of childcare, and there has been progress in achieving this. Working parents in Wales are entitled to 30 hours a week of a mixture of early education and childcare, with a minimum of 10 hours of early education and a maximum of 20 hours of childcare (Welsh Government, 2021b), over 48 weeks per year, which compares favourably to the 38 weeks in Scotland and England. During the school holidays, the full 30 hours can be taken up as childcare by eligible parents. Unlike in other countries of the UK, this is mainly accessed through local authorities.

A number of other policy initiatives highlight how Wales has continued to develop distinctive policies within the UK. A feature of devolution in Wales has been continuity of a Labour government (majority or in coalition) since 1998. In the 2016 election, the Labour Party saw a widespread fall in its share of the vote, but in the 2021 Welsh Parliament election, the Party won half of the 60 seats, 1 short of a majority. Following the election, Labour signed a three-year *Co-operation Agreement* with Plaid Cymru (Welsh Government, 2021b), which commits to a more distinctly Welsh social policy programme. It covers 50 policy areas, including the extension of free school meals to all primary schools over the lifetime of the agreement, the setting up of an expert group to support the creation of a National Care Service, the expansion of free childcare to all two-year-olds and radical action to address unaffordable housing and homelessness. A review of child policy in Wales (Smith, 2022) concludes that a distinctive character to child policy in Wales has emerged centred on the promotion of children's rights, child poverty and educational reform. It also draws attention to the constraints on Welsh Government initiatives, some due to limits of devolved powers but others relating more directly to how the implementation of policy fell short of policy intentions.

The introduction of the Wellbeing of Future Generations (Wales) Act 2015 made Wales the first government in the world to enshrine in law a duty on public bodies to safeguard the well-being of future generations. Based on the principle of sustainable development, the well-being duty covers economic, social, environmental and cultural factors and aims to address short-termism in policy making (Welsh Government, 2015). Public bodies in Wales have to consider the long-term impact of their decisions, work more collaboratively with citizens and prevent persistent problems such as poverty, health inequalities and climate change, and a Future Generations Commissioner was appointed to monitor progress (Welsh Government, 2015). While undoubtedly a visionary piece of legislation, the pace of progress has been slow, with scrutiny bodies finding much to be done for the Act to deliver on its aims (Audit Wales, 2020; Public Accounts Committee (Wales), 2021). The Public Accounts Committee (Wales) (2021) found that public bodies across Wales have not done enough to change their organisational cultures to align with the principles of the Act or to build awareness and understanding among their service users about the shift to sustainable development across public services. They also point to challenges emanating from short funding cycles and a complex and bureaucratic landscape of partnership bodies, plus the lack of sufficient funding to ensure principles of sustainable development can be embedded within public bodies.

Another distinctive feature of the social policy agenda in Wales since 2015 has been the continuance and development of an equality focus and policies to strengthen and advance human rights. A gender equality review was established to set out how the Welsh Government could become a 'feminist government' (Davies et al, 2018, p 49; Davies and Furlong, 2019). The government accepted most of the recommendations and published a policy and implementation plan to take them forward (Welsh Government, 2020). As in Scotland (in 2018), the Welsh Government made the decision to commence s 1 of the Equality Act 2010, known as the 'socioeconomic duty', on 31 March 2021. It requires that public bodies, when making strategic decisions, have regard to the need to reduce the inequalities of outcome resulting from socioeconomic disadvantage (Equality and Human Rights Commission, 2021). The UK government has no plans to introduce a socioeconomic duty in England, although a number of English local authorities have adopted the duty voluntarily. The public duty in NI (s 75 of the Northern Ireland Act 1998) does not include a socioeconomic duty and there are no proposals to plans to change this.

The Auditor General for Wales (Audit Wales, 2022a), in the first of three reviews on the challenge of alleviating and tackling poverty, noted that all local authorities undertook some form of assessment to determine the likely socioeconomic impact of decisions, but that these were highly variable. The duty is only one tool in addressing poverty, but it is potentially important in the context of a quarter of the population living in poverty, a proportion which has barely changed in the decade from 2010 (Matejic, 2020).

While there had been long-term improvements in health outcomes prior to the COVID-19 pandemic, the sustainability of health and social care services is a challenge facing all four countries in the UK. Despite some divergence in policies, structures and spending, the evidence up to 2020 suggests no significant difference in performance between the UK countries (Organisation for Economic Co-operation and Development, 2016; Atkins et al, 2021). This is due in part to the limited impact which health policy has on health outcomes. The number of people in each jurisdiction on waiting lists has increased rapidly since the start of the pandemic, but while this is a growing problem, it is not a new one. Waiting time standards have not been met for several years in England (The King's Fund, 2022), Scotland (Public Health Scotland, 2022) or Wales (Audit Wales, 2022b). However, NI has, by some margin, the longest waiting lists in the UK (Department of Health (NI), 2022).

It is perhaps in social care that more recent examples of divergent policy can be found. The *Independent Review of Adult Social Care in Scotland* (Feeley, 2021) outlined significant challenges in the social care system, including the creeping in of stricter eligibility criteria and growing levels of unmet need. In response, in the National Care Service (Scotland) Bill, the Scottish Government proposed the creation of a new National Care Service body which will see responsibility for social care shift from local authorities to central government ministers. This does not represent a new care service free at the point of use. There is no indication of changes to current arrangements; personal and nursing care will remain free and a means test will continue to apply to all other services. There is also potential for social care policies in Wales to diverge more significantly from policy in England and NI. An expert group was established to provide recommendations on the practical steps which can be taken towards the creation of a National Care Service where 'care is free at the point of need. These practical steps must be consistent with social care remaining a responsibility of local government and its continuance as a public service, taking account of the spending framework set by the Draft Budget 2022–2025' (Welsh Government, 2022). It reported in November 2022 and the government has yet to respond. Whether these proposals in Scotland and Wales will result in tangible outcomes remains to be seen, and there is little information on the funding of either policies. The repeal of a planned National Insurance levy by the Westminster government will mean little extra money in the block grant for social care.

There has been much less evidence of a distinctive NI social policy approach. This is not just the result of the lack of political stability, but also the outworking of a mandatory coalition consisting of parties with different ideological perspectives. The Northern Ireland Executive has struggled to make progress on a number of substantive policy issues, including health and social care reform, educational underachievement, the persistently high rate of economic inactivity and major deficiencies in social infrastructure – especially childcare, as outlined earlier. Despite seven major reviews all indicating the need for transformation of acute health care, implementation of reform has been slow. Only in 2022 did the Department of Health publish a consultative document on reform of adult social care (Department of Health (NI), 2022), despite primary legislation being more than forty years old.

When the Northern Ireland Assembly resumed in January 2020, it was in the context of the UK exiting the EU and was close to the start of the COVID-19 pandemic. The return of the institutions was accompanied by a plan, *New Decade, New Approach*, published by the UK and Irish governments (Northern Ireland Office, 2020). This listed agreed policy priorities and was to form the basis of a programme for government (though no such programme had been signed off on by the time the Assembly collapsed again in February 2022). Initially, despite the continuing difficulties in the relationship between the DUP and Sinn Féin, there was some indication of a stronger focus on social policy. The Northern Ireland Executive commenced work on a suite of equality strategies on gender, disability and sexual orientation and on an anti-poverty strategy committed to in *New Decade, New Approach*, commissioning expert reviews to inform each strategy and setting up co-design groups. In 2016, it put in place a number of welfare mitigation schemes designed to alleviate the impact of specific changes to social security benefits as a result of welfare reform. These were initially to last until 2020 but were then temporarily extended. Prior to the collapse of Assembly in 2022, the Department for Communities had appointed an independent advisory panel to review the welfare mitigation measures and provide recommendations with regard to future mitigations. This group reported in October 2022 (Department for Communities, 2022), but with no ministers in place, decisions were unable to be made on the recommendations.

An indicator of a greater interest in and focus on social policy could also be seen in the increase in Private Members Bills in the 2017–20 mandate and the number of these which made their way into legislation – 9 out of a total of 45 primary legislation bills, including on organ donation, tackling child holiday hunger, domestic abuse, climate change and carers rights. In the May 2022 elections to the Northern Ireland Assembly, a nationalist party, Sinn Féin, was returned as the largest party for the first time, allowing them to provide the First Minister. The DUP was relegated to second place. However, in the immediate aftermath of the election, the DUP declined to provide a Deputy First Minister, saying it would return to power sharing with nationalists only on removal of the EU Protocol.

What has been interesting to observe is that while the UK Conservative governments have been reluctant to introduce direct rule, they have appeared increasingly willing to intervene on some NI social policy issues by legislating at Westminster. The Northern Ireland (Executive Formation etc) Act 2019 decriminalised abortion in NI and legalised same-sex marriage. Westminster had previously been resistant to the idea that it should exercise powers to legislate for these issues, repeatedly arguing that they were devolved matters. The prospect of the Northern Ireland Assembly legislating on these issues was remote given the strong opposition of the DUP, although there was evidence of strong public support for reforms in both these areas (ARK, 2018). In addition, the United Nations Committee on All Forms of Discrimination Against Women (2018) had conducted an inquiry under the Optional Protocol to the Convention, which concluded that abortion law in NI had resulted in women being subject to grave and systematic abuse. It made a number of recommendations for action by the UK government as the state party to the Convention on the Elimination of All Forms of Discrimination Against Women.

The COVID-19 pandemic

The COVID-19 pandemic raised the profile of devolution and provided something of an insight into intergovernmental relations between the UK government and the devolved governments. In the early weeks of the pandemic, there were very visible signs of collaboration and coordination. The Johnson government introduced new legislation, the Coronavirus

Act 2020, which was supported by the four governments. The *Coronavirus Action Plan* (Department of Health and Social Care, 2020) was accompanied by parallel announcements of key decisions, and the announcement of the first lockdown in March 2020 was supported by all parliaments in the UK. Treasury schemes to address the economic impact of COVID-19 were rolled out across the UK; the Coronavirus Job Retention Scheme provided 80 per cent of employee salaries up to £2,500 per month, Value Added Tax and Income Tax deferrals were introduced, and people in receipt of Universal Credit and Working Tax Credit received an uplift of £20 per week (Mackley, 2021). Additional funding was also received by the devolved administrations via Barnett consequentials.

Whereas the first wave of the pandemic saw a high level of intergovernmental collaboration and coordination, policy divergences soon appeared. The devolved governments generally adopted a more cautious approach to the easing of restrictions and used their powers to deviate from UK government policy on the timing and stringency of responses. Each published their own roadmap for emerging from the pandemic and used devolved powers to establish local support measures for businesses and discretionary social security compensation schemes. While the profile of the devolved governments with regard to the pandemic response was high in their jurisdictions, the national media largely focused on Westminster policy, and UK government announcements were not always clear on the territorial reach of data, policy or guidance. Basta and Henderson argue that the crisis 'demonstrated the limits of the governing elite's perception of the UK as a multinational and multilevel state with inconsistent attention to the relationship between reserved and devolved powers' (2021, p 302). It is difficult to establish direct effects of the differences in guidance and restrictions between the countries of the UK. To date, analysis indicates limited variation in public health outcomes (Scobie, 2022), although the UK infection and death rates are high in international rankings (Office for National Statistics, 2021). Of relevance is the extent to which the policy responses of the devolved administrations may have been limited by fiscal constraints. Bell et al's (2021) analysis of the devolved nations' policy responses to the pandemic discusses the Treasury's reticence to commit to furlough where a devolved government imposed a full lockdown but England did not. They conclude that the pandemic has exposed limitations and risks of the devolved funding arrangements regarding the adequacy of block grant adjustment arrangements to cope with such shocks. An inquiry into the response to the pandemic in the UK commended in June 2022. It will examine and report on preparations and the response to the pandemic in England, Wales, Scotland and NI, including reserved and devolved matters across the UK. The Scottish Government has established a public inquiry to examine the handling of the pandemic in Scotland, but there will not be separate inquiries in Wales and NI

Looking ahead

The SNP was returned in 2021 for a fourth consecutive term in office, albeit needing the support of the Scottish Greens. The shared policy agreement included rent controls, new rights for tenants and green energy and renewables. In the *Programme for Government (2022–23)*, the focus was firmly on cost of living issues (Scottish Government, 2021). In September 2022, Nicola Sturgeon announced a rent freeze on public and private properties to last for two years, until rent controls are introduced in 2024, and an extension of free school meals to primary 6 and 7 pupils (from January 2022, all children in years 1 to 5 in local authority schools were eligible for free school meals). A key thread in the SNP narrative is that Scottish independence is necessary to deliver the scale of social policy changes needed post pandemic. However, Sturgeon's resignation as First Minister in the spring of 2023, along with other developments, led to disagreements within the SNP about the path to independence.

The full impact on the devolved countries of the loss of EU funding and the implementation of the UK Shared Prosperity Fund, put in place by the UK government to replace EU funding, are yet to be seen. The devolved administrations have two key concerns about the fund – the level of funding and the control the UK government is exercising over devolved jurisdictions in the allocation and running of it. Under the EU structural funding arrangements, devolved administrations had the role of 'managing authorities' and were responsible for allocating funding internally. These funds, which were designed to support economic development and targeted at disadvantaged communities, were worth in the region of £1.3 billion a year. The European Social Fund, in particular, had been strongly focused on employment and skills, with 66 per cent of the fund between 2014 and 2022 spent on 'inclusive labour markets' (Brien, 2022, p 7). The control over the allocation and spending of the £2.6 billion UK Shared Prosperity Fund in the devolved nations by the UK Department for Levelling Up, Housing and Communities has been highly contentious – indeed, the Welsh Government has referred to it as an 'attack on devolution' (Drakeford, 2017, p 5).

As has been seen, intergovernmental relations in the UK have been stretched since 2016. The *Review of Intergovernmental Relations* published in January 2022 (Cabinet Office and the Department for Levelling Up, Housing and Communities, 2022) may offer some prospect of improvement. Signed up to by the UK and devolved governments, it establishes a number of new structures and the principles which should underpin these: 'maintaining positive and constructive relations, based on mutual respect for the responsibilities of the governments and their shared role in the governance of the UK' (Cabinet Office and the Department for Levelling Up, Housing and Communities, 2022, p 1). The First Minister for Wales has said that 'the package has the potential to deliver significant improvements, if the spirit and content as set out in the package is translated through into consistent approaches and actions' (Drakeford, 2022).

Conclusion

A defining feature of the period since 2015 has been the changing relationships between the devolved governments and Westminster, which will contribute to constitutional changes in coming years. The Brexit and EU withdrawal process saw the UK government assert dominance through control over negotiations, repatriation of competences to domestic institutions and allocation of finances.

Consideration of the social policies of the devolved governments suggests that Scotland and Wales have maintained a social democratic ethos, favouring higher public expenditure than England or NI and having a continuing emphasis on equality and inclusion (Table 17.1). A number of factors suggest this will be the future trajectory, not least the continuing impact of Brexit, support for more devolved powers in Scotland and Wales and calls for another referendum on Scottish independence. Even in NI, where political disputes have greatly impacted the working of the devolved institutions, there is some indication of a greater focus on social policy. However, it is not always evident that divergent policies in the devolved nations have resulted in more positive outcomes, leading to the question of whether policies have been radical enough within the scope of devolved powers.

Even in the context of enhanced devolution in Scotland and Wales, and arguably more transformative policies emerging, it is difficult to assess whether the outcomes in the devolved administrations will be significantly better in the coming years given the exceptional challenges posed by the COVID-19 pandemic and the economic crisis (Sinclair, 2022).

Table 17.1: Dimensions of political approaches and the devolved administrations

Dimension	Conservative government, 2015–16 (Cameron)	Conservative government, 2016–19 (May)	Conservative government 2019–22 (Johnson)	Conservative government 2022 (Truss)	Conservative government 2022 (Sunak–)	Scotland	Wales	Northern Ireland
Approach	Deregulator	Deregulator	Deregulator	Deregulator	Deregulator	Leveller	Leveller	Elements of deregulator and leveller
Citizenship	Responsibilities	Responsibilities	Responsibilities	Responsibilities	Responsibilities	Rights	Rights	Responsibilities/ pragmatic
Outcome	Inequality	Inequality	Inequality	Inequality	Inequality	Inclusion	Inclusion	Some inequality
Mixed economy of welfare	Private	Private	Private	Private	Private	State/private/ civil society	State/private/ civil society	State/private/civil society
Mode	Competition	Competition	Competition/ cooperation	Competition	Competition	Cooperation/ partnership	Cooperation/ partnership	Centralised
Expenditure	Low	Low/pragmatic	Low/pragmatic	Low	Low/pragmatic	Medium/high	Medium	Pragmatic
Benefits	Low	Low/pragmatic	Low/pragmatic	Low	Low/pragmatic	Medium/high	Medium	Pragmatic
Services	Low/medium	Low/medium	Low/medium	Low/medium	Low/medium	Medium/high	Low/medium	Low/medium
Accountability	Market	Market	Market	Market	Market	Devolved	Devolved	Devolved
Politics	Right	Right	Right/pragmatic	Right	Right	Left	Left	Right/pragmatic

Source: Adapted from Powell (1999) and Chapter 1 of this volume

References

Adam, S. and Phillips, D. (2021) *Scottish tax, benefits and public spending – what's happened and what do the parties propose?* London: IFS.

ARK (2018) *Recording social attitudes and informing social policy in Northern Ireland: key findings from 20 Years of ARK's Life and Times Surveys*, Belfast: Ulster University and Queen's University Belfast.

Atkins, G., Dalton, G., Phillips, A. and Stojanovic, A. (2021) *Devolved public services: the NHS, schools and social care in the four nations*, London: Institute for Government.

Audit Scotland (2021) *Improving outcomes for young people through school education*, Edinburgh: Audit Scotland.

Audit Wales (2020) *So, what's different? Findings from the Auditor General's Sustainable Development Principle Examinations*, Cardiff: Audit Wales.

Audit Wales (2022a) ' "Time for change" – poverty in Wales, Cardiff, Audit Wales'. Available at: https://www.audit.wales/publication/time-change-poverty-wales (accessed 3 August 2023).

Audit Wales (2022b) 'Tackling the planned care backlog in Wales, Cardiff, Audit Wales'. Available at: https://audit.wales/sites/default/files/publications/Tackling_the_Planned_Care_Backlog_in_Wales.pdf (accessed 3 August 2023).

Basta, K. and Henderson, A. (2021) 'Multinationalism, constitutional asymmetry and COVID: UK responses to the pandemic', *Nationalism and Ethnic Politics*, 27(3): 293–310.

Bell, D., Eiser, D. and Phillips, D. (2021) *Designing and funding the devolved nations' policy responses to COVID-19*, Glasgow: University of Strathclyde Business School.

Birrell, D. (2009) *The impact of devolution on social policy*, Bristol: Policy Press.

Birrell, D. and Gray, A.M. (2016) 'Social policy, the devolved administrations and the UK Coalition government', in H. Bochel and M. Powell (eds) *The Coalition government and social policy*, Bristol: Policy Press, pp 325–46.

Birrell, W. and Gray, A.M. (2017) 'Devolution: the social, political and policy implications of Brexit', *Journal of Social Policy*, 46(4): 765–82.

Brien, P. (2022) *The UK Shared Prosperity Fund*, Research briefing, London: House of Commons Library.

Cabinet Office and Department for Levelling Up, Housing and Communities (2022) *Review of intergovernmental relations*, London: Cabinet Office.

Cairney, P., Russell, S., and St Denny, E. (2016) 'The "Scottish approach" to policy and policymaking: what issues are territorial and what are universal?' *Policy and Politics*, 44(3): 333–350.

Coghlin, P., O'Brien, U. and MacLean, K. (2020) *The Report of the Independent Public Inquiry into the Non-domestic Renewable Heat Incentive (RHI) Scheme*, Belfast: Department of Finance. Available at: https://cain.ulster.ac.uk/issues/politics/docs/rhi/2020-03-13_RHI-Inquiry_Report-V1.pdf.(accessed 18 August 2023).

Commission on Devolution in Wales (2014) *Empowerment and responsibility: legislative powers to strengthen Wales* (Chair: Paul Silk), Cardiff: Commission on Devolution in Wales.

Committee on the Elimination of Discrimination Against Women (2018) *Inquiry concerning the United Kingdom of Great Britain and Northern Ireland under article 8 of the Optional Protocol to the Convention on the Elimination of All Forms of Discrimination Against Women*, Geneva: Committee on the Elimination of Discrimination Against Women.

Davies, N. and Furlong, C. (2019) *Deeds not words: review of gender equality in Wales (phase two)*, Cardiff: Chwarae Teg.

Davies, N., Furlong, C. and Wharfe, H (2018) *Rapid review of gender equality 2018: phase one*, Cardiff: Chwarae Teg.

De Henau, J. (2022) 'Simulating employment and fiscal effects of public investment in high-quality universal childcare in the UK', *International Journal of Childcare and Education Policy*, 16: 3. doi: 10.1186/s40723-022-00096-y

Department for Communities (2022) *Welfare mitigations review: Independent Advisory Panel report*, Belfast: Department for Communities.

Department of Education (NI) (2022) 'McIlveen announces move towards 22.5 hours of funded pre-school for all children', *Department of Education*, 7 September. Available at: www.education-ni.gov.uk/news/mcilveen-announces-move-towards-225-hours-funded-pre-school-all-children (accessed 19 July 2023).

Department of Health and Social Care (2020) *Coronavirus action plan: a guide to what you can expect across the UK*, London: Emergency and Health Protection Directorate.

Department of Health (NI) (2022) *Consultation on the reform of adult social care*, Belfast: Department of Health.

Drakeford, M. (2017) *Regional investment in Wales after Brexit: securing Wales' future*, Cardiff: Welsh Government.

Drakeford, M. (2022) 'Written statement: review of intergovernmental relations', *Welsh Government*, 13 January. Available at: https://gov.wales/written-statement-review-intergovernmental-relations-0 (accessed 19 July 2023).

Education, Children and Young People Committee (2022) *Scottish attainment challenge*, Edinburgh: Scottish Parliament.

Equality and Human Rights Commission (2021) *Evaluating the socio-economic duty in Scotland and Wales*, London: Equality and Human Rights Commission.

Feeley, D. (2021) *Independent review of adult social care in Scotland*, Edinburgh: Scottish Government.

HM Government (2023) *The Windsor framework: a new way forward*, CP 806, London: HMSO.

House of Lords EU Committee (2017) *Scrutiny of Brexit negotiations*, London: House of Lords.

Kidner, C. (2022) 'Scottish social security in six charts', *Scottish Parliament, SPICe Spotlight*, 4 October. Available at: https://spice-spotlight.scot/2022/10/04/scottish-social-security-in-six-charts/ (accessed 19 July 2023).

Kings Fund (2022) *NHS waiting times: our position*, London: Kings Fund. Available at: https://www.kingsfund.org.uk/projects/positions/nhs-waiting-times (accessed 6 August 2023).

Mackley, A. (2021) *Coronavirus: Universal Credit during the crisis*, London: House of Commons Library.

Matejic, P. (2020) *Poverty in Wales*, York: Joseph Rowntree Foundation.

May, T. (2017) 'The government's negotiating objectives for exiting the EU: PM speech', *Gov.uk*, 17 January. Available at: www.gov.uk/government/speeches/the-governments-negotiating-objectives-for-exiting-the-eu-pm-speech (accessed 19 July 2023).

Northern Ireland Office (2020) *New decade, new approach*, Belfast: Northern Ireland Office.

O'Cinneide, C. (2019) 'The Social Security (Scotland) Act 2018 – a rights based approach to social security', *Edinburgh Law Review*, 23(1): 117–23.

Organisation for Economic Co-operation and Development (2016) *OECD reviews of health care quality: United Kingdom 2016*, Paris: OECD. Available at: www.oecd.org/els/health-systems/oecd-reviews-of-health-care-quality-united-kingdom-2016-9789264239487-en.htm (accessed 19 July 2023).

Office for National Statistics (2021) 'Comparisons of all-cause mortality between European countries and regions: 2020', *Office for National Statistics*, 19 March. Available at: www.ons.gov.uk/releases/comparisonsofallcausemortalitybetweeneuropeancountriesandregions2020 (accessed 19 July 2023).

Pascal, C., Bertram, T. and Cole-Albäck, A. *What do we know about the 30 hour entitlement? Literature review and qualitative stakeholder work*, London: Sutton Trust.

Phinnemore, D. (2018) 'Brexit and the "backstop"', *UK in a Changing Europe*, 7 November. Available at: http://ukandeu.ac.uk/explainers/brexit-and-the-backstop/ (accessed 19 July 2023).

Powell, M. (1999) 'Introduction', in M. Powell (ed) *New Labour: new welfare state*, Bristol: Policy Press, pp 1–28.

Public Accounts Committee (Wales) (2021) *Delivering for future generations: the story so far*, Wales: Welsh Parliament.

Public Health Scotland (2022) *NHS waiting time*, Edinburgh: Public Health Scotland, available at https://www.publichealthscotland.scot/publications/nhs-waiting-times-stage-of-treatment/stage-of-treatment-waiting-times-inpatients-day-cases-and-new-outpatients-30-september-2022/ (accessed 6 August 2023).

Rummery, K. and McAngus, C. (2015) 'The future of social policy in Scotland: will further devolved powers lead to better social policies for disabled people?', *The Political Quarterly*, 86(2): 234–9.

Sargeant, J. and Stojanovic, A. (2020) *The United Kingdom Internal Market Act 2020*, London: Institute for Government.

Scobie, S. (2022) 'Covid-19: How has the pandemic differed across the four UK nations?', *British Medical Journal*, 377: o1482. doi: 10.1136/bmj.o1482

Scottish Government (2016) *A new future for social security: consultation on social security in Scotland*, Edinburgh: Scottish Government.

Scottish Government (2021) *A fairer, greener Scotland: programme for government 2021–22*, Edinburgh: Scottish Government.

Simpson, M. (2022) *Renegotiating social citizenship in an age of devolution*, Oxford: Hart Publishing.

Simpson, M., McKeever, G. and Gray, A.M. (2019) 'From principles to practice: social security in the Scottish laboratory of democracy', *Journal of Social Security Law*, 26(1): 13–31.

Sinclair, S. (2022) 'Challenges to the strategic state: welfare reform lessons from a devolved polity', *Journal of Social Policy*. doi: 10.1017/S0047279422200068X

Smith, S. (2022) *The childhood policy landscape in Wales: a case study*, London: The British Academy.

Smith Commission (2014) *Report of the Smith Commission for further devolution of powers to the Scottish Parliament*, Edinburgh: The Smith Commission.

SNP (Scottish National Party) (2016) *SNP manifesto 2016*, SNP.

Social Security Scotland (2019) *Our charter*, Edinburgh: Scottish Government.

Sturgeon, N. and Jones, C. (2017) 'EU (Withdrawal) Bill: joint letter to Prime Minister', *Scottish Government*, 19 September. Available at: www.gov.scot/publications/eu-withdrawal-bill-joint-letter-to-prime-minister/ (accessed 19 July 2023).

Welsh Government (2015) *Wellbeing of Future Generations (Wales) Act 2014: essentials guide*, Cardiff: Welsh Government.

Welsh Government (2016) *Taking Wales forward, 2016–2021*, Cardiff: Welsh Government.

Welsh Government (2019) *Reforming our Union: shared governance in the UK*, Cardiff: Welsh Government.

Welsh Government (2020) *Advancing gender equality in Wales plan*, Cardiff: Welsh Government.

Welsh Government (2021a) 'Independent Commission on the Constitutional Future of Wales'. Available at: https://gov.wales/independent-commission-constitutional-future-wales (accessed 19 July 2023).

Welsh Government (2021b) *The co-operation agreement 2021*. Available at: https://gov.wales/sites/default/files/publications/2021-11/cooperation-agreement-2021.pdf (accessed 19 July 2023).

Welsh Government (2022) *Wales budget 2022–2025*, Cardiff: Welsh Government. Available at: https://www.gov.wales/sites/default/files/publi cations/2022-01/budget-leaflet-2022-25.pdf (accessed 3 August 2023).

Zolle, N. (2016) *Implications of Brexit on public services in Wales*, Cardiff: Wales Public Services.

18

Conclusions

Hugh Bochel and Martin Powell

Introduction

This chapter draws together the arguments presented throughout this book and relates them to the framework introduced in Chapter 1. In particular, it considers the main approaches underpinning the Conservatives' social policies since 2015, covering five prime ministers, albeit that is particularly complicated given the impacts of Brexit (Chapter 4), the COVID-19 pandemic (Chapter 5) and the period of high inflation from 2022. It is also important to recognise that in many areas of social policy, the remit of the Conservative governments was limited to England, although the main driver of levels of public expenditure across the UK remains the decisions of central government as it largely determines the funding available to the devolved administrations.

Locating the Conservative governments, 2015–23

As discussed in Chapter 1, this section draws on Powell's (1999) analysis of New Labour and Bochel and Powell's (2016) consideration of the Coalition government to examine social policies by setting them against the framework of alternative political approaches and drawing on the analyses provided by the contributors of each chapter for this book. It expands on Table 1.1 to look at the governments as led by David Cameron, Theresa May, Boris Johnson, Liz Truss (briefly) and Rishi Sunak, and it summarises their approaches to social policy in Table 18.1.

While there are, perhaps inevitably, some differences, our assessment is largely in line with the views of the other contributors to this book, with the Conservative governments being largely seen as having significant similarities with New Right thinking, but nevertheless having been greatly affected by 'events', meaning that successive prime ministers and their cabinets found it hard to clearly set out, let alone achieve, their social policy goals.

As discussed earlier, the 'Coalition' years cover the period with Cameron as Prime Minister in coalition with the Liberal Democrats, while the 'Conservative' years cover the period following the general elections of

2015, 2017 and 2019, under the leadership of Cameron (2015–16), May (2016–19), Johnson (2019–22), Truss (2022) and Sunak (2022–). However, it is very difficult to discuss the extremely short period of Truss as Prime Minister (although there appeared to be a clear preference for a smaller, deregulatory state and a relaxed view of inequality, even if aspects of policy had to be rolled back extremely rapidly) and the relatively short period (at the time of writing) of Sunak as Prime Minister. Looked at overall, and taking up some of the themes summarised in Table 1.1, in most respects, the Conservative governments, under successive prime ministers, as with their Coalition predecessor, can be seen as having significant similarities with the New Right, although the impact of events, such as Brexit, the COVID-19 pandemic and the effects of the Russian invasion of Ukraine, clearly pushed them in different directions in areas such as public expenditure (Table 18.1). In other words, it could be argued that it is difficult to work out what they would have done in a 'counterfactual' of no 'external shocks'. While many of the dimensions in Table 18.1, and the application to the Conservative governments' policies, inevitably overlap, they help provide a framework for comparison with some key ideas and with other governments.

Approach

The government's opening statement in the Grenfell Tower Inquiry (2021a) said that it was 'deeply sorry' for 'past failures in relation to the oversight of the system that regulated safety in ... high-rise buildings', while the Queen's Council appearing for one group of bereaved and survivors, pointed to successive governments' 'unbridled passion for deregulation' (Grenfell Tower Inquiry, 2021b).

As made clear in a number of chapters, the Conservatives' policy preferences seem to have been closer to the 'deregulatory' stance of the New Right-influenced Thatcher governments than the 'investor' approach of the Third Way, or even that of One Nation Conservatism. While it might be claimed that there has been a rise of regulators and regulation, this seems to have been paralleled by an increase in regulatory failure, with examples in health and social care, and pensions. Despite this, and central government criticisms of other providers for 'failures', such as the death of Awaab Ishak in mouldy housing run by Rochdale Boroughwide Housing, in many areas the government continued to cite the benefits of deregulation. In public health, for example, despite evidence of growing inequalities, there was a clear and continued reluctance to support measures that might be seen as impinging on individuals' 'freedom' (Chapter 7). More broadly, the Sunak government's Autumn Statement in November 2022 saw the Chancellor, Jeremy Hunt, promising 'big bang' deregulation (including lifting any cap on bankers' bonuses), apparently referencing the changes under Margaret

Table 18.1: Dimensions of political approaches

Dimension	Old Left	Third Way	One Nation	New Right	Coalition	Conservative government, 2015–16 (Cameron)	Conservative government, 2016–19 (May)	Conservative government 2019–22 (Johnson)	Conservative government 2022 (Truss)	Conservative government 2022– (Sunak)
Approach	Leveller	Investor	Investor	Deregulator	Deregulator	Deregulator	Deregulator	Deregulator	Deregulator	Deregulator
Citizenship	Rights	Rights and responsibilities	Rights and responsibilities	Responsibilities	Responsibilities	Responsibilities	Responsibilities	Responsibilities	Responsibilities	Responsibilities
Outcome	Equality	Inclusion	Inclusion/some inequality	Inequality	Inequality	Inequality	Inequality	Inequality	Inequality	Inequality
Mixed economy of welfare	State	State/private and civil society	State/private	Private	Private	Private	Private	Private	Private	Private
Mode	Command and control	Cooperation/ partnership	Command and control/ cooperation	Competition	Competition	Competition	Competition	Competition/ cooperation	Competition	Competition
Expenditure	High	Pragmatic	Pragmatic	Low	Low	Low	Low/pragmatic	Low/pragmatic	Low	Low/pragmatic
Benefits	High	Low/medium	Low/medium	Low	Low	Low	Low/pragmatic	Low/pragmatic	Low	Low/pragmatic
Services	High	Medium	Medium	Low	Low/medium	Low/medium	Low/medium	Low/medium	Low/medium	Low/medium
Accountability	Central state/ upwards	Central state/ upwards and market/ downwards	Central state/ upwards and market/ downwards	Market/ downwards	Market/ downwards and civil society	Market	Market	Market	Market	Market
Politics	Left	Left/post ideological	Right/ pragmatic	Right	Right	Right	Right	Right/pragmatic	Right	Right

Source: Adapted from Bochel and Powell (2016, p 9, Table 1.1) and Powell (1999, p 14, Table 1.1)

Thatcher that affected the financial markets and allowed the City to boom. Like other Conservatives, Hunt suggested that freedom from European Union 'red tape' in areas such as digital, life sciences and financial services would lead to innovation and growth. Critics, however, questioned the efficacy of such deregulation and pointed to the variety of risks associated with it, including boom and bust and unethical behaviour.

However, as Chapter 13 notes, for example, in some areas data and 'evidence' have effectively been used to create a new, or at least expanded, form of regulation of the behaviour of certain families frequently referred to by government as 'troubled'. While families may have been a particular focus for the Conservatives (see also Chapter 14), as Chapter 6 points out, politicians over the last two decades, perhaps notably David Cameron, have sometime seen 'data' as providing ways of monitoring not only the behaviour of individuals but also the work of some agencies, including by providing information through which the public might themselves raise questions. However, the extended use of data, algorithms and predictive analysis for families, linked with the portrayal of those families as dysfunctional and outside the mainstream, does raise important questions about the increased use of digital surveillance and control.

In contrast, the language of 'investment', let alone policies designed to achieve it, were scarce under the Conservatives, unless ideas such as 'levelling up' can be seen as such. Even in areas such as work and employment, and children and families, where the Coalition government had paid at least cursory attention to the notion of social investment, from 2016 onwards this largely petered out.

Citizenship

In terms of citizenship, while much of the discourse, such as 'making work pay', might appear similar to the Third Way, under the Conservatives responsibilities seemed to clearly trump rights, with smaller carrots (such as the minimum wage) and larger sticks (including cuts, caps and freezes for working-age benefits; Chapter 11). Similarly, in terms of timescale, it could be argued, on the one hand, these continued Labour's stress on 'conditionality', but on the other hand, there were more deep-rooted and longer historical resonances with the New Poor Law of 1834, which differentiated between the 'deserving' (older people) and 'undeserving' (working-age people) poor (see also Chapter 10) and attempted to ensure that those who 'could but did not' work were made 'less eligible' (that is, treated more harshly) so that people would always be better off working than not working, as discussed in Chapter 3. However, it should be noted that some of the government's emphasis on 'conditionality' was in line with much of public opinion, particularly with regard to those in low-paid jobs.

In addition, a number of chapters recognise the emphasis on a particular neoliberal view of how lives should be lived, whether that is in families, education or housing, and the development of tools to regulate the poor. The ongoing financial pressures on local authorities have meant that many have had to focus on areas where they have statutory responsibilities, and even there they have been under pressure.

Citizenship, in a strict sense, was also important during this period in having an impact on the labour market, with the UK having 'taken back' control of immigration following Brexit and the reduction in immigration, and particularly European Union immigration, contributing to the challenges faced by some employers in filling vacancies (Chapter 11). It was also reflected in debates around 'foreign criminals', including arguments about the forms and rates of deportation (Chapter 15).

Outcome

For outcome, there was considerable rhetorical reference to the importance of equality of opportunity and social mobility – for example, 'burning injustices' (May) and 'levelling up' (Johnson) – under successive prime ministers (see also Chapter 16 and its discussion of 'equalities'), perhaps reflecting some awareness of growing public concern about such issues (see Chapter 3). However, the central conclusion of Vizard and Hills is that 'the second decade of the 21st century was in many respects a decade of going backwards rather than forwards in terms of reducing social disadvantage and social inequalities through social policy making' (2021, p 8). While the UK saw a high level of many different types of inequalities in different spheres, it is clear that the main 'lens' of equality of government was focused on comparing the conditions of those on working-age benefits with those on low pay. In terms of poverty, it was not until 2019 that real wages attained the levels of 2007. While unemployment fell, with the proportion out of work reaching its lowest level since 1975 at the end of the decade, job security declined considerably, with the number of zero-hours contracts increasing from around 168,000 in late 2010 to more than one million by the end of 2021 (Office for National Statistics, 2022).

There was considerable evidence that the four-year benefit freeze from 2016 to 2020 increased poverty significantly (see Chapter 10) and that by 2021 there would be more than 400,000 more people in poverty than there would have been had benefits kept pace with inflation (Barnard, 2021), an issue manifest in the large increase in 'food banks' and the numbers using them (House of Commons Library, 2022). Income inequality, as measured by the Gini coefficient, has remained largely stable over the last decade. However, it is often closely linked to inequality in other domains, such as health and education. Moreover, there are also inequalities in terms of race and gender. It is generally considered that recessions and austerity often have the greatest impact on the less well off. Chapter 14 highlights the impact of years of austerity on children and families, with the poorest families having been hardest hit. Moreover, despite the use of the furlough scheme and the temporary uplifting of Universal Credit (see Chapters 10 and 11), the COVID-19 pandemic seemed to amplify pre-existing inequalities (see Chapter 16) both in terms of morbidity and mortality – with groups such as those on lower incomes and some ethnic groups (for example, Blundell et al, 2020) and those in poorer areas (for example, Kontopantelis et al, 2022) being worst affected – and in relation to the impact on employment and incomes (Blundell et al, 2020). Other pressures, particularly the highest inflation levels for thirty years, and high fuel prices, led to calls for action by the government in early 2022, but the main response in the Chancellor's Spring Statement was to raise the National Insurance threshold by £3,000, a change which largely benefits better-off individuals and families, although Sunak did also double the level of the Household Support Fund, which is intended to help local authorities in England support the most vulnerable households. Under Truss, there was the initial announcement of a two-year package of support for energy costs, although that was somewhat overshadowed by the proposal to reduce higher-rate Income Tax and to cut the standard rate by 1p, and the desire to remove the cap on bankers' bonuses. However, within weeks, following a tumultuous response by the financial markets and much public and political opinion, the energy support package was reduced to six months and the Income Tax reductions were cancelled or postponed. The Autumn Statement of 2022 included a mixture of tax increases and spending cuts, although many of the latter were delayed until 2025. The 2023 Budget included measures hoped to encourage people over 50 back into the workforce and provided a further expansion of childcare in England.

In so far as one existed, levelling up, largely associated with Boris Johnson, was arguably the key overarching idea in relation to inequality, although, as a number of contributors note (see, for example, Chapter 6), it was far from fully formed, many of the initiatives associated with it were simply reannouncements of existing policies, and the level and distribution of funding were widely seen as problematic in relation to its aims. As a result, even five years on from Johnson introducing his idea, little tangible progress could be identified.

Mixed economy

With the exception of some elements of the response to COVID-19, during this period the mixed economy of welfare in England clearly favoured the market and civil society over the 'big state'. While little government rhetoric on the 'Big Society' remains, it is clear that its apparent antithesis of 'big government' is not favoured and that market-type activity is preferred (see Chapter 6). As Chancellor, Rishi Sunak regarded the COVID-19 response as necessary in the short term, but in the longer term he wished to get his party back on track as 'tax-cutting Conservatives'. There was a significant departure from the early New Labour 'Third Way' focus on collaboration (or partnerships or networks) as the Coalition and Conservatives continued the emphasis of Conservative administrations from the 1980s, and later New Labour governments, on choice and competition in delivering social policies and, in particular, the importance of individual choice (and multiple providers) in health (Chapter 7), social care and education (Chapter 8) and markets for homeownership and renting in housing (Chapter 9). Much activity was subcontracted to commercial entities, sometimes on a 'payment by results' basis, although some 'results' were disappointing. However, the stress on 'integration' has increased over time, with recent moves in the National Health Service (NHS) arguably again moving away from competition (Chapter 7).

Mode

While the preference of the Conservative governments was generally for competition and the use of the private sector, such as in education (Chapter 8), the impact of the COVID-19 pandemic meant that for much of 2020 and 2021 the government was forced to make substantial use of the public sector, not just for the delivery of health care and the use of benefits, the furlough system and support for private businesses, but also, as Chapter 5 highlights, because of the impact that years of austerity had on organisations such as Public Health England and public health laboratories, as well as local authority services, which meant that the UK was arguably less well prepared to respond to the pandemic than some other countries.

Even after the pandemic, and under successive prime ministers and chancellors, the financial pressure on local authorities from 'austerity' continued (and the effects were similar, if sometimes slightly less marked, in the devolved administrations). Although the 2022 Autumn Statement allowed for somewhat higher increases in Council Tax, these were widely seen as passing the buck for tax increases from central to local government, and as insufficient to meet the needs of services, including social care.

As with previous governments, even where a multiplicity of providers is present, this did not automatically translate directly into greater choice for users, with examples from housing, education and social care. It is difficult to talk of meaningful choice when there are record waits for hospital services, care homes and domiciliary care.

Expenditure

Public expenditure was generally low in the period from 2010, largely as a result of political choices around austerity, and eased a little from about 2015 onwards (see Chapter 2; see also Vizard and Hills, 2021). In terms of total expenditure, the onset of the COVID-19 pandemic marked an end to austerity, as explained and explored in Chapters 2 and 5. Indeed, as Chapter 3 notes, the public have been divided over the desirability and impact of austerity. At the same time, public support for 'tax and spend' has increased over time, with particular preferences for health and education but even some softening of attitudes to some categories of benefits claimants, while maintaining or increasing the level of the State Pension has become less of a priority.

The government's interventions in relation to COVID-19, and then the support for fuel bills as part of the 'cost of living crisis' brought a huge increase in debt that will need to be repaid over a long period. In his Chancellor's Spring Statement in March 2022, Rishi Sunak reiterated his desire to be a low-tax chancellor, even promising a cut in Income Tax by the end of 2024 (Bell et al, 2022). However, the state of the economy, internal and external pressures, and not least the brief period of 'Trussonomics' meant that Sunak's Chancellor, Jeremy Hunt, in his Autumn Statement set out tax rises, with any promise of tax cuts retreating into a very distant future.

The 2022 Autumn Statement also further delayed the introduction of the social care cap (see Chapter 11) until 2025, with the Chancellor arguing that the move would allow additional funding for social care in 2023 and 2024, although critics accused the government of failing some of the most vulnerable in society and questioned whether the reform would ever be introduced.

Benefits

There are arguably two main reasons for low benefits under these governments. First, this was a major component of the aim of reducing public expenditure. Second, there was the 'moral' purpose of reducing welfare dependency. Indeed, the Coalition and Conservative governments were more successful in cutting public expenditure than had been the 1979 Thatcher government. However, there was a significant variation between favoured (the NHS and education) and less favoured (housing and local government) sectors, and universal benefits and 'unpopular' targeted benefits such as working-age benefits. As with New Labour's Third Way, there was a tendency to prioritise services such as health and education, which can be seen as preventive in nature and increasing human capital, over reactive cash benefits that provide 'relief'. For example, as noted elsewhere, there was some increase in free childcare as a 'social investment'.

Services

One of the ongoing effects of austerity was that some 'protected' services, such as the NHS and education, while by no means well resourced, were less badly affected by resource constraints. Even in those areas, schools and health services were under significant pressure before the COVID-19 pandemic, and in the following years continuing tight budgets meant that there was little scope to catch up, let alone to expand and improve services.

In addition, an inevitable consequence of protecting some areas was that others were particularly badly affected. Chapter 2 highlights the differential impact of public expenditure decisions on government departments and services, with benefits and local government services being particularly hard hit. It is unsurprising, therefore, that many contributors see services as under great pressure. Chapter 15, for example, argues that not only was the criminal justice system under pressure due to cuts in its funding, but also reductions in wider service provision, such as community health, youth services, local authority housing and social services, meant that more social problems were creating additional challenges.

Accountability

As implied in earlier discussion, the Conservatives' preference for accountability tended to be 'downward' to the market – for example, through the use of 'free' schools and commercial providers in health care and the Work Programme, and local bodies, such as academy schools (although those increasingly became part of national chains), and NHS trusts – rather than upwards to the central state, with a greater role for civil society organisations in providing services for and being accountable to their local areas.

Politics

Many of the contributors to this book have pointed to New Right and neoliberal influences on policy. However, during this period the internal politics of the Conservative Party clearly played a very significant role. As noted in the Introduction, at least three prime ministers – Cameron, May and Johnson – made rhetorical nods to One Nation Conservative ideas and also suggested that they would tackle (at least some) inequalities, even if actual policy change was limited at best. However, after Johnson's resignation, the contest for the leadership of the Conservative Party could largely be seen as the candidates seeking to make claims to ideas associated with the political Right, not least in attempting to appeal to Conservative Members of Parliament (MPs) and the Party membership. That culminated in Liz Truss defeating Rishi Sunak for the leadership and becoming Prime

Minister in September 2022. However, it also illustrated that the economic ideas of Truss, and her Chancellor, Kwasi Kwarteng, were unpalatable to the financial markets and to large sections of the public, so that when Sunak subsequently became leader and Prime Minister, he and his Chancellor, Jeremy Hunt, were forced to put forward a financial strategy that implied stability rather than radical change, and a mix of tax increases and public expenditure cuts. This is in contrast to the claims of a social democratic ethos from the administrations in Scotland and Wales (Chapter 17). However, it is difficult to point to many clear resulting differences in terms of outputs and outcomes in the devolved nations.

Comparisons with previous governments

Conservative governments under Thatcher and Major

While many contributors note the influence of ideas that might be associated with the New Right and neoliberalism, as was often the case during the Thatcher and Major governments, whether it was a result of the personalities in government, the disruption caused by events or simply a lack of drive and clarity in policy terms, across many policy areas there was no clear ideological underpinning other than broad preferences, and the governments from 2015 have tended to respond to pressures in relatively pragmatic and sometimes passive ways. However, in practice, it is possible to identify a range of similarities with the Conservative governments of the 1980s and 1990s, whether it be cuts in benefits, 'making work pay', emphasising particular notions of 'the family' and how it should behave (although arguably not the same version of the family that many Conservatives of the Thatcher period favoured), deregulation or the residualisation of services provided by local government.

New Labour under Blair and Brown

While the Coalition government almost inevitably demonstrated some areas of continuity after 13 years of Labour governments, by 2015, and certainly 2019, any influence of New Labour was arguably wearing off, although some awareness of the role of certain inequalities, such as those legislated for in the Equalities Act 2010, did appear to persist. However, in certain areas, ideas such as social mobility (or perhaps rather some concern with the lack of it) and how to deal with 'troubled families' persisted. At the same time, however, even where some of the rhetoric remained similar, such as in education, health care, social care and the labour market, ideological preferences and policy choices frequently differed from New Labour, with, for example, much less emphasis on 'partnership' and a greater reluctance to conceive of a substantial role for the state in many areas of welfare.

The Coalition government

As noted in Chapter 1, even with the Liberal Democrats' removal from government, there was initially a considerable degree of continuity of both personnel and policies following the 2015 general election, with the dominant austerity narrative continuing. That began to change following the Brexit vote, with the departure of David Cameron as Prime Minister and George Osborne, often seen as the architect of austerity, as Chancellor of the Exchequer. However, as reflected throughout this volume, while there were changes under subsequent prime ministers, the broad ideological preferences of the Conservative governments remained similar. As Table 18.1 suggests, while there were some differences from the Coalition government, these were largely as a result of 'external' forces rather than ideological or policy preferences.

Arguably, the May government was forced to take a more pragmatic approach in many areas following the loss of a House of Commons majority at the 2017 general election and the dominance of Brexit in parliamentary and policy terms. Under Boris Johnson, although the Conservatives won a handsome victory at the 2019 general election, the impact of COVID-19 only months later, perhaps together with Johnson's character and instincts, again saw something of a more pragmatic approach, particularly with regard to public expenditure and the delivery of benefits and services. However, the ongoing impacts of austerity, including the effect of spending cuts and constraints in many policy areas from 2010, continued to affect social policies. That said, in some areas, where policies could clearly be seen to be failing, the Conservatives did reverse some Coalition policies, as with the rolling back of Health and Social Care Act reforms (Chapter 7) and bringing criminal justice rehabilitation services back within the national Probation Service (Chapter 15).

Conclusion

The social policies of the Conservative governments since 2015 have clearly been shaped by the dominant theme of the Coalition government, austerity, and its implications for all areas of welfare policy. Even protected areas such as the NHS have been under very significant financial pressures, not least as a result of rising demand, while others, such as benefits and services provided by local authorities, have seen large real terms cuts. The clear exception to this has been the State Pension, whether the previous or new State Pension version, where the 'triple lock' has been maintained, although increasingly obviously at a cost to other areas of welfare provision.

At the same time, the governments have been buffeted by major changes, with Brexit arguably having been of the Conservatives' own making, while the COVID-19 pandemic was largely external (although the government did clearly choose to make particular decisions about how to respond, and in the early months of the pandemic these had a considerable impact). The cost of living crisis can largely be seen as resulting from a mix of external circumstances (the war in Ukraine and rising energy prices) and particular UK circumstances (such as decisions about how to respond to energy price increases and the short-lived Truss government's attempt to shift fiscal policy).

In addition, a major knock-on effect of these concerns was that the time devoted to Brexit and COVID-19 by politicians and civil servants meant that there was little scope for further policy development. Constant changes of ministers also had an impact, as noted for housing policy in Chapter 9, so that in many areas the status quo largely remained, even if ministers' rhetoric often suggested greater ambition.

The contributors to this book tend to follow a broadly critical line, with many identifying strong New Right tendencies in the government's policy approaches, although in some areas, not least because of Brexit and COVID-19, and then the cost of living crisis, the government has been forced to respond in a more pragmatic way which has, at times, appeared to clash with its ideological preferences. As Chapter 8 illustrates with regard to education policy, the mix of rhetorics alone, such as about equity, performance and autonomy, are hard to join up in policy, but when these are added to a government with no clear sense of direction, and which is pushed around by internal and external pressures, there is little scope for meaningful policy development and implementation.

The overall broad conclusion of the period may be that events or external shocks made it difficult to identify clear ideological positions underpinning the Conservatives' approach to social policy. First, the short tenures of many prime ministers and secretaries of state made spotting any 'isms' (such as Thatcherism) problematic. Second, events such as Brexit, the COVID-19 pandemic and the war in Ukraine becalmed 'normal policy making', with much energy devoted to 'emergency fire-fighting'. There is also the issue of the extent to which periods can be examined in terms of 'events'. Was it as simple as ABC, or perhaps AA, BB, and CC? Was it 'austerity = adversity' followed by 'Brexit = becalming of policy' and 'COVID-19 = crisis'? Even if this argument is not accepted, it might be difficult to disagree with the alphabetical sequence that the period may end with D, for something between dismal or perhaps disaster?

References

Apps, P. (2021) *Show me the bodies: how we let Grenfell happen*, Oneworld: London.

Barnard, H. (2021) *End the benefit freeze to stop people being swept into poverty*, York: Joseph Rowntree Foundation. Available at: www.jrf.org.uk/rep ort/end-benefit-freeze-stop-people-being-swept-poverty (accessed 21 November 2022).

Blundell, R., Joyce, R., Costa Dias, M. and Xu, X. (2020) *COVID-19 and Inequalities*, London: Institute for Fiscal Studies. Available at: https://ifs.org.uk/inequality/covid-19-and-inequalities/ (accessed 21 November 2022).

Bochel, H. and Powell, M. (eds) (2016) *The Coalition government and social policy*, Bristol: Policy Press.

Grenfell Tower Inquiry (2021a) 'Evidence on behalf of the Department for Levelling Up, Housing and Communities', 7 December, p 29. Available at: https://assets.grenfelltowerinquiry.org.uk/documents/transcript/Transcript%207%20December%202021.pdf (accessed 1 August 2023).

Grenfell Tower Inquiry (2021b) 'Module 6 opening on behalf of Bindmans, Hickman & Rose and Hodge Jones & Allen', 6 December, p 1. Available at: https://assets.grenfelltowerinquiry.org.uk/BSR00000096_BSR%20Team%201A%20-%20Phase%202%20Module%206%20Written%20Opening%20%28Government%2C%20FRA%2C%20Testing%20and%20Certification%29%20Submissions%20%5BBindmans%2C%20Hickman%20%26%20Rose%2C%20Hodge%20Jone (accessed 1 August 2021).

House of Commons Library (2022) *Food banks in the UK*, London: House of Commons. Available at: https://researchbriefings.files.parliament.uk/documents/CBP-8585/CBP-8585.pdf (accessed 21 November 2022).

Kontopantelis, E., Mamas, M., Webb, R., Castro, A., Gale, C., Ashcroft, D., Pierce, M., Abel, K., Price, G., Faivre-Finn, C., Van Spall, H., Graham, M., Morciano, M., Martin, G., Sutton, M. and Doran, T. (2022) 'Excess years of life lost to COVID-19 and other causes of death by sex, neighbourhood deprivation, and region in England and Wales during 2020: a registry-based study', *PLOS Medicine*. Available at: https://journals.plos.org/plosmedicine/article?id=10.1371/journal.pmed.1003904 (accessed 23 June 2022).

Office for National Statistics (2022) 'Dataset EMP17: People in employment on zero hours contracts'. Available at: www.ons.gov.uk/employmentandlabourmarket/peopleinwork/employmentandemployeetypes/datasets/emp17peopleinemploymentonzerohourscontracts (accessed 14 December 2022).

Powell, M. (1999) 'Introduction', in M. Powell (ed) *New Labour: new welfare state*, Bristol: Policy Press, pp 1–28.

Vizard, P. and Hills, J. (eds) (2021) 'Introduction and overview', in P. Vizard and J. Hills (eds) *The Conservative governments' record on social policy from May 2015 to pre-COVID 2020: policies, spending and outcomes*, London: Centre for Analysis of Social Exclusion, LSE, pp 1–12.

Index

References to figures appear in *italic* type; those in **bold** type refer to tables.

A

abortion 111–12, 307
'Academic Mentors' 144
Accelerated Construction Programme 154
Accounts Commission (Audit
   Scotland) 107–8
active labour market policies 193–7, 199
Adam Smith Institute 65
'administrative earnings threshold' 184
adult obesity 120
adult social care 208–21
  Coalition government 208–10
  Conservative approaches 219–20
  and COVID-19 215–16
  families providing care 218–19
  and NHS 214
  personalisation 209–10
  see also social care
Adult Social Care Discharge Fund 217
Advancing our Health (Cabinet Office &
  DHSC) 120
Affordable Homes Programme 155–6,
  165–6
affordable renting programme 160
Albania 268
Allen, N. 12, 13
alt-finance 68
Amess, David 267
Andersen, K. 284
antisocial behaviour 265
anti-welfare attitudes 45
Apple, M. 135
arm's-length bodies (quangos) 106–8
Article 50 5, 69
artificial intelligence (AI) 232
Association of Directors of Adult Social
  Services 215–16, 217
Association of Police and Crime
  Commissioners 271
Asthana, A. 219
asylum seekers 73, 268
Atlas Foundation 66–7
attitudes to tax and spend 47–8, *49*
Auditor General for Wales 305
austerity 2–3, 129
  benefit cuts 245
  and the Care Act 2014 209
  Coalition government 15, 262
  and COVID-19 pandemic 83, 96
  economic inactivity 199–200

Philip Hammond's Chancellorship 6, 30
  neoliberal 'market society' 229
  'over but not undone' 104
  public attitudes 47, 59
  and public expenditure 103–4
'austerity mark 2' (2022) 15
'authoritarian populism' 94
auto-enrolment pensions 175, 186–7
Autumn Budget 2021 104–5
Autumn Statement 2022 11–12, 15, 35
  Council Tax 323
  deregulation 318–20
  efficiency savings 105
  NHS budget 127
  One Nation approaches 20, 36
  social care charging reforms 217
  tax and spending 322, 324
  Universal Credit 184–5, 201–2
  see also Hunt, Jeremy
Avon and Somerset Police 235

B

'back to basics' agenda 271–2
Bailey, D. 40
Baker, Kenneth 134
Baker, Steve 35
Bambra, C. 292
Bangladeshi British working-age men 290
Bank of England 37
Banks, Arron 68
Bara, J. 12, 13
Barclay, Steve 126–7
Barran, Diana, Baroness Barran 137
Basta, K. 308
BBC 215
Beating Crime Plan (Home Office) 263,
  265, 271, 272
The Behavioural Insight Team 109
behaviour change 109
Bell, D. 308
benefit caps 175–6, 181–2, 245, 247
benefit cuts 194–5, 245–6, 247–8
  see also spending cuts
benefit fraud 176
benefit freezes 178–80, 321
benefit poverty traps 248
benefits
  benefit-sanction-oriented 203–4
  changes 247–8
  inadequate 188

perceptions of benefit levels 51, *52*
public expenditure 324
public priorities 48–54
rates of increase **179**
welfare provision 203–4
see also Universal Credit
benefit sanctions 200, 203, 287
Bennett, F. 181
Benquet, M. 67
The Best Start for Life report
 (DHSC) 254–5
'big bang' deregulation 318–20
'big data' 226
big government 244–7, 323
'Big Society' (Cameron) 2, 4, 105, 323
Bill of Rights Bill (2022) 111
biopolitics 139, 140, 147n1
Black and Asian households 280
Black and Minority Ethnic (BAME)
 communities 281, 283
Black Caribbean people 289–90
Black Lives Matter 270
Blair, Tony 226, 326
block grant adjustments 308
Blundell, J. 284
Bochel, H. 13, 208, 317
Boiler Upgrade Scheme 164
Bottery, Simon 217
Bourgeron, T. 67
Braverman, Suella 11, 269, 272
Brexit 65–78
 BAME groups 283
 devolved governments 75–6
 economic impact 71–2
 equality analysis 285
 health care 129
 immigration and work 73–4
 Leave campaign 68
 legislating for 110
 negotiations 69–70
 and the NHS 74–5
 no-deal preparedness' 30
 Northern Ireland 300–1
 regulatory alignment 72
 rise in unfilled vacancies 199–200
 social rights 72, 72–3
 and trade 38–40
 Withdrawal Agreement 70, 72, 75, 77
 see also European Union (EU); 'get Brexit
  done' slogan
'Brexit means Brexit' 69
Brexit referendum 2016 26, 67–9, 247, 300
Brien, P. 32
Bristol City Council 235
Britannia unchained (Kwarteng &
 Truss) 184, 201
British Empire 66
British Social Attitudes 47–51, **49**, **52**,
 54–7, 59

Brown, Gordon 326
Budget 2015 (Osborne) 4, 22, 181
Budget 2018 (Hammond) 26–30
Budget 2019 (Javid) 26–30
Budget 2023 (Hunt) 15, 20, 36–7, 322
budget deficit 2
Building Back Better (Johnson) 125
building control systems 163–4
Burnham, Andy 112
Burns, R. 141
business investment 37–8, *38*
Butler, Judith 140
buy-to-let properties 161

C

C2K Services for Schools 141
Cabinet Office
 Advancing our Health 120
 The Coalition 209
 *Declaration on Government
  Reform* 102, 107
 Government Transformation Strategy 229–30
 *Investigation into alleged gatherings
  on government premises during
  Covid restrictions* 8
 Review of Intergovernmental Relations 309
Cairney, P. 85
Cameron, David
 'Big Society' 2, 105
 Brexit referendum 67–8, 247
 dimensions of political approaches **319**
 intergenerational social mobility 227
 resignation 4, 247
 territorial inequalities 202
Campaign to Protect Rural England 157
Care Act 2014 208–9, 213, 219
care homes 213, 214
Care Quality Commission (CQC) 127
Carers Allowance 284
carers' leave 210, 212, 219, 221n1
Carozzi, F. 154
Centre for Ageing Better 108
Centre for Homelessness Impact 108
Centre for Social Justice (CSJ) 201,
 281, 282–3
The Charter for Social Housing Residents
 (MHCLG) 160
chauvinist populism 66
Child Benefit 179, **179**, 245, 247
childhood obesity 117–18, 120, 128
Childhood Obesity (HM Government)
 117–18, 128
child poverty 187, 245, 248, 250–1,
 252, 256
Child Poverty Act 2010 248
Child Poverty (Scotland) Act 2017 302
Child Poverty Strategy (HM
 Government) 245
child protection 246

children 243–56
  having the same opportunities 252
  'level up' socioeconomic
    opportunities 252
  local services for 246
  lockdowns 232, 252–3
  school closures 140, 142–3, 232
  welfare concerns 254
Child Tax Credit 247
citizenship 320–1
cladding materials 163
Clegg, Nick 227
The Coalition (Cabinet Office) 209
Coalition government 2010–15 2–3,
  174–5, 317, 327
  adult social care 208–10
  arm's-length bodies (quangos) 107
  benefit system 193–4
  big government 244–7
  Care Act 2014 reforms 209
  Child Poverty Strategy 245
  council housing 159
  criminal justice 260–1
  dimensions of political
    approaches 14, 319
  education policies 138
  family and welfare benefits 245
  family-centred investment state 227
  family policies 228
  Public Bodies Reform Programme 107
  public services reform agenda 246
  public spending cuts 101, 244–5
  public spending strategy 21
  Universal Credit 3, 174, 246
Coffey, Thérèse 126, 177, 182, 196, 198, 200
Collins, Sir Kevan 144–5
'combined authority mayors' 112–13
combustible facades 163
Commission on Devolution in Wales
  (Silk Commission) 299
Commission on Race and Ethnic
  Disparities (Sewell report) 280–3
Committee on Climate Change 164–5
community cohesion 265
Community Renewal Fund 9, 106
compassionate Conservativism 3, 244–5
  see also One Nation Conservatism
Comprehensive and Progressive Agreement
  for Trans-Pacific Partnership 71
conditionality 199, 200–2, 203, 320
Conservative Home 219
Conservative Party
  'compassionate' party 2
  conference 2018 6
  conference 2022 217
  health papers 117
  ideological transformation 76–7
  leadership contests 104, 216, 255
  post-Thatcherite social conservativism 244

Conservative Party manifestos 12–13,
  32, 175–6
Conservative Party manifesto 2010 208
Conservative Party manifesto 2015 3–
  4, 103
  child poverty debates 248
  criminal justice system 261–2
  disability employment gap 287
  new homes commitments 151
  social care system 211
  social security 175–6
  working-age benefits 194
Conservative Party manifesto 2017 5,
  176, 195
  disability discrimination 287
  new homes commitments 151–3
  NHS 118–19
  One Nation Conservativism 250
  social care system 211–12
Conservative Party manifesto 2019 6–7,
  12–13
  criminal justice system 262–9
  'get Brexit done' 6–7, 103, 176, 251–2,
    263, 268
  labour groups 12
  landlords and tenants 161–2
  NHS 123
  social care system 212–13
  'strong state conservatism' 263
  welfare reform 196
'Conservative' years 317–18
Consumer Prices Index 34, 179
contact-intensive occupations 199
control 265–6
  see also 'law and order' politics
Convention on the Elimination of All
  Forms of Discrimination Against
  Women 307
Co-operation Agreement with Plaid Cymru
  (Welsh Government) 304
Corbyn, Jeremy 68, 103
core homelessness 162–3
Coronavirus Act 2020 307–8
Coronavirus Action Plan (DHSC) 308
Coronavirus Job Retention Scheme 31,
  51–3, 78, 183, 197, 253, 290, 308
'cosmopolitan-traditionalist' 13
cost of living crisis 10, 20, 183, 189,
  201–2, 324
council housing 158, 159–60
  see also local authorities
Council Tax 35, 183, 323
council tenants 152
coupled mothers 284
Courts Service 262
'COVID-19 cost tracker' (NAO) 31
COVID-19 pandemic
  and 'austerity' 83
  and Brexit 7–8, 56, 110

care homes 220
cases per million 89, *91*
deaths 87–9, *88*, *90*, 290, 292
differential morbidity 289–91
disabled people 199, 291–3
economic inactivity 199
education 139–45
education inequalities 139
excess deaths 129
inequalities 95, 292–3, 322
mental health 291–2
morbidity and mortality 289–90
worker preferences 199
'in-work poverty' 198–9
COVID-19-related spending (NAO) 31–2, *32*, *33*
COVID-19 responses 91–7
  closed networks 93
  complacency period 82–3
  contracts for PPE and testing 128–9
  cronyism 92
  deficit 30
  devolution 112–13, 307–8
  effective responses 95
  evidence-informed policies 108–9
  'Freedom Day' 89
  getting a grip 86–7
  getting back to normal 87
  health systems 85
  'herd immunity' 84
  hospitals discharging untested patients 215
  'immunity passports' 140
  large-scale interventions 91
  living with the virus 89–91
  lockdowns 232, 252, 270
  misreporting data 92
  NAO criticisms 85
  New Right government 188
  NHS and older people 215
  One Nationism 20
  panic 83–6
  policy making 15
  and populism 93–4
  poverty reduction 198
  PPE and testing contracts 93
  protecting jobs 197
  public expenditure 104
  public finances 31–5, 103
  public opinion 51–4
  Rishi Sunak as Chancellor 323
  safety net 197–200
  school closures 140, 232
  social security 174
  testing and tracing 84, 86
  travel restrictions 86
  two-tier claimant hierarchy 199
  Universal Credit 182–3, 193, 196–7
  use of public sector 323
  Winter 2020 87–9

Covid Recovery Group 77–8
Cox, Jo 267
Crabb, Stephen 83–6, **177**
Cribb, J. 187–8
crime 269
Crime Survey for England and Wales 2019–20 285
criminal justice system 262
'crimmigration control' 267–8
cronyism 92
cronyist populism 81, 93–5, **95**
Crown Courts 262
Crown Prosecution Service 262
CT scanners 120
Cullinane, C. 142
Cummings, Dominic 30, 87, 109, 232
curriculum decision-making 134–5
curriculum restorationism 134
Curtice, J. 53

D

Daily Telegraph 7
Data Accelerator Fund 233
data-centric approaches 236–7
data-driven governance 229, 230
'data-driven policy making' (van Veenstra and Kotterink) 226
datafication and automation 232
datafication of families 231, 236, 237
'data lake' systems 234, 235
data-led family intervention projects 235
dataveillance 234, 236
Davis, David 70
debt-to-GDP ratios 2, 36
Decent Homes Standard (DCLG) 163
Decent Homes Standard (DLUHC) 160, 164
Declaration on Government Reform (Cabinet Office) 102, 107
deep poverty 199, 203
  see also poverty
deficit *24*, 32
  see also public sector debt
deficit reduction plans 3–4, 22, 35–6, 247
deficit spending limits 67
Defined Contribution pensions 188–9
'dementia tax' 288
Democratic Unionist Party (DUP) 5, 69, 112, 300–1, 307
Department for Communities and Local Government (DCLG) 21, 228
  Decent Homes Standard 163
Department for Digital, Culture, Media and Sport (DCMS) 231
Department for Education (DfE)
  education recovery plan 255
  Get Help with Technology scheme 253
  proscriptions and prescriptions 134

Realising the potential of technology in education 141
Schools Bill 2022 136–7
Transforming Children and Young People's Mental Health 251
Understanding progress in the 2020/21 academic year 139
Department for Levelling Up, Housing and Communities (DLUHC)
  Decent Homes Standard 164
  'Renters' Reform' White Paper 161–2
  Review of Intergovernmental Relations 309
Department for Work and Pensions (DWP)
  COVID-19 pandemic 183, 197–8, 199
  post-Brexit approaches 193
  Secretaries of State 176–7, **177**, 195
  social security spending 177
Department of Health, *Transforming Children and Young People's Mental Health* 251
Department of Health and Social Care (DHSC)
  Advancing our Health 120
  The Best Start for Life report 254–5
  Coronavirus Action Plan 308
  Integration and Innovation White Paper 124–5
  'Next steps to put people at the heart of care' 217–18
  Our Plan for Patients 217
  People at the heart of care 214–15, 217
  Prevention Is Better than Cure 119–20
  Reforming the Mental Health Act 124
  Women's Health Strategy for England 126
depoliticising policy decisions 232
deporting foreign criminals 261
deregulation and responsibilities 128
'deserving' poor 193, 203, 320
'destatalisation' of education services 134
destitution 199, 203
developers 156–7
Developing People – Improving Care (National Improvement and Leadership Development Board) 118
devolution 3, 4, 298–311
  block grants 308
  COVID-19 pandemic 9, 307–8
  education policies 134
  EU funding 309
  health and social care services 305
  innovation and divergence 9, 101, 301–7
  intergovernmental relations 309–10
  internal trading relationship 301
  political approaches 310, **311**
  and the Union 111–13
  see also Northern Ireland (NI); Scotland; Wales
'Devo Manc' (Greater Manchester) 116–17
de Vries, R. 53–4

digital academy 143–4
digital-centred governance 226
digital exclusion 142, 253–4
digital governance of family problems 237
digital poverty 142
digital technology 230–1
Dilnot, A. 3, 127, 288
dimensions of political approaches 13, **14**, 103, 128, 220, 317–18, **319**, 327
direct commissioning new homes 153, 154
disability benefits 175, 182
Disability Benefits Consortium 199
Disability Discrimination Act 1995 288–9
disability employment gap 287
Disability Living Allowance 175, 287–8
Disability News Service 182
Disability Rights Commission 288
disabled people 199, 214, 286–9, 291–2
disabled women pay gap 284
disadvantaged households 234
Dissolution and Calling of Parliament Act 2022 110
domestic abuse 254, 285
Domestic Abuse Act 2021 254, 285
Domestic Abuse Bill 2019 251, 252
Domestic Abuse Commissioner 285
Downing Street lockdown parties 8, 10, 261, 270
Du, J. 38
Duncan Smith, Iain 35, 174, 177, **177**, 181, 195, 248
Dunn, A. 201
Dwyer, P. 181, 287

E

Early Years Pupil Premium 246
early years services 234–5, 254–5
earnings-related pensions 186
East Kent 127
economically inactive individuals 193, 203
Economic and Fiscal Outlook (OBR) 32–4, 38–40
economic and social inequalities 13–15
Economic and Social Research Council 220
economic pessimism and uncertainty 12, 57
education
  attainment gaps 139, 281, 302
  BAME communities 281
  COVID-19 pandemic 139
  ethnicity and class 281
  inequalities and levelling up 138–9, 255
  market-type mechanisms 104
Education Endowment Foundation 108, 142, 144–5
education policies 133–47
  COVID-19 pandemic 139–45
  devolution and 'destatalisation' 134

incoherence and contradictions 146
levelling up 138–9
policy and profit 143–5
'policy hyperactivity' 145–6
privatisation and marketisation 146
'restorationism' 134
Education Recovery Commissioner 144–5
education recovery plan 255
Education Reform Act 1988 134
Efficiency and Savings Review 105
efficiency savings 104–5
election manifestos *see* Conservative
    Party manifestos
Employment and Support Allowance
    (ESA) 287
Employment Bill 210, 219, 221n1
Employment Equality Framework
    Directive 2000 289
employment policies post-Brexit 192–3
employment rates 281–2
'end of austerity' (May) 26
Energy Company Obligation 165
Energy (Oil and Gas) Profits Levy 35
energy price cap 34–5
Energy Price Guarantee 12
England
    Brexit 2016 referendum 300
    devolution 112
    Help to Buy 154
    national edtech platform 141
English Channel migrant crossings 268–9
English nationalism 66–7, 68
epidemic 'preparedness' 82
Equality Act 2010 75, 286, 288–9, 305
Equality and Human Rights Commission
    (EHRC) 288, 289
equality in education 138–9
'Equality: Positive' (Conservative
    manifestos) 12–13
'*étatisation du biologique*' (Foucault) 139–40
ethnicity-based inequalities 280–3
European Convention on Human
    Rights 101, 111
European Economic Area (EEA)
    migrants 73
European Parliament elections 2014 65
European Research Group (ERG) 36, 66,
    77, 192
European Social Fund 75, 309
European Social Model 67
European Union (EU)
    COVID-19 deaths *90*
    disabled people's rights 289
    'human capital development' 227
    neoliberalism 67
    social and employment standards 72
    structural funds 76, 78, 301
    withdrawal negotiations 300–1
    see also Brexit

European Union (Withdrawal) Act
    2018 289
Euroscepticism 66
Eurosceptic libertarian authoritarian
    factions 70
Eurosceptic MPs 65, 67–8
Eurozone 67
EU (Withdrawal Agreement) Bill 70, 300
Evaluation Task Force 108
Everard, Sarah 264
Everyone In initiative 162
'exceptional police powers' 271

F

Fairer care funding (Dilnot) 3, 127, 288
A fairer, greener Scotland (Scottish
    Government) 309
family benefits 247
family governance techniques 226
Family Hubs 232–3, 234–5, 252
family policies 228, 231–6
family profiling and risk scoring 235–6
family services 246
family support 232
'family values' 219
Farage, Nigel 68
Farnsworth, K. 71–2
'fast policy' (Peck and Theodore) 144
'fast-track' supplier links 96
Fawcett Society 284
feedback loops 236
Feeley, D. 305
Field, Frank 68
financial crisis 2007—2008 46, 76, 244
financial statement September 2022
    see mini-budget September 2022
    (Kwarteng)
First Homes policy 153–4
Five Year Forward View (NHS
    England) 116–17, 118–19, 121, 124
Fixed-Term Parliaments Act 2011 110
flagged families 234, 235
flood defence programmes 163
food and energy prices 34
foreign criminals 267
Foucault, M. 139–40, 147n1
France *39*, 89, *90*, 164, 269
Frankfurt, H. 94
freedom
    and COVID-19 89, 93
    from EU 'red tape' 320
    and public health 318
free markets 100–1
Freud, David 195
funding reforms 213–14
'furlough' scheme *see* Coronavirus Job
    Retention Scheme
Future High Streets Fund 9
Future Homes Standard 165

G

Gamble, Andrew 6, 263
Gauke, David **177**, 195, 261
gender 283–6
gender inequalities 321–2
gender pay gap 284
Gender pay gap inquiry (Women and Equalities Select Committee) 284
General Data Protection Regulation 237
general election 2010 2, 101
general election 2015 1, 3, 65, 68, 103, 117, 247
general election 2017 5–6, 69
general election 2019 1, 6, 30, 70, 103, 123, 251–2, 327
'get Brexit done' slogan 6–7, 70, 103, 123, 176, 251–2, 263, 268
see also Brexit
Get Help with Technology scheme (DfE) 253
Gibbons, A. 141
Givan, Paul 10, 300
Glasby, J. 208, 209–10
'Global Britain' (branding) 30, 71, 72
Global Britain (think tank) 65
Glow Connect (Education Scotland) 141
Good Friday Agreement 75
Good Law Project 92
Google 140–2, 144
Google Classroom 141
Gove, Michael 11, 68–9, 106, 135
Government of Wales (Devolved Powers) Bill 299
Government Transformation Strategy (Cabinet Office) 229–30
Gray, Sue 8
Great British Insulation Scheme 165
Green, A. 202
Green, Damian **177**
Green Homes Grant scheme 164
greenhouse gas emissions 164
Greening, J. 135
Grenfell Tower fire 6, 159, 163
Grenfell Tower Inquiry 318
'gridlock' NHS (CQC) 127
Grimshaw, D. 229
gross domestic product (GDP) 2, 21, *22*, 26, 105
gross fixed capital formation (GFCF) 37–8, *38*, *39*
G Suite for Education (Google) 141
The Guardian 137–8, 145
Guiney, T. 263

H

Halfon, Robert 134
Ham, C. 117
Hammond, Philip 6, 26, 30

Hancock, Matt 119
'hard Brexit' 26–30, 69, 77
Harris, N. 197
Havas SA 144
Health and Care Act 2022 125
Health and Social Care Act (HSCA) 2012 116, 124
    Section 75 125
Health and Social Care Levy 34, 35, 36, 125, 213, 216
health care
    Brexit 129
    COVID-19 85
    market-type mechanisms 104
    policies 2015–23 117–27
    sustainability 305
Health Foundation 220
Health Service Safety Investigations Body 125–6
'health tourism' 74
Help to Buy 154–5, 158
Help to Buy Individual Savings Accounts 4
Henderson, A. 308
'herd immunity' 84
Hervey, T. 129
Hewitt, Patricia 127
Hills, J. 2, 321
HM Inspectorate of Constabulary (HMIC) 271
Hobson, F. 194–5
Hogan, A. 140
homelessness 162–3
Homelessness Reduction Act 2017 162
Home Office
    Beating Crime Plan 263, 265, 271, 272
    Modern Crime Prevention Strategy 261–2, 263
    New Plan for Immigration 268
    Serious Violence Strategy 264
    Tackling Violence Against Women and Girls 285
homeownership 158–9
Horizon 2020 research funding 75
'hostile environment' policies 267–8
household allowances 194
households in England 151, **152**
Household Support Fund 183, 322
House of Commons 285–6
House of Commons Committee of Public Accounts 166
House of Commons Library 8
House of Commons Public Accounts Committee 105
House of Lords 110, 137–8
House of Lords Built Environment Committee 156, 157
House of Lords Select Committee on the Equality Act 2010 and Disability 288

Housing Act 1988 161
Housing and Planning Act 2016 153, 159
housing associations **152**, 160–1
Housing Benefit 181, 186, 247
housing completions 151–3, **152**, 155, 158, 160
housing policies 165–6
housing quality 163–5
housing tenure **152**, 158–62
'hub and spoke' governance 232
Hudson, J. 45
Hull and East Riding of Yorkshire 112
Human Rights Act 1988 101, 261
Hunt, Jeremy
  'big bang' deregulation 318–20
  Budget 2023 36
  as Chancellor 10–11
  Health Secretary 119
  see also Autumn Statement 2022

I

illegal immigrants 73, 268
Illegal Migration Bill 269
immigration 267–9, 321
'immunity passports.' 140
IMPACT ('IMProving Adult Care Together') 220, 221n3
income inequality 321
income poverty 187–8
Income Support 178–80, **179**
Independent Commission on the Constitutional Future of Wales 299
independent medicines and medical devices safety review 123–4
Independent Review of Adult Social Care in Scotland (Feeley) 305
Independent Review of Children's Social Care (MacAlister) 255
Independent Review of Maternity Services at The Shrewsbury and Telford Hospital NHS Trust (House of Commons) 126
Independent Review of the Mental Health Act 1983 118–19
Indian British working-age adults 282
inequalities 13–16, 54–9, 321–2
  Conservatism and cronyist populism **95**
  COVID-19 pandemic 95
  dimensions of political approaches **14**
  education 139
  levelling up 58
inflation 12, 34, 322
information technology (IT) 229
Inheritance Tax 4, 12, 157
'insider' model of scientific advice 83
Insight Bristol 230, 235
Institute for Employment Studies 199–200
Institute for Fiscal Studies (IFS) 9, 35, 104, 142–3, 301–2

'integrated care' 210
Integrated Care Boards 125, 127
Integrated Care Systems 125
Integration and Innovation White Paper (DHSC) 124–5
Intensive Work Search labour market regime 184
interagency data warehouses 235
intergenerational social mobility 227
Interim NHS People Plan (NHS) 121–2, 123
internet access 142, 253–4
Investigation into alleged gatherings on government premises during Covid restrictions (Cabinet Office) 8
'in-work poverty' 198–9
iPLM 144
Ipsos Economic Optimism Index 57
Ipsos MORI polls 261
Ipsos polls 58
Irish backstop 70
Ishak, Awaab 318
issue salience 12

J

Jacobs, M. 184
Jamaica 268
Javid, Sajid 26–30, 125, 219
Jenrick, Robert 34
job security 321
Jobseeker's Allowance 178–80, **179**, 201
Johnson Banks (agency) 144
Johnson, Boris 6, 30–1, 327
  Beating Crime Plan 263
  COVID-19 advice 84–5
  COVID-19 response 91–2, 95, 198
  data-driven policy making 231–4
  dimensions of political approaches **319**
  equality in education 138–9
  family policy 231–4
  'get Brexit done' 70, 103, 251–2
  levelling up 8–9, 26, 103, 106, 202
  long-term care funding reforms 210
  NI protocol 300–1
  'no confidence' vote 10
  One Nation Conservative 7
  'Partygate' 10, 261, 270
  populism and COVID 93–4
  as Prime Minister 70, 110
  public attitudes to rhetoric 59–60
  Queen's Speech 2019 122
  resignation as Foreign Secretary 70
  resignation as Prime Minister 10
  social care 212
  Vote Leave campaign 68–9
  welfare reform 196
Joint Ministerial Committee 300
Joseph Rowntree Foundation (JRF) 250, 253

K

Keddell, E. 230
Keegan, Gillian 138, 146–7
Keep, M. 32
Kerr, Sir Ron 118
Khan review (2022) 126
Khan, Sadiq 112
Kingdon, J. 264
King's Fund 216, 217
knowledge-rich curricula 134–5
Kotterink, B. 226
Kwarteng, Kwasi
  Britannia Unchained 184, 201
  mini-budget 10–11, 36, 58, 78, 102,
    104, 184–5, 192, 272

L

labour groups 12, 13
labour market 192–204
  Brexit 72
  conditionality and levelling up 200–2
  COVID-19 pandemic 197–200
  over 50s leaving 185
  welfare reform 193–7
Labour Party 66, 68, 101, 107, 189
  see also New Labour
land value tax 157
Lansley reforms (2012) 209–10
large-scale government interventions 91
'law and order' politics 260–72
  Conservative manifesto 2015 261–2
  Conservative manifesto 2019 262–9
  control 265–6
  crime 269
  police 262, 263
  prisons 266–7
'lead carers' 227
*Leadership for a collaborative and inclusive
  future* (Messenger and Pollard) 126
Leadsom, Andrea 254, 255
Leave campaign 68
  see also Brexit
Leave-voting English constituencies 30
'left behind' areas 202
'left-right' scale (Manifesto Project) 13
legacy benefits 199, 254
Legal Aid 262
Leonard, James 141
'levelling up' agenda 6–7, 54–9, 105–6, 322
  BAME communities 283
  Budget 2019 26
  children 252
  and conditionality 200–2
  Conservative manifesto 2019 12, 176
  decline of towns and cities 265
  education policies 138–9
  general election 2019 103
  housing 165 6

Queen's Speech 2021 8–9
  social mobility and life chances
    policies 255
  Supporting Families 228
Levelling Up and Regeneration Bill 166
Levelling Up Fund 9, 76, 105–6, 202
Levelling Up the United Kingdom (HM
  Government) 9, 106, 112, 139, 165–6
'Lexit' (Left exit) 67
'liberal collectivism' 229
Liberal Democrats 4, 138, 209, 244, 245
  see also Coalition government 2010–15
libertarian authoritarianism 65, 66–7, 77
Liberty 271
Life Chances Fund (DCMS) 231
'life chances policies' 249
'life' sentences 266
Light Touch labour market regime 184
Loader, I. 269, 272
local authorities 101
  care homes 214
  central government funding 245
  council housing 159–60
  'data lake' systems 234, 235
  'left behind' areas 202
  payment-by-results system 228–9
  permitted development rights 156
  political representation 286
  support for children and families 253–4
  and TFP 229
Local Government Chronicle 215
Local Housing Allowance 163, 247
'localism' 105
'localist' crime and disorder agendas 265–6
local planning 157
local welfare support 254
lockdowns 84
  children and youths 232, 252–3
  government breaking guidance 87
  parties in Downing Street 8
  recorded crime 270
  school closures 140, 142–3, 232
London 154–5
lone-parent family households 248
long-term unemployed 185
Lorenzini, D. 139–40
low-income families with children 245
Low Income Family Trackers (Policy in
  Practice) 234
Lund, B. 157

M

Maastricht Treaty 1992 66, 67
MacAlister, J. 255
machine learning techniques 232
Major, John 326
Making smoking obsolete (Khan review) 126
'making work pay' 320
Manchester 112, 116–17

manifesto commitments 32, 175–6
Manifesto Project 12–13
manifestos 12–13
  see also Conservative Party manifestos
market-type mechanisms 104
Marmot, M. 129
Marr, Andrew 136
Maternity Allowance 284
maternity services reports 126–7
Maude, Francis. Baron Maude of
  Horsham 102
May, Theresa
  Brexit 'deal' and resignation 6
  Brexit negotiations 69–70, 75–6, 300
  digital transformation 229–31
  dimensions of political approaches 319
  'end of austerity' 6, 20, 26, 103
  general election 2017 110
  long-term care funding 210
  Northern Ireland 'backstop' 75, 300
  One Nation Conservatism 20, 202,
    249–50
  'place agenda' 202
  as Prime Minister 4–5, 247
  public attitudes 59–60
  reducing territorial inequalities 202
McIntosh, K. 283
McKay, S. 178
McVey, Ester 177, 195
men
  predatory behaviour 264–5
  State Pension ages 187
Mental Health Act 1983 118
MERS (Middle East respiratory
  syndrome) 83
Messenger, G. 126
'metro mayors' 112–13
Microsoft 140–2
Midlands 40
Mid-Staffordshire NHS Hospital Trust
  Inquiry 128
migration 38, 73, 268
Millar, J. 181
mini-budget September 2022
  (Kwarteng) 10–11, 36, 58, 78, 102,
  104, 184–5, 192, 272
Ministry of Housing, Communities and
  Local Government (MHCLG)
  The Charter for Social Housing
    Residents 160
  A New Deal for Social Housing 159–60
Ministry of Justice, Prisons Strategy 266–7
mixed economy 322–3
Modern Crime Prevention Strategy (Home
  Office) 261–2, 263
Modernising the Mental Health Act
  (Independent Review of the Mental
  Health Act 1983) 119
Montacute, R. 142

Morgan, N. 135
Morgan, Rhodri 299
Morozov, E. 229, 234
Morrison, L. 219
'muddling through' trope 92–3
'multiple streams' model of policy
  development (Kingdon) 264
Munro, E. 246
The Munro review of child protection
  (Munro) 246

N

National Academy 139
  see also Oak National Academy
National Assembly for Wales 111,
  286, 298
National Audit Office (NAO) 105
  'COVID-19 cost tracker' 31, 31–2,
    32, 33
  government spending 108
  government's response to COVID-19 85
  Starter Home initiative 153
National Care Service (England) 288
National Care Service
  (Scotland) 221, 305–6
National Health Service (NHS) 4
  and adult social care 214
  and Brexit 74–5, 123
  budget 7, 83, 127
  Conservative manifesto 2017 118–19
  Conservative manifesto 2019 123
  Interim NHS People Plan 121–2, 123
  job vacancies 73–4
  neoliberal approaches 101
  'permacrisis' 127
  public/private mix 128–9
  rhetoric of prevention 116
  scandals 128
National Housing Federation 161
National Improvement and Leadership
  Development Board 118
National Institute for Health and Care
  Excellence 108
National Insurance 322
  see also Health and Social Care Levy
nationalism and populism 66, 94
National Living Wage 248
National Planning Policy Framework 157
National Police Chiefs' Council 262
National Tutoring Programme 144
neoconservative approaches 134, 256
'neoliberal austerity' 20
neoliberalism 13, 65–7, 325
  approaches to social policies 101
  commercialisation of education 134
  EU 67
  housing policies 166
  and libertarian authoritarianism 76–7
  and the New Right 100–1

and One Nation Conservativism 129
welfare state cutbacks and reforms 256
neoliberal 'market society' 229
neoliberal Right 35–6
Net Zero Strategy 164
A New Deal for Social Housing
  (MHCLG) 159–60
New Deal for Working People
  (Labour) 189
New Decade, New Approach (Northern
  Ireland Office) 300, 306
New Labour 326
  education policies 138
  'human capital development'
    spending 226–7
  'nudging' citizens 109
  see also Labour Party; Third Way
New Plan for Immigration (Home
  Office) 268
New Poor Law 1834 320
New Right
  COVID-19 188
  dimensions of political approaches 13,
    14, 104
  neoliberal influences 100–1, 325–6
  Thatcher governments 3
  welfare post COVID-19 201
New Right thinking 16, 317
new State Pension **179**, 180, 185–6
  see also State Pension
'Next steps to put people at the heart of
  care' (DHSC) 217–18
NHS England
  Five Year Forward View 116–17, 118–19,
    121, 124
  We Are the NHS 123
*NHS Long Term Plan Implementation
  Framework* (NHS England) 122
NHS Long Term Plan (NHS England)
  120–2, 124
Nightingale hospitals 85, 92
non-decent rented homes 164
non-EU migration 73
non-state pensions 186–7
Northern Ireland Assembly 10, 111, 286,
  301, 306
Northern Ireland Executive 300, 306
Northern Ireland (Executive Formation)
  Bill 112
Northern Ireland (Executive Formation
  etc) Act 2019 307
Northern Ireland (NI) 75–6, 111–12, **311**
  abortion 111–12, 307
  Brexit 9–10, 300
  C2K Services for Schools 141
  childcare strategies 256, 303
  devolution 299–300
  direct rule 307
  prison population 266

same-sex marriage 307
social policies 306
waiting time standards 305
welfare mitigation schemes 306–7
see also devolution
Northern Ireland Office 300, 306
Northern Ireland Protocol 112, 300–1
Northern Research Group 78
'nudging' citizens 109
nursing homes 85

O

Oak National Academy 143–4
The Observer 272
occupational pensions 186
occupational segregation 282
Ockenden Report (2022) 126
Office for Budget Responsibility
  (OBR) 8, 12
  Economic and Fiscal Outlook 32–4, 38–40
  Restated March 2019 Forecast 26
Office for Health Improvement and
  Disparities 107, 125
Office for Health Promotion 125
Office of National Statistics (ONS) 281–2,
  290–1
office-to-residential development
  schemes 156
'official knowledge' (Apple) 135
Ofgem 107
Ofqual 107
Ofwat 107
Old Left 13, **14**, **319**
One Nation Conservatism 16, 20–1, 129,
  192, 193, 244–5
  Brexit 30
  Budget 2023 36–7
  Conservative manifesto 2017 250
  COVID-19 support packages 20
  dimensions of political approaches **14**,
    15, **319**
  Boris Johnson 7
  Theresa May 20, 195, 249–50
  as rhetorical 203, 325
  Rishi Sunak 35
  territorial inequalities 202
  see also compassionate Conservativism
OneView package (Xantura) 230, 234
online lessons 143
Online Safety Bill 255
Open Government Data 108
Open Government Partnership 108–9
Operation Vigilant (Thames Valley
  Police) 264–5
'opting out' (contracting out) 186
Organisation for Economic Cooperation
  and Development (OECD) 120
'Osborne economics' 20
Osborne, George 4, 22, 194

Our Plan for Patients (DHSC) 217
owner-occupiers **152**

P

Pakistani/Bangladeshi British employment
    rates 282
pandemic preparedness 82
    see also COVID-19 responses
parenting programmes 232
Parliament 70, 109–11
Parole Board 266
'Partygate' 8, 10, 261, 270
Patel, Priti 268
Paterson, Owen 10
'pathways to poverty' discourse 245
pay disparities 282
payment-by-results system 228–9
Peck, J. 144
Pension Credit 175, **179**, 185, 186
pensions 175, 185–7
    see also auto-enrolment pensions; new
        State Pension; non-state pensions;
        State Pension; 'triple lock' guarantee
Pensions Act 1995 187
People at the heart of care (DHSC) 214–15, 217
'permacrisis' 127
permitted development rights 156
Perry, Ruth 147
personal allowance (Universal Credit) 194
Personal Independence Payments 175, 287–8
personal protective equipment (PPE) 85–6,
    92, 93, 128–9
'the philanthro-capitalism of digital
    humanitarianism' (Burns) 141
Pincher, Chris 10
'place agenda' (May) 202
'plan for growth' (2022) *see* mini-budget
    September 2022 (Kwarteng)
planning reforms 156–8
Platt, L. 290
points-based immigration policy 73, 268
police 262, 263
Police and Crime Commissioners 265–6
Police, Crime, Sentencing and Courts Act
    2022. 271
Policy in Practice 234
policy turn to data 234
political representation 285–6
Pollard, L. 126
poor families 236
populism 66, 93–4, **95**
'post-austerity' policies 256
post-COVID-19
    attitudes to work 38
    labour market 199–200
    spending 26
post-Thatcherite social conservativism 244
poverty 56–7, 187–8, 198–9, 281, 321
    see also deep poverty; digital exclusion

Powell, M. 13, 208, 317
Powering up Britain (HM Government) 160
pre-COVID-19 spending 26, 30
predatory male behaviour 264–5
predictive analytics 233–4, 235
Prevention Is Better than Cure (DHSC)
    119–20
prison conditions 266
prison population 266–7
Prison Reform Trust 266
Prisons Strategy (Ministry of Justice) 266–7
Private Members Bills 307
private pensions 186
private rented housing 161–2, 164
private sector new housing
    completions 158
private tenants **152**
Probation Service 261
Programme for Government (Coalition) 209
Programme for Government (Scotland) 309
programme for government (Wales) 303
proroguing Parliament (2019) 70
Public Accounts Committee (House of
    Commons) 215
Public Accounts Committee (Welsh
    Parliament) 304
public attitudes 45–6, 47
Public Bodies Reform Programme
    (Coalition government) 107
Public Health England 83, 107, 125
public opinion 53–4, 60
public sector debt 2, 22, 25
    see also deficit
public spending 20–40, 324
    ambivalence 2022 34
    and austerity 103–4
    benefits 324
    COVID-19 pandemic 8, 31–5,
        96, 103–4
    dimensions of political approaches 14
    evaluation 108
    pre-COVID-19 2015–20 30
    public attitudes 45–6, 60
    Ukraine 34
public trust in government 87
Pupil Equity Funding (Scotland) 302
Pupil Premium funding 138, 246
Purcell, C. 246–7

Q

quangos (arm's-length bodies) 106–8
Queen's Speech 2019 123
Queen's Speech 2021 8–9
Queen's Speech 2022 210, 219, 221n1
Quince, Will 233

R

Raab, Dominic 11, 102, 266
race 280–3, 321–2

radical Right 65–7
Rajic, I. 40
Randstad NV 145
rape prosecutions 262
The Reach Foundation 143
Realising the potential of technology in education (DfE) 141
'red wall' constituencies 30, 176
Rees-Mogg, Jacob 72–3
reforming social care 5
Reforming the Mental Health Act (DHSC) 124
Refugee Council 268
refugees and migrants 268
regional economic disparities *see* 'levelling up' agenda
regional police forces 235
'rehabilitation revolution' 260
rehabilitation services 261
remote education 142, 143
'rendition' of illegal immigrants 73, 268
Renewable Heat Incentive scheme ('RHI scandal') 300
'Renters' Reform' White Paper (DLUHC) 161–2
Republic of Ireland 300
Resolution Foundation 10, 184, 196
responsible carers 283–4
Restated March 2019 Forecast (OBR) 26
'restorationism' in education policies 134
Retained EU Law (Revocation and Reform) Bill 72–3
Review of Intergovernmental Relations (Cabinet Office and DLUHC) 309
'revolt on the Right' (UKIP) 67–8
Richards, D. 100
Right to Buy 4, 159
Right-wing news media 66
Rochdale Boroughwide Housing 318
Rotheram, Steve 112
rough sleeping 163
Rowlingson, K. 178
Royal Institution of Chartered Surveyors 156
Rudd, Amber **177**, 195–6
Russian invasion of Ukraine 15, 20, 34, 183, 318
Rwanda 73, 268

S

'SAGE' advisory committee 85
same-sex marriage 307
SARS (severe acute respiratory syndrome) 83
school closures 140, 142–3, 232
school inspection grades 147
schools 133–6, 253
Schools Bill 2022 134, 136–9

Scotland 75–6, 111–13
    Accounts Commission 107
    arm's-length external organisations 107–8
    Brexit 2016 referendum 300
    childcare 303
    child poverty 256
    dimensions of political approaches **311**
    education 302
    Equality Commission 289
    free school meals 309
    Glow Connect 141
    independence referendum 2014 111, 298
    National Care Service 221, 305–6
    policy directions 9
    Poverty and Inequality Commission 303
    prison population 266
    Pupil Equity Funding 302
    rent freeze 309
    second independence referendum 75
    social care system 305–6
    social policies 301–2
    social security charter 303
    social security policies 256, 302–3
    tax and benefits 301–2
    universal childcare 303
    waiting time standards 305
    see also devolution
Scotland Act 2012 111
Scotland Act 2016 111
Scottish Attainment Challenge 302
Scottish Greens 309
Scottish National Party (SNP) 302, 309
Scottish Parliament 286, 298
Select Committee on Work and Pensions 197
'selective austerity' (Vizard and Hills) 2
Self-Employment Income Support Scheme 31, 183
Senedd Cymru (Welsh Parliament) 111, 286, 298
Senned and Elections (Wales) Act 2020. 299
Serious Violence Strategy (Home Office) 264
Sewell report (Commission on Race and Ethnic Disparities) 280–3
sex offenders 285
sexual harassment 285
Shakespeare, T. 292
Shared Prosperity Fund 252, 301, 309
Shepotylo, O. 38
Shrewsbury and Telford Hospital NHS Trust 126
Sibieta, L. 142–3
Silk Commission (Commission on Devolution in Wales) 299
single parents 50
Sinn Féin 300, 307
Skinns, D. 261
'smart governance' (Cummings) 232

Smith, Chloe **177**
Smith Commission 298, 302
Smith, M.J. 100
social care
  Conservative manifesto 2010 208
  Conservative manifesto 2015 211
  Conservative manifesto 2017 211–12
  Conservative manifesto 2019 212–13
  'Dilnot reforms' 127
  leadership contest 2022 216
  local models of support 220
  Queen's Speech 2019 123
  Scotland 305–6
  sustainability 305
  see also adult social care
social care charging reforms 217
Social Care Institute for Excellence 220
social contract and welfare state 76
Social Housing Decarbonisation Fund 164
Social Housing (Regulation) Bill 160
social impact bonds (SIBs) 231
Socialist Workers Party 67
social liberalism 244
Social Mobility Commission 251
social policies
  1979–2015 100–1
  2015–2023 102–13
  devolution 301–7
  'hard Brexit' 77
social rights 72
social security
  COVID-19 pandemic 8, 174, 188
  rates of increase **179**
  spending 177, **178**
Social Security Advisory Committee 201
Social Security (Scotland) Act 2018 302
social workers 246
sofa surfing 163
'soft Brexit' 69
Somerville, P. 154
special schools 140
spending cuts 37, 46–7, 54, 280
  see also benefit cuts
spending departments 21
spending restraint 47–8
Spending Review 2020 9, 103–4,
  105–6, 202
Spending Review 2021 104–5, 232
Spring Statement 2022 (Sunak) 10, 35,
  322, 324
Stability and Growth Pact 67
Starmer, Keir 74
Starter Home initiative 153–4
Start for Life 232
state–family relations 229
State Pension 4, 175, 178–80, **179**, 186–7
  see also new State Pension; 'triple
  lock' guarantee
statutory homelessness 162

Statutory Maternity Pay 284
Statutory Paternity Pay 284
Statutory Shared Parental Pay 284
STEM subjects 146
Stevens, Simon 116
Stewart, K. 73
Stride, Mel **177**
'strong state conservatism' (Gamble) 7
Sturgeon, Nicola 111, 302, 309
The Sun 271
Sunak, Rishi
  cost of living crisis 34–6
  COVID-19 pandemic 8, 31, 323
  data innovation 237
  dimensions of political approaches **319**
  low-tax chancellor 7, 324
  as Prime Minister 11, 104, 272
  social care charging reforms 217
  technocratic competence 113
  and Liz Truss' economic and fiscal
    strategies 272
  welfare post COVID-19 201
Supporting Families Programme 225,
  228, 233
  see also Troubled Families Programme
  (TFP)
Sure Start 233
Sutton Trust 142, 144

T
Tackling Violence Against Women and Girls
  (Home Office) 285
'taking back control' agenda 267, 268
tax and spend and priorities 46–8
tax credits 245–6, 247–8
tax cuts 20, 47, 184
TaxPayers' Alliance 65
Teach First 144
'technological solutionism'
  (Morozov) 229, 234
'Technology and Infrastructure'
  (Conservative manifestos) 12–13
TES magazine 141
Thames Valley Police 264–5
Thatcher governments 3, 107, 326
'Thatcherites' 7, 66
Theodore, N. 144
Think Family database (Avon and Somerset
  Police) 235
Third Way 13, **14**, 226, 320, 323, 324
  see also New Labour
Tier 4 lockdown restrictions 270, 272n3
The Times 216
top-down approaches 101
total managed expenditure (TME) 21, 22,
  23, 27, 28, 37
Towns Fund 9, 106
toxic deportation narratives 268
trackable digital trails 230

Trades Union Congress 285
Transforming Children and Young People's Mental Health (Department of Health and DfE) 251
'transforming rehabilitation' 260
'triple lock' guarantee 4, 175, 176, 193
  see also pensions; State Pension
Troubled Families Programme (TFP) 227–9, 230, 246, 252, 254
  see also Supporting Families Programme
Truss, Liz
  cost of living crisis 34–5
  dimensions of political approaches **319**
  as 'education prime minister' 146
  law and order agenda 271–2
  New Right policies 201
  as Prime Minister 10–11, 78, 110, 318
  social care 216–17
  'tax cuts now' approaches 36
  see also mini-budget September 2022 (Kwarteng)
Tucker, J. 245, 247–8
Tuition Partners 144
'two-child benefit cap' 175, 181, 227

U

UK Border Control 268
UK Health Security Agency 107, 125
UK Open Government National Action Plan 2021–2023 (Open Government Partnership) 108–9
Ukraine 15, 20, 34, 183, 318
Understanding progress in the 2020/21 academic year (DfE) 139
'undeserving' poor 203, 320
  see also 'deserving' poor
United Kingdom Independence Party (UKIP) 65, 66, 67–8
United Kingdom Internal Market Act 2020 301
United Nations Committee on All Forms of Discrimination Against Women 307
United Nations Convention on the Rights of Persons with Disabilities (CRPD) 289
United Nations Special Rapporteur on Extreme Poverty and Human Rights 187
Universal Credit 3, 202–3
  'administrative earnings threshold' 184
  assessment period 198
  Autumn Statement 2022 184–5, 201–2
  basis for and introduction 193–4
  benefit cuts 194, 247, 248
  Conservative manifestos 176
  COVID-19 pandemic 51, 53, 182–3, 193, 196–8, 253
  cutbacks 2018 250
  deficit reduction plan 247

devolved powers 298–9
internet-only benefit 230
legacy benefits 196, 201
'managed migration' 201
personal allowance 194
rates 180, **180**
reasons for 174
rollout 180–1
shortcomings 254
'two-child benefit cap' 175, 181, 227
women 283
  see also benefits
Urban, J. 128

V

vaccination programme 94
vaccines 87
Vallance, Sir Patrick 108
Veenstra, A.F. van 226
violence against women and girls (VAWG) 261, 262, 264–5, 285, 286
Violence Reduction Units 264
violent crime 265
Vizard, P. 2, 321
'voluntary right to buy' 160–1
Vote Leave campaign 68
vulnerable pupils 140

W

waiting time standards 305
Wales
  behaviour change 109
  Brexit referendum 75–6, 300
  child policies 256, 303, 304
  devolution 9, 111–13, 299
  dimensions of political approaches **311**
  Future Generations Commissioner 304
  Labour and Plaid Cymru 304
  National Care Service 304
  social policy programme 304–5
  waiting times 305
  well-being duty 304
  see also devolution
Wales Act 2014 111
Wales Act 2017 111, 299
Warren, S. 213–14, 216
Warwick, R. 290
We Are the NHS (NHS England) 123
Webster, David 200
welfare
  benefit-sanction-oriented 203–4
  effects of changes 247–8
  post-Brexit 192–3
  post COVID-19 201
  public support 45
  reforms 193–7
welfare chauvinism 74
welfare conditionality 284, 287
welfare dependency 324

welfare governance 96
Welfare Reform Act 2012 174
Welfare Reform and Work Act 2016 174, 194–5, 196, 248
'Welfare State Expansion' (Conservative manifestos) 12–13
welfare-to-work measures 249
Wellbeing of Future Generations (Wales) Act 2015 304
Welsh Parliament (Senedd Cymru) 111, 286, 298
What Works Network 108
White British children 281
White British employment rates 281–2
Whitty, Chris 84, 108
Williamson, B. 140
Williamson, Gavin 11, 135–6, 143
'Windrush scandal' 268
The Windsor Framework (HM Government) 75–6, 301
Withdrawal Agreement 70, 72, 75, 77
see also Brexit
'woke' opposition 94
women
    burden of spending cuts 280
    COVID-19 pandemic 291
    domestic abuse 285
    gender pay gap 284
    Northern Ireland 307
    political representation 285–6
    predatory male behaviour 264–5
    sexual harassment 285
    State Pension ages 187
Women and Equalities Select Committee (House of Commons) 284
Women's Health Ambassador for England 126
Women's Health Strategy for England (DHSC) 126
Work and Pensions Secretaries 195–6
Work and Pensions Select Committee (House of Commons) 182
Work Capability assessments 287
'Work ethic' (*Britannia Unchained*) 201
'work first' policy 193
working age benefits 175, 177–85, 245, 247
working from home 290–1
Working Tax Credit 31, 253
Working Time Directive 67
Work Related Activity Group (ESA) 287
World Health Organization (WHO) 82, 83–4
Wright, S. 181, 266

X

Xantura 230, 234

Y

York and North Yorkshire 112
YouGov 46–7, 51, 54, *55*, 58–9
Youth Futures Foundation 108
youth services 246

Z

Zahawi, Nadhim 134, 136
zero-hours contracts 321

www.ingramcontent.com/pod-product-compliance
Lightning Source LLC
Chambersburg PA
CBHW070609030426
42337CB00020B/3730